"Judges play critical roles as custodians of law and justice. The judicial oath places a duty on judges to apply the law equally, and without fear or favor. The generally held view on gender and judging, however, indicate that the law may not always be applied fairly in matters relating to women and other minorities. This book comes at a time when the world is reawakening to discussions on the rights of women, especially during the Covid-19 pandemic. The chapters provide theoretical and practical analyses and entry points for expanding our understanding of how judges apply the law and the potential for judicial interpretation to either promote women's rights or diminish them. This book is a must-read for judicial officers, gender advocates, experts interested in judicial policy, judicial training, and judicial institutional development. It touches on issues at the intersection of gender, law, and development across Africa."

Justice Georgina Theodora Wood *(Rtd.) (SOG, LLD (honoris causa),*
Former Chief Justice of the Republic of Ghana

"A rich, timely, thoughtful, lively and diverse compendium of papers examining the multiplicity of questions at the core of constitutional rights and freedoms across the African continent today. The book excellently captures the main issues raised at the conference in Arusha which illuminated the gaps in law and practice towards full and meaningful achievement of women's rights. It highlights the slow but steady advances being made in the gender awareness of judges in Africa, while calling to action the need for more gender-sensitive training for judicial officers."

Justice Albie Sachs *(Rtd.), Constitutional Court of South Africa*

Gender, Judging and the Courts in Africa

Edited by J. Jarpa Dawuni

Women judges are playing increasingly prominent roles in many African judiciaries, yet there remains very little comparative research on the subject. Drawing on extensive cross-national data and theoretical and empirical analysis, this book provides a timely and broad-ranging assessment of gender and judging in African judiciaries.

Employing different theoretical approaches, the book investigates how women have fared within domestic African judiciaries as both actors and litigants. It explores how women negotiate multiple hierarchies to access the judiciary, and how gender-related issues are handled in courts. The chapters in the book provide policy, theoretical and practical prescriptions to the challenges identified, and offer recommendations for the future directions of gender and judging in the post-COVID-19 era, including the role of technology, artificial intelligence, social media, and institutional transformations that can help promote women's rights.

Bringing together specific cases from Kenya, Uganda, Ghana, Nigeria, Zambia, Tanzania, and South Africa and regional bodies such as ECOWAS and the African Commission on Human and Peoples' Rights, and covering a broad range of thematic reflections, this book will be of interest to scholars, students, and practitioners of African law, judicial politics, judicial training, and gender studies. It will also be useful to bilateral and multilateral donor institutions financing gender-sensitive judicial reform programs, particularly in Africa.

J. Jarpa Dawuni is an Associate Professor of Political Science at Howard University, United States and the Founding Director of the Howard University Center for Women, Gender and Global Leadership. She is the founder and Executive Director of the non-profit organization, the Institute for African Women in Law (IAWL).

Gender, Judging and the Courts in Africa

Selected Studies

Edited by J. Jarpa Dawuni

Routledge
Taylor & Francis Group
LONDON AND NEW YORK

THE WORLD BANK
IBRD • IDA | WORLD BANK GROUP

First published 2021
by Routledge
2 Park Square, Milton Park, Abingdon, Oxon OX14 4RN

and by Routledge
605 Third Avenue, New York, NY 10158

Routledge is an imprint of the Taylor & Francis Group, an informa business

British Library Cataloguing-in-Publication Data
A catalogue record for this book is available from the British Library

Library of Congress Cataloging-in-Publication Data
A catalog record has been requested for this book

ISBN: 978-0-367-34458-0 (hbk)
ISBN: 978-1-032-12952-5 (pbk)
ISBN: 978-0-429-32786-5 (ebk)

DOI: 10.4324/9780429327865

Typeset in Goudy
by Deanta Global Publishing Services, Chennai, India

Contents

Acknowledgments x
List of contributors xii
Note from Chief Justice of Tanzania xiv
Foreword xv

1 **Introduction: Gender and judging across Africa: A case of old wine in new skins or new wine in old skins?** 1
J. JARPA DAWUNI, PHD

PART I
Women and gender-related jurisprudence in the courts 23

2 **An analysis of gender equality jurisprudence by Kenyan courts since the enactment of the 2010 constitution** 25
NANCY BARAZA, PHD

3 **To win both the battle and the war: Judicial determination of property rights of spouses in Ghana** 40
MAAME YAA MENSA-BONSU AND MAAME A.S. MENSA-BONSU

4 **"Judging" lesbians: Prospects for advancing lesbian rights protection through the courts in Nigeria** 57
PEDI OBANI, PHD

PART II
Emerging gender issues in the courts 77

5 **Femicide and judging: Social media as an alternative online court in Kenya** 79
STEPHEN MUTHOKA MUTIE, PHD

6 Judging beyond gender: Maternal and infant mortality as an emerging gender-related issue in Ugandan courts 99
W. NAIGAGA KYOBIIKA

7 Revenge pornography as a form of sexual and gender-based violence in Ghana: Emerging judicial issues 123
MAAME EFUA ADDADZI-KOOM

8 Litigating gender discrimination cases before the ECOWAS Community Court of Justice and the African Court on Human and Peoples' Rights 142
OSAI OJIGHO

PART III
Judicial appointments and gender representation in regional bodies and national courts 159

9 The feminine face of the African Commission on Human and Peoples' Rights 161
REINE ALAPINI-GANSOU

10 Pursuing gender equality through the courts: The role of South Africa's women judges 189
PENELOPE ANDREWS

11 One sauce for the goose, another for the gander: Zambian women judges and perceptions of illegitimacy 209
TABETH MASENGU, PHD

PART IV
Judicial training and gender 231

12 Unlocking gender inequality through judicial training: Insights from Tanzania 233
JULIANA MASABO, PHD

13 Gender awareness training in Judicial Training Institutes in Kenya and Uganda 254
NIGHTINGALE RUKUBA-NGAIZA, PHD

PART V
COVID-19 pandemic and gender-related judicial issues 277

14 The COVID-19 pandemic, courts, and the justice system 279
MUNA NDULO, DPHIL

15 Sexual and gender-based violence in Uganda during the COVID-19 pandemic: New and old lessons for the criminal justice system 297
LILLIAN TIBATEMWA-EKIRIKUBINZA, PHD

Index 321

Acknowledgments

The preparation and publication of this book would have been inconceivable without the foresight and vision of several Chief Justices and heads of judiciaries across Africa who came together in Arusha, Tanzania, in June 2018 for the first Gender and Judiciary Conference in Africa to explore avenues for addressing a myriad of issues and devise strategies for protecting women's fundamental rights in Africa. Special thanks to Chief Justice Ibrahim Hamis Juma of Tanzania and Dr. Sandie Okoro, Senior Vice President and General Counsel of the Legal Vice Presidency, World Bank, who hosted the conference and have continued to champion judicial reform efforts, including ensuring more inclusive judiciaries.

Her Excellency, President Samia Suluhu, Tanzania's first female Vice President (Vice President at the time) opened the conference and set the tone for this book by calling on the courts in Africa to examine and develop gender-responsive solutions to overcome gender inequality and to end the impunity enjoyed by perpetrators of violence against women.

I would like to extend my thanks to the contributors to the book, who carefully analyzed the issues presented at the conference, and the Chief Justices, judges, academics, and various development practitioners who agreed to be interviewed on these chapters at a time when the world is grappling with a pandemic with social, health, and personal challenges. A special thanks to Judge Albie Sachs (Rtd), Constitutional Court of South Africa, and Chief Justice Georgina Theodora Wood (Rtd), of Ghana, who reviewed and endorsed the book.

To the World Bank colleagues who contributed to the preparation of this book, thank you. I would like to recognize Nightingale Rukuba-Ngaiza, who contributed a chapter and task managed the preparation of the book, Francesca Daverio, who coordinated the peer reviews of the articles, Tamika Zaun, who meticulously handled the administrative details, Rowena Gorospe, who handled the copyright and other legal aspects in connection with the publication of the book, and other colleagues in other parts of the World Bank, including Nichola Smithers and her team from Governance; Markus Goldstein and his team in the Africa Gender Innovation Lab, Governance, who peer reviewed and provided invaluable insights on the chapters; and Mayya Rezvina, who handled the publication aspects.

Last but not least, I am grateful for the coordination, solicitation of quality papers, and editorial support provided by the Institute for African Women in Law, led by Jarpa Dawuni.

Sheila Braka Musiime
Chief Counsel
The World Bank

Contributors

Maame Efua Addadzi-Koom is a Lecturer at Kwame Nkrumah' University of Science and Technology, Kumasi and Co-Founder and Managing Partner at Grasil Consult.

Reine Alapini-Gansou is a Judge at the Pre-Trial Division of the International Criminal Court.

Penelope Andrews is a Professor of Law at New York Law School and is Co-Director of New York Law School's Racial Justice Project.

Nancy Baraza is a Professor of Law at the University of Nairobi School of Law.

J. Jarpa Dawuni is an Associate Professor of Political Science at Howard University, United States, and the founder and Executive Director of the non-profit organization the Institute for African Women in Law.

W. Naigaga Kyobiika is a Magistrate in Uganda and is Co-founder of a non-profit, Wanawake Kwanza—Women First.

Juliana Masabo is a Justice of the High Court of Tanzania and a Senior Lecturer at the University of Dar es Salaam.

Tabeth Masengu is an External Collaborator for the GLOBALCIT program at European University Institute and is an Honorary Research Associate at the University of Cape Town.

Maame Abena Mensa-Bonsu is a D&D Fellow in Public Law and Justice at the Center for Democratic Development in Ghana. She is currently pursuing a Doctor of Philosophy (DPhil) in Law at the University of Oxford.

Maame Yaa Mensa-Bonsu is a Lecturer at the University of Ghana and is a Legal Consultant.

Stephen Muthoka Mutie is a Lecturer and Researcher at Kenyatta University School of Humanities and Social Sciences.

Muna Ndulo is a Professor of Law at Cornell Law School.

Pedi Obani is an Assistant Professor at the University of Bradford School of Law and Visiting Researcher at the University of Leeds.

Osai Ojigho is the Country Director at Amnesty International—Nigeria.

Nightingale Rukuba-Ngaiza is a Senior Counsel at the World Bank's Legal Vice Presidency.

Lillian Tibatemwa-Ekirikubinza is a Justice of the Court of Appeal and Constitutional Court Judge in Uganda and is an experienced legal scholar in judicial and legal matters.

Note from Chief Justice of Tanzania

I am happy to note that my conversation with Ms. Sandie Okoro, Senior Vice President and General Counsel for the World Bank Group, in Washington DC during the Law, Justice and Development Week in November 2017 led to the conference on *Gender and the Judiciary in Sub-Saharan Africa* in June 2018 in Arusha, Tanzania. The conference brought together chief justices, judges, magistrates, and other concerned stakeholders to discuss ways judiciaries can guarantee every woman's fundamental right to live free of discrimination and violence and promote women's pivotal role in social and economic development. This book and its fourteen authors confirm that the conversations on gender equality and gender justice continued beyond the Arusha Conference.

A few examples from the chapters underscore the need to sustain conversations on gender equality and gender justice. Ms. Maame Efua Addadzi-Koom takes us through revenge pornography, an emerging form of sexual and gender-based violence, and how the courts and existing laws in Ghana have responded. Dr. Penelope Andrews takes us through South Africa's Constitution, which she describes as transformational. She looks at female judges' roles through their decisions and distinct ways to frame and analyze gender-related legal issues. Dr. Nancy Baraza discusses the Constitution of Kenya. Apart from applauding it for having made significant gains for gender equality and equity and protecting the human rights of all women and men in Kenya, she faults the Judiciary of Kenya for using its interpretive authority under the Constitution not to advance but to undermine gender equality.

As the world is living through the disruptions caused by the COVID-19 pandemic, Dr. Lillian Tibatemwa-Ekirikubinza shares with us her experience in Uganda. She examines the effects of pandemic-related restrictions on the incidence of sexual assault and evaluates the response of Uganda's justice system to the imposed limits.

The fourteen chapters of this book open up new frontiers for further conversations. *I commend the authors* for contributing to the discussion on gender equality and justice in Africa. My final note is that *conversations about* gender equality and justice *must continue*, and we all have a duty to both encourage and be a part of such conversations if we are to achieve meaningful change and create more opportunities for women's access to justice.

Prof. Ibrahim Hamis Juma
CHIEF JUSTICE OF TANZANIA

Foreword

Sandie Okoro
Senior Vice President and General Counsel for the World Bank Group

Gender inequality remains a threat to sustainable development worldwide. Ensuring gender equality is not only a matter of human rights, it is also "smart economics." It is evident that "gender-smart development" policies have the ability to enhance productivity and improve development outcomes. The benefits of gender equity are echoed in a number of World Bank publications, including the World Bank's *Women, Business and the Law* reports, which analyze countries' legislation to assess the legislative differences in the treatment of men and women in accessing economic opportunities. These reports have repeatedly found that economies become more resilient when societies pursue and implement policies aimed at achieving gender equality. As such, attaining gender equality is at the heart of the World Bank's twin goals of ending extreme poverty and boosting shared prosperity.

Over the years, the World Bank has embarked on a number of gender-responsive reforms, not only to mainstream gender in its policies, programs, and projects but also to monitor the development outcomes of its gender-related interventions. The Legal Vice Presidency has supported these efforts by strengthening knowledge and awareness of gender issues through the implementation of various initiatives. In particular, it has made progress in improving women's access to justice by combining efforts focused on Sustainable Development Goal (SDG) 5, which relates to gender equality, and SDG 16, which relates to peace, justice, and strong institutions. The World Bank's Legal Vice Presidency has also published a series of legal compendia on the pressing issues of child marriage, female genital mutilation, and sexual harassment. It co-convened the High-level Group on Justice for Women, where, together with its partners, it developed two key reports on women's access to justice. Moreover, it has also launched the *Empowering Women by Balancing the Law* initiative, which aims at identifying, addressing, and revising existing laws that impede the voice and agency of women and girls around the world.

The idea to write this book emerged from one of the World Bank's efforts to improve women's access to justice, namely the Gender and the Judiciary in Sub-Saharan Africa Conference, which was held in Arusha, Tanzania between June 11–13, 2018. The Arusha Conference, which was jointly hosted and sponsored by the Judiciary of the United Republic of Tanzania and the World Bank, stemmed from a candid discussion I had with the Chief Justice of Tanzania Ibrahim Hamis Juma during the World Bank's Law, Justice and Development Week in 2017. We shared a common concern: we both wanted to gain a better understanding of the factors that affect African women's access to justice, including violence against women, barriers to the recruitment and retainment of women judges, and the consequences of excluding women from the workforce.

The Arusha Conference convened over 200 participants, ranging from chief justices and delegates from various African judiciaries to presidents of regional courts and tribunals. We shared rich discussions on a range of issues, including gender equality, access to justice, judicial education, and the recruitment and promotion of female judicial officers. This resulted in the identification of several recommendations, including the need to raise gender awareness to eliminate stereotypes and unconscious biases; implement gender-responsive training; establish "justice on wheels," or mobile courts; review how customary laws are applied to women; and ensure that gender parity is attained by appointing more women judges to local, regional, and international courts and tribunals.

The analytical papers in this book follow up on some of the issues raised during the conference. They provide an interesting set of theoretically informed and empirically grounded analyses on sexual and gender-based violence; the role and representation of women in national and regional courts; gender-training and its potential to influence judicial outcomes; progressive gender equality jurisprudence; and emerging gender issues and the response from courts. In light of the COVID-19 pandemic, they also examine the changing environment of the justice sector and the challenges faced by justice sector institutions and the judiciaries in particular.

I thank the editor, and the contributors—the academicians, lawyers, judges, and various justice-sector professionals—who have shared their incredible knowledge and experience and without whom we would not have this book.

I would also like to thank my World Bank colleagues Sheila Braka Musiime, Nightingale Rukuba-Ngaiza, Francesca Daverio, and Tamika Zaun for shepherding this work, as well as Markus Goldman and the Africa Gender Innovation Lab, Nicola Smithers, Deborah Hannah Isser, Manuel Vargas, Christine Owuor, Nyandeng Gajang, Imani Paige Jaoko, and Lyatitima Ernest Mate who provided critical input along the way.

I hope that this book can help increase our understanding of women's justice needs, particularly in Africa, and the ways in which the justice system can be improved. Change doesn't happen overnight. But as a Tanzanian proverb goes, "Little by little, a little becomes a lot." May we always strive for more equality, through both the large and small steps we take.

1 Introduction

Gender and judging across Africa: A case of old wine in new skins or new wine in old skins?

J. Jarpa Dawuni, PhD

Every society has multiple and often intersecting ordering principles. Research has shown that gender is one major socially constructed ordering principle that has found its way into what we perceive as law and how we interpret, apply, and enforce these laws. Societal ordering principles are intrinsically present in institutions, and the judiciary is no exception. Judiciaries are institutions that are slow to adapt to change. Judiciaries across Africa, like those in other parts of the world, continue to evolve, albeit at a much slower pace than the lawyers and litigants who use these courts would like.

Across Africa, the emergence of judiciaries as we know them today is linked to the colonially imposed imported legal systems and traditions, which radically disrupted and replaced existing systems, understandings, and manifestations of justice and human rights (An'Naim, 2002; Juma, 2002; Murungi, 2013; Pimentel, 2011). The presumptive roles of women and men in these societies were also affected and re-engineered, leading to new forms of gendered division of labor, revised societal expectations, and ultimately, new and reimagined rights and obligations (Steady, 2011; Tamale, 2020). African legal systems are currently anchored in, and operating largely within, pluralistic normative legal structures. African legal systems are derivatives of imported legal systems and living customary laws, a combination that sometimes has deleterious effects on human rights and on women's rights (Banda, 2005; Ndulo, 2011).

The role of women and the gendered expectations of women in society continue to evolve across the continent in time and space. These evolutionary patterns can be traced through the precolonial, colonial, and independence movement phases, leading up to the current phase of the post-democratic period (Achebe, 2020; Chukwu, 2002; Tamale, 2020). These shifts in gender constructs and the ensuing rights and freedoms women enjoy have taken different forms under political transitions that span everything from military and quasi-authoritarian dictatorships to democratic systems in the wake of the fourth wave of democratization (Mama & Okazawa-Rey, 2012). Closely linked to the fourth wave of democratization across Africa was the promulgation of new constitutions promising, among other things, liberalization, freedoms, rights, and equal representation. Democratization introduced various changes in judicial functions; some were subtle, whereas others were abrupt—such as the total overhaul

DOI: 10.4324/9780429327865-1

and expansion of existing fundamental notions of equality (Fombad, 2011; Klug, 2010; Ndulo, 2001).

Democratic constitutions promised fundamental changes, but the extent to which these promises have materialized over time varies. The failure to implement these principles of good governance has led to an abdication of the executive's role of enforcing constitutionally guaranteed human rights and freedoms (Ndulo, 2001). Consequently, most African constitutions exist on a skeletal phantom of many unmet rights, resulting in a poor translation of the letter of the constitution (text) into the spirit of constitutionalism (actual guarantees and protections) (Okoth-Ogendo, 1988; Prempeh, 2007). Across Africa, constitutional changes and the ongoing legal transformations vary from one country to another and from one political regime to another. Constitutional transformation projects must juggle competing constituency interests such as religion, ethnicity, disability, and gender (Ndulo, 2001). Race is an extra consideration in the context of countries in Southern Africa, and in South Africa, to be precise (Klug, 2010). In most of these countries, gender is often not prioritized in discussions of human rights, or more specifically, of women's rights (Banda, 2005).

Notwithstanding the seismic constitutional changes that gained ground in the mid-1990s, the question of gender as a defining feature of many African constitutional transformation projects holds less primacy in the larger discourse on judicial politics in Africa (Andrews, 2001; Cassola et al., 2014; Tripp, 2016). Often, in popular parlance and even in written discourse, gender is confused with sex, leading most analysts, policymakers, and laypersons to think and act in ways that promote the ideology that "gender" is a women's issue and to therefore dismiss "gender" as a woman "problem." For the purposes of the discussions in this book, I conceptualize gender as the socially constructed ideas, beliefs, and practices of societal expectations regarding women and men. This conceptualization locates and challenges the prevailing binary distinctions between the normative question of "what ought to be," translated as *how women ought to behave or be*, against the empirical question of "what is"—in other words, *what is the status of women?* Normativity does not operate in a vacuum but is built on a matrix of historical, cultural, social, and political trajectories—which often intersect while being powering and disempowering for different constituents. In this matrix is located the question of how gender is constructed, reconstructed, and exported across time and space.

As a social construct, gender lends itself to multiple interpretations based on the historical, cultural, political, class, and social structures across different temporal spaces. Definitively, what are perceived as the "rights" of women differ from one community to the next. African feminist/womanist perspectives on gender and judging must be formed from a premise cognizant of the matrix of gender visibility/inclusion or invisibility/exclusion in negotiating constitutional transformations. Any discussion of the historical development of legal and judicial systems, and of subsequent constitutional transformation projects propelled by the tide of democratization, must be analyzed against the backdrop of how socially constructed gender norms affect what is perceived as gender equity or equality by the law, the courts, and judges.

Kenney (2013, p. 24) captures the essence of gender and judging when she notes, "Gender differences thus do not flow inevitably from sex differences; rather, gendering is the process by which we attach meaning to sex differences, most often to devalue whatever society associates with women." Using gender as a measure of value makes sense when one examines the gendered outcomes of laws on multiple issues, such as women's access to sexual and reproductive health, divorce, alimony, and equal pay. However, Kenney's qualified assertion that gender is "most often" used to devalue requires a nuanced examination in a plethora of matriarchal traditional African systems and customs replete with examples of gender constructs that accord women value and respect (Steady, 2011; Tamale, 2020; Tripp et al., 2009). Therefore, in the process of reimagining law and gender, more research is needed to understand the ways in which traditional notions of womanhood, often couched as "motherhood," can be harnessed to inform legal practices and judicial decision-making.

Focusing on gender as an integral part of the judging process, the chapters in this volume are guided by two interrelated questions: *To what extent does gender matter in the construction of law?* and *What role does gender play in judicial interpretation of the law?* The first question broadly explores questions regarding how laws (such as constitutions and treaties) are crafted and whether their crafters consider the gendered aspects of social expectations and the attendant legal and judicial outcomes for women. The second question examines the extent to which the courts have applied a gendered lens in their interpretative role when deciding cases.

Empirical and normative assumptions regarding what the law *is* and what the law *ought to be* have traditionally been excluded from theorizing on how law functions (Kenney, 2013). Therefore, it is imperative for any discussion on the connections between law and gender to acknowledge the role of gender constructs in the making of laws by legislatures, interpretation of the laws by the courts, and enforcement of such laws by the executive. Judicial outcomes require a nuanced approach that examines not only the existence of laws but also their effect on promoting rights. The chapters in this book engage with these nuances from different perspectives and with a focus on the relationship between laws and judicial outcomes for women.

Setting the context: Gender and judging

The nexus between gender and judicial outcomes (judging) has been explored by many studies, conducted largely in the global north. For ease of classification, I focus on three broad categories emerging out of this rich body of scholarship. First is the category of *gender and judicial diversity*—which has tended to focus on the question of "why not women?" Led primarily by socio-legal scholars, the analyses were driven by the noticeably paltry number of women acting as judges (Malleson, 2006). These studies centered on the issue of symbolic representation, often advocating for the appointment of women to the bench as emblematic of democratic values of equality, institutional legitimacy, and representation. Thus, although representation was the driving force behind the initial questions, the discussion was not so much about women's value-addition to justice but rather, about the right of women to serve as judges.

Subsequent studies expanded the issue of judicial diversity beyond symbolic representation of women to include how women judges substantively represent the needs of women. This category of studies focused on *gender* and *difference*. Drawing largely from sociologist Carol Gilligan's (1982) work on the "ethic of care," these studies sought to "justify" the demands for diversity on the bench by advocating the "difference" women judges bring to judicial decision-making processes (Boyd et al., 2010; Coontz, 2000; Cowan, 2013; Kenney, 2013; Miller & Maier, 2008; Wilson, 1990). The debate moved from a focus on symbolic representation grounded in equality of representation to addressing substantive representation of women's issues on the bench. In other words, what do women do differently that justifies adding them to the bench? The authors of these studies examined the gendered outcomes of judicial-making processes to determine whether women judged cases differently from men. The case studies ranged from gender-specific cases of marriage, divorce, and alimony to other issues less related to gender, such as criminal cases, immigration, and the environment (Coontz, 2000; Hunter, 2015; Songer & Crews-Meyer, 2000). Most of these studies were inconclusive: most of them found no discernable gendered pattern in decision-making and little or no evidence suggesting that women were genetically or socially predisposed to ruling in a certain way. It soon became apparent that arguing that women should be present on the bench because they would make a difference was a false start and a limited entry point for making the case for judicial diversity (Malleson, 2003; Rackley, 2013; Hunter, 2008, 2015).

The third category of *gender and judicial outcomes* moved beyond women's roles as judges to an expansive inclusion of male judges by disaggregating the framing and understanding of gender in judicial decision-making (Boyd et al., 2010; Sherry, 1986). This category may be considered a more viable body of scholarship in that it moves from the normative aspects of justifying "why" women ought to be on the bench to a more empirical and inclusive analysis of "what" the courts ought to do to advance the rights of minority groups (in this case, women). Within this category, most of the studies examined how, and whether, judges—both female and male—apply a gendered analysis (whether consciously or unconsciously) to the interpretation of law to determine the rights of women, men, and other genders (Albertyn & Bonthuys, 2016; Baines & Rubio-Marín, 2005; Cowan, 2013).

The chapters in this volume touch on each of the three gender-related categories: *representation*, *difference*, and *judicial outcomes*. However, it is within the third category of *gender and judicial outcomes* that this book is framed. By examining the centrality of gender as a social construct and unpacking how it affects judging, this book adds to the emerging scholarship on gender and judging in Africa pioneered by *Gender and the Judiciary in Africa: From Obscurity to Parity* (Bauer & Dawuni, 2016), the first edited volume on women in African judiciaries.

Collectively, the chapters in this book touch on four central issues. First, the book recognizes that although laws are central to advancing gender-equitable outcomes, the role of courts (and judges) in interpreting and breathing life into gender equity requires an understanding of how gender constructs affect law-making and judicial interpretation processes. Second, gender-equitable judicial outcomes and achieving gender equality should be the duty of all judges—both men and women—as is seen in the cases on maternal mortality in Uganda, matrimonial cases in Ghana, and land issues in Kenya, where male judges were pro-women in their rulings. Third, it underscores the need for judicial training on gender to be a centralized component of legal education curriculum generally and should specifically be embedded as a core aspect of continuous judicial training for judges, with appropriate monitoring and evaluation. Fourth, African judiciaries need to stay ahead of the curve in providing access to justice, especially for women, during times of crises. The current COVID-19 global pandemic has demonstrated how fragile judiciaries remain in Africa and the impact of such fragility on further restricting women's access to justice through the courts.

Progress, process, and prospects for gender-equitable judicial outcomes

The chapters in this book are guided by three main questions. First, what *progress* has been made in crafting gender-inclusive laws? Second, what role does gender play in judicial interpretation *processes*? Third, what are the *prospects* for centralizing gender as an integral part of judicial decision-making and appointment processes? In principle, the aspiration that constitutions will promote gender equality has been enthusiastically received by women and gender rights activists. However, the record shows mixed outcomes on how the courts have interpreted the constitutional rules on equality to promote gender equity. On the one hand is the question of whether constitutions have gone far enough in making gender-specific judicial provisions for issues affecting women and other minorities. On the other hand is the question of what judiciaries are doing to sensitize judicial officers to the role of gender as a social construct in existing laws and in the interpretation of such laws. In the ensuing section, I discuss the four key themes running through the book: legal instruments as *progress* toward achieving gender equality; judicial interpretation as a *process* for achieving gender equality; judicial training as a *prospect* for gender equality; and judicial appointments and gender diversity as *progress*, *process*, and *prospect* for gender-equitable outcomes.

Legal instruments as *progress* toward gender equity

The third wave of democratization, which began in the 1990s, saw countries across Africa adopting new constitutions that granted varying levels of freedoms and rights (Ferejohn & Pasquino, 2003). Legal scholars have long debated the role of law in achieving equity, justice, and order in societies. Law has traditionally been assumed to embody norms grounded in neutrality, impartiality, and rationality (Murphy, 1991). If these assumptions are taken to be true, then there is an expectation that these principles would lead courts to accord women the same rights as men. By examining three legal instruments—constitutions, legislative acts, and treaties—this section analyzes the potential and challenges of using these legal instruments to achieve gender equity. Whereas domestic and international legal instruments have provisions seeking to protect and safeguard against gender-based discrimination, the analyses in these chapters demonstrate that the *progress* made through the enactment of laws is only the first step toward achieving gender equality.

As part of its post-apartheid democratic aspirations, South Africa embarked on an ambitious project of judicial transformation. The Constitution of South Africa (1996) has been hailed globally as a progressive constitution with provisions for achieving equality and justice for all. As in all other constitution-making projects, at the center of the constitutional debates in South Africa were questions about how to achieve diversity and equality across all aspects of South African institutions and practices. Achieving diversity and equality was a mechanism to correct the past injustices inflicted by racial oppression in the country (Klug, 2010).

Although racial equity was a primary focus, women's rights groups made a strong case for including gender diversity in the Bill of Rights as a fundamental tool for achieving diversity and equality (Albertyn, 2009; Andrews, 2001). Despite the inclusion of constitutional provisions in efforts to transform the judiciary, including the establishment of the Judicial Service Commission (JSC) in Section 178, the pace at which women have been appointed to the judiciary has been much slower than anticipated. The path for black women and other women of color has been particularly narrow (Masengu, 2016).

In Kenya, Article 27 of the 2010 Constitution of Kenya (Kenya Constitution, 2010) aims to correct past discrimination against minority groups. Of interest to this discussion is Article 27 (6), which obligates the state to use affirmative action policies to correct past wrongs. Additionally, Article 27 (8) provides that no more than two-thirds of one sex shall hold any particular public office, a provision commonly referred to as the two-thirds rule for gender equality (Aura-Odhiambo, 2018). Some progress has been made in the Kenyan judiciary, with a narrowing of the gap between women and men; but much remains to be done to create a gender-inclusive institutional culture that accepts women as equal to men in the context of judicial leadership (Dawuni, 2020).

The Constitution of Ghana (1992) does not have a specific provision on affirmative action for gender equality to correct past gender-discriminatory practices. The rights of women can be inferred broadly from Chapter 5 of the constitution, which guarantees human rights generally. Article 17 (2) states: "A person shall not be discriminated against on grounds of gender, race, colour, ethnic origin, religion, creed or social or economic status." Another general provision on nondiscrimination based on sex is Article 35 (6)(b), which obligates the state to "respond appropriately to achieve reasonable gender balance in the recruitment and appointment to public offices," and a third is Article 27 (3), which guarantees women "equal rights to training and promotion without any impediments from any person." The Directive Principles of State in Chapter 6 of the constitution shift the obligation to the legislature and other organs of government to pass laws and policies that promote gender equality. The Directive Principles of State provided the grounds for the advocacy and eventual passage of the Domestic Violence Act (Act 732) of 2007. These principles have also been used by women's groups to advocate for the Affirmative Action Bill, which was stalled in parliament for several years (Skinner, 2020; Tsikata, 2009).

Constitutions are often the supreme law of the land, safeguarding, among other things, the principles of fairness, equality, justice, and representation. Evidence from judicial interpretation often shows the contrary, lending support to the argument that constitutions without constitutionalism are an empty promise of the law (Fombad, 2014; Ndulo, 2001; Prempeh, 2007). Consequently, constitutions depend on courts to set the wheels of justice rolling. As the fundamental law of the land, constitutions can either promote or impede the rights of women and other minority groups. Further, constitutions can provide radical shifts for gender-equitable opportunities through gender-sensitive constitution-making processes, a point discussed later in the chapter.

As research examining the role of women in constitution-making has shown, constitutions have the potential to reproduce and create new gender inequities when gender-responsive actors, women, and gender-neutral processes are not central to the constitution-making processes (Maingi, 2011; Tripp, 2016). The prospect for the constitutional realization of gender-equitable outcomes is closely linked to gender-inclusive constitution-making. The United Nations Women Global Gender Equality Constitution Database provides a comprehensive overview of countries whose constitutions contain provisions on women's equality and for the protection of women's rights (UN Women, 2016). These "women-responsive" constitutional provisions are closely linked to the active participation of women's groups in constitution-making processes (Andrews, 2001; Cassola et al., 2014; Ezeifeka & Osakwe, 2013; Jagwanth & Murray, 2005).

From a legislative perspective, acts of parliament are generally binding sources of law. Parliaments can pass laws to address loopholes in existing laws or create new ones where no law exists on a subject matter. Globally, more than 140 countries have passed some form of law related to domestic and gender-based violence (Htun & Weldon, 2012; Klugman, 2017). Yet, available data indicate that across the globe, domestic violence cases continue to rise (Tavares & Wodon, 2018). In many countries where domestic violence and sexual harassment laws have been passed, Richards and Haglund (2015) find, an effective enforcement mechanism is crucial to ensuring that the rights are protected. The chapter in this volume by Addadzi-Koom on revenge pornography in Ghana demonstrates the current shortcomings of using the Domestic Violence Act 2007 (732) to protect women victims of technology-induced violence. In the Nigerian context, Obani's chapter shows how the Same Sex Marriage Prohibition Act 2014 is used to effectively deny sexual minority rights. As I write this chapter, the novel coronavirus pandemic is still raging across the world, and the continent of Africa has not been spared from the rise in domestic violence cases (Mlambo-Ngcuka, n.d.). Tibatemwa-Ekirikubinza's chapter on sexual violence in Uganda and Ndulo's comparative study of judiciaries during the global pandemic collectively demonstrate the inadequacy of laws to protect women *before* and *during* times of crisis.

Operating within the African regional context, the Protocol to the African Charter on Human and Peoples' Rights on the Rights of Women in Africa of 2003 (the Maputo Protocol) is hailed as a regional legal instrument critical to grounding the equality of women across Africa. To date, it remains the most comprehensive body of law at the African regional level led by women, and for women, in addressing women's issues across a broad spectrum of rights and freedoms. Across Africa, women have demanded their right to participate in the lawmaking processes—in national constituent assemblies or in treaty-making processes (Eziefeka, 2013; Mutua, 2006; Tripp, 2016). Advocacy by women's organizations in the mid-1990s for women's inclusion in constitution-making processes demonstrated unequivocally that when given the chance to participate, women generate and support gender-responsive constitutions (Bond, 2008). Women's groups have made demands for women-inclusive provisions and in some cases have radically rejected less optimal outcomes (Maingi, 2011; Tripp, 2016). As the chapter by Ojigho on two regional courts demonstrates, regional treaties on women's rights require gender-sensitive judicial interpretation if they are to move beyond their mere existence. Alapini-Gansou's chapter on the African Commission on Human and Peoples' Rights provides a potent analysis of women commissioners' roles in capitalizing on available legal instruments to advance human rights generally.

These three categories of legal instruments—constitutions, acts of parliament, and international treaties—provide glimpses into the progress made in passing laws that address gender inequities at the national and regional levels. Notwithstanding these developments, this chapter offers three conditions for their effectiveness. In the first place, these three legal instruments collectively highlight the need to center the experiences and voices of all minority groups in the lawmaking processes. These voices should be allowed not only to be present but also to be heard. As the United Nations Security Council Resolution on Women, Peace and Security, Resolution 1325 (2000), has shown, women must be included as active agents in finding solutions to peace and security. Furthermore, involving women in the lawmaking processes should not be mere window dressing, as we have seen in the context of the domestic violence laws passed by African countries. These laws must be backed by strong enforcement mechanisms through budgetary allocation and the training of judicial and police staff. Finally, laws passed in the international and African regional contexts should be used by courts in judicial decision-making processes. Judicial use of treaty instruments requires the implementation of active and ongoing judicial training mechanisms to ground international and regional laws in domestic legal and judicial practices.

Studies conducted in Argentina, Chile, South Africa, and Botswana strongly suggest that gender-specific provisions in constitutions provide women's advocacy groups with stronger entry points for demanding women's rights (Lambert & Scribner, 2018). Through gender-responsive constitutional transformation, some countries, such as South Africa, Rwanda, Kenya, and Uganda, have lifted the veil of gender neutrality and gender blindness by inserting specific provisions in their constitutions that support gender equality, yet the full realization of these provisions is yet to be seen (Kabira, 2012; Mutua, 2006).

Judicial interpretation as a *process* for gender equity

Central to the aspirations driving the discourse and support for democratic change is the hope that constitutional transformation will lead to substantive equality for all citizens. Although these liberal constitutional aspirations may sound idealistic to some, they nonetheless provide the guarantees and safeguards for citizens to advocate for equitable opportunities for all (Abbiate et al., 2018; Mbondenyi & Ojienda, 2013). The drafting of constitutions, legislative instruments, and international treaties is not an automatic guarantee of women's rights. The inherent continuity of the lawmaking process holds a legacy in common law countries, where judges have a bigger role in lawmaking through their setting of precedents that are binding on lower courts. However, which cases will make it to the highest courts probably depends on the prioritization of the appeal process by the higher or superior courts; the salience for the public of the issues at stake; and the existence of strong pressure groups, such as civil society. In Benin, Kang and Wing (2021) find that more civil and political issues and fewer economic and social issues affecting women make it to the Constitutional Court. Judicial interpretation of existing laws can lead to progressivity in gendered realities via decisions that advance women and the rights of gender minorities—or it could lead to a regression or stagnation of women and gender rights. I conceptualize this dichotomy as old wine in new skins versus new wine in old skins.

A case of old wine in new skins or new wine in old skins?

Constitutional transformations are of no use if the old methods of judicial function and judicial interpretation have not changed to fit the letter and the spirit of new circumstances and aspirations for democratic equality. In this analogy, constitutional changes and transformations are the new skins—promising, among other things, equality, fairness, and justice. As alluded to earlier, where constitution-making processes fail to involve women as contributors or listen to the concerns of gender minority groups, it can lead to a case of old wine—the reproduction of existing gender inequities. The old wine scenario arises through carrying over archaic, hegemonic imperialistic colonial rules or laws and discriminatory cultural practices that are often presented as principles of customary law and advanced as cultural relativist arguments to protect the "cultures" of non-Western societies (Bond, 2008; Obiora, 1997).

The South African Constitution of 1996 and the Kenyan Constitution of 2010 have been heralded as progressive constitutions with provisions for achieving gender-equitable outcomes (Andrews, 2001; Kabira, 2012). At the regional level, the Maputo Protocol is significantly symbolic as a progressive instrument for women's empowerment at the continental level. To what extent have these laws moved the scales of justice toward gender-equitable judicial outcomes? Pouring new wine (new constitutions) into old wineskins—in this case, stagnant judicial interpretation processes—does not provide optimal outcomes for achieving the spirit of constitutional gender equality. The paradox of constitutions without constitutionalism is highlighted in several chapters in this book. Baraza on Kenya and Mensa-Bonsu and Mensa-Bonsu on Ghana, respectively, examine a litany of cases on women's rights and find instances where the courts failed to pronounce on women's constitutional rights. In the context of Nigeria, Obani characterizes the persistent violation of sexual minority rights as a blatant violation of the Nigerian constitution. And Kyobiika shows how judges in Uganda are beginning to acknowledge maternal and infant mortality as a constitutional issue.

A systematic review of how judiciaries are using laws to decide gender-based cases is important in ascertaining the progress being made or the lack thereof. The litany of constitutional cases discussed by the various chapters in this book is by no means exhaustive of all the constitutional cases across the continent or even in one country. The cases in this book present mixed outcomes. The chapters on Kenya and Uganda highlight progressive developments in advancing women's rights in land and in health, respectively. On the other hand, in both Kenya and Ghana, we witness the current failure of the courts to pronounce on important emerging issues such as technology-enabled gender-based violence. To push the issue onto the judicial agenda, Addadzi-Koom in this volume challenges the courts in Ghana to recognize revenge pornography as a form of gender-based violence, often perpetrated against women, with debilitating effects, including the loss of life.

As the chapters in this book demonstrate, reversing the stagnation of old wine in new skins places an obligation on judiciaries to hear and pronounce on emerging gender-related cases, such as those involving social media–induced violence in Kenya and Ghana. Ironically, the substance of these cases is by no means new; these forms of violence have always been perpetrated against women. What may be new and therefore justifies their being classified as "emerging" is the increased frequency of their occurrence as they become more violent and widespread. If gender is to be centered in judicial interpretation, judges—both men and women—must be sensitized to the gendered dimensions of the cases they adjudicate. I turn to the issue of judicial training, presented as a prospect for achieving gender-equitable judging.

Judicial training as a *prospect* for gender equity

How do socially constructed gender norms influence the law? To what extent does the social conditioning of judges affect judicial interpretation processes?

Existing studies suggest that these and many other questions surrounding gender as a social construct and an ordering principle in law appear not to have been prioritized by judiciaries across Africa (Bauer & Dawuni, 2016).

Judicial training is necessary to keep judicial officers abreast of new laws and procedural rules. In most instances, judges receive their first judicial training when they are inducted into the judiciary. These trainings are often carried out by Judicial Training Institutes (JTIs) or via on-the-bench training through attachment to other judges (Goldbach, 2016). Judicial training may be offered as part of continuous judicial training by the judiciary or through individual activities and initiatives such as conference participation and acceptance of invitations to dialogues and seminars (Oxner, 2001). The World Bank has incorporated judicial training as part of the broader goal of justice sector reform (Laver, 2012).

Judicial training programs have also been carried out by international organizations, such as the United Nations Office on Drugs and Crime (UNODC) Global Judicial Integrity Network (GJIN). The GJIN provides training to supplement or complement what is offered at the national levels. Additional judicial training programs involving African judiciaries are implemented through collaborative site visits to the U.S. Federal Judicial Center, The Hague in the Netherlands, and other countries in the global north. The Judicial Institute for Africa (JIFA), based at the University of Cape Town, South Africa, is one of the few regional hubs that cut across national jurisdictions, even though most of the work is carried out in the Southern Africa region. With a plethora of issues to be covered during judicial training programs, judiciaries across the globe are becoming aware of the need for gender-sensitive judicial training; but this awakening has not come without its own challenges (Schafran, 2001). In Germany, Schultz (2013, p. 597) observes that "deficits in the initial legal education than in further training" are to blame for the difficulty in infusing gender into the judicial decision-making process.

In the Philippines, Miwa (2013) credits the relative success of gender-sensitive training to judicial leadership and to extra mechanisms such as the Gender Justice Award for judges who produce gender-sensitive decisions and demonstrate gender sensitivity to women litigants. Minamino's (2014) study of employment discrimination cases in Japan elucidates how systematic gender bias is reproduced in judicial decision-making when judges follow social mores that position men as the "male breadwinners" in the family. Minamino (2014) notes that democratic principles of openness and transparency in judicial decision-making processes can be fulfilled if judicial education programs and training opportunities challenge the gendered aspects of the law.

Judicial training efforts across Africa have been anchored within the larger democratic development discourse on the need for judicial reform as a precursor to promoting democratic values and development. Driven by the law and development discourse that emerged in the late 1980s, the push for judicial reforms has been spearheaded by development agencies, multilateral financial organizations such as the World Bank, and philanthropic organizations such as the Ford Foundation (Trubeck, 2006). These externally funded and often externally led trainings tended to focus on strengthening judiciaries to promote liberal democratic values and were largely driven by capitalist norms of trade liberalization (World Bank, 2012). Feminist critiques of development policies nestled within the Women and Development (WAD) and Gender and Development (GAD) discourses provide better insights into how gender and women's issues had traditionally not been prioritized in these law and development and judicial transformational processes (Nyamu-Musembi, 2006).

To be effective, judicial training must be localized and practical. Judicial training requires resources, but judicial leaders across Africa are saddled with meager budgets; for that reason, deciding what topics to prioritize in judicial training becomes an issue. In addition, the problem of resource allocation means that judiciaries are susceptible to external pressures and influence by funding agencies, meaning that those agencies often determine what topics should be covered (Trubeck, 2006).

As the chapters by Masabo on Tanzania and Rukuba-Ngaiza on Uganda and Kenya, respectively, show, gender has not been prioritized in judicial training programs. The idea that the law is rational and that judges will remain neutral, unbiased, and impartial may partly explain the continuity of a blind gaze on the role of gender constructs in decision-making processes. Correcting the "gender-blind gaze" requires an investigation into how judicial training can be made gender responsive. Masabo's outline of the history of judicial education and judicial training in Tanzania shows a longstanding absence of gender concerns in all judicial training programs. Masabo argues that although gender can be introduced as a stand-alone course in training programs, the gendered aspects of judicial decision-making should be incorporated into all other judicial training topics.

As Masabo notes in her chapter, the failure of judiciaries to provide gender sensitization training to judges has not been lost on women judges' associations, because it has reproduced the "double care burden" of women's issues on women judges—a situation where women must do the double work of care at home and at work. The Tanzania Women Judges Association has taken on an extra burden of care work by providing gender-sensitive training to members of the judiciary and the public. Other studies confirm the double burden of care; for instance, in Ghana, the women judges' association has provided gender sensitization training to members of the judiciary and has raised awareness of women's rights among members of society (Dawuni, 2016). To foreground the understanding of gender issues and to lessen the burden placed on women judges in leading the fight for gender equality, Masabo advocates for making courses on gender mandatory in the law school curriculum rather than mere electives. Using the examples of Kenya and Uganda, Rukuba-Ngaiza demonstrates how judicial training on gender-related issues has not been provided by the judiciary, partly because of budgetary constraints but also a result of low prioritization. She argues that inclusion of gender training in the performance contracts of judicial officers is imperative and robust evaluation of the limited gender training and the effectiveness of the JTIs is necessary to justify a continuous investment in both. Nevertheless, through the chapters on Tanzania, Uganda, and Kenya, we do find that judges who received gender-sensitive training testified to the impact of that training on their later rendering of gender-sensitive decisions.

Training of judges regarding unconscious gender bias will help to illuminate the gender-blind spots in judicial decision-making. The absence of judicial training on the impact of gender bias will invariably reproduce existing gender inequities in society. As Ojigho potently argues, in the Economic Community of West African States (ECOWAS) and African Court scenarios, of the few cases that were decided in favor of women, the judges did not focus on gender as a defining feature of the reliefs sought. Rather, the decisions were located within the larger human rights framework. Although the decisions need to be commended, the fact that the courts are failing to prioritize gender as a determinative factor in the biases and discrimination women suffer in society requires urgent attention. For the sake of reversing the gender gaze, I argue for the necessity of shifting the duty of understanding gender as the burden of "women" judges to understanding it as a (hu)man-made problem requiring sensitivity on the part of both female and male judges.

Consequently, dismantling the masculinist practices, beliefs, and privileges that contributed to producing these inequitable gender constructs should equally be the responsibility of men. A key strategy for alleviating the problem requires intentionality in adhering to gender-focused judicial training that aims to deconstruct inequitable gender norms through the lawmaking and judicial interpretation processes. To borrow from Audre Lorde (1984), the "master's tools will not dismantle the master's house." In the analogy as used here, the master's house refers to the existing gender inequities in law, and the master's tools represent the usual judicial training programs that do not incorporate gender sensitivity. These chapters insist that gender-sensitive judicial training must become the new tools for gender-conscious judicial interpretation. Thus, gender sensitivity training can be the sledgehammer used to break down the master's house.

Gender-sensitive judicial training increases the prospects for gender-equitable judicial outcomes. However, gender-sensitive judicial training is not a sufficient condition; nor can it singularly ordain gender-responsive and progressive outcomes. Other intervening factors are at play, including the level of executive interference in judiciaries, along with the presence of an active civil society and media creating awareness of gender cases that come to the judiciary. Additionally, an active public interest litigation bar that brings gender cases to court and an engaged public that scrutinizes and reacts to judicial decisions are key players. Discerning the impact of these factors requires further research.

To draw the curtain on this discussion, I postulate that judicial training is one tool that is largely within the control of national judiciaries, which gives them enormous leeway in deciding what trainings are offered to judges. Gender-awareness training can illuminate gender gaps in the law, which could in turn lead to gender-responsive judicial outcomes. This trajectory is by no means linear, as externalities such as a judge's predisposition to change can alter the course of the linear projection presented. Nevertheless, providing gender-inclusive judicial training is still a good way to start.

Gender diversity as *progress, process and prospect*

In this section, I briefly discuss the importance of gender parity and gender diversity as necessary conditions for inclusive and progressive judging. Across Africa, a body of scholarship on women in African judiciaries is emerging (Bauer & Dawuni, 2016; Cowan, 2013; Kamau, 2013; Klibi, 2016; Masengu, 2016). Notwithstanding the progress made in some countries, the process for appointing women and their promotion to higher courts remains contested in some jurisdictions, including Egypt, Algeria, Namibia, and Sudan. Even in countries where women have made gains as judges, as Masengu's chapter brings home, the reality is that lingering societal perceptions of gender bias have led to perceptions of women judges as being illegitimate occupiers of the bench.

Considering the emergence of the postcolonial state in the mid- to late 1950s, available studies suggest that across the continent, women judges have made tremendous progress at domestic (Bauer & Dawuni, 2016) and international courts (Dawuni & Kuenyehia, 2018). In addition to their progression in judicial appointments, women judges have made commendable gains as leaders of judiciaries across both civil and common law countries (Dawuni & Kang, 2015). In tracing women's access to the bench in Nigeria, Uzebu-Imarhiagbe concludes that

> the history of women in the legal profession is not a history of exclusion but of reception and advancement. In the admission and appointment of women lawyers into the bar and the bench, there was no deliberate consensus or policy by government to achieve gender integration. The driving force was need, the need for qualified legal practitioners.
>
> (Uzebu-Imarhiagbe, 2020, p. 11)

In a few countries, such as Egypt, women continue to fight for their right to be judges (Hamad, 2016). In Uganda, although women represent more than 40% of the judiciary, access to the highest judicial office as Chief Justice has yet to be realized, with women going only as far as occupying the deputy Chief Justice position (Dawuni, 2020). Despite the progress women have made in becoming judges, women judges are not immune to gender-based discrimination during judicial appointment commission hearings, as the chapters by Andrews and Masengu show. Andrews provides evidence showing how in South Africa the intersectional nature of historical racial discrimination against blacks and "colored" people, and of gender discrimination against women, is slowing the opportunities for black women to be appointed as judges.

Similarly, Masengu's chapter sounds the alarm on the unfounded perceptions of illegitimacy women judges in Zambia continue to face. Media representations of women judges during appointment processes tend to reinforce the perception that women are "outsiders" coming to the bench, a perception that leads to harsher lines of questioning by appointing bodies (Escobar-Lemmon et al., 2016).

Masengu's chapter is by no means invoking "the difference women make" argument for women's appointment to the bench, as doing so would lead us down the slippery road of essentialism—the idea that all women are the same and will make a difference for all women (Kenney, 2013). Evidence from Constitutional Court decisions has shown that women judges on constitutional courts have effectively adjudicated cases that advance the rights of both women and men (Baines & Rubio-Marín, 2005). The chapter by Andrews shows that despite being few, women judges on the Constitutional Court of South Africa have delivered some progressive judgements on women's rights issues.

Diversity in the composition of the bench matters for promoting democratic principles of equality, representation, and inclusion. Zambia and Zimbabwe have achieved gender parity, with more than 50% representation of women within all levels of the judiciary. Yet, other Southern African states are struggling, including Namibia, which, at the time of this writing, has no woman on the Supreme Court. These examples, though relatively few when compared across all 54 states, do signal that we cannot yet conclude that sex diversity does not matter. More studies are needed to understand the changing dynamics in different countries and the struggles women face in judicial appointment processes.

Although progress has been made in diversifying the sex composition of some benches, the process of making judicial appointments should be closely and constantly monitored. Women judges have made valuable contributions to the bench through jurisprudence, socialization of male colleagues on gender-related matters, and challenges to enshrined male institutional structures (Dawuni, 2016). Gender diversity on the bench signals *progress* toward gender equity in representation. Women and men should have equal access and opportunity to be judges and to adjudicate cases; because when they do, understanding of the *process* of using gender as an ordering principle in judicial appointments increases, as do the prospects for gender-responsive judging.

Contributions of the book

The selected essays in this book make important contributions to theory, practice, and policy by broadening our understanding of the nexus between gender and judging within the African context. Additionally, the findings are relevant for policymakers interested in understanding how laws affect women's rights and women's access to justice through the judiciary. These policy implications are instrumental in expanding the Women in Law and Business project of the World Bank by moving the discussion beyond examining the existence of laws to taking a closer look, by measuring judicial outcomes, at what these laws mean for women.

Additionally, the contributions in this volume provide important entry points for the operation of the World Bank and other development agencies by highlighting the need to reform the justice sector and to prioritize institutional reforms that are gender inclusive. These changes can be implemented through programs aimed at promoting gender-inclusive lawmaking and gender-inclusive judicial training.

Taken individually and collectively, the chapters in this book cover several important debates by providing contextualized analyses within specific countries. First is the lingering question of what happens to women's rights after the promulgation of constitutions. Second, how are courts handling emerging gender issues such as the use of social media to inflict gender violence? Third, some chapters focus on the need to develop an expansive judicial interpretation that allows inclusivity in the definition of "gender" to protect non-gender binaries. Fourth, the trans-nationalization of gender beyond domestic courts is evident in the chapters on the African Commission and the ECOWAS Court, where we witness the roles women play in justice delivery, and how gender is constructed in judicial decisions, respectively. Fifth, two chapters—Tanzania, and Kenya and Uganda—underscore the importance of putting gender on the agenda of judicial training. Sixth, the chapters on Zambia and South Africa highlight the continued significance of promoting gender diversity in judicial appointments. Seventh, the chapters on the COVID-19 pandemic drive home the need for courts to be well equipped to deal with cases of violence against women, both during times of peace and more so during times of crises.

Organization of the book

The chapters in this book bring together socio-legal academic scholars, members of the judiciary, human rights defenders, and development policy analysts to examine a broad range of issues on gender and judging. All the chapters are grounded in different theoretical and methodology frameworks. Some are written from a highly academic perspective, and others are more policy oriented. Woven through each narrative are policy, judicial, and legal recommendations. Together, these chapters provide specific case studies from which patterns emerge for further exploration and for extrapolation to appropriate contexts. Although these case studies may not be, and do not claim to be, generalizable across the continent, this book is the first volume to provide a selection of comprehensive studies on gender and judging within the African context—and that is a significant contribution.

The 14 chapters in this volume have opened new frontiers for research on gender and judging across Africa. By emphasizing how gender as an ordering principle affects judicial interpretation processes within domestic and regional courts, this book has broadened the discussion on gender and the judiciary beyond a narrow focus on the symbolic representation of women as judges in African judiciaries. In examining judicial decision-making processes and outcomes, the chapters have queried the centering or decentering of gender in court cases, judicial training, and judicial appointments. Through the case analyses, we see both what happens when judges fail to recognize gender as an ordering principle in judicial decision-making processes and the critical role judicial training plays in making judges gender aware. The book is organized into four interrelated categories. These categories are not mutually exclusive but cover themes that run concurrently across some chapters. The case studies in this book do not promise to exhaust the plethora of gender-related issues across the continent. Neither do they provide definitive answers to the complex questions concerning gender and judging. Instead, the book makes an important contribution to our understanding of gender and judging by highlighting the loop-back mechanism between the *process* of lawmaking as a necessary condition for gender-sensitive judicial decision-making, the essential elements for achieving *progress* in judicial interpretation of gender-sensitive cases, and the *prospects* for achieving gender equity by centering gender in judicial training of judges and promoting gender diversity on the bench. This book breaks new ground as the first volume to examine the nexus between gender and judging from African perspectives. The individual chapters presented will no doubt open new research avenues and generate more research questions about gender and judging across Africa. The findings will also inform judiciaries, policymakers, and judicial trainers about the need to pay closer attention to gender as an ordering principle of women's access to justice, equality before the law, and equitable representation in judicial decision-making.

References

Abbiate, T., Bockenforde, M., & Federico, V. (Eds.). (2018). *Public Participation in African Constitutionalism*. Routledge.

Achebe, N. (2020). *Female Monarchs and Merchant Queens in Africa*. Ohio University Press.

Albertyn, C. (2009). The stubborn persistence of patriarchy? Gender equality and cultural diversity in South Africa. *Constitutional Court Review*, 2, 165–208. https://hdl.handle.net/10520/EJC28139

Albertyn, C., & Bonthuys, E. (2016). South Africa: A transformative constitution and a representative judiciary. In G. Bauer & J. Dawuni (Eds.), *Gender and the Judiciary in Africa: From Obscurity to Parity?* (pp. 49–66). Routledge.

An'Naim, A. (Ed.). (2002). *Cultural Transformation and Human Rights in Africa*. Zed Books.

Andrews, P. (2001). The stepchild of national liberation: Women and rights in the new South Africa. In P. Andrews & S. Ellmann (Eds.), *Post-Apartheid Constitutions* (pp. 326–358). Witwatersrand University Press and Ohio University Press.

Aura-Odhiambo, R. (2018). Gender equality: Integration of women in the judiciary in Kenya. In K. Wanjiku, P. Mbote, K. Nkatha & A. Meroka (Eds.), *Changing the Mainstream: Celebrating Women's Resilience* (pp. 93–122). University of Nairobi Press.

Baines, B., & Rubio-Marin, R. (Eds.). (2005). *The Gender of Constitutional Jurisprudence*. Cambridge University Press.

Banda, F. (2005). *Women, Law and Human Rights: An African Perspective*. Hart.

Bauer, G., & Dawuni, J. (Eds.). (2016). *Gender and the Judiciary in Africa: From Obscurity to Parity?* Routledge.

Bond, J.E. (2008). Constitutional exclusion and gender in commonwealth Africa. *Fordham International Law Journal*, *31*(289), 292–293. https://ssrn.com/abstract=1662654

Boyd, C.L., Epstein, L., & Martin, A. (2010). Untangling the causal effects of gender on judging. *American Political Science Review*, 54(2), 389–411. https://doi.org/10.1111/j.1540-5907.2010.00437.x

Cassola, A., Raub, A., Foley, D., & Heymann, J. (2014). Where do women stand? New evidence on the presence and absence of gender equality in the world's constitutions. *Politics & Gender*, *10*(2), 200–235. https://doi.org/10.1017/S1743923X1400004X

Chukwu, G. (2002). Women and nationalist movements in Africa. In T. Falola (Ed.), *The End of Colonial Rule: Nationalism and Decolonization* (Vol. 4, pp. 109–130). Carolina Academic Press.

Constitution of Kenya (2010). Available at https://www.constituteproject.org/constitution/Kenya_2010.pdf?lang=en. Retrieved, October, 3, 2020.

Coontz, P. (2000). Gender and judicial decisions: Do female judges decide cases differently than male judges? *Gender Issues*, *18*, 59–73. https://doi.org/10.1007/s12147-001-0024-7

Cowan, R. (2013). Do women in the judiciary make a difference? In U. Schultz & G. Shaw (Eds.), *Gender and Judging* (pp. 26–37). Hart.

Dawuni, J., & Kuenyehia, A. (Eds). (2018). *International Courts and the African Woman Judge: Unveiled Narratives*. Routledge Press.

Dawuni, J. (2016). To "mother" or not to "mother": The representative roles of women judges in Ghana. *Journal of African Law*, 60(3), 419–440. https://doi.org/10.1017/S0021855316000115

Dawuni, J. (2020). Women in judiciaries across Africa. In: O. Yacob-Haliso & T. Falola (Eds.), *The Palgrave Handbook of African Women's Studies*. Palgrave Macmillan. https://doi.org/10.1007/978-3-319-77030-7_75-1.

Dawuni, J., & Kang, A. (2015). Her ladyship the chief justice: The rise of female leaders in the judiciary in Africa. *Africa Today*, 62(2), 45–69. https://doi.org/10.2979/africatoday.62.2.45

Escobar-Lemmon, M.C., Hoekstra, V., Kang, A., & Kittilson, M. (2016). Just the facts? Media coverage of female and male high court appointees in five democracies. *Politics and Gender*, *12*(2), 254–274. https://doi.org/10.1017/S1743923X16000234

Ezeifeka, C., & Osakwe, N.N. (2013). Gender representation in the 1999 Nigerian constitution: A critical discourse analysis for socio-political equity. *Discourse & Society*, *24*(6), 687–700. https://doi.org/10.1177/0957926513486221

Ferejohn, J., & Pasquino, P. (2003). Rule of democracy and rule of law. In J. Maravall & A. Przeworski (Eds.), *Democracy and the Rule of Law* (pp. 242–260). Cambridge University Press.

Fombad, C.M. (2011). Constitutional reforms and constitutionalism in Africa: Reflections on some current challenges and future prospects. *Buffalo Law Review*, 59(4), 1007–1108. https://digitalcommons.law.buffalo.edu/buffalolawreview/vol59/iss4/4

Fombad, C.M. (2014). Constitution-building in Africa: The never-ending story of the making, unmaking and remaking of constitutions. *African and Asian Studies*, *13*(4), 429–451. https://repository.up.ac.za/handle/2263/43423?show=full

Gilligan, C. (1982). *In a Different Voice*. Harvard University Press.

Goldbach, T. (2016). From the court to the classroom: Judges' work in international judicial education. *Cornell International Law Journal*, 49(3), 617–682. https://scholarship.law.cornell.edu/cilj/vol49/iss3/3

Hamad, M. (2016). Egypt: The lingering battle for female judgeship. In G. Bauer & J. Dawuni (Eds.), *Gender and the Judiciary in Africa: From Obscurity to Parity?* Routledge.

Hunter, R. (2008). Can feminist judges make a difference? *International Journal of the Legal Profession*, *15*(1–2), 7–36. https://doi.org/10.1080/09695950802439759

Hunter, R. (2015). More than just a different face? Judicial diversity and decision-making. *Current Legal Problems*, 68(1), 119–141. https://doi.org/10.1093/clp/cuv001

Jagwanth, S., & Murray, C. (2005). "No nation can be free when one half of it is enslaved": Constitutional equality for women in South Africa. In B. Baines & R. Rubio-Marín (Eds.), *The Gender of Constitutional Jurisprudence* (pp. 230–255). Cambridge University Press.

Juma, L. (2002). Reconciling African customary law and human rights in Kenya: Making a case for institutional reformation and revitalization of customary adjudication processes. *St. Thomas Law Review*, *14*, 459–512.

Kabira, W.. (2012). *Time for Harvest: Women and Constitution Making in Kenya.* University of Nairobi Press.

Kamau, W. (2013). Women judges and magistrates in Kenya: Challenges, opportunities, and contributions. In U. Schultz & G. Shaw (Eds.), *Gender and Judging* (pp. 167–232). Hart.

Kang, A. (2016). Benin: Women judges promoting women's rights. In G. Bauer & J. Dawuni (Eds.), *Gender and the Judiciary in Africa: From Obscurity to Parity?* (pp. 108–119). Routledge.

Kang, A., & Wing, S. (2021). Constitutionalism constrained: The constitutional court of Benin and defense of human rights. *African Affairs* (in press).

Kenney, S.J. (2013). *Gender and Justice: Why Women in the Judiciary Really Matter.* Routledge.

Klibi, S. (2016). Tunisia: A new constitution and more women judges. In G. Bauer & J. Dawuni (Eds.), *Gender and the Judiciary in Africa: From Obscurity to Parity?* (pp. 80–92). Routledge.

Klug, H. (2010). *The Constitution of South Africa: A Contextual Analysis*. Hart Publishing.

Klugman, J. (2017). *Gender Based Violence and the Law.* World Development Report Background Paper. World Bank. https://openknowledge.worldbank.org/handle/10986/26198

Lambert, P., & Scribner, D. (2018). Constitutions and women's rights advocacy: strategic uses of gender provisions in Argentina, Chile, Botswana, and South Africa. *Politics, Groups, and Identities*, 8(2), 228–247. https://doi.org/10.1080/21565503.2018.1449759

Laver, R. (2012). The World Bank and judicial reform: Overcoming "blind spots" in the approach to judicial independence. *Duke Journal of Comparative and International Law*, *22*(2), 183–238. https://heinonline.org/HOL/LandingPage?handle=hein.journals/djcil22&div=9&id=&page=

Lorde, A. (1984). The master's tools will never dismantle the master's house. In *Sister outsider: Essays and speeches* (pp. 110–113). Crossing Press.

Maingi, G. (2011). The Kenyan constitutional reform process: A case study on the work of Fida Kenya in securing women's rights. *Feminist Africa*, *15*, 63–81. http://awdflibrary.org:8080/xmlui/handle/123456789/435

Mala Htun, M., & Weldon, S.L. (2012). The civic origins of progressive policy change: Combating violence against women in global perspective, 1975–2005. *American Political Science Review*, *106*(3), 548–569. https://doi.org/10.1017/S0003055412000226

Malleson, K. (2003). Justifying gender equality on the bench: Why difference won't do. *Feminist Legal Studies*, *11*(1), 1–24. https://doi.org/10.1023/A:1023231006909

Malleson, K. (2006). Rethinking the merit principle in judicial selection. *Journal of Law and Society*, 33(1), 131–140. https://doi.org/10.1111/j.1467-6478.2006.00351.x

Mama, A., & Okazawa-Rey, M. (2012). Militarism, conflict and women's activism in the global era: Challenges and prospects for women in three West African contexts. *Feminist Review*, *101*, 97–123. http://www.jstor.org/stable/41495235

Masengu, T. (2016). It's a man's world: barriers to gender transformation in the South African judiciary. Perspectives from women advocates and attorneys. *International Journal of the Legal Profession*, *23*(3), 305–319. https://doi.org/10.1080/09695958.2016.1179639

Mbondenyi, M.K., & Ojienda, T. (Eds). (2013). *Constitutionalism and Democratic Governance in Africa: Contemporary Perspectives from Sub-Saharan Africa*. Pretoria University Law Press (PULP).

Miller, S., & Maier, S. (2008). Moving beyond numbers: What female judges say about different judicial voices. *Journal of Women, Politics & Policy*, *29*(4), 527–559. https://doi.org/10.1080/15544770802092691

Minamino, K. (2013). Gender and judicial education in Japan. In U. Schultz & G. Shaw (Eds.), *Gender and Judging* (pp. 167–232). Hart.

Minamino, K. (2014). Introducing gender training in judicial education in Japan to support the judiciary. *International Journal of the Legal Profession*, *21*(3), 297–306. https://doi.org/10.1080/09695958.2015.1036869

Miwa, A.. (2013). Gender and judicial training: Lessons from the Philippines. In U. Schultz & G. Shaw (Eds.), *Gender and Judging* (pp. 167–232). Hart.

Mlambo-Ngcuka, P. (2020, April 6). Violence against women and girls: the shadow pandemic. *UN Women*. https://www.unwomen.org/en/news/stories/2020/4/statement-ed-phumzile-violence-against-women-during-pandemic

Mohammed, W.F. (2020). Deconstructing homosexuality in Ghana. In S.N. Nyeck (Ed.), *Routledge Handbook of Queer African Studies* (Chapter 13). Routledge.

Mohanty, C.T. (1984). Under Western eyes: Feminist scholarship and colonial discourses. *Boundary 2*, *12*(3)–*13*(1), 333–358. https://doi.org/10.2307/302821

Murphy, W.F. (1991). Civil law, common law, and constitutional democracy. *Louisiana Law Review*, *52*(1). https://digitalcommons.law.lsu.edu/lalrev/vol52/iss1/6

Murungi, J. (2013). *An Introduction to African Legal Philosophy*. Lexington Books.

Mutua, A. (2006). Gender equality and women's solidarity across religious, ethnic, and class differences in the Kenyan constitutional review process. *William & Mary Journal of Race, Gender, and Social Justice*, *13*(1), 1–128. https://scholarship.law.wm.edu/wmjowl/vol13/iss1/2

Ndulo, M. (2001). Constitution-making in Africa: Assessing both the process and the content. *Public Administration & Development*, *21*(2), 101–117. https://doi.org/10.1002/pad.163

Ndulo, M. (2011). African customary law, customs and women's rights. *Indiana Journal of Global Legal Studies*, *18*(1), 87–120. https://scholarship.law.cornell.edu/facpub/187

Nyamu-Musembi, C. (2006). Ruling out gender equality? The post-Cold War rule of law agenda in sub-Saharan Africa. *Third World Quarterly*, *27*(7), 1193–1207. https://doi.org/10.1080/01436590600933289

Obiora, L.A. (1997). Feminism, globalization, and culture: After Beijing. *Indiana Journal of Global Legal Studies*, *4*(2), 355–406, 388–406. https://www.repository.law.indiana.edu/ijgls/vol4/iss2/5

Okoth-Ogendo, H.W. (1988). *Constitutions Without Constitutionalism: Reflections on an African Paradox*. American Council of Learned Societies.

Oxner, S. (2001). The many facets of training. In R.V. Van Pumbroeck (Ed.), *Comprehensive Legal and Judicial Development: Toward an Agenda for a Just and Equitable Society in the 21st Century*. World Bank.

Oyeronke, O. (Ed.). (2003). *African Women and Feminism: Reflecting on the Politics of Sisterhood*. Africa World Press.

Pimentel, D. (2011). Legal pluralism in post-colonial Africa: Linking statutory and customary adjudication in Mozambique. *Yale Human Rights & Developmental Law Journal, 14*(1). https://digitalcommons.law.yale.edu/yhrdlj/vol14/iss1/2/

Prempeh, K. (2007). Africa's "constitutionalism revival": False start or new dawn? *International Journal of Constitutional Law, 5*(3), 469–506. https://doi.org/10.1093/icon/mom016

Protocol to the African Charter on Human and Peoples' Rights on the Rights of Women in Africa. (2005). Available at https://www.un.org/en/africa/osaa/pdf/au/protocol_rights_women_africa_2003.pdf

Rackley, E. (2013). *Women, Judging and the Judiciary: From Difference to Diversity*. Routledge.

Richards, D., & Haglund, J. (2015). *Violence against Women and the Law*. Paradigm Books.

Schafran, L.H. (2001). Promoting gender fairness in the courts through judicial education. In *Toward Elimination of Gender Bias in the Courts*. Working Women's Network and Women's Voice.

Schultz, U. (2013). Do German judges need gender education? In U. Schultz & G. Shaw (Eds.), *Gender and Judging*. Hart.

Schultz, U., & Shaw, G. (Eds.). (2013). *Gender and Judging*. Hart.

Sherry, S. (1986). Civic virtue and the feminine voice in constitutional adjudication. *Virginia Law Review, 72*(3), 543–616. https://doi.org/10.2307/1072973

Skinner, K. (2020, March 6). International Women's Day: What is happening with affirmative action in Ghana? *Democracy in Africa*. http://democracyinafrica.org/international-womens-day-happening-affirmative-action-ghana/

Songer, D., & Crews-Meyer, K. (2000). Does judge gender matter? Decision making in state supreme courts. *Social Science Quarterly, 81*(3), 750–762. http://www.jstor.org/stable/42864001

Steady, F. (2011). *Women and Leadership in West Africa: Mothering the Nation and Humanizing the State*. Palgrave Macmillan.

Tamale, S. (2020). *Decolonization and Afro-Feminism*. Daraja Press.

Tavares, P., & Wodon, Q. (2018). Ending violence against women and girls: Global and regional trends in women's legal protection against domestic violence and sexual harassment. *Children's Investment Fund Foundation, Global Partnership for Education, & The World Bank*. http://pubdocs.worldbank.org/en/679221517425064052/EndingViolenceAgainstWomenandGirls-GBVLaws-Feb2018.pdf

Tripp, A. (2016). Women's movements and constitution making after civil unrest and conflict in Africa: The cases of Kenya and Somalia. *Gender and Politics, 12*(1), 78–106. https://doi.org/10.1017/S1743923X16000015

Tripp, A., Casimiro, I., Kwesiga, J., & Mungwa, A. (2009). *African Women's Movements: Transforming Political Landscapes*. Cambridge University Press.

Trubeck, D. (2006). The "rule of law" in development assistance: Past, present, and future. In D. Trubeck & A. Santos (Eds.), *The New Law and Economic Development: A Critical Appraisal* (pp. 74–94). Cambridge University Press.

Tsikata, D. (2009). *Affirmative Action and the Prospects for Gender Equality in Ghanaian Politics*. Friedrich Ebert Stiftung.

UN Women. (2016, May 6). UN Women's Constitutional Database boosts efforts towards women's rights. https://www.unwomen.org/en/news/stories/2016/5/un-womens-constitutional-database-boosts-efforts-towards-womens-rights

United Nations. (2000). United Nations Security Council Resolution on Women, Peace and Security, Resolution 1325. Retrieved from https://www.un.org/womenwatch/osagi/cdrom/documents/Background_Paper_Africa.pdf

Uzebu-Imarhiagbe, E. (2020). Women in the Nigerian judiciary: Considerable headway or organised progress? *International Journal of the Legal Profession*, *27*(2). https://doi.org/10.1080/09695958.2020.1750410

Wilson, B. (1990). Will women judges really make a difference? *Osgoode Hall Law Journal*, *28*(3), 507–522. https://digitalcommons.osgoode.yorku.ca/ohlj/vol28/iss3/1

World Bank. (2012). Initiatives in justice reform 1992–2012. Justice Reform Practice Group. http://documents1.worldbank.org/curated/en/575811468175154113/pdf/707290WP0Full000Box370050B00PUBLIC0.pdf

Part I

Women and gender-related jurisprudence in the courts

2 An analysis of gender equality jurisprudence by Kenyan courts since the enactment of the 2010 constitution

Nancy Baraza, PhD

Introduction

Since independence, gender inequality due to patriarchy were the norm in Kenya. Generally, society was characterized by a discriminatory social system coupled with negative stereotypes against women (Nzomo, 2018, p.54). Kenyan courts sustained these social norms by failing to protect the human rights of women (Kameri-Mbote, 2018, p.23). Women suffered unmitigated discrimination, especially in matters of inheritance, land ownership, marriage, and sharing of matrimonial property, among other areas. This exposed the majority of them to poverty (McCullough et al., 2016, p.4). Discrimination against women was caused partly by the normative deficiencies of the then Constitution and a lack of judicial will and know-how on the part of judges to interpret the law to favor promotion of human rights, especially those of women. Nzomo rightly notes that the independence Constitution provided for and legitimized patriarchy and discrimination against women in issues of matrimonial property ownership, and devolution of property on the death of a spouse, by allowing customary law to apply to the detriment of the female gender (Nzomo, 1991, p.3).

The economic impact of discrimination against women with regard to property ownership in Kenya has persisted to date. A 2016 Gender and Poverty Assessment by the World Bank (World Bank, 2018), for instance, found that currently, Kenyan women are less likely than men to own land or housing property. Only 12% of women between the ages of 20 and 49 reported any individual ownership of land, compared with 39% of men. In the realm of housing, men are 32% more likely to have sole ownership. The implications of women's marginalization in property and land ownership cannot, therefore, be overstated. Research carried out by the World Bank has shown that insecure land tenure can lead to economic inefficiency, especially for women, who have in some countries in Africa been shown to under-invest in their land, which can lead to them realizing substantially lower agricultural yields. This is true of Kenyan women, who are condemned to poverty due to precarious land ownership and access.

The Constitution of Kenya 2010 (hereinafter referred to as the Constitution), however, seeks to change this paradigm. Normatively, the constitution contains far-reaching commitments to a wide range of rights and an ambitious vision of social equity and has the potential to address historical injustices and grievances

DOI: 10.4324/9780429327865-3

suffered by women (Baraza, 2018a, p.75). It provides for national values and principles of governance that bind all state organs and state officers, including the courts and judicial officers (Fitzgerald, 2010, p.62). These values and principles include human dignity, equity, social justice, inclusiveness, equality, human rights, non-discrimination, and protection of the marginalized. State organs are enjoined by the constitution to take all these values into account whenever they interpret or apply the Constitution (Fitzgerald, 2010, p.3). Further, the Constitution requires the judiciary to promote the gender equality principle and fairness through transformative judicial decision-making (Baraza, 2018a, p.76). Article 259 specifically lays down the rule of judicial interpretation as follows:

> This Constitution shall be interpreted in a manner that promotes its purposes, values, and principles; advances the rule of law, and human rights and fundamental freedoms in the Bill of Rights; permits the development of the law, and contributes to good governance.

To buttress the Constitution, the Supreme Court of Kenya has reaffirmed the requirement under Article 259. In its Advisory Opinion No. 2 of 2011 (*In the Matter of Interim Independent Electoral Commission [2011] eKLR*), the Supreme Court ruled that the constitution, which is the supreme law of the country, calls for a transformative and purposive approach in their judicial decision-making. In a unanimous decision, the seven justices of the Supreme Court, Justices Willy Mutunga (Chief Justice), Nancy Baraza (Deputy Chief Justice), Jackton Ojwang, Smokin Wanjala, Philip Tunoi, Njoki Ndungu, and Mohammed Ibrahim affirmed the provisions of the constitution on interpretation, noting that it should be transformative. The Supreme Court confirmed that the Constitution requires the courts, in interpreting the Bill of Rights, to promote the values that underlie an open and democratic society, based on human dignity, equality, equity, and freedom, and the spirit, purport, and objects of the Bill of Rights, thus setting the pace for other courts to adopt transformative decision-making in interpreting the principles of the Constitution.

Consequential legislation to the Constitution has also been enacted since 2010. This includes the Marriage Act, the Matrimonial Property Act, the Protection from Domestic Violence Act, and the Land Act, among others. Together with the constitution, these laws are crucial to addressing women's marginalization. Since 2010, the courts have been making decisions in matters critical to gender equality and gender justice in line with the constitutional and the new laws (Kameri-Mbote & Muriungi, 2016, p.93). Opinions, however, vary on how well these recent court decisions uphold gender equality in areas that have perpetuated discrimination and gender inequality. There is scanty literature analyzing judicial decisions since 2010 to gauge the courts' fidelity to the Constitution's principles of gender equality. This chapter seeks to fill that gap.

The chapter is organized in six parts. The first part gives an overview of the constitutional provisions relevant to gender equality. The second part discusses transformation as a theory and its relevance to the discussions at hand. The third part is an exploration of the courts' decisions on marriage, inheritance, domestic violence, access to matrimonial property, and inheritance prior to the enactment of the 2010 constitution. The fourth part explores court decisions in similar areas since the promulgation of the Constitution in 2010. The fifth part discusses some possible threats to the transformative work by the judiciary. The sixth part gives a conclusion to the chapter.

Gender equality in the Constitution

The vision of social equity and gender justice enshrined in the Constitution marks a break from a past characterized by gender discrimination and inequality (Mutunga, 2015, p.5). Several articles of the constitution entrench gender equality and the demands of social justice in areas of equal treatment with men, equitable access to land, recognition of equality of ownership of matrimonial property, protection from gender-based violence (GBV), inheritance and equality in marriage, and women's equitable participation in elective and appointive positions in the country (Fitzgerald, 2010, p.3). Equality is listed as one of six essential values upon which governance should be based. These expressions of principle are given legal force in Article 10, which includes equity, social justice, equality, non-discrimination, and "protection of the marginalized" among the national values and principles of governance that are to be used in applying and interpreting the Constitution and other laws, and in making or implementing policy decisions.

Of importance is Article 27 of the Constitution. The right to equality and non-discrimination as expressed in Article 27 of the Constitution represents a substantial improvement on the right as provided in Article 82 of the previous constitution (Fitzgerald, 2010, p.3). The Article begins with a guarantee of equality before the law and equal protection and benefit of the law, a guarantee that was not present in the previous constitution. Moreover, equality is defined as including "full and equal enjoyment" of all rights and freedoms. These provisions provide important additional protection, which goes beyond the protection from discrimination provided in Article 27 (4). Article 27 (4) prohibits discrimination on an extensive list of specified grounds: "race, sex, pregnancy, marital status, health status, ethnic or social origin, color, age, disability, religion, conscience, belief, culture, dress, language or birth." The list grants substantially increased protection to women (Fitzgerald, 2010, p.3). Article 27 (6) creates a duty of affirmative action, a concept defined in Article 260, which obligates the State to take legislative and other measures, including but not limited to affirmative action programs and policies designed to redress any disadvantage suffered by individuals or groups as a result of past discrimination. Article 27 (8) requires the state to take measures to ensure that "not more than two-thirds of the members of elective or appointive bodies" are of the same gender. Separate provisions create reserved places for women in the National Assembly, Senate, and County Assemblies. These provisions should have a substantial positive effect on women's representation and role in the decision-making process at all levels of government (Fitzgerald, 2010, p.4).

The Constitution in Article 2 (5) and (6) adopts international treaties ratified by Kenya before 2010. Notable among the conventions is the Convention on the Elimination of All Forms of Discrimination against Women (CEDAW), which calls upon States Parties to take all appropriate measures to eliminate discrimination against women in the political and public life (Nzomo, 2016, p.45). Kameri-Mbote and Muriungi rightly argue that the 2010 Constitution heralded a new era, as it re-envisioned the governance charter by revamping fundamental rights and freedoms and providing for far-reaching institutional reforms. It expanded the purview of and made provision for affirmative action and social justice (Kameri-Mbote & Muriungi, 2016, p.93). Mutunga posits that the Constitution is a radical document, which looks to a future that is very different from the past in its values and practices. It seeks to make a fundamental change from colonialism and repressive post-colonial years of independence (Mutunga, 2015, p.5). He further states that Kenya has moved from a past characterized by much, which was arbitrary and unequal in the operation of the law to a present and a future in a constitutional state where state action must be such that it is capable of being analyzed and justified rationally. The idea of a constitutional state presupposes a system whose operation can be rationally tested against or in terms of the law (Mutunga, 2015, p.5).

In stark contrast to the independence Constitution, the 2010 Constitution sets up an institutional framework of checks and balances, including through strengthened judicial review, something for which women activists actively lobbied (Baraza, 2018, p.3). In a nutshell, the Constitution potentially provides an enabling institutional architecture for the realization and protection of women's rights and gender equality principles. Such was the extent of its reform in favor of gender equality that the 2010 constitution is known informally as "the women's constitution" (Baraza, 2018, p.3). Additionally, the Constitution spells out how the judiciary is to interpret its robust Bill of Rights. Article 259 states that the Constitution shall be interpreted in a manner that promotes its purposes, values, and principles; advances the rule of law, and the human rights and fundamental freedoms; permits development of the law; and contributes to good governance (Mutunga, 2015, p.5).

There is no doubt that the Constitution offers the courts an opportunity to break from the old way of judicial interpretation, which failed to consider societal values as the basis for decision-making. The courts are expected to "liberate themselves from previously self-imposed restraints that undermined their position in the equilibrium of governmental power" (Mutunga, 2015, p.5). Such restraints included a legal culture in which judges and lawyers failed to relate their actions to the purposes of a Constitution in any functional democracy. Muigai notes that the Kenyan courts have previously adopted a positivist approach to judicial interpretation, which ignored constitutional values such as equality and social justice (Muigai, 2004, p.45).

The realization of gender equality under the Constitution is a possibility but it requires innovative and transformative judicial decision-making by the judiciary. The framers of the 2010 Constitution were alive to feminist approaches to the interpretation of the Constitution when they entrenched a method of interpretation in the constitution (Baraza, 2018a, p.75). The constitutional requirement for transformative judicialism seeks to diminish the difficulty that courts have previously faced by setting parameters for purposive interpretation. According to Baraza (2018a, p.76), this interpretive approach considers societal values and requires judges to be the guardians of the socio-political transformation project of the country. Difficulties in judicial interpretation require all provisions of the Constitution to be construed according to the doctrine of interpretation that the law is always speaking, thus avoiding doctrinal and textual capture (Mutunga, 2015, p.5).

The argument in this chapter is that the Constitution's normative provisions, coupled with the imperative of purposive interpretation placed on the judiciary, offer an excellent opportunity for the judiciary to move away from the past and uphold gender equality and the human dignity of all people. However, the chapter is also aware that the purposive role of the judiciary faces threats not just from itself but from parliament and executive arms of government, as will be discussed elsewhere in the chapter. The following section examines the meaning and theoretical perspectives of transformation.

Transformation

The Cambridge dictionary, 1995 edition, defines transformation as "a complete change in the appearance or character of something or someone, especially so that that thing or person is improved." This definition of the concept of transformation is reflected in the design and spirit of the Kenyan Constitution, considering the historical inequalities in Kenya and the intention of the constitutional purpose of shaping a new and different future that is anchored in social justice. Klare, who coined the term "transformative constitutionalism," says that transformative constitutionalism means a long-term project of constitutional enactment, interpretation and enforcement committed (not in isolation, of course, but in a historical context of conducive political developments) to transforming a country's political and social institutions and power relationships in a democratic, participatory, and egalitarian direction (Klare, 2012, p.146). He further states that transformative constitutionalism is anchored by progressive jurisprudence from the judiciary and observance of the Constitution by other state organs, and indeed all Kenyans (Klare, 1998, p.152). In this view, achieving equality in the context of transformation requires an understanding by lawmakers, judges, and those in charge of institutions of society that equality forms the center of the constitutional vision and promise of transformation, as well as an understanding of equality as a value and equality as a right.

Langa also argues that transformation is a social and an economic revolution, while. Albertyn and Goldblatt perceive transformation to be a movement from the one side of the bridge to the other, and this would have to be radical movement which requires a complete reconstruction of the state and society, including a redistribution of power and resources along egalitarian lines. The challenge in achieving equality within this transformation project involves the eradication of systemic forms of domination and material disadvantage based on race, gender, class and other grounds of inequality. It also entails the development of opportunities which allow people to realize their full human potential within positive social relationships (Langa, 2017, p.353).

Transformative judicial interpretation is premised on the concept of transformation. It draws from Ronald Dworkin's theory of constructive interpretation, which posits a principle-based mode of interpretation (Zegrebelsky, 2001, p.621). Dworkin's principle-based approach to interpretation considers societal values and principles as foundational to judicial decision-making. This approach faults the positivist approach, which considers interpretation as merely guided by rules, precedents, and procedures, and judges as mere mouthpieces of the legislature (Zegrebelsky, 2001, p.622). The positivist approach, however, remains common among judges and lawyers, especially in the common law systems, and dominated judicial thought among most Kenyan judges, especially before 2010. Dworkin's approach leads to transformative constitutionalism, the very expectation of the constitution of Kenya. A transformative Constitution and its attendant transformative constitutionalism are both about a change from a status quo that is neither acceptable nor sustainable (Mutunga, 2015, p.5).

The Constitution of Kenya is transformative and aims at changing the society to make it more egalitarian and alive to gender equality. Although the word "transformation" does not appear in the Constitution of Kenya, it has now been widely accepted that the Constitution aims at radically changing or transforming the political, social, cultural, and economic space in Kenya (Mutunga, 2015, p.5).

Judicial decisions on gender issues in Kenya prior to 2010

Patriarchal decision-making in matters of succession arising out of a narrow judicial interpretation of the law by the courts was rampant in the judiciary prior to 2010. Property of a deceased patriarch customarily devolved to the male members of a household, principally the sons of the deceased (Kamau, 2015, p.4). Where a deceased person had no son, such property devolved to the deceased person's brothers. It was assumed that girl children or women could not inherit, at least under customary law, on the basis that women never really belong to any clan, as they move from their clan of birth to their husband's clan. Most customs only allow some inheritance to unmarried daughters and divorced women when they return to their parents' home, but even in such instances, the inheritance given to such women is small compared with that of sons or men. These practices serve to entrench gender inequality further, as they peg what a person may inherit from their parents' estate on their gender without referring to other relevant factors (Baraza, 2008, p.5).

An examination of some cases demonstrates the skewed nature of judgments, mostly against women, prior to 2010. In the case of *Mary Rono v Jane Rono & another, [2008] 1 KLR 803*, for instance, the High Court awarded a lesser share of the deceased father's estate to the girls and a bigger share to the brothers, agreeing with the brothers that the girls would get married elsewhere and get property from their husbands (Baraza, 2008, p.5). The sons had based their argument on tribal culture, which did not permit girls to inherit land from their father. Upon appeal, the Court of Appeal reversed the High Court decision, noting that the law of succession in Kenya did not discriminate against girls. Although the High Court decision was overturned by the Court of Appeal in *Eldoret High Court Civil Appeal 66 OF 2002), [2005] eKLR*, the case reflected the common judicial attitude at the time.

Regarding division of matrimonial property, until 2013, when the Matrimonial Property Act was enacted, Kenya relied on an old 1882 piece of legislation—the Married Women Property Act (MWPA) of England—to find relief for women seeking a share of matrimonial property. The Act laid the ground for a consideration of women as legally distinct individuals, contrary to the situation prevailing under the doctrine of coverture that underpinned the old English law (Kameri-Mbote & Muriungi, 2016, p.45). Judicial construction of the provisions of the MWPA presented mixed but dismal results in terms of delivering property rights for married women. For instance, in *Echaria v Echaria, Civil Appeal 75 of 2001 (2007) eKLR (C.A.)*, the court held that a married woman had to prove financial contribution in order to get a share of the matrimonial property upon divorce. Given the injustice and harshness visited on married women, who mainly performed unpaid household chores, the court in *Kivuitu v Kivuitu Civil Appeal 26 of 1985, eKLR* had earlier remarked *obiter* that contribution need not be financial.

According to Kameri-Mbote and Muriungi, there were many instances of women and children being disinherited when male members of households or husbands opted to dispose of the matrimonial property with the concurrence of the courts (Kameri-Mbote & Muriungi, 2016, p.45). This was the position in *Jacinta Wanjiku Kamau v Isaac Kamau Mungai, Civil Appeal 59 of 2001 (2006) 59 K.L.R*, where the court emphasized that the husband was under no legal obligation to seek the consent of the wife before disposing of the land that was used as matrimonial property as long as it was registered solely in the husband's name. Though the wife worked to maintain the land, she was only awarded 0.25 acres of the land to enable her to fend for herself and the eight children. A similar holding regarding the interest of a married woman was made in *Margaret Mumbi Kagiri v Kagiri Wamairwe & 3 others. (2007) 181 K.L.R. 8 (C.A. K)*.

In the case of *Kamore v Kamore [2000] 1* EA 80, the court considered the principle or doctrine of trust. It held that there was a need to show evidence of contribution by a spouse and thus departed from Nderitu. The court held that it could not make a finding of a resulting trust in favor of the wife without evidence of either express or implied intention of the donor. It further noted that there was a need to demonstrate contribution for a share of matrimonial property to vest and that section 17 of the MWPA gave no power to the court to pass any proprietary interest from one spouse to another (Kameri-Mbote & Muriungi, 2016, p.45).

In *Kimani v Kimani, [2000] 1 EA 80, 81, 85*, the parties had undergone a Christian marriage and were blessed with two children but later lived separately after strains in their relationship. After alleged battery, the wife left the matrimonial home for good and later filed for divorce. Within the pendency of the divorce proceedings, she brought an application for a share of property. During trial, the husband was able to prove that he contributed to the purchase of the property alone. Kuloba J, unconvinced that the wife had made any financial contribution toward the acquisition of the property, held that contribution must be proved on evidence (Kameri-Mbote & Muriungi, 2016, p.45). The trial equated the behavior of the wife wanting to share in the matrimonial property with her "riding on the husband's back with her hands in his pocket." This decision was reversed by the Court of Appeal, on the basis that the trial judge was biased generally against women, and remitted to another trial judge for retrial.

Customary marriages in their several variants have existed in Kenya alongside their formal and religious counterparts. However, customary law generally, and customary marriages in particular, have, until the 2010 constitution, been assigned an inferior status to civil and religious marriages (Osogo & Ahaya, 2015, p.47). Customary marriages include polygamous unions, woman-to-woman marriages, and widow inheritance, among others. Subjugation of customary marriages, expressed through court decisions, has previously caused a lot of suffering to the concerned parties. From the onset of colonialism, courts have entrenched a dim view of African forms of marriage, and in most cases, they have declared them either immoral or not worth being called marriages (Cotran, 1983, p.42).

In *R v Amkeyo [1917] 7 EALR 14*, the question that arose during the trial was whether a woman married under African customary law could testify against her husband in a criminal case in which she was the only witness. The husband had been charged with stealing an animal skin, which he hid in the matrimonial house. Applicable common law deemed a husband and wife as one person, and neither could be compelled to give evidence against the other. In this case, the court found that the African wife could give evidence against her husband because the two did not meet the criteria of being considered married. According to Hamilton, CJ, a wife married under African customary law was not a legal wife or spouse under the formal law. Consequently, the court compelled her to give evidence against her husband. This case is indicative of how African customary law was degraded to the bottom of the legal rules hierarchy and made way for judicial precedence, ordinances, and statutes (Osogo & Ahaya, 2015, p.47).

In *Maria Angoi v Macella Nyomenda, Civil Appeal No.1 of 1981(unreported)*, the court was faced with the question of whether a woman-to-woman marriage custom among the Kisii tribe was repugnant to justice and morality. A woman-to-woman marriage is a customary practice whereby a woman whose husband is dead "marries" another woman and chooses a male figure from her husband's clan to sire children for the dead husband. The High Court held that the practice was repugnant to justice and morality, since it prevented the other woman from freely choosing whom to marry. Thus, there was no marriage. The decision did not consider the circumstances of the local community and the intention underlying the woman-to-woman practice in African communities, whose perpetuity was guaranteed through children (Baraza, 2018, p.71).

Judicial decisions since 2010

Since the promulgation of the Constitution in 2010, some Kenyan courts have begun to embrace transformative and purposive judicial interpretation of cases and this has led to significant strides toward realizing gender equality in marriage, access to matrimonial property, protection against gender-based and domestic violence, and inheritance. Courts have been developing jurisprudence with some radical judgments that have upheld the principles of equality (Kameri-Mbote & Muriungi, 2016, p.45). The following part discusses some of these cases.

Inheritance

Since 2010, the courts have been emphatic that all children, whether male or female and irrespective of their marital status or financial status, are eligible to inherit in equal shares unless they indicate to the court that they do not wish to inherit. These decisions have been made as a result of women challenging being disinherited by their brothers and uncles. In *re Estate of Francis Mbaria (Deceased) [2018] eKLR*, one of the female children filed an application for revocation of a grant that had been issued and confirmed to one of the male children (her brother). She protested the mode of distribution of the estate of her deceased father, citing unfairness, and principally on the ground that the female children had each been allocated 1 acre of land, unlike the male children, who were given a bigger portion. The brothers had argued that the female children were happily married and had property of their own and thus ought to be satisfied with the 1 acre of the land that they had been allotted. The court, in considering the argument that married female children should not inherit from their parents, as doing so is unfair to their brothers, rejected the argument as being based on backward and patriarchal customs. Accordingly, the court held that all the children were entitled to an equal share (Kameri-Mbote & Muriungi, 2016, p.45).

Similarly, in *Joshua Cheruiyot v Rachel Korir [2017] eKLR*, six sisters in their old age who had been totally disinherited by their brothers were able to successfully apply for revocation of grant and obtain a declaration that all the children were to have an equal share of their deceased father's property. The rationale for providing for equal inheritance for both male and female children in the spirit of gender equality was aptly put by Justice Kimaru in *Peter Keingati & 4 Others Vs Ann Nguthi & 3 Others [2014] eKLR*, where he stated that due to "the promulgation of the constitution 2010, particularly Article 27 that prohibits discrimination of persons on the basis of their sex, marital status or social status, among others, the time has now come for those discriminative cultural practices against women be buried in history."

Gender-based violence (GBV)

Gender-based violence (GBV) is one of the most prevalent human rights violations in Kenya. Violence against women is perhaps the most widespread and socially tolerated human rights violation, cutting across borders, race, class, ethnicity, and religion. GBV in Africa, as elsewhere in the world, is a complex issue that has at its root structural inequalities between men and women, young and old. This results in the persistence of power differentials between the sexes. World Bank research has indicated that in 2014, 22% of Kenyan women and 19% of Kenyan men agreed with the statement that if a wife went out without informing her husband, he would be justified in hitting or beating her. The social norms justifying GBV in Kenya appear to have been changing: the share of the population who agreed with the above statement fell by about half between 2003 and 2014 (DHS, 2018). However, in 2014, about half of all women (45%) between the ages of 15 and 49 reported having experienced physical violence (World Bank, 2018).

The Kenyan state has, in most cases, perpetrated or tolerated violence against women, through either action or non-action, by prioritizing custom or tradition over the respect of fundamental freedoms and rights belonging to women. Previously, there had been little commitment from the state to protect citizens from the vice of GBV; the existing criminal laws were not adequate to address the issue, and in any event, they were ignored in favor of customs by law enforcers. The Constitution recognizes several important general principles that are of importance to gender equality and that have a general bearing on GBV in the country (Aura, 2015). These principles were either not given recognition by the previous Constitution or were given inadequate treatment.

A significant development consequential to the 2010 constitution was the enactment of the Protection from Domestic Violence Act of 2015. The Act is fundamental, as it is the only piece of legislation that addresses violence within the family set-up. The Constitution at Article 29 provides expressly for the freedom and security of the person. Article 29 (c) protects all persons from any form of violence from either public or private sources, and Article 29 (d) prohibits any manner of torture, whether physical or psychological. The Constitution further places the duty on the state and its organs to ensure that the Bill of Rights is followed. Article 21 (3) of the Constitution places this duty on all public officers. The state and public officers are required to address the needs of vulnerable groups within the society, including women, older members of the society, persons with disabilities, children, youth, members of minorities or marginalized communities, and members of particular ethnic, religious, or cultural communities (Aura, 2015, p.4). Since 2010, the courts have been developing jurisprudence in the area of GBV. In *NML v Peter Petrausch [2015] eKLR*, Rika J held that "gender-based violence is the most prevalent human rights violation in the world. No other form of sex discrimination violates so many fundamental rights as articulated in the 1948 United Nations Universal Declaration of Human Rights". The claimant, in this case, was a domestic worker who was consistently sexually harassed and threatened by her employer. The case indicates the gravity of domestic violence matters.

The recent case of *C.K. (A Child) Through Ripples International as Her Guardian and Next Friend) & 11 Others v. Commissioner of Police/Inspector General of The*

National Police Service & 3 Others [2013] eKLR is significant. In this case, the High Court's finding that the failure of the police to enforce Section 8 of the Sexual Offences Act 2006 effectively infringed upon the petitioners' right to equal protection and benefit of the law, contrary to Article 27 (1) of the Constitution of Kenya, 2010, was a step in the right direction. Also, the court observed that by failing to enforce existing defilement laws, the police contributed to the development of a culture of tolerance for pervasive sexual violence against girl children with impunity (Aura, 2015, p.4).

On the other hand, Wakiaga J in *Republic v Johana Mweni [2018] eKLR*, while commenting on the issue of domestic violence, stated that

> The court is alive to the rise in the number of deaths arising out of domestic violence or in the family setting and therefore any Judgement/Sentence meted out by the court should send a warning that the home is a city of refuge and not a place where one has to be on his/her guard as was in the case herein.

These are profound sentiments by the courts, not previously known for regarding domestic violence, because it afflicts mostly women, as a serious offense, and demonstrate transformative decision-making. Within a patriarchal society, it should be noted that although the Protection from Domestic Violence Act of 2015 is a great milestone in addressing GBV, the vice still persists due to ignorance of the law among many Kenyans and the perseverance of socio-cultural habits that still condone such violence.

Sharing of matrimonial property

Matrimonial property is now governed by the Matrimonial Property Act of 2013. This legislation replaced the old English Married Women's Property Act of 1882, which was introduced in Kenya in the colonial period as an Act of general application. The 2013 law recognizes non-monetary contributions, such as housework, toward the acquisition of matrimonial property. The introduction of non-monetary contributions in consideration of marital property distribution upon divorce is a shift from earlier case law, which was seen in *Peter Mburu Echaria vs. Priscilla Echaria [2007] eKLR* before the enactment of this Act, and set out the direct financial contribution of a spouse in a marriage as the basis of determination of the distribution of marital property in divorce cases (Kameri-Mbote & Muriungi, 2016, p.17). *In ZWN v PNN* [2012] eKLR, the court shared the properties equally between the spouses.

Equality in marriage

Courts have also since 2010 affirmed equality of parties in a marriage, a departure from the past. In the case of *Agnes Nanjala -vs- Jacob Goes, Appeal No. 127 of 2011* (UR), the court affirmed equality of spouses and appreciated that the

Constitution guarantees equality of parties to a marriage and both are entitled to equal rights at the time of the marriage during the marriage and at the dissolution of the marriage.

There have also been progressive court decisions on matters of the rights of women in customary marriages. Courts had previously failed to protect women in polygamous unions. They had also been inconsistent in articulating the position of customary practices such as the much-respected woman-to-woman marriage, which is a reality among several communities (Baraza, 2018a, p.71). Departing from the court's attitude in *R. vs. Amkeyo* discussed earlier, the courts have dealt positively with polygamy and the institution of woman-to-woman marriage. In the case of *Eunita Geko & Another v Philip Orinda Petition No. 237 of 2014 [2015] EKLR*, the court upheld the validity of a woman-to-woman marriage under the Kuria customs, a clear departure from the decision in *Gisege Angoi v Macella Nyomenda*, discussed earlier, in which the court had declared woman-to-woman marriage immoral and repugnant to morality. The "repugnancy" clause in the Kenyan Judicature Act, chapter 8 of the Laws of Kenya, was a colonial requirement as a criterion for the application of African customary laws.

Threats to the judiciary's efforts to uphold gender equality

Although the Constitution has the potential for realization of gender equality, customary law, which has historically held *de facto* sway over formal law (Hallward-Driemejer & Hasan, 2012), still threatens to lessen the impact of the transformative constitution, especially in matters of inheritance of land by women. Kamau (2011a, p.4) acknowledges that customary law contains aspects that often run counter to principles of gender equality and non-discrimination espoused in the constitution, especially the right of women to inherit equally with men. Indeed, World Bank research (World Bank, 2015) has also found that Kenya is indeed notable as one of a minority of African countries where there are formal inheritance rights. However, the research also notes that though the Constitution establishes non-discrimination articles, some subordinate statutes do have lingering gender biases. For example, the Law of Succession Act distinguishes between male and female surviving spouses. It is also worth noting that since the promulgation of the Constitution, the right guaranteed to women to inherit land from their parents has hardly benefited them due to hostility from their male siblings against allowing them to inherit, basing their arguments on customary practices (Kamau, 2011b, p.4).

Although the judiciary has been transformative in its decisions, the legislature and the executive pose a real threat to its efforts, particularly given that one of the key distinctive features of the constitution relating to gender equity is the not more than two-thirds gender rule, which is meant to ensure fair representation of women in the legislature and appointed positions. The provision has been repeatedly undermined and contested by both the legislative and executive branches, and no enabling legislation has been enacted or implemented. This spells real danger to women's representation in elective and appointive positions envisaged under the constitution. Further, Kenya is currently considering constitutional amendments, and women fear that the entire not more than two-thirds gender rule might be repealed if men's current attitude toward it is anything to go by (Kamau, 2011b, p.4).

Conclusion

This chapter set out to examine the nature of judicial decisions on gender equality since the promulgation of the constitution of Kenya 2010. It has highlighted the normative and procedural provisions that are of importance for equality generally and for gender equality in particular. Further, it explored the duty that the constitution imposes on the courts in decision-making. It examined relevant decided cases before the 2010 constitution and demonstrated how narrow approaches to interpretation by the courts sustained gender inequality. It noted that the courts are under an obligation to depart from the positivist approach of the past when making decisions that touch on the rights of men and women. A significant part of this chapter was then devoted to an analysis of jurisprudence on gender equality on disparate areas of law as emanating from the various courts of law. The analysis has shown that in the majority of cases, the courts have been transformative and bold in asserting themselves and giving effect to constitutional provisions on gender equality. It also noted that although the judiciary has been transformative, both the legislature and the executive threaten to derail equal participation of men and women in all spheres of life.

References

Aura-Odhiambo, R.A. (2015), *Situational Analysis and the Legal Framework on Sexual and Gender-based Violence in Kenya: Challenges and Opportunities*. Nairobi: National Council for Law Reporting.

Baraza, N. (2008). Lost Between Rhetoric and Reality: What Role for the Law and Human Rights in Redressing Gender Inequality? *Kenya Law Review Journal*, 11, 16–27.

Baraza, N. (2018a). Supreme Court of Kenya Advisory Opinion on the Two-Thirds Gender Principle: A Critique Through Dworkin's Constructive Interpretation. *East African Law Journal, 150*, 150–165.

Baraza, N (2018b). The Institution of Woman to Woman Marriage in Kenya: Navigating Between Culture and Human Rights. *Africa Nazarene University Law Journal*, 6(2):71–91

Cotran, E. (1983). *The Development and Reform of the Law in Kenya*. Cambridge: Cambridge University Press.

Demographic Health (DHS) (2018). The Kenya National Bureau of Statistics (KNBS), https://dhsprogram.com/pubs/pdf/fr308/fr308.pdf.

Fitzgerald, J. (2010). The Road to Equality? The Right to Equality in Kenya's New Constitution. *The Equal Rights Review*, 5, 55–69.

Hallward-Driemeier, M., & Hasan, T. (2013). A Copublication of the Agence Franceise de Developpment and the World Bank. Available at www.worldbank.org

Kamau, W. (2011a). Customary Law and Women's Rights in Kenya. http://theequalityeffect.org/wp-content/uploads/2014/12/CustomaryLawAndWomensRightsInKenya.pdf

Kamau, W. (2011b). Women Judges and Magistrates in Kenya: Challenges, Opportunities and Contribution. In U. Schultz & G. Shaw (eds.), *Gender and Judging. Overview and Synthesis* (pp. 167–190). Oxford: Hart.

Kamau, W. (2015). Women's Representation in elective and Appointive Offices in Kenya: Towards Realization of The Two-Thirds Gender Principle. In M.K Mbondenyi, E.O. Asaala, T. Kabau, & A. Waris (eds.), *Human Rights and Democratic Governance in Kenya: A Post-2007 Appraisal*. Pretoria University Law Press (PULP). https://www.pulp.up.ac.za/edited-collections/human-rights-and-democratic-governance-in-kenya-a-post-2007-appraisal

Kameri-Mbote P. (2018). Constitutions as pathways to gender equality in Plural legal systems. *Oslo Law Review*, 5, 21–41.

Kameri-Mbote, P., and Kabira, N. (2018). Woman of Law: Kenyan Women's Triumph in the Constitution of Kenya. In W. Kabira, P. Kameri-Mbote, N. Kabira, & A. Meroka (Eds.), *Changing the Mainstream: Celebrating Women's Resilience*. Nairobi: African Women Studies Centre, University of Nairobi.

Kameri-Mbote, P., and Muriungi, M. (2016). Much ado about Nothing; A Critical analysis of the Matrimonial Property Law in Kenya. *Zanzibar Yearbook Law Journal*, 6, 71–102.

Klare, K.E. (2012). Legal Culture and Transformative Constitutionalism. *South African Journal on Human Rights*, *14*(1), 146–188.

Langa, P. 2017. Transformative Constitutionalism. 17 Stellenbosch L. Rev. 351, 2006, 351–360.

McCullough, A., Simbiri, F., & Wanjala, B. (2016). *Women and Power: Shaping the Development of Kenya's 2010 Constitution*. London: Overseas Development Institute.

Muigai, G. (2004). Political Jurisprudence or Neutral Principles: Another Look at the Problem of Constitutional Interpretation. *The East African Law Journal*, *1*, 40–60.

Mutunga, W. (2015). The 2010 Constitution of Kenya and Its Interpretation: Reflections from the Supreme Court's Decisions. *Speculum Juris* 6, 29(1), 1–20.

Nzomo M. (1991). The Role of Women in Politics and Public Decision Making Positions. Paper presented at the United Nations Expert Group Meeting on the Role of Women in Politics and Public Decision Making, Vienna, Austria, 21–24 M. http://erepository.uonbi.ac.ke/handle/11295/46061

Nzomo M, (1993). The Gender Dimension of Democratization in Kenya: Some International Linkages. *Alternatives*, *18*(1), 61–74. University of Nairobi.

Nzomo, M. (2016). *The Status of Women's Human Rights in Kenya and Strategies to Overcome Inequalities*. Cambridge: Cambridge University Press.

Nzomo M. (2018). Gender and Governance in Kenya: Women's Journey Beyond Numbers. In *Changing the Mainstream: Celebrating Women's Resilience* (Kabira W, Kameri-Mbote P, Kabira N and Meroka A eds). Nairobi: African Women Studies Centre, University of Nairobi.

Osogo A.J., & O. Ahaya. (2015). The Wretched African Traditionalists in Kenya: The Challenges and Prospects of Customary Law in the New Constitutional Era. *Strathmore Law Journal*, *1*(1), 41–58.

Patricia Kameri-Mbote, P. (2016). The quest for equal gender representation in Kenya's Parliament: Past and present challenges. In Japhet Biegon (ed.), *Gender Equality and Political Processes in Kenya* (39–64). Strathmore University Press.

Procter, P. (1995). *Cambridge International Dictionary of English*. Cambridge: Cambridge University Press.

World Bank, 2015. Women, Business and the Law Report. Available at http://pubdocs.worldbank.org/en/810421519921949813/Women-Business-and-the-Law-2016.pdf

World Bank, 2018. Http:/documents 1.worldbank.org,/pdf/kenya-poverty-and-gender-assessment-2015-2016-reflecting-on-a-decade-of-progress-and-the-road-ahead.pdf

Zegrebelsky, G. (2001). *Ronald Dworkin's Principle-based Constitutionalism*. London: Oxford University Press.

Constitutions

The Constitution of Kenya 2010
The Independence Constitution of Kenya 1963

Statutes

Judicature Act, chapter 8 of the Laws of Kenya
Matrimonial Property Act of 2013.
Protection from Domestic Violence Act of 2015
2014 Marriage Act, the 2013

Cited cases

Agnes Nanjala -vs- Jacob Goes, Appeal No. 127 of 2011 (UR)

C.K. (A Child) Through Ripples International as Her Guardian and Next Friend) & 11 Others v. Commissioner of Police/Inspector General of The National Police Service & 3 Others [2013] eKLR.

Echaria v Echaria, Civil Appeal 75 of 2001 (2007) eKLR (C.A.).

Eunita Geko & Another v Philip Orinda Petition No. 237 of 2014 [2015] EKLR.

Joshua Cheruiyot v Rachel Korir [2017] eKL.,

Kimani v Kimani, [2000] 1 EA 80.

Kamore v Kamore [2000] 1 EA 80.

Lucy Wanjiru Kariuki v Republic, Criminal Revision 12 of 2014 [2015] eKLR.

Maria Angoi v Macella Nyomenda, Civil Appeal No.1 of 1981(unreported).

Margaret Mumbi Kagiri v Kagiri Wamairwe& 3 others. (2007) 181 K.L.R. 8 (C.A. K).

Mary Rono v Jane Rono & another, [2008] 1 KLR 803.

Mary Rono v Jane Rono & another, Eldoret High Court Civil Appeal 66 OF 2002), [2005] eKLR,

MJK v FML Civil Suit 39 of 2012.

NML v Peter Petrausch [2015] eKL.,

Peter Mburu Echaria vs. Priscilla Echaria [2007] eKLR.

Peter Keingati & 4 Others Vs Ann Nguthi & 3 Others [2014] eKLR.

Republic v Amkeyo [1917] 7 EALR 14.

Republic v Johana Mweni [2018] eKLR.

Republic v Collet Wafula [2016] eKLR.

Re Estate of Francis Mbaria (Deceased) [2018] EkL.

Supreme Court of Kenya Advisory Opinion No. 2 of 2011(In the Matter of Interim Independent Electoral Commission [2011] eKLR.

3 To win both the battle and the war

Judicial determination of property rights of spouses in Ghana

Maame Yaa Mensa-Bonsu and Maame A.S. Mensa-Bonsu

Introduction

Customary law has long been problematic for wives seeking access to marital property in Ghana. In both matrilineal and patrilineal family systems, marriage does not entail the self-acquired estates of the spouses (Mensa-Bonsu, 2012). The self-acquired property, therefore, became family property on the intestate death of the owner, leaving the surviving spouse without an interest in the property which they should rightfully own. The cultural bias in favor of males in succession and other customary laws have served to widen the economic chasm between males and females, with the latter often unable to enjoy the products of their labor. From pre-independence times until the 1992 constitution, Ghanaian courts determined disputes involving marital property largely under customary law, which, as noted, is often disadvantageous to wives. What progress was made toward parity resulted from judges' reliance on their own culturally shaped notions of fairness, and standards of progressive thinking. The 1992 Constitution of Ghana has provided Ghana's legal order with a new and apparently more just standard for the distribution of marital property. This chapter evaluates seminal cases from before and since 1992 to establish the practical impact of Article 22 of the 1992 constitution on the financial fortunes of ex-wives (i.e., widowed or divorced). We seek to answer the following questions:

1. Have judicial outcomes improved for women since the 1992 constitution took over the regulation of spousal property rights?
2. Has the rhetoric of judicial law-making in fact evolved along the lines of the 1992 constitution?

The chapter is divided into three sections. The first briefly examines the state of Ghana's law prior to the coming into force of the 1992 constitution. It outlines the customary law position and the judicial efforts at progressing beyond this position through the substantial contribution doctrine, statute law, and the application of equitable principles. The second provides an extensive review of the trends in the outcomes and rhetoric since 1993, when the constitution came

DOI: 10.4324/9780429327865-4

into force. Of particular interest is the import of Article 22 on the judicial determination of spousal rights to marital property. Finally, we consider the challenges posed by judicial interpretation of the relevant provisions and caveats applied by subsequent courts. We provide a critical analysis of the potential tensions between Article 22 and other constitutional provisions. While not proposing specific reforms, the insights this chapter will achieve are critical for accurately assessing the progress we have made toward creating a just and equitable society and how much remains to be done. We advance these arguments with the goal that they will contribute to the evolution of Ghana into a consciously shaped, rather than reactionary, society, with the full intent to advance the rights of women.

Property rights of wives: Before 1992

This section provides an overview of the state of the law up until the 1992 constitution entered into force by looking first at the outcomes and then at the rhetoric under which the said outcomes were achieved. The goal is to contextualize any changes that the 1992 constitution has achieved in respect of both the guiding principles for the distribution of property between spouses upon the dissolution or determination of marriage, and the portions of the estate that have typically fallen to the female spouse. We do this by examining the landmark cases from Ghana's independence in 1957 until December 1992, when the last dictatorship ended.

Judicial rhetoric

The rhetoric of the pre-1992 regime on spousal rights was centered on three things: customary law, equity, and statute law. In that era, both the rhetoric and consequent outcomes were based exclusively on customary law. The experience of ex-wives and widows was especially dire under these laws, leading to court-led initiatives to soften the impact of customary law on them. But as the court would not depart too far from the customary law rule, the improvement was not overwhelming. The statutory interventions, though helpful, did not apply to every ex-wife/widow in every circumstance (Watnizek, 1991). Equity was also sometimes invoked to provide relief in particularly unjust situations. However, customary and statute law could not be entirely sidestepped. Equity could, therefore, not serve as a wholesale rectifier of the harsh impact of customary law and statute law. Thus, the situation until the 1992 constitution entered into force was one of inconsistencies and inequality for wives. We now examine briefly how women fared in terms of outcomes under each of these three sources of judicial rhetoric.

Customary law

The decision in *Quartey v. Martey* (1959) set out the judicial understanding of customary law in respect of the property rights of widows. In that case, the plaintiff, who had been married to the intestate under customary law for over 25 years, sued her deceased husband's family for expenses incurred in the course of the funeral and for a one-third share in his estate. She argued that as she had assisted her late husband both in his work and financially, and as he had by such assistance acquired the properties, she was entitled to a share thereof.

Ollennu J held that by customary law, it was the duty of a man's wife and children to assist him in carrying out the duties of his station in life. The proceeds of that joint effort, and any property acquired with such proceeds, were by customary law the property of the man and not the joint property of the spouses.[1] The only right of a widow, the court further held, was to maintenance and support from the family of her deceased husband. Unsupported by evidence (Daniels, 1972), *Quartey v Martey* nevertheless became firmly entrenched in the jurisprudence and was followed in a long line of cases, including *Yaotey v. Quaye* (1961), *Adom v Kwarley* (1962), *Manu v. Kuma* (1963), and *Jonas v. Ofori* (1988). *Ayer v. Kumordzie* (1964) held that even the chattels a husband provided to his wife for her personal use were limited to the duration of the marriage and save for those expressly declared to be gifts, fell to be returned upon its dissolution.

The case of *Quaico v. Fosu* (1965) ameliorated the condition of widows. There, the court found, for the first time, that under Akan customary law, a widow, while she remained unmarried, had a proprietary interest equivalent to a determinable life tenancy in her deceased husband's property. Further, and perhaps more importantly, she did not have to live in the property; she could rent it out and enjoy the rental income therefrom. While the family acquired title to the late husband's estate, it was subject to the life interest of his children and the occupational rights of the widow. *Quaico v. Fosu* not only gave widows, at last, a proprietary right, albeit only a non-heritable, inalienable, potentially temporary one; it also provided a potential source of income for the widow. As for ex-wives, they remained firmly under the *Quartey v. Martey* regime until the doctrine of substantial contribution was adopted by the courts.

Substantial contribution doctrine

In the 1970s, the courts introduced the doctrine of substantial contribution, which deemed a wife to have acquired a proprietary interest in property if she had contributed to its acquisition (financially or in-kind) to a degree exceeding the duty of wifely assistance contemplated by customary law. The scope of this interest, however, was to be determined by the court on a case-by-case basis. In *Yeboah v. Yeboah* (1974), where the doctrine was first espoused, the wife had, at her own expense, flown repeatedly to Ghana from their London residence to supervise the construction of the property in dispute and paid the costs of structural changes thereto. The court held that the wife was a joint owner of the house and further, that the conduct of the parties prior to, during, and subsequent to the acquisition of the property displayed an intention to own the matrimonial home jointly.

What the principle of substantial contribution entailed was elucidated by *Abebreseh v. Kaah* (1976), *Clerk v. Clerk* (1981), and *Achiampong v. Achiampong*

(1983). In *Abebreseh,* the court found that part payment for the land and sole support of the family during the construction period amounted to a "substantial contribution." In *Clerk,* the court stated that it would, or at least could, hold the overwhelming role in family life played by a stay-at-home wife and mother as a substantial contribution; but only if the wife, having had the option of a career, had forfeited it to take care of the home needs of the family. *Achiampong* added the rule that the substantial contribution could be established by proving either an agreement between the couple giving the wife some beneficial interest in the matrimonial home, or the wife's direct financial improvements, renovation, or extensions to the property, or that she had applied her income for the family upkeep, thereby financially enabling the husband to acquire the property in dispute.

Substantial contribution continued as the guiding principle of a wife's rights in marital property acquired until 1993, when the Fourth Republic began. But it had unclear thresholds, and each judge relied on their own estimation of what acts exceeded the *Quartey v. Martey* standard. In some cases, contributions that were held not to be insubstantial were nonetheless not held to be enough to convey an interest in the property to the wife; for example, paying in part for and personally supervising the construction of the property (*Abobor v. Abobor,* 1987) and paying all household bills and the children's school fees to enable the husband to devote his earnings to the property (*Otoo v Otoo,* 1984, *Odoteye v. Odoteye,* 1984–86). In others, contributions of the same kind and in some cases to an even lesser extent were held to suffice (*Anang v. Tagoe,* 1989–90, *Domfe v. Adu,* 1986). The case law was thus very inconsistent.

Statute law

The three pieces of legislation that had the greatest impact on the fortunes of wives prior to the birth of the 1992 constitution are §48 of the Marriages Act 1884-1985,[2] (Cap 127), the Matrimonial Causes Act, 1971 (Act 367), and the Intestate Succession Act, 1985 (PNDCL 111). All three created rather complex legal regimes, an exhaustive overview of which is beyond the scope of the present chapter. It is important to note, however, that Cap 127 created monogamous unions, and, by its §48, gave the widow acknowledged under it a third of the husband's estate. By creating the possibility of a man supporting his ex-wife financially, Act 367 seemingly reversed the customary law rule in *Ayer v. Kumordzi.* But it did not apply automatically to all forms of marriage in Ghana.[3] Even among those to which it applied, it operated to reverse the rule only in "deserving" cases. This subjective standard led to more inconsistency. In *Beckley v Beckley* (1974), the court made an order of maintenance in favor of the wife. By contrast, in *Happee v Happee* (1974), the wife was awarded a lump-sum payment but, being held to have been a poor example of a wife, was not granted maintenance. Nevertheless, the impact of Act 367 must not be under-appreciated. For, although it did not have much of an impact on women's property rights, it did, practically speaking, improve their daily economic circumstances by making it possible for them to receive lump-sum settlements[4] or periodic financial support for themselves and/or their children.[5] PNDCL 111 gave widows a tangible proprietary interest in their husband's estate. But the impractical mandatory apportionment made sale of the property inevitable, and being insubstantial, particularly in polygamous unions,[6] the widow's portion was hardly ever sufficient (Mensa-Bonsu, 1994).

Equity and/or the judge's own conscience

Writing in 1972, Daniels, noted that bill-paying wives had become so common that the courts had shaken off the constraints imposed on them by the strict doctrine of customary law (Daniels, 1972). But, absent clear legislative guidance, these equity-based decisions only compounded the deep inconsistency in the case law. In *Deborah Takyiwa v. Kweku Adu* (1971), a customary law wife was awarded half the farm she had jointly cultivated with her husband on her own land. Would she have been awarded half the farm if it had been jointly cultivated on his land? It is doubtful. Indeed, in *Owusu v. Nyarko* (1980), decided nine years later, the *Quartey v. Martey* position was reiterated.

In *Bulley-Neequaye v. Acolatse* (1969), and also in *Reindorf alias Sacker v. Reindorf* (1974), property bought by a wife in her husband's name was found by the court to be held in trust for her. In *Domfe v. Adu* (1986), the court found that the respondent having contributed the initial working capital, and having worked jointly to establish the business, the husband, in whose sole name the business was registered, held it and the profits in trust for himself and his wife. A trend clearly emerges from these cases. Only where the wife had purchased the property or had held the financial power that culminated in the property acquisition were the pre-1992 courts unhesitating in granting a proprietary interest to the wife. Wives who could not prove financially quantifiable contributions did not find the courts so protective.

In sum, prior to the 1992 constitution, Ghana's legal regime on property distribution upon the dissolution or termination of marriage was not exceptionally kind to wives. Though the initial starkness of their position under customary law had been somewhat ameliorated under the substantial contribution doctrine, statutory interventions, and equity, the situation was still far from ideal.

Property rights of wives after the 1992 constitution

Since January 1993, the 1992 constitution has been the fundamental law in Ghana and has amended all legal regimes to remove any inconsistency with itself. For clarity, we reproduce Article 22, the relevant provision for our purposes.

Article 22

1) A spouse shall not be deprived of a reasonable provision out of the estate of a spouse whether or not the spouse died having made a will

2) Parliament shall, as soon as practicable after the coming into force of this constitution, enact legislation regulating the property rights of spouses
3) With a view to achieving the full realization of the rights referred to in clause (2) of this article
   (a) spouses shall have equal access to property jointly acquired during marriage
   (b) assets which are jointly acquired during marriage shall be distributed equitably between the spouses upon dissolution of the marriage

While the language of the provision is gender neutral, its genesis is not. Article 22 originally appeared under the section titled "women's rights" in the proposals upon which the Constitution was drafted (Government of Ghana, 1991). The section's preamble acknowledges the "great sorrow and distress" that the then state of the law caused widows and recommended that it be changed permanently through constitutional entrenchment (Government of Ghana, 1991).

In this section, we study a number of important decisions to answer the research questions. We ascertain whether judicial outcomes have truly improved for women since the 1992 Constitution took over the regulation of spousal property rights. We also evaluate whether the rhetoric of judicial lawmaking in fact aligns with the 1992 Constitution. This is not an exhaustive review of every case that has been decided under the Constitution. Rather, it is an evaluation based on a group of cases, which together demonstrate the potential viewpoints from which Article 22 could be interpreted.

Substantive judicial outcomes

Judicial outcomes have generally been better for wives since the coming into force of the 1992 constitution. In a number of important cases, the court has held that the wife was entitled to a share of the matrimonial estate. The interest awarded her has ranged from one-third to half of the matrimonial estate. It is worth noting that in all those cases, the wife was held to have made a substantial and pecuniary contribution to its acquisition. Still, this is quite an improvement on the *Quartey v. Martey* regime, under which her contribution, regardless of its magnitude or proof, entitled her to nothing.

In another line of cases, the court has, while pronouncing a significant settlement figure, refused to treat the relevant properties as jointly owned at all. In all those cases, too, that decision turned on the wife not having made a substantial financial contribution to their acquisition. This second line of cases shows that the court does not, or has not yet begun to, fully match its rhetoric to its decisions. For though it has said more than once that it is willing to consider non-quantifiable contributions to the family life as a contribution to the family asset portfolio, when this has been all that the applicant relied on, the court has not yet found that a non-pecuniary contribution created a proprietary interest. Nevertheless, it is a credit to the courts that post 1992, they have been more open to viewing such actions as potentially entitling wives to some interest in marital property. And it must not be understated how much better wives in such a position have fared post 1993 than their counterparts under the *Quartey v. Martey* regime did.

The circumstances of the cases and the profiles of the women who bring these cases have not changed much. In the post-1992 cases, the partner claiming is still more frequently the one with significantly less earning power. In *Quartson* (2012), the claimant was a housewife, while her husband was a sailor. In *Katey* (2016), she was a beautician; he was a geodetic engineer. In *Arthur* (2013), the wife was a housewife; the husband was an international footballer. The applicant in *In Re George Ntim* (2012) was primarily a subsistence farmer. In these cases, the contribution proved by the wives was largely of domestic services rendered by them. The cases align with the findings of sociological studies: economic inequality of spouses continues to be a feature of Ghanaian marriages, and women are more frequently the vulnerable partner (Deere et al., 2013). One new development is the phenomenon of the man as a plaintiff/petitioner seeking an interest in the property, as in the case of *Mensah* (1993). But this remains rare. Again, this confirms the data that women are still largely lower than men on the employment/economic hierarchy. That, in turn, implies that female spouses are more dependent than male spouses on judicial largesse in determining their entitlement to the property.

Like the pre-1992 wives, these post-1992 wives did not act to ensure that their joint ownership was reflected in the title documents, though they were usually aware of the disputed properties at the time of their acquisition. Admittedly, in a good number of cases, the wife was so unevenly matched with her husband economically that it was not necessarily an option for her to get her name onto the paperwork. This was the case in *Arthur*, *Katey*, and *In Re George Ntim*. But this is not the scenario in other cases. Gladys Mensah was an equal partner and manager of the business they established jointly. She collected monies and kept the accounts. Yet, she let her husband put 4 houses totaling 16 bedrooms, several plots of vacant land, a 20-foot container, and several cars in his name only. In *Quartson*, the sailor-husband was away for long stretches of time; several years in one instance. The wife, with the money he remitted to her, purchased materials and supervised the construction of the matrimonial home to its completion. She also claimed to have acted as a director in a jointly run company, yet her name was conspicuously missing from the title documents, and the court found from the evidence a discernible intention in the absent partner to hold the house as sole owner. The wife in *Tabury* (2013) was just as industrious and as involved in the business that made them rich as Gladys Mensah. Yet, she too let her husband vest all properties acquired with the proceeds from their joint enterprise in his name. It cannot be said, therefore, that the vulnerability of wives in respect of the matrimonial property is entirely a function of economic inequality. There are clearly social and cultural factors at play that are beyond the reach of the law that must be addressed in the larger society. In particular, the cultural narratives on women, personal responsibility, and property must be rethought.

Where the husband is the petitioner in respect of the settlement of matrimonial property, two outcome trends are visible. In one line of cases, the husband is petitioning to be named sole owner of the property to which he held the title and which he also built or helped to build (*Verdose v Verdose-Kuranchie*, 2009 and *Esseku v. Inkoom*, 2013). The wives, inevitably, failed in a similar counterclaim. However, where the wife was the owner of the land and constructed the house either solely or with minimal participation of the husband (as occurred in *Kwawukume*, 2009, *Owusu*, 2011, and *Nanor*, 2018), the wives succeeded in holding on to their property as sole owners. These cases are far away from the injustice that *Quartey v. Martey* spawned. But they remain a small minority.

The final observation we make about the outcomes for wives in the Fourth Republic is this: while more wives have got higher percentages of the matrimonial property, the situation is not as heartening as it may appear at first glance. This is because now, as then, such wives often face a great challenge of providing proof of contribution, especially in respect of property other than the matrimonial home. Thus, the court might award 50% of the matrimonial property to her. But more than 50% of the assets under contention may remain completely outside the definition of matrimonial property. Given the similarity between fact trends of pre- and post-1992 cases, a wife's chance of profiting from the asset portfolio of the couple beyond just the matrimonial home is still minimal. On the outcomes front, therefore, it is fair to say that we are almost as far away from the constitutional ideal as we are from the *Quartey v Martey* days. That means the journey is far from over.

Rhetoric

The 1992 constitution is barely mentioned in the earliest cases of the Fourth Republic. Rather, equity and the substantial contribution doctrine are the principal points around which the decisions are made. The rhetoric changed noticeably in *Mensah v. Mensah* (1993), where the 1992 constitution made its first, albeit peripheral, appearance as a guiding principle in a matter of property distribution between spouses. The court held that in the absence of clear equities in matrimonial property, the court would treat equality as equity. But even with marginal mention, the role the constitutional terminology played in pulling out the entrenched roots of customary law and replacing it with constitutional compliance should not be overlooked. In *Boafo v Boafo* (2005), the court held that the *Mensah* rule of "equality is equity" is not what it called "a blanket" rule applying blindly and in all cases. Instead, the equities of each case were to be considered. The court then reintroduced the language of the substantial contribution doctrine but collocated it under Article 22 and the "equality is equity" rubric (Barnes, forthcoming, 2020)[7]; a development discussed more fully later on in this chapter.

The constitutional rhetoric finally comes into its own in *Gladys Mensah v. Stephen Mensah* (2012), where the Supreme Court not only dwelt extensively on Articles 22 and 35[8] but expressly pronounced the substantial doctrine rule unconstitutional. *Quartson v. Quartson* is alone in this line of cases. Although, again, the outcome is not undesirable, the language is puzzling and disappointing, because the Supreme Court oddly ascribed the birth of the substantial contribution rule to Parliament's inaction in respect of its Article 22 obligation to regulate the distribution of marital property upon dissolution or determination of marriage. It is important to note that the court expressly spoke of substantial *financial* contribution. It then, confusingly, held that the Court of Appeal was wrong to hold that the wife had no interest in the matrimonial home and yet refused to give her a share therein. Fortunately, *Arthur v. Arthur* (2013) set things right again. In that case, the court found the wife's performance of her housekeeping duties and as the personal driver (to her husband) sufficient to amount to such substantial contribution as to grant the wife an interest in the matrimonial home. This position has been followed in a number of cases, including *Kofi Tabury*. *Arthur* further established the assumption, albeit rebuttable, that property acquired during the subsistence of the marriage is marital property and therefore should be shared between the parties. The court found that to hold otherwise, as the Court of Appeal had in the same case, would be inconsistent with the Constitution. However, this is not to be taken as inconsistent with the constitutional right to own property alone. The Supreme Court indicated that some categories of properties could be excluded from this presumption, as determined on a case-by-case basis.

In the second line of cases discussed in the preceding section, the court once again relied heavily on the constitution to reach its decision. Although the women in these cases did not succeed in their requests, the language of the judicial decision-making is consistent with that of the first line of cases, in which the women succeeded at least in part. In *Fynn*, for example, the meaning of the relevant constitutional provisions was discussed quite extensively and was central to the decision. Additionally, the court discussed Article 18 and concluded that the property in question was not jointly owned. *Electroland v Adomako* (2019) saw an interpleader by a husband succeed on the ground that the property sought to be attached was his personal property, not jointly owned property, and as such could not be used in satisfaction of his wife's business debts.

It is interesting to note that in both lines of cases, the courts continue to search for proof of contribution or the intention of the parties at the time of acquisition as discernible from the couple's conduct at the time. In *Gladys Mensah*, the court makes a radical move away from the substantial contribution doctrine and reframes the principles within the language of the constitution, thereby extending and strengthening the equality principle. To go contrary to this new exposition of the law was no longer merely a departure from equitable principles. It was, per *Arthur*, in contravention of the constitution. In the decade since *Gladys Mensah*, the court has reiterated its position that a substantial, and specifically a financial, contribution is not required to create a proprietary interest in matrimonial property. Yet, there remains a marked insistence on the contribution (the desirability of which we discuss in subsequent paragraphs) that belies Dotse JSC's conviction that the post-1992 precedents had "sounded the death knell of the substantial contribution doctrine" (*Gladys Mensah v. Stephen Mensah*, 2012). The early post-1992 decisions give no real explanation of why the court could not seem to get beyond proof of contribution even as it waxed eloquent about equality and equity. In the later cases, however, the courts have attempted to explain both why they accept housekeeping as contribution and why they still require proof of contribution. In these discussions, the Constitution and its dictates have dominated the dialogue and the decision.

The foregoing discussion has reviewed and reflected on the case law on the property rights of wives. It has examined the trends in outcomes to know whether wives are faring better in the Fourth Republic and if so, how much. The discussion has also assessed the rhetoric of judicial reasoning to determine its commensurability with the outcomes. Our discussion leads us to answer both the research questions posed earlier in the affirmative. Yes, the likelihood that a widow or ex-wife will be sent away empty-handed has reduced considerably. Yes, the rhetoric on judicial equity for spousal rights has become increasingly centered on the Constitution. In spite of some lingering challenges, there has been a marked movement in the rhetoric toward recognizing the rights of wives to marital property irrespective of financial contribution, or indeed, any contribution. But the outcomes have not always been as consistent as one would expect, nor have they always matched the rhetoric. Nevertheless, from the preceding discussion, it is beyond debate that the 1992 constitution has had a palpable and positive impact on the fortunes of wives when a marital property falls to be distributed.

Outcomes versus rhetoric: Where are we now?

We have seen that the outcomes for women have improved in actions for the distribution of matrimonial property. We have also noted how the rhetoric has evolved from the harsh rule of *Quartey v. Martey* through the substantial contribution doctrine to the present position, touted as the "Jurisprudence of Equality," which, according to the courts, aligns with the purposes of the 1992 constitution. This section evaluates the truth of that assertion. We examine *Nanor v. Nanor* and *Electroland v. Adomako* (*supra*) to assess the validity of the courts' parameters when called to determine whether the matrimonial property is jointly owned. While conceding their necessity, we draw attention to the problematic nature of these parameters.

The relevant facts of *Nanor* are as follows: the husband sought, upon divorce, the matrimonial home, another of his wife's three houses, and a plot of her land. He did not deny that all the property was acquired by his wife with her own funds alone. But he argued that because he had run some of the purchasing errands and had done some amount of the construction supervision, he had contributed to the completion of the matrimonial home and should be granted a half share. In respect of the other properties, his argument was that he had married her under the Marriage Ordinance (Cap 127) and that it was he who introduced his wife to the person who helped her acquire goods on credit to begin her textile business. For those reasons, he invited the court to hold him the owner of half of her wealth. The High Court rightly rejected his arguments.

Article 22 concerns

Of interest to this chapter is the court's reasoning for refusing to hold that the matrimonial home was joint property. The court held that being married *ipso facto* could not create a proprietary interest in each other's assets. The husband's involvement in the construction of the matrimonial home had been no more than what his duty to care for his partner entailed. Therefore, it did not create title in him. This decision, on the facts presently given, is not very different from *Clerk*, where the court ruled that the acts of the wife, which were pleaded as giving rise to entitlement in the marital property, were merely what was expected of a "good wife," or indeed *Ribeiro*,[9] where the minority argued that the bare domestic services rendered by the wife did not give her rights to her husband's property. Yet, it is hard to say it was untenable. If it is not, then in principle, neither were the two earlier cases. In that case, *Mensah* and *Arthur* are by implication wrong.

But there are additional facts to *Nanor* that help shape the discussion. The husband had essentially been supported by his wife for almost the entirety of their marriage. She had borne all the bills of their joint life and family. The husband even admitted that all sums he had expended personally on the matrimonial home had been reimbursed to him by his wife at his instance. Nor did he claim to have borne the larger share of the domestic or child-raising duties. His wife's success was in spite of, rather than because of, him. It is clear, then, that the husband of the marriage had not conducted himself in such a way that it was reasonable to hold him co-owner of his wife's property. The point is this: the requirement of contribution to the acquisition of the property is not unreasonable even in a constitutional era that promotes spousal rights to the property. By necessary implication, then, it is possible, even if not easy, to determine the facts of each case: whether the conduct of a spouse exceeds what is a reasonable minimum and attains a level that gives the other spouse an advantage or opportunity to acquire assets.

Even so, there are two opposite but equally grave concerns with the substantial non-pecuniary contribution requirement. On the one hand, given Ghana's history of cultural and customary law bias against wives' property interests, there is a high risk of retrogression to the old forms if the terminology of the new era resembles or even echoes the terminology of the old days. It makes it easier for the old rules to creep into the workings of the new ones, thereby eroding all the benefits of the 1992 constitutional regime. For example, in a significant number of the cases discussed, the court sought or somehow managed to quantify the non-pecuniary contributions proved by a party. The judges' discussions and assessments of the wife's claim of financial contribution would not, in some instances, sit awkwardly in *Abebereseh* or *Yeboah*.

But on the other hand, without further clarification on where parenting and home management, as a duty of the couple, end, and where title-creating housekeeping and parenting begin, the court appears to be saying that no duties of parenting or cohabiting exist in the absence of property. We illustrate with *Quartson*, where the wife pleaded her housekeeping and childrearing as contribution sufficient to create a title in her. The court found that Mrs. Quartson's assumption of her husband's parental duties in addition to her own amounted to a contribution to its acquisition. For the purposes of this chapter, and, without endorsing the traditional view of gender roles, we shall assume, as the case law does, that in a Ghanaian marriage, the woman's role is to keep the house and raise the children, while the man's is to pay the bills. On that premise, it is tempting to think that Mrs. Quartson succeeded because she was playing the other parent's role in addition to her own. But as we demonstrate, deeper engagement with the facts will show this reasoning to be only superficially attractive.

First, if there had been no matrimonial home, would Mrs. Quartson not have cared for the children when her husband failed in doing his part? If she would have, then the court ought to have been clearer as to what extent her care of her children differed from what she would have given them if there had been no property. This distinction must be discernible, it is argued, for the line between parenting/partnering *simpliciter*, and parenting/partnering as the root of title, not to be arbitrary. Mrs. Quartson rose to the occasion when she was made a single parent. The paradox here is that it does not mean necessarily that she contributed to his assets. But it also does not necessarily mean that she did not. The court should have engaged more fully with the facts to explain how they met the threshold of contribution. For example, what if a housewife pays school fees for a long period of financial difficulty and then is reimbursed by the husband and after that reimbursement, he acquires properties? Do the school fees years count as her contribution to those houses or not?

The effort required for a housewife to step into her husband's shoes is significantly greater than what would be required for the managing director of a transnational bank to do the same. It seems unfair to undervalue the housewife's effort simply because it was reimbursed. It also seems unfair to say the wife, who is the managing director, had no interest in her matrimonial home because stepping into her errant husband's shoes had been easier for her. Moreover, the court should not appear to be relieving parents whose union has acquired no property from the ordinary obligations of parenthood. It is concerning that *Mensah* and, especially, *Arthur* do not draw the line clearly between partner/ parent duties *simpliciter* and partner/parent acts creating title in the matrimonial property.

We do not by this analysis either endorse or reject the rightness of the view that marriage should *ipso facto* render all assets of both parties jointly held. That rule exists in several countries on other continents, and as with all things, has its merits and demerits. However, an evaluation of these is, for want of space, beyond the scope of this chapter. What we seek to do by this analysis is to assess whether what the court has been saying and doing is indeed what the 1992 constitution of Ghana requires it to do. Our answer is that the court must, with the greatest respect, reflect on and clarify where the ceiling of wifely/husbandly duty ends and where the floor of property-creating duty begins. Otherwise, improved outcomes notwithstanding, it cannot claim to have aligned the legal order with the constitutional purposes for which Article 22 was enacted.

Article 18 concerns

In *Fynn*, the Supreme Court first grappled with the effect of their broad interpretation of Article 22 on Article 18. In that case, a husband sold a store, and his wife sought to have the sale overturned on the grounds that the store was jointly owned property and the sale was without her knowledge and consent. The court held that parties within a union retained their Article 18 right to own property alone. As such, the property of one spouse did not automatically become the property of the couple, and the spouse retained the power to dispose of such property unilaterally. The court refused, therefore, to overturn the sale.

Fynn was applied in *Electroland v Adomako* (*supra*). The facts of that case and the court's reasoning are helpful aids to understanding the import of the *Mensah* rule as it would have operated had the caveats not tempered it. In *Electroland*, where the husband successfully resisted the attachment of his house in the satisfaction of a judgment debt against his wife, the court discussed extensively the practical implications of *Mensah* for Article 22 and concluded that the right to equitable distribution of marital property did not arise while the marriage subsisted. The court held further that absent proof of contribution to its acquisition, property did not become jointly held only because of the continued subsistence of the marriage. To hold otherwise would have amounted to removing the right of a married person to hold property alone under Article 18, and that would, of course, be unconstitutional.

Again, premised on the model of the Ghanaian marriage as described earlier, it is immediately evident that there is tension between Articles 18 and 22. As noted earlier, to hold, as the court did in *Mensah* and *Arthur*, that housekeeping and childrearing duties suffice as contribution to property acquisition is to hold that all property acquired during marriage is marital property unless one spouse is a bad partner. Indeed, the court held it to be a rebuttable presumption in *Arthur*.

This, in turn, means that no party in a union may dispose of their property alone. While it could be argued that it is ideal for a married couple to make decisions about their individual property jointly, it can hardly be argued that the law should compel them to. Such a legal state of affairs would, in addition to discouraging citizens from legally combining their estates, have the most deleterious effect on commerce. In the *Fynn* case, the third party had diligently conducted her enquiries into the ownership of the store before proceeding with the sale. To reverse it because of an undiscoverable third-party interest would have been inequitable and would have set a poor precedent for the sanctity of commercial transactions.

Be that as it may, the question of what the Constitution requires the courts to do is easily answered in respect of Article 18. It requires the courts to uphold and protect the sole ownership of self-acquired property. To do this, the courts have had to introduce some limits on their own jurisprudence under Article 22 in order to prevent a headlong collision of the two constitutional provisions. Seen in that light, the limitations on the *Mensah* and *Arthur* principle are not unreasonable, even if, as discussed, they may be problematic.

Conclusion

This chapter has been driven by three critical inquiries. First, we juxtaposed the landmark cases decided before the 1992 constitution entered into force with those decided thereafter to determine whether outcomes have truly improved for women since the 1992 constitution took over the regulation of spousal property rights in Ghana. We then examined the rhetoric of the post-1992 jurisprudence to ascertain whether the dictates of the 1992 Constitution have attained a centripetal role in judicial reasoning and decision-making in this sphere of the law. Finally, we tested the constitutional compliance of the judicial reasoning in the jurisprudence by examining its implicit and explicit ramifications. We found that the language of judicial reasoning was undoubtedly in consonance with the Constitution. The answer to the question on outcomes was more complicated, being at once yes and no. While fewer women are walking away empty-handed from the fruits of their efforts, they are not necessarily getting the full value of their labor. We conclude that the court needs to further illuminate both its rules under Article 22 and the limitations it has put on its interpretation. We note that the profiles of the wives indicate clearly that there are problems of socialization that need to be tackled if Article 22 is to be fully realized; there is only so much the law can do. Parliament's deplorable failure to enact the legislation envisioned in Article 22 has ensured that the court's journey toward constitutional implementation will be a muddled, stumbling journey. But even so, it is on its way. And, in spite of the rough terrain, it is a worthy path the court is charting.

Notes

1 Ollennu based his decision on *Okwabi v. Adonu* (2 W.A.L.R 268), which decided that a child did not become co-owner of property acquired from the joint industry of the child and the father. The case had nothing to do with marriage, yet the learned judge found that the principle could apply to property acquired by the husband from the proceeds of joint efforts of himself and his wife.
2 Formerly known as the Marriage Ordinance.
3 Act 367 applies to marriages other than monogamous ones only on application by a party to the marriage. See Section 41.
4 e.g., *Clerk v Clerk* (n 13), *Ribeiro v. Ribeiro* (n 14), *Gyang v. Gyang* (Accra H.C., Jan. 30, 1987), *Okang v. Okang*, (Accra H.C., Sept. 3, 1985).
5 e.g., *Abobor v. Abobor* (n 12), *Ahmed v. Ahmed* (Accra H.C., Oct. 4, 1988), *Addai v. Addai* (Accra H.C., Sept. 16, 1983).
6 Further, HJAN Mensa-Bonsu has argued that the conflation of the widows' and children's interests in a polygamous society has eroded the benefits of the Act when (as is commonly the case) there are multiple spouses or children of multiple mothers. See Henrietta Mensa-Bonsu, "The Intestate Succession Law of Ghana: Practical Problems in Application" (1994) 8 *Yearbook of African Law*, 105.
7 Some writers have criticized the judgment as reintroducing the language of substantial contribution—and by extension, its challenges—into the post-1992 era. See M.Y.A Barnes, "Equality is Equity...or is it? A critical Examination of the Equality Principle in Distribution of Marital Property." In C. Dowuona-Hammond et al, *Ghana@60: Mobilising the Law for Ghana's Future* (Wildy, Simmonds and Hill, forthcoming, 2020).

8 Which allows the court to enforce any other internationally recognized human rights not expressly provided for in the Constitution.

9 This was an application for financial provision under the Matrimonial Causes Act. However, the court discussed the point and intimated that it would have been willing to grant her a proprietary interest had she applied for one.

Constitutions and legislation

Ghana Constitution, 1992
Intestate Succession Act, 1985 (PNDCL 111)
Marriage Ordinance (Cap 127)
Matrimonial Causes Act, 1971 (Act 367)
Property Rights of Spouses Bill
Intestate Succession Bill
Lands Bill

Other

Government of Ghana, Accra Report of the Committee of Experts on draft Proposals for the Constitution, 1991, Assembly Press.

Case law

Abebreseh v. Kaah [1976] 2 GLR 46-42
Abobor v. Abobor (Accra H.C., Feb. 16, 1987)
Achiampong v. Achiampong [1982-83] GLR 1017-1039
Adom v. Kwarley [1962] 1 GLR 112
Amissah-Abadoo v. Abadoo [1974] GLR 110
Anang v. Tagoe [1989–90] 2 GLR 8
Arthur v. Arthur [2013–2014] SCGLR 543
Ayer v. Kumordzie [1964] GLR 622
Beckley v. Beckley [1974] 1 GLR 393
Boafo v. Boafo [2005–2006] 705
Bulley-Neequaye v. Acolatse (1969) C.C. 51
Clerk v. Clerk [1981] GLR 583
Deborah Takyiwa v Kweku Adu, Unreported judgment of the High Court (Sunvani Suit No. L.C. 7/66) May 18,1971
Domfe v. Adu [1986] 1 GLR 653
Happee v. Happee [1974] 2 GLR 186
Electroland v. Adomako Unreported, decided April 22, 2009 HC
Fynn v. Fynn [2013–2014] 1 SCGLR 727
Gyang v. Gyang (Accra H.C., Jan. 30, 1987)
In re George Ntim: Marfoa v. Agyeiwaa, unreported suit no J2/42/2012 SC
In re Kofi Antubam (decd); *Quaico v. Fosu* [1965] GLR 138
Kofi Tabury v. Adwoa Yeboaba unreported, decided January 24,2013 CA
Kwawukume v. Kwawukume unreported, July 30, 2009 (CA)
Jonas v. Ofori (Accra H.C., Jan II 1988)

Manu v. Kuma [1963] 1 GLR 464
Mensah v. Mensah [1993–94] 1 GLR 111
Mensah v. *Mensah* [1998–99] SCGLR 350
Mensah (Gladys) v. Mensah (Stephen) [2010–2012] 1 GLR 204
Odoteye v. Odoteye [1984–86] GLRD 61
Okang v. Okang (Accra H.C., Sept. 3, 1985)
Okwabi v. Adonu 2 W.A.L.R 268
Otoo v. Otoo (Unreported, June 26, 1984 H.C.)
Owusu v. Nyarko [1980] GLR 428
Owusu v. Owusu March 17, 2011 (CA)
Nanor v. Nanor Unreported, decided November 19, 2018
Quartey v. Martey [1959] GLR 377-383
Quartson v. Quartson [2012] 2 SCGLR 1077
Reindorf alias Sacker v. Reindorf [1974] 2 GLR 38
Ribeiro v. Ribeiro [1989–90] 2 GLR 109 SC
Shardow v. Shardow unreported, July 31, 2009, High Court
Sykes v. Abbey [1995–96] 1 GLR 81-90
Yaotey v. Quaye [1961] GLR 573
Yeboah v Yeboah [1974] 2 GLR 114

Bibliography

Agyeman-Budu K. (2017) "The pursuit of actual equality: Women's matrimonial property rights in Ghana since independence." in *Ghana @ 60: Governance and Human Rights in Twenty-First Century Africa*, M. Addaney & M.G. Nyarko (eds.). Pretoria: Pretoria University Law Press.

Appiah, E.M., Oduro, A.D., Baah-Boateng, W., & Boakye-Yiadom, L. (2011) *Situation Analysis of the Intestate Succession and Property Rights of Spouses Legislation in Ghana.* Legon: Department of Economics, University of Ghana.

Archampong, E.A. (2007/8) "Matrimonial property division at marriage breakdown: *The* way forward." *KNUST Law Journal*, *4*, 78–98.

Barnes, M.Y.A. (in press) (2020) "Equality is equity…or is it? A critical examination of the equality principle in distribution of marital property." in *Ghana@60: Mobilising the Law for Ghana's Future*, C. Dowuona-Hammond et al. (ed.). London: Wildy, Simmonds and Hill.

Daniels, E.W.C. (1972) *The Legal Position of Women Under our Marriage Laws*. (Vol IX No. 1), UGLJ, 1.

Daniels, WC. (1965) "Towards the integration of the laws relating to husband and wife in Ghana" *University of Ghana Law Journal, 20*(2): 22

Daniels, WC. (1976) "Marital family law and social policy in WC Daniels, essays in Ghanaian law." *University of Ghana Law Journal*, 92–117.

Daniels, WC. (1977) "Notes and comments: Dissolution of customary law marriages by the court." 9 *Rev. GHANA L.*, *71*, 76.

Dankwa E.V.O. (1982–85) "Property rights of widows in their deceased husbands' estate." *University of Ghana Law Journal, XVI*, 1–24.

Deere C.D., Oduro A., Swanamithan H., Doss, C. (2013) "Property rights and the gender distribution of wealth in Ecuador, Ghana and India." *The Journal of Economic Inequality*, *11*(2) 249–265.

Doss, C.R., Deere, C.D., Suchitra, J.Y., Oduro, A.D., Hillesland, M. (2012) *Lessons from the Field: Implementing Individual Asset Surveys in Ecuador, Ghana, India and Uganda.* Bangalore: Indian Institute of Management

Fenrich, J, & Higgins TE. (2001) "Promise unfulfilled: Law, culture, and women's inheritance rights in Ghana." *Fordham International Law Journal, 25*(2): 259.

Kuenyehia A., & EO Aboagye (2004) "Family law in Ghana and its implications for women." In Akua Kuenyehia (ed.), *Women and Law in West Africa Situational Analysis of Some Key Issues Affecting Women*, 23. Legon: University of Ghana.

Mensa-Bonsu, H.J.A.N. (1994) "The intestate succession law of Ghana: Practical problems in application." *Yearbook of African Law*, 8, 105–127.

Mensa-Bonsu H.J.A.N. (2011–2012) "Ensuring equitable access to marital property; when the holy estate becomes an unholy ex- state- will the legislature walk the road paved by the courts?" *University of Ghana Law Journal* 99(1).

Oduro, A.D., Baah-Boateng, W., Boakye-Yiadom, L.(2011) *Measuring the Gender Asset Gap in Ghana.* Legon: Department of Economics, University of Ghana. Accra: Woeli Publishing Services.

Watnizek, U. (1991) "Integration of personal laws and women's access to property in Ghana: The matrimonial causes act of 1971." *Third World Legal Studies, 10*, 75–107.

Woodman, G. (1974) "The rights of wives, sons and daughters in the estates of their deceased husbands and fathers." *Legon Family Research Papers, No. 1*. Legon: University of Ghana.

Woodman, G. (1982) "The adaptation of customary law to the matrimonial causes act, 1971." *Review of Ghana Law, 13–14*, 218, 219.

Woodman, G. (1985) "Ghana reforms the law of intestate succession." *Journal of African Law*, 29(1): 118.

4 "Judging" lesbians

Prospects for advancing lesbian rights protection through the courts in Nigeria

Pedi Obani, PhD

Introduction

The year 2020 marks two and a half decades since the United Nations Fourth World Conference on Women, popularly called the Beijing Conference. The ensuing Beijing Declaration and the Platform for Action marked a significant milestone in the global gender equality discourse and still significantly influence the international and various national agendas for women's empowerment and gender equality. In addition to legal reforms, courts represent an important forum for promoting gender equality issues. In Nigeria, the courts play an important role of denying enforcement to discriminatory customary practices and statutes entrenching gender inequality (Ekhator, 2015; Enabulele & Bazuaye, 2019). Nonetheless, issues of women's sexual and reproductive health and rights are still impacted by legal, cultural, and religious factors, among others, including the legal restrictions on same-sex relations (Anozie, 2020). In addition to the extant criminalization of sexual offenses against the "order of nature" under the Criminal Code Act (1916) and more recent Penal Code provisions, Nigeria has in recent decades witnessed more restrictive legal changes on non-heterosexual relations, which have in turn spurred the LGBT (lesbian, gay, bisexual, and transgender) movement (Sogunro, 2017). This is not unconnected with the trends of increasing focus on lesbian, gay, bisexual, transgender, and queer (LGBTQ) issues in the global political discourse and in social justice movements (Amaya & González, 2019; Ashford, 2010; United Nations, 2013).

The attributes and experiences of non-heterosexual sexualities and non-binary genders in Nigeria are often homogenized under the description of "gay" or LGBT, whereas the term LGBT itself "encompasses a complex and contradictory set of identities, political agendas and collective actors" (Amaya & González, 2019: 372; Namwase et al., 2017). At the same time, the LGBT movement in Nigeria has been expanding in recent years to include emerging gender identities and sexualities (Sogunro, 2018). There is also growing reference to the term "queer" in the LGBT movement in Nigeria, and across the African continent, in relation to deconstructing sexuality (Massaquoi, 2013; Matabeni, 2014; Moreau & Tallie, 2019). Lesbians[1] specifically face intersecting forms of discrimination that impact their access to justice (CEDAW, 2017). However, lesbians have

DOI: 10.4324/9780429327865-5

been historically under-represented in the scholarly literature on sexual minorities (Currier & Migraine-George, 2017), and feminist literature exploring themes around sexual minorities has been disapproved of in mainstream scholarship (Malumfashi, 2019; Whitsitt, 2003). Lesbians are also under-represented in the LGBTQ movement in Nigeria. To date, there has only been one decided case by a Nigerian court that specifically involves lesbian rights (freedom of association), the case of *Pamela Adie v Corporate Affairs Commission* (2018), which will be discussed in more detail further on in the chapter. In contrast, there are currently 15 cases before the Federal High Court in Lagos, all on issues involving the rights of gay men.[2] This also makes it even more likely that the recognition of sexual minority rights in Nigeria may come through a case on gay rights.

Adopting a feminist intersectional perspective, this chapter uses qualitative research methods to address the question: *how can courts protect lesbians in Nigeria against discrimination on the grounds of their gender identity?* The research combines analysis of legislation and case law, interview data, and participant observations to understand the links between the legal framework and experiences of lesbians in the society (Venturi, 2017; Ashford, 2010). Attempts were made to secure interviews with members of the lesbian community (including self-identifying lesbians and LGBTQ advocates), being mindful of the heterogeneity of the community and how intersecting identities might affect an individual's experiences of discrimination. Initial attempts to contact LGBTQ organizations in Nigeria through emails were unsuccessful. The experience revealed the challenges of conducting qualitative research on LGBTQ issues due to the sensitive nature of the subject and the vulnerability of members of the community (Suen, 2015). Another round of attempts was made using the snowballing technique. This involved contacting LGBT scholars and advocates outside Nigeria, who assisted with identifying willing respondents in Nigeria. Through this, it became possible to gain access to key actors in the LGBTQ community in Nigeria and have meaningful engagements for this research. In the end, five key informant interviews were conducted with two self-identified Nigerian lesbians who have themselves experienced various forms of discrimination in Nigeria and are leading activists, one Nigerian lawyer who has been directly involved in LGBTQ advocacy and seeking justice for lesbians through both formal and informal justice mechanisms in Nigeria, and two queer scholars.

The chapter is divided into four sections. The first section presents the grounding of the research in intersectionality theory. The second section highlights two levels of discrimination experienced by lesbians through expounding on social discrimination and forms of violence, and discrimination and erasure in legislations. The third section focuses on access to justice in the courts and draws from the jurisprudence of the African Charter on Human and Peoples' Rights system and domestic courts in African countries such as Botswana and South Africa for the analysis of constitutional rights protections. The fourth section builds on the research findings to make pragmatic recommendations for a multi-stakeholder approach and judicial activism for the protection of lesbians against discrimination in Nigeria.

Framing intersectionality as context and reality

Situating this study in intersectionality theory is necessary to support analyzing and framing of how lesbians experience intersecting forms of vulnerability to violence and discrimination and inequality, which also creates barriers to accessing justice. The relationships between inequality and social identities, such as gender and sexual orientation, are interactive rather than additive (Bowleg, 2008). As such, a generalized human rights analysis for female sexual minorities is only a first step toward understanding the diverse experiences occasioned by respective multiple identities and would not capture the cumulative effects of the interactions between inequality and social identity. Generally, negative attitudes toward minority sexual orientations often converge with other social identities, including age and economic status, to occasion human rights violations (Biddulph, 2006; Afe et al., 2019). Even within similar settings, the experiences of sexual minorities are known to differ based on multiple identities such as ethnicity, religion, social class, income, geographical location, health status, age, educational qualifications, race, and more (Meyer, 2012; McGuffey, 2018).

In the African context, some of the nuances are mostly reflected in tensions between the regulation of female sexuality in formal institutions, particularly "Westernized" settings, versus more traditional societies. For instance, while female nakedness has been used as a sign of protest (Tamale, 1996) and connotes a spiritual dimension in some traditional settings, it is common to have women's dress codes regulated in churches, schools, and other formal settings as a means of upholding "morality." Moreover, the history of lesbianism in African societies has been characterized by fluidity and complex meanings beyond the simplistic and rigid binary understanding of same-sex relations in Western literature. In addition to women engaging in same-sex relations, the concept of minority female identities is further complicated by men who adopt feminine roles or attributes or are sexually attracted to other men—such as the "Yan Daudu" in northern Nigeria (Ayeni, 2017; Gaudio, 2009) and the "Gor-Digen" in Senegal (M'Baye, 2013). "Yan Daudu" describes cross-dressing males who also display sexual ambiguity and are associated with feminine attributes. "Gor-Digen" means "man-woman," who are also cross-dressing or gender non-conforming. The complexity of meaning around gender and sexuality is well covered in the African queer literature (Amadiume, 1987; Gay, 1985; Kendall, 1999; Oyèrónkẹ́, 2005).

Intersectionality theory expands our understanding of the location of multiple identities and how they intersect while opening up possibilities for exploring the links between the identities and individual or group experiences (Crenshaw, 1991). Intersectionality itself is rooted in the experiences of women of color and the limitations of homogeneous feminist approaches, which did not account for the different yet convergent social identities of women (Crenshaw, 1991; Schiller, 2000). McCall (2005) identifies three approaches adopted by intersectionality theory scholars to manage the complex intersecting social relations in social life: anticategorical complexity; intracategorical complexity; and intercategorical complexity. Anticategorical complexity challenges set categories because "social life is considered too irreducibly complex … to make fixed categories anything but simplifying social fictions that produce inequalities in the process of producing differences" (McCall, 2005, p.1773). Intracategorical complexity acknowledges established social categories and mainly manages complexity by focusing on particular social groups at neglected points of intersection, represented by individuals. Intercategorical complexity similarly acknowledges established social categories and analyzes relationships of inequality along multiple and conflicting dimensions rather than focusing on complexities within a single group.

The application of intersectionality in this chapter is "group-centered" (Choo & Ferree, 2010) and falls under McCall's (2005) intercategorical approach. This group-centered intersectionality analysis has been applied by scholars to understand the experiences of individuals who belong to a single group, such as black lesbians, but have experiences differentiated by the other categories with which they also identify—such as race, class, or ethnicity (Moore, 2012; Collins, 2004). The racial dimension is not a major concern for the LGBTQ movement in Nigeria. However, other categories such as gender, sex, ethnicity, class, age, education, and location (in urban or rural areas) are some of the prominent categories experienced. This research considers how intersecting categories (such as gender, sexual orientation, class, and location) experienced by lesbians in Nigeria affect discrimination and access to justice.

Lesbians' experiences of discrimination

Social experiences

Overall, lesbians experience diverse forms of vulnerability to violence and discrimination in different spheres of life (Azuah, 2016; The Initiative for Equal Rights, 2018). There are two main angles to the consideration of lesbian vulnerability and discrimination in society; one is in connection with the wider Nigerian LGBTQ community, and the second is in relation to heterosexual women. Within the LGBTQ community, lesbian issues generally receive less attention, as the focus is mainly on gay and bisexual men. This is attributed first to the patriarchal foundations of the Nigerian society and the fact that women's issues are generally not prioritized in the public domain. In the words of Interviewee 1:

> The idea that gay men are a direct breach to patriarchal notions means that even people who are ordinarily anti-LGBT don't often see women as a threat to this social understanding of what sexuality means, it's this whole patriarchal system. If anything, even lesbian sexuality is considered entertainment for men.

Another possible explanation is that the origin of the LGBTQ movement in Nigeria is connected to the prevention of the spread of HIV/AIDS among gay and bisexual men, while lesbian issues have emerged more recently in the public domain (Interviewee 5).

The second angle questions whether lesbians, and indeed other queer women, face forms of vulnerability and discrimination that are either distinct from and/or additional to those experienced by heterosexual women. Two perspectives emerge in connection with this. First, lesbians face similar forms of vulnerability and discrimination as most women, irrespective of their sexuality. This perspective was not popular among the key informants connected to the LGBTQ community compared with other lawyers working in specialized areas (including land law, customary succession, and adoption rights issues) who were contacted for this study (cf. Ayebazibwe, 2019). Conversely, the more prevalent view among the key informants is that lesbians face additional forms of discrimination compared with heterosexual females simply because of their sexual orientation. For Interviewee 5:

> The discriminations that lesbians face in Nigeria which I have recognized is literally all the kind of discrimination that women face. (What) queerness does to that is only to deepen such discrimination. The only thing you may add to that in respect of women who are gender non-conforming is they experience a piled on layer of violence which is both systemic and social, … and basically amplifies the effect of the baseline discriminations that women already face.

Within the home, lesbians, particularly young lesbians who are closeted or whose families do not approve of their sexual orientation, are exposed to various forms of abuse, including financial, physical, and social stigmatization. In some cases, it is family members who perpetrate social stigmatization, rejection, and various forms of violence against lesbians. Interviewee 4:

> And so we see a lot of things like "corrective rape" happening within our community, where your family member can arrange somebody for you, someone that is going to rape you in an attempt to "correct" your sexual orientation and to make you straight. And we see people suffer from that. We see people go to the churches for so-called "deliverance" and sometimes the church that is supposed to protect you (is) the one that violates you. So, we hear cases of rape again…, cases of sexual assault.

Additionally, there is workplace discrimination, with lesbians experiencing unwanted social advances from men in the workplace and being denied opportunities for career advancement on grounds of their sexual orientation; indiscriminate arrest on grounds of perceived sexual orientation; blackmail and extortion from persons threatening to expose their sexual orientation to their families or the public; pathologization of lesbianism as a condition that needs to be treated; and trivialization as something that is "not to be taken seriously" or "a form of entertainment for men" (The Initiative for Equal Rights, 2019a; Human Rights Watch, 2016). Lesbians in Nigeria appear to be additionally vulnerable to poverty and physical assault and other forms of discrimination and human rights abuses, especially when they are forced out of home and have to live with strangers or miss out on educational and livelihood opportunities as a result. Also, on the political level, even though there is no rule against participation in electoral processes, there is no record of a lesbian running for political office, and they remain under-represented in the political space, where laws affecting them are made mainly by men (The Initiative for Equal Rights, 2019a).

Erasure in statutes

Within domestic laws in Nigeria, there are instances of tacit forms of erasure of women and non-gender-conforming persons. This commonly occurs where legal provisions relating to sexual minorities directly address men only, even though the spirit of the law is understood to cover sexual minorities generally. Instances are found in the Criminal Code Act (1916), the Armed Forces Act (1993), and the Same Sex Marriage (Prohibition) Act (2013). The Criminal Code Act (1916) provisions sanctioning offences "against the order of nature" do not expressly mention women as "perpetrators" except when the female involved "permits a male person to have carnal knowledge of … her against the order of nature" (Criminal Code Act (1916) s. 214). The Criminal Code Act (1916) s. 217 expressly states: "Any male person who, whether in public or private, commits any act of gross indecency with another male person, or procures another male person to commit any act of gross indecency with him, or attempts to procure the commission of any such act by any male person with himself or with another male person, whether in public or private, is guilty of a felony, and is liable to imprisonment for three years."

Remarkably, similar prohibitions of unnatural offenses have in recent times been declared unconstitutional in countries such as India (Misra, 2009; Rudueša, 2019) and Botswana (Montz, 2019), particularly in cases involving consensual sexual relations between adults that are held in private. In contrast, Shari'a laws of some states in northern Nigeria criminalize lesbianism. For instance, the Shari'a Penal Code Law 2000 (Zamfara State) prohibits both sodomy (*Liwat*), defined as having "carnal intercourse against the order of nature with any man or woman" (Shari'a Penal Code Law (2000) s. 130), and lesbianism, defined narrowly as sexual acts between two women (Shari'a Penal Code Law (2000) s. 134). Paradoxically, the punishment for sodomy is more severe (100 lashes and one year's imprisonment for the unmarried, and stoning to death for the married) than that for lesbianism (50 lashes and a term of imprisonment of up to six months).

Having "carnal knowledge against the order of nature" is also prohibited under the Armed Forces Act (1993) s. 81 with respect to persons subject to the service law under the Act. This offense renders the perpetrator liable, upon conviction by a court martial, to imprisonment for a term of seven years or any lesser punishment under the Armed Forces Act. Interpreting the provision of the Armed Forces Act (1993) s. 81, the Supreme Court of Nigeria in *Magaji v. The Nigerian Army* (2008) defined the order of nature as "carnal knowledge with the female sex." It is possible that there was no reference to sex between females in the case because the appellant before the court was a male. Nonetheless, the court in this case missed an opportunity to proffer an inclusive definition of "carnal knowledge against the order of nature" in the context of diverse sexual identities of both males and females.

The Same Sex Marriage (Prohibition) Act (2013) s. 4 generally criminalizes the contracting of same-sex marriage or civil union, social activities, or public display of amorous relations by same-sex couples, or any form of support for these activities. The Same Sex Marriage (Prohibition) Law (2007) for Lagos State contains similar provisions as the national Same Sex Marriage (Prohibition) Act (2013) (Sogunro, 2017). The Same Sex Marriage (Prohibition) Act (2013) s. 5(3) directly sanctions a person or group of persons who administers, witnesses, abets, or aids the solemnization of a same-sex marriage or civil union, or supports the registration, operation, and sustenance of gay clubs, processions, or meetings, liable on conviction to ten years in prison. Although there is no mention of lesbians or bisexual or queer women throughout the law, it was applied by the court in the *Pamela Adie* case to uphold the Corporate Affairs Commission's refusal of registration to a non-governmental organization for lesbian rights. The Same Sex Marriage (Prohibition) Act (2013) is seen as critical to addressing issues of discrimination and violence against lesbians and other sexual minorities in Nigeria (Ayeni, 2017; Human Rights Watch, 2016). Interviewee 2:

> It is with the Same Sex Marriage (Prohibition) Act that even just holding hands in public can be seen as a criminal activity. Previous legal provisions on homosexuality and carnal knowledge against the order of nature focus on the sexual act itself and not on identifying as a gay or lesbian. When people know that same sex cannot display affection in public, people take advantage of it. Just on the basis of perceived sexual orientation, people mob a suspect, a gay man or a lesbian. People are emboldened to carry out these atrocities, because they feel society supports them, they feel religion supports them, they feel the law supports them. The law, the Same Sex Marriage (Prohibition) Act and others, has emboldened perpetrators of violence.

Moreover, in the Nigerian setting, where there is a lot of pressure on young women to get married (Ntoimo & Isiugo-Abanihe, 2014), the Same Sex Marriage (Prohibition) Act (2013) restriction on same-sex marriage exposes lesbians to additional layers of stigmatization, vulnerability, and rights violations. Interviewee 3:

> Sometimes, due to the pressures, they are forced to get married and end up in a dysfunctional relationship. This confuses their children. They are hardly home and they expose themselves to health infections because they cannot be in stable relationships. It is multilayered because even to be in a relationship is a problem. For instance, one of my friends had to pretend and say that her lover is her sister. Her landlady went as far as making enquiries and

> decided that she cannot continue renting out her house to two women who are together. You cannot be open about the relationship. At some point, you have to prove that the person is your sister. You have to be cautious; you have to live correctly, if you are with your girlfriend, there are certain things you cannot do in public.

Despite the challenges noted by interviewees, a recent survey of social perception on LGBT rights indicates changing attitudes and a slight (7%) decrease in the level of support for the Same Sex Marriage Prohibition Act: 75% support in 2019 compared with 90% support in 2015 (The Initiative for Equal Rights, 2019b). Former President Goodluck Jonathan, who signed the Same Sex Marriage Prohibition Act into law in 2014, declared two years later, in 2016, that "in the light of deepening debates for all Nigerians and other citizens of the world to be treated equally and without discrimination, and with the clear knowledge that the issue of sexual orientation is still evolving, the nation may, at the appropriate time, revisit the law" (Feder, 2016). Nonetheless, the Same Sex Marriage Prohibition Act remains in force throughout Nigeria, being a federal-level law, subject to judicial or legislative review.

Access to justice in the courts

It is difficult to conclusively assess the judicial attitude to lesbian rights in Nigeria for several reasons. First, most cases do not make it to court either because the victims are closeted and do not wish to press charges or because the justice delivery system, particularly the police, has failed to diligently investigate and prosecute the matter, thereby effectively "revictimizing" the victim. Illustrating an instance of workplace discrimination that went unreported, Interviewee 2:

> This happened because she (the victim) would have to narrate what has happened and the fact would include revealing her own sexual orientation. Was she ready? She was not ready. Would the table turn? Possibly, yes, the table could turn! They (the police) leave the investigation and start discussing her sexual orientation.

Second, the chance of obtaining justice also varies according to the rights violations alleged. For Interviewee 1:

> If you are using your sexuality as the focal point, the Nigerian court system has so far proven to be inhospitable to recognizing that same sex relationships exist and that there are people who go beyond the binaries of male/female identity or the straight sexual orientation.

The perception is, therefore, that cases of police brutality or unlawful arrest would likely be "easier" to establish in court and obtain justice. A ready example is the case of *Ifeanyi Orazulike v. Inspector General of Police & Abuja Environmental*

Protection Board (2014). Ifeanyi Orazulike (the applicant), a renowned LGBT advocate, filed a motion on notice in the Federal High Court in Abuja for the enforcement of his fundamental rights. The applicant claimed that he was arrested by the police during his birthday celebration in his office in Abuja and subjected to humiliating and dehumanizing treatment during the raid of his office and his detention. The raid occurred after the enactment of the Same Sex Marriage (Prohibition) Act (2013). The police did not bring any charges against the applicant that warranted the raid. The court ruled in favor of the applicant, stating that his rights to personal liberty, dignity, and freedom of movement had been violated.

There are also laws protecting against discrimination and violence that extend to everyone in the society and can form the basis for instituting related actions in court. An example is the HIV/AIDS (Anti-Discrimination) Act (2014) for the prevention of discrimination based on real or perceived HIV status and the provision of access to healthcare and other services to everyone. Another is the Violence against Persons (Prohibition) Act (2015), which "prohibits all forms of violence against persons in private and public life and provides maximum protection and effective remedies for victims and punishment of offenders" (Explanatory Memorandum, n.p.). The Violence against Persons (Prohibition) Act (2015) is only applicable in the Federal Capital Territory Abuja and needs to be enacted by the house of assembly of each of the remaining 36 states to became effective in other parts of the country.

A third factor affecting access to justice is linked to how personal attributes, such as wealth, income, level of education, and overall status in the society, offer intersecting layers of protections to the LGBTQ community in general and influence the decision to even engage the justice systems. Interviewee 3: "*the more visible you are, the easier it gets.*" This is seen as a critical deciding factor in instances of successful enforcement of fundamental rights protection by the LGBTQ community, as in the *Ifeanyi Orazulike* case. Most lesbians in Nigeria live in vulnerable situations, including those in rural or remote areas with limited availability of justice, and most who cannot afford the high cost of legal representation are unable to access justice systems without external support from nongovernmental organizations. Heterosexual women in Nigeria face comparable barriers to accessing justice (CEDAW, 2017). This informs the expectation that progress with gender equality issues, including sexual and reproductive autonomy for women in Nigeria, might culminate in a recognition of lesbian sexuality. Interviewee 1:

> This [advancement of lesbian right issues in close connection with sexual and reproductive rights from women] is different from the way gay issues are evolving. Because women have long faced this whole idea of your body is not yours. It's either your father's or your husbands or just society's decision to decide (that) you can't show this, you can't show, you can't wear that, you can't be seen here, you can't open your hair here. Women's bodies have been policed for such a long time that if there is any breakthrough in that

> it is much more likely that that is where you will have that breakthrough in women's sexuality.

The only case so far decided on lesbian issues in Nigeria is *Pamela Adie v. Corporate Affairs Commission*. In the *Pamela Adie* case, the respondent (the government agency in charge of company registration and related matters in Nigeria) had rejected the registration/reservation of the applicant's proposed name of an organization that was to be called "Lesbian Equality and Empowerment Initiatives." The applicant requested the court to declare that the respondent's refusal was a violation of her rights to freedom of expression and association under the Constitution of the Federal Republic of Nigeria (1999) and the African Charter on Human and Peoples' Rights (Ratification and Enforcement) Act (1983). The applicant sought a court order enforcing her right to assemble and associate under the stated name and to have the name registered. Additionally, the applicant requested an order of *mandamus* directing the respondent to issue a notice of approval of the proposed name for registration. The court held that "so far as the Same Sex Marriage (Prohibition) Act is still operative in Nigeria and has not been repealed, the case of the Applicant must fail." This justifies the following observation by Interviewee 2:

> If the Same Sex Marriage (Prohibition) Act can be systematically addressed, then the problem is half solved. The next issue would be the Criminal Code, and this is deeply engrained in the religious nature of the Nigerian society.

Other decided cases on gay rights also allow a preliminary assessment of indications of justiciability of sexual minority issues in Nigerian courts.[3] In an earlier case, *Teriah Joseph Ebah v Federal Government of Nigeria (FGN)* (2014), the applicant instituted the action on behalf of the "Gay Community in Nigeria" and asked the court to consider the constitutionality of the Same Sex Marriage Prohibition Act. The case was dismissed for lack of *locus standi* because the court noted that there was no such community in Nigeria. The applicant had instituted the originating summons before the Federal High Court of Abuja under the Fundamental Rights (Enforcement Procedure) Rules (2009). The Fundamental Rights (Enforcement Procedure) Rules (2009) requires the court, among others, to encourage and welcome public interest litigation on human rights and provides that no human rights case may be dismissed or struck out for lack of *locus standi* (Onuora-Oguno, 2017). In fact, the court in the *Pamela Adie* case noted that one of the fundamental changes brought about by the Fundamental Rights (Enforcement Procedure) Rules (2009) was a move away from procedural technicalities and that the court, being a court of justice, "will not allow technicalities to stand in the way of substantial justice," contrary to the *Teriah Joseph Ebah* decision. The *Pamela Adie* case is therefore still considered by some of the key informants in this study as an instance of access to justice in the court. The perception of the interviewees is in line with the idea that justice is not tantamount to victory in court: existing layers of discrimination against lesbians would need to be progressively dismantled one at a time, and every "victory" is an important milestone to accessing justice.

Constitutional rights protection

Cases on LGBTQ issues in Nigeria have been mainly argued on the grounds of constitutional rights. Although the courts are yet to declare on the constitutionality of legislative restrictions on same-sex relations, human rights protections and the enforcement procedures feature prominently in the court decisions on LGBTQ-related issues in Nigeria. Much of the scholarly focus on LGBTQ issues in Nigeria has also been on the implications of laws sanctioning homosexuality on constitutionally guaranteed human rights (Akogwu, 2018; Anozie, 2020), the right of the Nigerian government under international law to legitimately exercise national sovereignty to impose the restrictions in the Same Sex Marriage Prohibition Act (Nnamuchi, 2019), and the cultural and moral dimensions of the restrictions (Arimoro, 2018).

The Constitution of the Federal Republic of Nigeria (1999) s. 42 prohibits any form of discrimination against any citizen of Nigeria "of a particular community" or "sex" on the basis of being a member of the particular community, sex, or other listed group. The Nigerian Constitution does not expressly prohibit discrimination on the ground of sexual orientation, unlike the Constitution of South Africa 1996 s. 9(3), which prohibits the state from unfairly discriminating against anyone on one or more grounds, including sexual orientation. Nonetheless, the African Charter on Human and Peoples' Rights (1981) ("Banjul Charter") Art. 2, which has been enacted into law in Nigeria since 1983, requires that "every individual shall be entitled to the enjoyment of the rights and freedoms recognized and guaranteed in the present Charter without distinction of any kind such as …, sex, … or other status." The Banjul Charter Art. 2 does not expressly mention "discrimination," but the Banjul Charter Art. 6 refers to distinction and equality before the law. Any law prohibiting marriage on a "suspect ground" offends against equality and considering sexual orientation as a "suspect ground" also suggests discriminatory treatment (Rudman, 2015).

The Nigerian Constitution s. 37 also expressly guarantees and protects the right to private and family life of all citizens. In line with this, it is the right of citizens to enjoy their privacy, including the right to carry out sexual activities within their private spaces. In South Africa, in the case of *National Coalition for Gay and Lesbian Equality v. Minister of Justice* (1998), the Constitutional Court held that the offense of sodomy was inconsistent with the fundamental rights to equality, dignity, and privacy guaranteed in the country's constitution. The court distinguished between the right to hold religious beliefs and the state's ability to impose these beliefs on the entire population, "even in moderate and gentle forms." It further stated that there was no valid purpose suggested for the limitation and "the enforcement of the private moral views of a section of the community, which are based to a large extent on nothing more than prejudice, cannot qualify as such a legitimate purpose" (Jernow, 2011, p.18). Similarly, in the Botswana case of *Letsweletse Motshidiemang v Attorney General; LEGABIBO (Amicus Curiae)* (2019), the High Court held that the provisions of the Botswana Penal Code that criminalized (attempts to commit as well as commission of) unnatural offenses violated constitutional protections of the rights to liberty, dignity, privacy, and freedom from discrimination. The High Court of Botswana further held in that case that the Botswana Penal Code s. 167, which had hitherto criminalized "indecent" practices between persons, whether in public or in private, should be amended to exclude practices carried out in private in order to ensure compliance with the Constitution of Botswana.

The Nigerian Constitution s. 39 guarantees every person the freedom of expression, including the freedom to hold, receive, and impart ideas and opinions without interference. The Nigerian Constitution s. 40 also guarantees every person their freedom of association, including the freedom to "form or belong to any political party, trade union or any other association for the protection of" the individual's interests. The right to freedom from discrimination and rights to private and family life, freedom of expression, and freedom of association are, however, violated by laws criminalizing LGBTQ activities, with nuances for lesbians. In the Kenya case of *Eric Gitari v. NGO Board & 4 others* (2015), the Kenya High Court held on the basis of the proportionality principle that it was wrong for the national non-governmental organization (NGO) board to refuse to register an LGBT association on the basis of moral beliefs, as this was an infringement of the freedom of association of LGBT minorities. Notwithstanding, same-sex relations are still criminalized in Kenya. The High Court in the Kenya case of *EG & Ors. v. The Attorney General & Ors.* (2019) ruled against decriminalizing same-sex relations, stating that the extant restrictions do not violate the right to privacy and dignity enshrined in the Constitution of Kenya 2010 Arts. 28 and 31, and that a decision to the contrary would promote same-sex unions, which was against the values of the Constitution of Kenya.

The Nigerian Constitution s. 45(1) also provides that neither the right to privacy nor freedoms of thought, conscience and religion, expression, and peaceful assembly and association "shall invalidate any law that is reasonably justifiable in a democratic society: (a) in the interest of defense, public safety, public order, public morality or public health; or (b) for the purpose of protecting the rights and freedom of other persons." These grounds for limitation of human rights are far reaching and yet to be adjudicated by the courts in Nigeria, even though the links between law and morality in connection with sexuality remain topical (Agyeman-Budu, 2018; Meerkotter, 2019).

Nonetheless, based on the rule of law, arbitrary interference with human rights is not justifiable. Rather, any limitation of rights can only be justified if it is proportional, considering the extent of the limitation and the outcome. The principle of proportionality has been applied by national courts in other jurisdictions to assess restrictions on constitutional rights. In striking down the sodomy laws in the case of *National Coalition for Gay and Lesbian Equality v. Minister of Justice* (1998), the

Constitutional Court of South Africa considered the lack of valid purpose suggested for the limitation while also observing that "the private moral views of a section of the community..., cannot qualify as ... a legitimate purpose" (Jernow, 2011, p.17). Similar reasoning has also been applied by the African Commission of Human and Peoples' Rights in interpreting the impact of "claw-back clauses," which have a similar effect of limiting the applicable rights guaranteed in the Banjul Charter. A claw-back clause is a limitation clause that permits, under normal circumstances, the breach of a human rights obligation based on specific public reasons (Higgins, 1976; Udombana, 2000). This makes a claw-back clause distinct from a derogation clause permitting the breach or suspension of a human rights obligation only during war or public emergency, as special circumstances.

In line with the principle of proportionality, the African Commission on Human and Peoples' Rights in the case of *Constitutional Rights Project v. Nigeria* (1999–2000) declared: "[T]he justification of limitations (*under Article 27(2) of the Charter*) must be strictly proportionate with and absolutely necessary for the advantages which follow. Most important, a limitation may not erode a right such that the right itself becomes illusory." The Banjul Charter Art. 27 (2) reads: "[T]he rights, and freedoms of each individual shall be exercised with due regard to the rights of others, collective security, morality and common interest." Similarly, the African Court on Human and Peoples' Rights in the case of *Mtikila v The United Republic of Tanzania* (2013) held that

> the jurisprudence regarding the restriction on the exercise of rights has developed the principle that, the restrictions must be necessary in a democratic society; they must be reasonably proportionate to the legitimate aim pursued. Once the complainant has established that there is *prima facie* violation of a right, the respondent state may argue that the right has been legitimately restricted by "law," by providing evidence that the restriction serves one of the purposes set out in Article 27(2) of the Charter.

Furthermore, as the African Commission on Human and Peoples' Rights reiterated in *Article 19 v. Eritrea* (2007), "the Commission's jurisprudence has interpreted the so-called claw-back clauses as constituting a reference to international law, meaning that only restrictions on rights which are consistent with the Charter and with states parties' international obligations should be enacted by the relevant national authorities" (para. 92). Moreover, arbitrary deprivation of rights cannot be justified through "claw-back" clauses. It is therefore not enough for the state to rely on restrictions in existing domestic law, as the court mentioned in the Nigerian case of *Pamela Adie*. Rather, human rights restrictions must be shown to be necessary and proportional.

Recommendations and conclusion

Progress with women's rights issues in Nigeria, particularly around sexual and reproductive autonomy, benefits all women and can be expected to become a watershed for lesbian rights. This should therefore be a rallying point for both gender and sexuality rights advocates to promote strengthening of the legal framework for the protection of women's gender and sexuality rights. Given the unique positionality of lesbians, it is further necessary to unpack the social and legal drivers of vulnerability and discrimination, which lesbians experience differently, depending on their respective social identities. Although the institution of law, and justice systems, has in most cases primarily presented barriers to accessing justice for lesbians (and other sexual minorities), it also presents principles that can be drawn on for their emancipation.

Achieving social change for lesbians through the courts would require a proactive approach to the interpretation of fundamental rights guarantees in the Nigerian Constitution. Such a proactive approach could entail relying on the existing fundamental rights guarantees to protect lesbians from discrimination, various forms of violence, and outright human rights violations, which they experience because of their gender and sexual orientation, among other reasons. For this purpose, the interpretation of similar fundamental rights guarantees and the proportionality principle as applied in other jurisdictions to cases involving sexual minority rights offers elements for assessing the legality of any interference with rights on the grounds of gender or sexual identity. There is room for cross-jurisdictional learning drawing on the jurisprudence from the African Commission and domestic courts in other African jurisdictions on issues of proportionality in relation to the rights of sexual minorities.

Some skepticism exists over the value of law in addressing marginalization and violence against sexual minorities, and it is suggested that law reforms need to occur as a part of wider strategies for transformation (Spade, 2015; Devji, 2016). The law and the courts hold key places in addressing discrimination against sexual minorities in Nigeria. As currently constituted, the notorious Same Sex Marriage (Prohibition) Act (2013) and other similar criminal sanctions are largely blamed for recent incidents of violence and discrimination against sexual minorities in Nigeria. These discriminatory practices are reflected in the court cases, particularly the decision of the court in the *Pamela Adie* case. In line with these developments, the judiciary has a primary duty to enforce the rule of law—particularly the Nigerian Constitution—and nullify, rather than enforce, any legislative provision that is relied upon to justify arbitrary limitations or violations of fundamental rights.

From the few cases so far available on sexual minority rights in Nigeria, the law has been used to sometimes maintain the *status quo*, sometimes to remove technicalities that affect access to justice, and at other times to create a paradox whereby sexual minorities are granted audience in the courts but do not achieve their desired "justice" outcomes. In the words of Iñaki Regueiro De Giacomi, "[L]aw functions at the same time as a tool to maintain the status quo of a community—which is what it is often used for—but there are also some exceptional and wonderful cases where law proves to be the opposite, a tool for social change" (Lalor et al., 2016, p.37). In the Nigerian context, the current trend in advocacy for sexual minority rights has entailed legal challenge of a specific provision(s) of the Same Sex

Marriage (Prohibition) Act (2013) on grounds of incompatibility with fundamental rights guarantees and/or challenge against fundamental rights violations without any direct reference to the sexuality of the victims (usually of assault, unlawful arrest, or other forms of inhuman and degrading treatment). It is expected that the jurisprudence arising from such cases would eventually form the legal basis for a challenge to the constitutionality of the Same Sex Marriage (Prohibition) Act (2013) and other discriminatory laws highlighted in this chapter.

Overall, the domestic courts remain a "last hope," yet to be fully explored for access to justice for lesbians and many others in vulnerable situations in Nigeria because of both salient and underlying barriers to access to justice. Other quasi-judicial institutions and agencies that form part of the justice system, particularly the police, also play an intervening role and are more commonly involved in cases affecting lesbian rights. The police have been identified as playing an essential role in the investigation and prosecution of cases (especially criminal cases). As such, any reforms aimed at enhancing the role of the courts in protecting lesbians against discrimination in Nigeria will necessarily have to address other social and legal barriers that affect the capacity of women and lesbians to seek redress in courts and engage with the justice system.

Notes

1 The chapter adopts the definition of a lesbian as "[A] woman who is emotionally, romantically, sexually or relationally attracted to other women" (The Initiative for Equal Rights, 2019a).

2 Interviewee 2.

3 A case in which the issues of same-sex marriage was mentioned, specifically in connection with women, is *Mr. Afam Okeke v Madam Helen Okeke* (2017). In Okeke's case, one of the issues for determination in the appeal was the validity of a customary practice that allows a woman to have posthumous children for her deceased husband. In delivering the lead judgement, Yakubu JCA stated that while advances in technology and globalization influence societal culture, this should not compromise the value system and ethos through encouraging practices such as same-sex marriage. Although the condemnation of same-sex marriage in the *Okeke* case was by way of *obiter dictum*, as this was not an issue for determination in the present case, it reflects the judicial attitude toward same-sex marriage as an "alien" and "immoral" culture that is not to be encouraged in Nigeria.

References

Afe, T.O., Ogunsemi, O., & Oyelekan, A. (2019). Social distancing toward gays and lesbians among college students in Lagos, Nigeria. *Journal of Gay & Lesbian Social Services*, *31*(4), 546–557. doi: 10.1080/10538720.2019.1654424.

Agyeman-Budu, K. (2018). *Law & Morality in Africa: Towards a Rational Public Policy Framework for Regulating Intimate Human Conduct in Ghana* (Unpublished doctoral dissertation). Fordham University, New York.

Akogwu, A. (2018). *Assessing the Human Rights Implications of the Nigerian Law Dealing with Sexual Orientation* (Unpublished doctoral dissertation). University of Pretoria, Pretoria.

Amadiume, I. (1987). *Male Daughters, Female Husbands: Gender and Sex in an African Society*. New York: Zed.

Anozie, M.C. (2020). Abortion and homosexuality prohibitory regimes versus the right to privacy in Nigeria. *Commonwealth Law Bulletin*, 46, 483–518. DOI: 10.1080/03050718.2020.1774786

Arimoro, A.E. (2018). When love is a crime: Is the criminalisation of same sex relations in Nigeria a protection of Nigerian culture? *Liverpool Law Rev* 39, 221–238. https://doi.org/10.1007/s10991-018-9217-y

Ashford, C. Socio-Legal perspectives on gender, sexuality and law: Editorial. *Liverpool Law Rev* 31, 1–12 (2010). https://doi.org/10.1007/s10991-010-9069-6

Ayebazibwe, J.S. (2019). Traditional African systems of land ownership and their impact on lesbian women. In S.N. Nyeck (Ed.), *Routledge Handbook of Queer African Studies* (pp. 15–24). Routledge Handbooks Online. Retrieved from https://www.routledgehandbooks.com/doi/10.4324/9781351141963-3.

Ayeni, V.O. (2017). Human rights and the criminalisation of same-sex relationships in Nigeria. In S. Namwase & A. Jjuuko (Eds.), *Protecting the Human Rights of Sexual Minorities in Contemporary Africa* (pp. 203–237). Pretoria: Pretoria University Law Press.

Azuah, U.N. (ed) (2016). *Blessed Body: The Secret Lives of Lesbian, Gay, Bisexual and Transgender Nigerians*. Jackson, TN: Cookingpot.

Biddulph, M. (2006). Sexualities equality in schools: Why every lesbian, gay, bisexual or transgender (LGBT) child matters. *Pastoral Care in Education*, *24*(2), 15–21. doi: 10.1111/j.1468-0122.2006.00367.x.

Bowleg, L. (2008). When black + lesbian + woman ≠ black lesbian woman: The methodological challenges of qualitative and quantitative intersectionality research. *Sex Roles*, 59(5–6), 312–325.

Choo, H.Y. & Ferree, M.M. (2010). Practicing intersectionality in sociological research: A critical analysis of inclusions, interactions, and institutions in the study of inequalities. *Sociological Theory*, 28, 129–49.

Collins, P.H. (2004). *Black Sexual Politics: African Americans, Gender, and the New Racism*. New York: Routledge.

Committee on the Elimination of Discrimination against Women (CEDAW). (24 July 2017). Concluding observations on the combined seventh and eighth periodic reports of Nigeria. CEDAW/C/NGA/CO/7-8.

Crenshaw, K. (1991). Mapping the margins: Intersectionality, identity politics, and violence against women of color. *Stanford Law Review*, *43*(6), 1241–1300.

Currier, A., & Migraine-George, T. (2017). "Lesbian"/female same-sex sexualities in Africa. *Journal of Lesbian Studies*, *21*(2), 133–150. doi: 10.1080/10894160.2016.1146031.

Devji, Z.Z. (2016). Forging paths for the African queer: Is there an "African" mechanism for realizing LGBTIQ rights? *Journal of African Law*, *60*(3), 343–363. doi:10.1017/S0021855316000097.

Ekhator, E.O. (2015). Women and the law in Nigeria: A reappraisal. *Journal of International Women's Studies*, *16*(2), 285–296.

Enabulele, A.O., & Bazuaye, B. (2019). Validity and enforceability of customary law in Nigeria: towards a correct delimitation of the province of the courts. *Journal of African Law*, 63(1), 79–104. https://doi.org/10.1017/S002185531800030X

Feder, J.L. (2016). Nigeria's former president thinks anti-LGBT law could be revisited. *BuzzFeed News*, June 7, 2016. Retrieved from https://www.buzzfeednews.com/article/lesterfeder/nigerias-anti-lgbt-law-could-be-revisited-says-the-former-pr.

Gaudio, R.P. (2009). *Allah Made Us: Sexual Outlaws in an Islamic African City*. New York: Wiley-Blackwell.

Gay, J. (1985). 'Mummies and babies' and friends and lovers in Lesotho. *Journal of Homosexuality*, *11*(3–4), 97–116.

Higgins, R. (1976). Derogations under human rights treaties. *British Yearbook of International Law*, 48 (1), 281–319. https://doi.org/10.1093/bybil/48.1.281

Human Rights Watch. (2016). "Tell me where I can be safe": The impact of Nigeria's Same Sex Marriage (Prohibition) Act. Retrieved from https://www.hrw.org/report/2016/10/20/tell-me-where-i-can-be-safe/impact-nigerias-same-sex-marriage-prohibition-act#

Jernow, A. (2011). *Sexual Orientation, Gender Identity and Justice: A Comparative Law Casebook*. Geneva: International Commission of Jurists.

Kendall, K.L. (1999). Women in Lesotho and the (western) construction of homophobia. In E. Blackwood & S.E. Wieringa (Eds.), *Female Desires: Same-Sex Relations and Transgender Practices across Cultures* (pp. 157–178). New York: Columbia University Press.

Malumfashi, S. (n.d.). Zata Itaya: A history of Hausa feminist writings (The Republic) 13 December 2019. Retrieved from https://republic.com.ng/december-19-january-20/history-of-hausa-feminist-literature/

Massaquoi, N. (2013). No place like home: African refugees and the emergence of a new queer frame of reference. In S.N. Nyeck and M. Epprecht (Eds.), *Sexual Diversity in Africa: Politics, Theory, Citizenship* (pp. 37–53). Montreal: McGill-Queens University Press.

Matabeni, Z. (ed.). (2014). *Reclaiming Afrikan: Queer Perspectives on Sexual and Gender Identities*. South Africa: Modjaji Books.

M'Baye, B. (2013). The origins of Senegalese homophobia: Discourses on homosexuals and transgender people in colonial and postcolonial Senegal. *African Studies Review*, 56(2), 109–128.

McCall, L. (2005). The complexity of intersectionality. *Signs*, *30*(3), 1771–1800.

McGuffey, S.C. (2018). Intersectionality, cognition, disclosure and black LGBT views on civil rights and marriage equality: Is gay the new black? *Du Bois Review: Social Science Research on Race*, *15*(2), 441–465. doi:10.1017/S1742058X18000218.

Meerkotter, A. (2019). In defense of constitutional morality recent jurisprudence from the global south on LGBTI rights affirms constitutional morality. Retrieved from: https://www.southernafricalitigationcentre.org/wp-content/uploads/2019/07/Policy-brief-on-Constitutional-Morality.pdf

Meyer, D. (2012). An intersectional analysis of lesbian, gay, bisexual, and transgender (LGBT) people's evaluations of anti-queer violence. *Gender & Society*, 26(6), 849–873. https://doi.org/10.1177/0891243212461299.

Misra, G. (2009). Decriminalising homosexuality in India. *Reproductive Health Matters*, *17*(34), 20–28.

Montz, B. (2019). The fight to decriminalize homosexuality since the repeal of Section 377. *Outright Action International*, Retrieved from https://outrightinternational.org/content/fight-decriminalize-homosexuality-repeal-section-377?_ga=2.25522041.576645590.1592053775-486836106.1592053775.

Moore, M. (2012). Intersectionality and the study of black, sexual minority women. *Gender and Society*, 26(1), 33–39.

Moreau, J. & Tallie, T.J. (2019). Queer African studies and directions in methodology. In S.N. Nyeck (Ed.), *Routledge Handbook of Queer African Studies* (pp. 49–60). Routledge

Handbooks Online. Retrieved from https://www.routledgehandbooks.com/doi/10.4324/9781351141963-3.

Namwase, S., Jjuuko, A., & Nyarango, I. (2017). Sexual minorities' rights in Africa: What does it mean to be human; and who gets to decide? In S. Namwase & A. Jjuuko (Eds.), *Protecting the human rights of sexual minorities in contemporary Africa* (pp. 2–12). Pretoria: Pretoria University Law Press.

Nnamuchi, O. (2019). Nigeria's Same Sex Marriage (Prohibition) Act and threat of sanctions by western countries: A legitimate case of human rights advancement or what? *Southwestern Journal of International Law*, *25*(1), 120–154.

Ntoimo, L.F.C., & Isiugo-Abanihe, U. (2014). Patriarchy and singlehood among women in Lagos, Nigeria. *Journal of Family Issues*, *35*(14), 1980–2008. https://doi.org/10.1177/0192513X13511249.

Onuora-Oguno, A.C. (2017). Protecting same-sex rights in Nigeria: Case note on Teriah Joseph Ebiah v Federal Government of Nigeria. In S. Namwase & A. Jjuuko (Eds.), *Protecting the Human Rights of Sexual Minorities in Contemporary Africa* (pp. 238–244). Pretoria: Pretoria University Law Press.

Oyèrónkẹ́, O. (Ed.). (2005). *African Gender Studies: A Reader*. New York: Palgrave Macmillan.

Rudman, A. (2015). The protection against discrimination based on sexual orientation under the African human rights system. *African Human Rights Law Journal*, *15*, 1–27 http://dx.doi.org/10.17159/1996-2096/2015/v15n1a1

Ruduša, D. (n.d.). One year on since repeal of Section 377 in India: A third of the world's countries continue to criminalize same-sex relations. *Outright Action International*, September 5, 2019. Retrieved from https://outrightinternational.org/content/one-year-repeal-section-377-india-third-world%E2%80%99s-countries-continue-criminalize-same-sex.

Schiller, N. (2000). A short history of black feminist scholars. *The Journal of Blacks in Higher Education*, *29*, 119–125. doi:10.2307/2678863.

Serrano Amaya, J. F., & Ríos González, O. (2019). Introduction to the special issue: Challenges of LGBT research in the 21st century. *International Sociology*, *34*(4), 371–381. https://doi.org/10.1177/0268580919856490

Sogunro, A. (2017). *Discrimination against Persons Based on Sexual Orientation & Gender Identity Expression in Nigeria*. Lagos: Initiative for Equality.

Sogunro, A. (2018). Citizenship in the shadows: Insights on queer advocacy in Nigeria. *College Literature*, *45*(4), 632–640. https://doi.org/10.1353/lit.2018.0037

Spade, D. (2015). *Normal Life: Administrative Violence, Critical Trans Politics, and the Limits of Law*. Durham: Duke University Press.

Suen, T.Y. (2015). Methodological reflections on researching lesbian, gay, bisexual and transgender university students in Hong Kong: To what extent are they vulnerable interview subjects? *Higher Education Research & Development*, *34*(4), 722–734. DOI: 10.1080/07294360.2015.1051009

Tamale, S. (1996). Taking the beast by its horns: Formal resistance to women's oppression in Africa. *African Development*, *21*(4) 5–21.

The Initiative for Equal Rights. (2018). *Human, Not Number: Lived Experiences of Sexual Minorities in Nigeria*. Lagos: Initiative for Equal Rights.

The Initiative for Equal Rights. (2019a). *Human Rights Violations Report: Based on Real or Perceived Sexual Orientation and Gender Identity in Nigeria*. Lagos: Initiative for Equal Rights.

The Initiative for Equal Rights. (2019b). TIERs releases results from 2019 social perception survey on LGBT+ rights in Nigeria. June 12, 2019. Retrieved from https://theinitiativeforequalrights.org/2019-survey-released/

Udombana, N.J. (2000). Toward the African Court on Human and Peoples' Rights: Better late than never, *Yale Human Rights & Development law Journal*, 3(1) 45–111. Retrieved from https://digitalcommons.law.yale.edu/yhrdlj/vol3/iss1/2

United Nations (2013) Free and Equal campaigns. Retrieved from www.unfe.org/campaigns/

Venturi, D. (2017). Reflections on empirical research with LGBTI refugees: a legal scholar's perspective. *Oxford Monitor of Forced Migration*, 6(2), 20–23.

Whitsitt, N. (2003). Hausa women writers confronting the traditional status of women in modern islamic society: Feminist thought in Nigerian popular fiction. *Tulsa Studies in Women's Literature*, *22*(2), 387–408. doi:10.2307/20059159.

Cases

App. No. 011/2011—*Rev. Christopher R. Mtikila v. United Republic of Tanzania* (2013) (African Court on Human and Peoples' Rights)

Article 19 v. Eritrea (2007) AHRLR 73 (ACHPR 2007) (African Commission on Human and Peoples' Rights)

Constitutional Rights Project v. Nig., Comm. 140/94, 141/94, 145/95, 13th ACHPR AAR Annex V (1999-2000) (African Commission on Human and Peoples' Rights)

EG & Ors. v. The Attorney General & Ors. (2019) Petition No. 150 of 2016 (High Court of Kenya)

Eric Gitari v. NGO Board & 4 Ors. (2015) Petition No. 440 of 2013 (High Court of Kenya)

Ifeanyi Orazulike v. Inspector General of Police & Abuja Environmental Protection Board (2014) Suit No. FHC/ABJ/CS/799/2014. (Federal High Court of Nigeria at Abuja)

Letsweletse Motshidiemang v. Attorney General; LEGABIBO (Amicus Curiae) (2019) MAHGB-000591-16 (High Court of Botswana)

Magaji v. The Nigerian Army (2008) LPELR-SC.204/2004 (Supreme Court of Nigeria)

Mr. Afam Okeke v. Madam Helen Okeke (2017) LPELR-42582 (Court of Appeal of Nigeria)

National Coalition for Gay and Lesbian Equality v. Minister of Justice (1998) CCT 11/98 [1998] ZACC 15 (Constitutional Court of South Africa).

Pamela Adie v. Corporate Affairs Commission (2018) Suit FHC/ABJ/CS/827/2018 (Federal High Court of Nigeria at Abuja)

Strydom v. Nederduitse Gereformeerde Gemeente Moreleta Park [2008] 30 ILJ 868 (Equality Court of South Africa)

Teriah Joseph Ebah v. Federal Government of Nigeria (FGN) (2014) Suit FHC/ABJ/CS/197/2014 (Federal High Court of Nigeria at Abuja)

Treaties, constitution and statutes

African Charter on Human and Peoples' Rights (Ratification and Enforcement) Act (1981) Cap. A9 Laws of the Federation of Nigeria 2004

Armed Forces Act (1993) Cap. A20 Laws of the Federation of Nigeria 2004

Constitution of the Federal Republic of Nigeria (Promulgation Act) Cap. C23

Criminal Code Act (1916) Cap. C38 Laws of the Federation of Nigeria 2004

Organization of African Unity (OAU), *African Charter on Human and Peoples' Rights ("Banjul Charter")*, 27 June 1981, CAB/LEG/67/3 rev. 5, 21 I.L.M. 58 (1982)
Penal Code (Northern States) Federal Provisions Act (1960) Cap. P3 Laws of the Federation of Nigeria 2004
Same Sex Marriage Prohibition Act 2013 (Nigeria)
Shari'a Penal Code Law of 2000 (Zamfara State, Nigeria)
UN Human Rights Committee (HRC), *CCPR General Comment No. 13: Article 14 (Administration of Justice), Equality before the Courts and the Right to a Fair and Public Hearing by an Independent Court Established by Law*, 13 April 1984

Part II

Emerging gender issues in the courts

5 Femicide and judging

Social media as an alternative online court in Kenya

Stephen Muthoka Mutie, PhD

Introduction

When the hyena is the judge, the goat has no rights

Kenyan proverb

On December 10, 2019, a petition, which included five demands and a call for the Ministry of Education to commit to ensuring higher learning institutions uphold the laws on sexual harassment outlined in the Sexual Offences Act No. 3 of 2006 section 23 and 24, was delivered to the Cabinet Secretary in the Ministry of Education in Kenya. This petition was dubbed #CampusMeToo and was waged on social media. This petition came against the backdrop of the rising number of femicide[1] cases in the country. According to *Counting Dead Women – Kenya*, a nationally recognized and respected Twitter account that creates an online archive highlighting the number of Kenyan women who are victims of femicide reported in the Kenyan media, 108 women were victims of femicide between January 1, 2019, and December 30, 2019.

What is also problematic, however, is that when these deaths are reported in the Kenyan mainstream media, the facts are often one-sided, a distortion that directs the public conversation in the wrong direction. Inadvertently, this one-sidedness serves to disparage the reputations of victims, often portraying them as having contributed to their deaths by being involved intimately with other men apart from those who killed them, or by failing to requite affection from their partners (Mutune, 2019). While femicide victims are blamed, the killers are often sanitized as cool men who had never shown any signs of "stress" or staunch African men who could not bear "love gone sour."

Gender-based violence (GBV) has a long history in Kenya. It is a normalized violation of women dating back many decades (Morrison, 2007). The Kenyan communities uphold, practice, and normalize violence against women, mostly perpetuated as a form of discipline. It is noteworthy that the most practiced gender-based violence occurs in the family setting in the form of domestic violence, which is the use of force or threats by a husband or boyfriend to coerce or intimidate a woman into submission (National Gender and Equality Commission,

DOI: 10.4324/9780429327865-7

2016). According to the 2008–2009 Kenya Demographic and Health Survey, about 45% of women aged between 15 and 49 years had experienced gender-based violence. Some of these GBVs end up being femicide cases. The World Bank's Poverty and Gender Assessment report 2015–2016 notes that "in 2014, 22 percent of Kenyan women and 19 percent of Kenyan men agreed with the statement that a husband is justified in hitting or beating his wife if she goes out without telling him" (World Bank, 2018).

Historically, there has been a strong link between physical violence and marriage, with a prevalence of GBV among women who have been married. World Bank research has shown that "women who have ever been married, and especially those who have gone through a marital dissolution" are more likely to have experienced physical violence than women who had not been married, indicating that current or former spouses are often perpetrators of violence (World Bank, 2018). Additionally, age can also play a role in the risk that a woman experiences GBV, as well as whether the woman is remarried, and her employment status. Women who marry after the age of 25 are less likely to experience GBV than women who marry before they turn 15. In addition, women who have married more than once are almost four times more likely to have experienced GBV than women who have been in only one union (World Bank, 2018).

Whereas GBV and femicide may now be a national tragedy in Kenya, mainly rooted in exploitive power dynamics and entrenched by a cursory application of the law, there is a human rights need to spark a national conversation on these vices. This conversation has already begun in earnest in the new media, specifically in social media. Social media[2] in Kenya provides a national conversation that preserves the integrity of women's voices and builds a shared understanding that both men and women can speak up and speak out without the fear of reprisals. It provides an alternative space for articulating and amplifying resisting voices.

Femicide and GBV are unethical and illegal practices that hurt women and families. However, in most cases, the necessary measures are not taken to effectively enforce the Sexual Offences Act No. 3 of 2006, especially sections 3, 4, 5, 8, 9, 10, 11, 23, and section 24 on sexual offenses relating to positions of authority and persons in a position of trust, or to prevent femicide and violence against women in formal courts. In Kenyan parlance, statements like "no stone will remain unturned until we bring the culprits to book" are mostly used, and then forgotten. The national anger subsides until another femicide or GBV case is reported. According to *#CountingDeadWomenKenya*, eight Kenyan women are currently being killed every month by their boyfriends or husbands. While this "deliberate forgetting" has been propped up by the perennial lack of goodwill from advocates and judges in Kenya, another possible late entrant in this debilitating forgetting is the traditional media.[3] The traditional media is guilty because it portrays patriarchal notions, like violence against women, as the reality and recognized culture of the Kenyan people and taken over by the spirit of the Kenyan law. According to Fiske (1987, pp.4–5), "what passes for reality in any culture is the product of that culture's codes [...] 'reality' is always already encoded, it is never 'raw.'" Therefore, Kenyan traditional media has been able to define, package, and perpetuate masculinities that objectify, erase, and murder women while using the law to escape liability.

Hard questions, thus, need to be asked. If the Kenyan girl/woman cannot feel secure in the family[4] and in the formal courts, where else can she feel secure? Who watches over the watchman[5]? This chapter argues that in social media, Kenyan women, and those angered by the partial application of the law that denies women justice, use social media to provide the evidence needed to "bring the culprit(s) to book." In other words, social media "turns the stones for the law enforcers." This chapter thus discusses the connection between gender, judging, and the issue of femicide and GBV in Kenya.

Situating social media in feminist scholarship

Gusse (2016, p.2) argues that social media, specifically Twitter, has facilitated the rise of #BlackLivesMatter by creating an environment where social-political movements can flourish. These movements are accomplished by determining the unique characteristics of social media in activism (resistance to censorship, the efficiency of communication, horizontalist structure, and hashtag activism) and analyzing how #BlackLivesMatter has utilized these principles. According to scholars, social media outlets, that is, Facebook, Twitter, Tumblr, etc., employ a bottom-up structure to produce user-generated content and are therefore not subject to this degree of censorship (Gusse, 2016; Heather & McVey, 2016). Conversely, traditional mass media outlets like *CNN*, *The New York Times*, and *Vox* use a top-down format to produce content, allowing such content to be controlled and influenced by the political elite. Because of this, traditional mass media outlets are subject to a certain degree of censorship that makes them less likely to voice alternative viewpoints or run stories that may upset the political *status quo*.

In Kenya, social media has not only been used to express dissenting opinions on socio-political issues in the country but also serves as a platform where dissent can be circulated to the masses in a way that traditional mass media cannot. In essence, social media can give a voice to the voiceless. Jackson and Banaszczyk (2016) examine how hashtags have worked in the past to challenge dominant silences about gendered violence. Anchoring their study on the hashtags #YesAllWomen and #YesAllWhiteWomen, they powerfully contended that hashtags can be representative of a more traditional feminist counter-public seeking to influence, challenge, and rewrite dominant public narratives about violence against women. Social media can also reflect an oppositional counter-public that challenges the tendency in traditional feminist spaces to collapse women's experiences along the lines of gendered oppression.

In the same way, social media in Kenya manifests and articulates resistance on the miscarriage of justice in the formal courts, especially in femicide and GBV cases. Using hashtags #TotalShutDownKe, #HerLifeMatters, and #EndFemicideNow, social media provided spaces for, transformed, and influenced broader public narratives on issues central to women's lives. The cases in point were Winfred Mwende in Makueni County (who was captured on camera being beaten by her husband to unconsciousness), Sharon Otieno (who was allegedly killed by people known to her and closely linked to Migori County Governor Okoth Obado), and Ivy Wangechi (a final year Bachelor of Medicine student who was hacked to death by Naftali Kinuthia because he could not stand rejection). Social media played a central role in all these cases, although in varying degrees. One of the ways social media intervened was to bring these cases to the public. The traditional media got the information from social media. The public outrage that followed these cases was necessitated by social media. In these cases, social media was telling "their side of the story" in instances whereby the formality in the formal courts seemed to buy into the myth of "oppressed masculinity."

Using mixed methods as part of my methodology, I combined an examination of the text of tweets, the use of questionnaires with ten women judges, and an analysis of existing discourse on social media. I purposely sampled out tweets that engaged the Kenyan law by demanding justice for women who suffered the brunt of femicide or GBV. The research focused on the tweets that touched on and emanated specifically from the three cases under investigation here. The tweets sampled and interrogated were between September 2018 and May 2019. From each hashtag, and each case, I studied tweets within a month. The tweets were contained in the hashtags #TotalShutDownKe, #HerLifeMatters, and #EndFemicideNow. These online interlocutions were interpreted alongside what the ten female judges said offline in the questionnaire I circulated.

Social media, in my opinion, is the new judge in Kenya today. There has been a deliberate feminization of social media in Kenya, especially in matters of judging. Inside the suffocating "bricked walls of patriarchy" (Roy, 2019) that seem to define the Kenyan judicial system is a new light threatening to break down the Kenyan gender-blind judicial system. Mobile internet, especially in smartphones, has become the primary means by which new internet users are sharing information, particularly information that deals with issues of public concern, especially women's access to justice (Macharia, 2014; Napoli & Obar, 2014). As with the mobile phone, greater access to social media has the potential to create gender equity and access to justice (Liew et al., 2014).

My locus of enunciation in this chapter is that social media in Kenya provides a pool of knowledge that when given space in the judicial system, can contribute and restore the dignity of Kenyan women by bringing out particular kinds of memory production in ways that subvert normative temporalities. As it were, and following the above trajectory, social media can function as counter-publics for the debate and exchange of ideas and facilitate constructive dialogue about justice for women. Through social media, feminists can document what happens to Kenyan women daily and how their cases are handled in the formal courts. This documentation, I argue, provides a foundation for rewriting (her)stories and restores women within the discourse of gender, feminism, and the law. Handled well, social media can remove the veil of silence that has for so long been cast over the legal narratives that threaten to continue keeping the Kenyan woman marginalized by the same Kenyan law that is supposed to protect her, with the hope of increasing access to justice for women.

The "artifacts of political engagement"[6] in Twitter, showing women being molested by men and shared on social media, touch on collective memory in our lived realities. The use of social media shows how traumatic experiences are being viewed and remembered in Kenyan society today. By collecting and foregrounding these experiences in social media, Kenyans denounce the silencing of femicide and GBV cases in the formal court of law, where, in most instances, these cases are deemed private and relegated to the privacy of the family. By exposing these cases, social media maps directions for new forms of remembering and memory activism (Altinay & Pető, 2015, pp.379–385). In the hands of a feminist, social media is feminized and acquires a radical angle that refuses multi-faceted exclusions, intolerance, and erasure as well as the exclusion of challenging memories from women. At the same time, sharing these traumatic experiences and the dark sides of Kenyan law, social media produces new solidarities among and between feminists.

Conceptual and analytical framework

I draw on André Brock's (2012) critical technocultural discourse analysis (CTDA) framework to examine the complexities involved in social media communication with a particular focus on how Twitter hashtags can be used to help women access justice. According to Brock (2012), CTDA is a multimodal analytic technique for the investigation of internet and digital phenomena, artifacts, and culture. It integrates an analysis of the technological artifact and user discourse, framed by cultural theory, to unpack semiotic and material connections between form, function, belief, and meaning of information and communication technologies (ICTs). CTDA requires the incorporation of critical theories like feminism to integrate the epistemological standpoint of underserved ICT users to avoid deficit-based models of underrepresented populations' technology use. In the Kenyan case, the underserved populations are, due to the many patriarchal bottlenecks, women.

Locating itself within this framework, this chapter foregrounds the power of social media in constructing a new technoculture that resists the pernicious wave of violence and its normalization that has gripped the Kenyan socio-political spaces; a kind of culture that is genderless. Social media has the capacity of becoming a counter-public (Fraser, 1992; Farrell and Rabin, 1996). Women, who, as I have already argued, are newcomers and a minoritized community, utilize social media to display artifacts of their engagement in a patriarchal system. There is a culture that permeates the discourses in these artifacts of engagements. According to Williams (1977), these artifacts, i.e., the photos, videos, or even quotes that accompany these photos/videos, gain meaning because they are shared, oftentimes, by someone known to the recipient. Of course, the Kenyan case proves otherwise; most interlocutors are new to one another and only joined together by their chagrin about femicide and GBV cases. These artifacts, therefore, become imbued with meanings that are understood as actively lived and felt, yet are meanings that have not gained full expression but may lead to new starting points and new conclusions. Within this meaning creation, new cultures are formed in the form of online activism, a tsunami that can puncture patriarchal myths that normalize violence against women.

Pacey (1983) argues that technology is a construction of technical artifacts, practices, organizations, actors, and beliefs that are governed by a particular culture. This kind of formulation is advanced by CTDA, which focuses on representations within and of technology and is keenly interested in the technological artifact as a "set of rules and resources built into the technology by designers during its development which are then appropriated by users as they interact with the technology" (Orlikowski & Iacono, 2001). This definition is advanced in this research to accommodate the photos, memes, drawings, and streams of videos shared in the identified hashtags. These artifacts advance particular public discussions whose purpose is to resist patriarchal practices that dehumanize women. The culture constructed online, thus, humanizes women, giving not only voice but also life to female bodies. In this way, Brock (2012) argues that CTDA offers a critical approach to technology artifacts that reorients technocultural practice to the cultural context in which the artifact is being used.

Speaking and appealing to the emotion of the recipients, the culture of the social media hashtags draws people to action, bringing together online affective publics and counter-publics and propelling people toward participation in constructing contested public spaces (Papacharissi, 2014). Relying on feminist beliefs, CTDA draws directly from the perspective of the group under examination; the Kenyan feminist interlocutors in #TotalShutDownKe, #HerLifeMatters, and #EndFemicideNow platforms; and discussions meant to decenter theories of technological determinism (advancing misogynist notions that normalize violence against women) premised upon the beliefs of a dominant patriarchal Kenyan culture. The hashtags #TotalShutDownKe, #HerLifeMatters, and #EndFemicideNow platforms shaped online and offline activism in three cases: Winfred Mwende's, Sharon Otieno's, and Ivy Wangechi's cases. CTDA "formulates technology as cultural representations and social structures to simultaneously interrogate culture and technology as intertwined concepts" (Brock, 2018, p.1012).

This theoretical framework opens ways to analyze online discussions that touch on Kenyan law and its attendant opaqueness through a critical deconstruction of the activities of the discussants involved in engaging with seeking justice for women victims. In this sense, the theory can be seen as providing "a holistic analysis of the interactions between technology, cultural ideology, and technology practice" (Brock, 2018, p.1013). Within this framework, it is imperative to examine the intricacies of technology use by taking into consideration the actors involved and the cultural capital they possess (Nissenbaum & Shifman, 2017), their technological literacy skills, and the relationships between old and new media (Srinivasan, 2013). According to Mohammed (2019), who borrows from Brock (2012), Srinivasan (2013), and Pillay (2016), the new media use disrupts notions of binaries between old and new technology, online and offline affordances among others, because these binaries do not reflect the complexities of the relationships between digital technology and social movements in the physical world. This point will be pursued later in this chapter.

Social media provides the subaltern with a voice to discuss and articulate not only the daily lived realities of Kenyan women, especially bringing to light the many femicide cases, but also informally contravening the *sub judice* rule[7] to discuss miscarriage in justice or even lauding justice when well served. Importantly, the 2010 constitution of Kenya was born out of the need to ensure that all Kenyan men and women would be part of the process of telling a different story—a different narrative about how they wanted to be protected. It was a people-driven process that entailed several stages of civic education, collection, and collation of views, and I would add that at various stages of the process, it was indeed a women-driven process (see also Sivi-Njonjo, 2016; Kameri-Mbote, 2016; Omondi, 2016). Social media has been instrumental in bringing these cases to the public knowledge and ensuring that justice is served in the formal courts.

Social media and judging: Lived realities of a Kenyan woman

#When a woman goes to report some of these cases, she is told "Hii ni mambo ya nyumbani" [*these are family matters*]

#And here you talk of due process ... In Kenya, all that matters is the judge. Why hire a lawyer when you can buy the judge

The data from the femicide awareness platform *Counting Dead Women Kenya* paint a gloomy picture of the status of femicides in Kenya. Their report shows that 46 women were victims of femicide between January and May 2019. By November 16, this figure had risen to 82 cases of reported femicide (Mutune, 2019). Another strand of data from the *Open Africa* report on "Femicides in Kenya" shows that 84 women were murdered between January and October 2019 by their boyfriends and/or husbands (Odhiambo, 2018). The report indicates that Kenya is among the countries with the highest numbers of female homicides and abuse against women. For example, 38.5% of girls and women in Kenya aged 15 to 49 have experienced physical violence at least once in their lifetime, and 24% of these women experienced physical violence in 2018 alone (Mutune, 2019). This is despite having many laws in the country that aim to protect women from all kinds of harm.

In Table 5.1, I describe three particular cases that were discussed in the three hashtags, whether they went to court or not, and the outcome of the prosecution (convicted, acquitted, or otherwise).

It is noteworthy that before social media, many similar cases would take place, and even the police would not be informed (Chepkwony, 2016, p.12). It could be reported to the village head, then the chief, a process that could take weeks. In most cases, the village head would revert the case to the family (in case of battery) or the clan (in case of death) (Okoth-Ogendo, 1979; International Development

Table 5.1 Legal status of cases discussed in social media

Prosecution			
Cases	*Conviction*	*Acquited*	*Other*
Julius Nzomo Daudi against The Republic of Kenya (August 2018)	Convicted: Serving 12-year jail term		
Governor Zackary Okoth Obado against The Republic of Kenya (murder of Sharon Otieno) (Sept. 2018)			released on a Ksh5 million cash bail.
Naftali Kinuthia against the Republic of Kenya **(murder of Ivy Wangeci)** (April 2019)			**bond denied on 17th** day of **June** 2019 Could not start on March 6, 2020 as planned.

Source: *Kenya Law Cases Database, 2020*

Law Organization, 2020). However, due to social media, and through online activism, it took a few hours before the three cases in Table 5.1 were brought to the public. The mainstream media, the Director of Public Prosecution (DPP), the Inspector General's office, and all citizens were involved in the conversation. Hinging my discussion on the online conversations on the three cases presented in Table 5.1, I argue that the swift action of the arrest of the accused persons was engineered by social media. The discussion they led online approached the cases from all possible angles, interpreting the applicable laws and pointing out the potential loopholes. These conversations enlighten the public and educate women on the possible laws they can use to seek justice. This later function confirms the points made by judges F, G, and I (see the next section in this chapter) that one impediment of women's access to justice was a lack of information about the available laws that protect them.

Although there were many femicide cases in Kenya before social media, a paltry number of perpetrators were punished (Brown, 2020). For instance, if it were not for social media, the likes of Julius Nzomo, Zachari Obado, and Naftali Kinuthia would probably remain unprosecuted. Nzomo was captured on camera beating his wife Mwende unconscious. Images of the unconscious Mwende surfaced online, and this prompted the DPP to swing into action. Consequently, Nzomo, the perpetrator, was arrested, charged, and arraigned before court. He was convicted to serve 12 years' imprisonment.[8]

The hashtags #TotalShutDownKe, #HerLifeMatters, and #EndFemicideNow draw national attention to the violence and killings against women by amplifying the plight of Kenyan women. There follow samples of some of the online interlocutions, which I will interpret later alongside what the ten female judges said offline in the questionnaire I circulated:

#Straight members of the societies do not want to hear the reasons these criminals had for carrying out these heinous acts, we demand **justice** for the families of the victims. It is their **right** # TotalShutdownKe #SayHerNameKE [1]

#TotalShutdownKe #SayHerNameKE We are tired of being murdered. We can't even be safe in our own houses. We will not be silent anymore. Let's fight for our **right** to live. Let us rise and say [2]

#NoToFemicide, #TotalShutDownKe Women's **rights** are fundamental **rights**. [3]

#We salute all women & womxn for their bravery, determination and resolve; for breaking barriers and disrupting patriarchal spaces; for calling out **injustice** and demanding **transparency & accountability** among duty bearers; for their compassion & #SayHerNameKE **#TotalShutDownKE** [4]

#I am marching because I want to change the narrative and stop normalizing violence against womxn. What we want **accountability #TotalShutdownKe** #SayHerNameKe [5]

#Ivy's aunt is speaking, she wrote a paper on achieving **justice** for women and girls in Kenya, "I never expected that I would be living the story of my paper." **#TotalShutdownKE** #JusticeForIvy #SayHerName #HerLifeMatters [6]

#Don't say "died" when you mean "murdered." People die from old age. Or from terminal diseases. But it's not plain old death to be hacked by a machete in the head. The passive voice invisibilises murderers and does little to give victims **justice**. **#totalshutdownke** #sayhername [7]

#There should be a national inquiry to the killing of women, special courts to deal with SGBV issues, and the establishment of Gender Recovery Centers in all the 47 counties. We demand **accountability #HerLifeMatters [8]**

#One of the family members speaking had just come from a funeral to bury their daughter. Truly, this is a national tragedy. People should not have to go through this and with nil **justice**. **#HerLifeMatters [9]**

#The fact that #sexualviolence is being normalized is not only a grim representation of our realities but a serious injunction on what the Kenyan society is turning into. We demand state **accountability** for these violations. **#HerLifeMatters [10]**

#@CSMargaretKobia and @Rachelshebesh will today join other women leaders at a vigil night at @uonbi from 4-9 pm to protest against the widespread killing of women and girls and appeal for **justice**. @FredMatiangi will also be in attendance. **#HerLifeMatters [11]**

#Time has come for the government of #Kenya to live up to its obligations to protect, prevent against and punish perpetrators of #sexualviolence including femicide; and to collectively affirm the **rights** of women to self-determination and bodily autonomy. **#HerLifeMatters [12]**

#HerLifeMatters, it is indeed a tragedy that lives are lost in the name of love. we are watching because we could be the next victim and demanding **justice** before it all gets out of hand! [13]

#@CS Matiangi commits DCI effort and investment in tackling femicide, GBV, and reviving gender desks at police stations. Where are the commitment to paper and hard action? What are the timelines? We want to hold this to **account**. **#HerLifeMatters** #TotalShutdownKE [14]

#WE DEMAND TO LIVE We demand for a police department that solely deals with violence, femicide and rape cases against women. We demand **accountability**. We demand **justice #HerLifeMatters** #EndFemicideNow @ FeministsKE [15]

#When a woman goes to report some of these cases, she is told "Hii ni mambo ya nyumbani" #EndFemicideNow **#HerLifeMatters** #KTNNewsCentre @ Michellengele [16]

#Are there adequate laws protecting women from gender-based violence? We **demand justice** and **accountability**. **#HerLifeMatters [17]**

#We demand **accountability**. We want **justice**. There are more than enough laws that protect girls and women in Kenya, more than anywhere else in the world. Article 100 of the constitution is among them [18]

"GBV has been shrouded in a conspiracy of silence, thus perpetuating impunity. We need to strategise on how we can make laws more impactful to the lives of people,"@Rachelshebesh, @PSYGKenya #EndGBV #GBVConferenceKe **#HerLifeMatters [19]**

#Proving Malice aforethought is essential in murder cases … Now the narrative for the defense will be that Kinuthia had bought an Axe for his own use chopping firewood, and he visited Ivy, but a mob of irate guys thought they were thugs and beat them up. Kinuthia survived.

Ivy didn't … So the prosecution will have to prove beyond reasonable doubt this was not the case … it is a basic **right**. We want **justice**.

Remember the case of Matheri, Nyamwacha, all who had seemingly overwhelming evidence of murder … they were never convicted of murder … it all depends on the Judge. We demand **accountability** #kibetosh #HerLifeMatters [20]

#Apart from proving malice aforethought or premeditation, the rest of your submission is hogwash or at best muguka wisdom. Court process is not a circus where accused have time to come up with tales. The two incoherent cases you quoted are not in any way related and their verdict was never acquittal. Proving criminal case is easier than acknowledged. We demand a**ccountability** is the key #Jalaal Kafkaesque kibetosh #HerLifeMatters [21]

#Hahahahah …yet the cop who followed and killed Ainamoi MP together with his Female Companion in 2008, who happened to be the cop's lover only got 10 years in a case that put current CJ into ridicule a accused of favouring the cop because he was came from his tribe. The cop has now finished his ten-year sentence and is most likely out. In the meantime, two innocent people died, and the family was left to lick their wounds. We demand **Accountability**. **Accountability** is the key to **justice**. As a Precendent [Precedent] … what is the difference btwn that case and this one concerning Kinuthia ad Ivy.

Similarities. In both cases the victim was followed by her male lover.

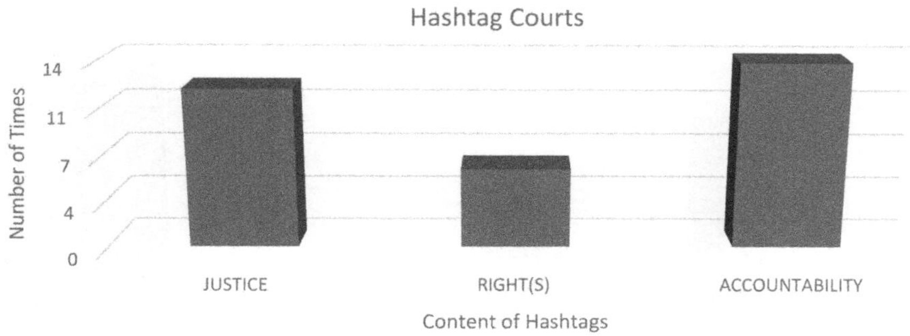

Figure 5.1 Hashtag Courts

In both cases the culprit was well armed

In both cases the culprit traveled hundreds of Kilometers in pursuit of the victim who did not know she was being followed.

And here you talk of due process … In Kenya, all that matters is the judge. Why hire a lawyer when you can buy the judge. @#kibetosh Jalaal Kafkaesque, #HerLifeMatters [22]

In these conversations, the word *justice* has been used 12 times in the 22 tweets. The word *right*(s) has been used 6 times and the word *accountability* 14 times. These three words are correlated. When the word justice is used, it is mostly introduced by the word no/nil,- or demand. This information is presented in Figure 5.1.

Some of the tweets have more reactions from the online publics, with 12 tweets (55%) interpreting applicable laws ([1], [2], [3], [4], [10], [11], [15], [18], [19], [20], [21], [22]), another 6 (27%) expressing disgust about the blindness of the Kenyan law on femicide cases ([10], [12], [15], [20], [21], [22]), one (5%) appealing for and 16 (73%) demanding action ([1], [4], [5], [8], [9], [10], [13], [14], [15], [17], [18], [20], [20], [21], [22]) against femicide and GBV cases. See Figure 5.2 for this information.

In Figure 5.2, 54% interpreted the Kenyan law, 27% expressed disgust about the opaqueness of the Kenyan law on femicide, 5% appealed for action, and 73% demanded justice and accountability. What becomes apparent is that the users of this platform make social media a site of engagement; a public platform where oppressive discourses can be contested and resisted. The result is a technoculture with a common purpose, demanding action. This technoculture is gender-inclusive, objective, and humane.

The aim of the hashtags is not only to honor femicide victims but also to use online activism to seek justice for women. For instance, in the first tweet in #TotalShutdownKE, Renoh Omollo said on the day of the protest on March 8, 2019, "there is a war against our bodies, there is a war against Kenyan womxn and together we are raising our voices to say no to this femicide and violence against womxn. No consequences befall these perpetrators. We note that violence

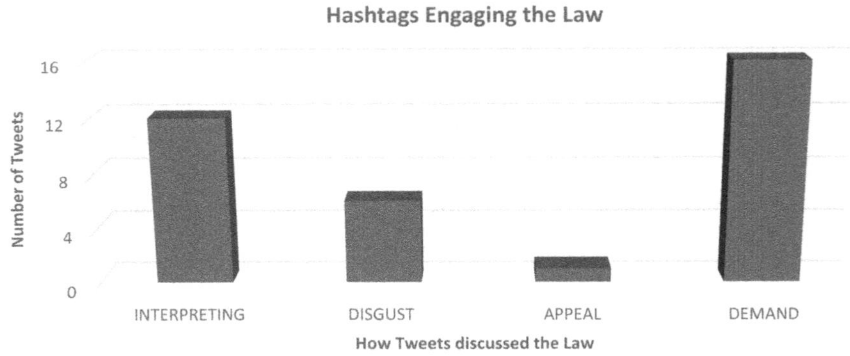

Figure 5.2 Hashtags Engaging the Law

against womxn has been normalized and, therefore, escalating because of the systemic power structures that favour men" (Feminist Collective, 2019). What can be seen from the tweet is the deliberate deletion of the vowel "e" in "women." The word is deliberately changed to "womxn." This refusal to be yoked together with the tormentor problematizes the general view in a patriarchal society; that women are appendages of men (daughter of so and so, wife of so and so, mother of so and so). This view can be seen through the rationalization that follows these murders, which as the women judges interviewed for this study suggested, affects the judgment that is meted out to the culprits in the formal court of law.

Perceptions of women judges

To supplement the data from Twitter, this study benefited from data collected using a questionnaire circulated and filled in by ten purposely sampled out female high court judges in Kenya. The study chose female judges due to their positionality and gender. Views from the ten judges are relatively representational. After the ten judges filed the questionnaires (typing their answers to the questions asked), I analyzed their responses and retyped them, following similarities and divergences in their responses. In this way, I was able to minimize unnecessary repetitions and redundancy. For anonymity, the judges are referred to as A, B, C, D, E, F, G, H, I, J.

The main question in the questionnaire was: does social media impact on justice in Kenya? The answer to this question was an affirmative yes: all ten judges agreed that social media can influence the outcome of court cases in Kenya. Seven out of the ten high court judges who answered the questionnaires said that one of the problems making femicide cases problematic to handle was the general public's rationalization of crimes against women and girls. Quoting the Naftali Kinuthia case against the Republic (refer to Table 5.1), judges A, B, and D blamed societal normativity as an impediment to justice for women. However, the same judges strongly agreed that it is wrong for any man to harm a woman, irrespective of the motivation, and any man who kills a woman for whatever reason deserves the full punishment provided by the law.

According to these judges, the public is always out to defend the perpetrator's action, even to the extent of working tirelessly to sanitize the killers. Others (mis) use the law to entrench male entitlement to the female body. The responses from judges A, B, and D were also noted in #HerLifeMatters and #EndFemicideNow, where approximately 5% of the tweets tried to sanitize Naftali Kinuthia as "a teetotaller who had never shown any sign of stress, a gentleman who was being misused by Ivy Wangechi, and a generous man who was always sending money to his cheating girlfriend." It is noteworthy that the use of the terms "teetotaller" and "gentleman" in the tweets contradicts research findings, which have noted that the risk of a woman being subject to GBV in Kenya "declines with the education level of her spouse but increases if her spouse has a history of alcohol abuse" (World Bank Group, 2018). This is because although the victim was highly educated, the perpetrator had no history of alcohol abuse.

It becomes clear that the use of the words "gentleman" and "teetotaller" serves to advance patriarchal interests in the case, as seen through the argument of the other 75% of the tweets, which contended that the problem with Naftali was his failure to stand rejection, a warped sense of male entitlement that can best be described as toxic masculinity. This latter group argued that the spirit of the law is very harsh on criminals like Kinuthia, men who justify murder or assault. Women are not and have never been chattels. Any man who harms a woman, irrespective of the motivation, deserves the full punishment provided by the law.

This latter group (75%) also blamed the law for being silent on issues of femicide. According to this group, by being silent on issues of GBV and femicide, the law itself was being toxic. Out of toxicity, the law becomes sensational and reactionary, and judgment is served overly from a patriarchal point of view aimed at disparaging the reputations of victims (Mutune, 2019). According to this toxic strand of the law, those killed by their husbands contributed to their murders by being involved intimately with other men apart from those that killed them, or by failing to reciprocate affection from their partners. Others, like Sharon Otieno, were being blamed for accepting monetary favors from the men who kill them. The killers are sanitized as men who had never shown any signs of "stress" or as men who could not bear "love gone sour" (Mutune, 2019).

One of the key demands for #TotalShutdownKE was that existing laws and action plans be reviewed to determine why they have failed to protect women from violence and murder. Approximately 30% of the tweets under this hashtag talked about the failure of Kenyan law to deal with this seemingly new occurrence in the Kenyan courts. This was also acceptable to three judges according to the way they answered the question of whether there was a possibility that laws can be misread to deny women justice. The judges, just like some of the tweets, discussed the failure of Kenyan laws to even define what constitutes femicide or what qualifies a case as femicide. There was agreement among the views of the female judges who filled in the questionnaire that social media, and especially these hashtags, amplified these femicide and GBV cases, a kind of activism that positively influenced the nature of judgment meted out to the culpable culprits. These hashtags did this by letting the public know what was going on in the court of law, and what the Kenyan law said about cases of similar nature.

To the question of how the judges dealt with femicide cases that are brought before them, all the ten female judges who filled in the questionnaires for this study agreed that the law on femicide in Kenya is governed under the murder regime. There is no law that specifically provides for femicide. Femicide is treated like any other murder case despite its uniqueness. The fact that judicial officers also exercise discretion in sentencing opens a door for the judicial officers to deal with every femicide matter independently. This has thus produced mixed results for the sentencing of convicts. What these honorable judges seemed to suggest, and frown upon, is that there is no consistent legal jurisprudence in Kenya on femicide. The same sentiments were expressed in the hashtags #TotalShutDownKe, #HerLifeMatters, and #EndFemicideNow.

Online discussions on these platforms about the inadequacies of the Kenyan law to combat femicide and GBV cases corroborated the offline response from the ten female judges. From the analysis of the data collected, the study argues that although there is legislation that criminalizes gender-based violence and codifies the rights of people to live free of violence, social media plays an emblematic role by amplifying the relevant clauses. The related sanctions may serve a deterrence function. Legislation can also be receptive to victims by providing protection and access to support services. Social media, as can be noted from the foregoing, enhances other interventions designed to reduce GBV in low- and middle-income countries. To wit, researchers have identified strategies, including group training, social communications, community mobilization, and livelihood strategies, which help in addressing underlying risk factors for violence, including social norms regarding gender dynamics and the acceptability of violence (Arango et al., 2014).

The problem of non-prosecution of femicide and GBV cases in Kenya presents a conundrum—the paradox between the existence of laws, on the one hand, and the lack of prosecution of cases, on the other hand. The Kenyan government has performed relatively well in the enactment of laws, policies, and regulations on the response, prevention, and management of gender-based violence. The problem therefore lies with the lack of effective implementation of the law. For instance, Article 29 (c) of the Kenyan constitution provides that every person has the right to freedom and security of the person, which includes the right not to be subjected to any form of violence from either public or private sources. Besides, many laws have been enacted in Kenya to protect people from gender-based violence. These laws include The Protection against Domestic Violence Act 2005, 2015; The Sexual Offences Act 2003; The Matrimonial Property Act 2013; The Marriage Act 2014; and Penal Code Cap 63 (Revised Edition 2012).

Other national instruments include the Criminal Procedure Code (Revised Edition 2012), the Prohibition of Female Genital Mutilation Act (2011), and the National Gender and Equality Commission Act (2011). Article 2 (5 and 6) of the Constitution of Kenya provides that all international laws, treaties, and conventions form part of Kenya's laws. Kenya has ratified several treaties that govern gender-based violence, including The Convention on the Elimination of All Forms of Discrimination Against Women (CEDAW), 1979; The Declaration on the Elimination of Violence Against Women (DEVAW), 1993; and The African Charter on Human and Peoples' Rights on the Rights of Women in Africa (known as the Maputo Protocol), 2005. By Article 2 (5 and 6) of the Constitution of Kenya, upon domestic ratification, these international treaties became part of the laws of Kenya and are applicable within the domestic arena. Despite the many laws governing gender-based violence, there is a likelihood of judicial officers misdirecting themselves on the laws. This can be attributed to various factors such as little knowledge about their existence. Also, the enactment of the Acts has not been matched with adequate training and dissemination of the Acts to law enforcement officers and relevant justice system agents, such as prosecutors, who have the responsibility to bring the right charges to court.

Although the government has audited various laws and repealed discriminatory provisions, subsequent legislations have remained gender neutral in their language, thus making it difficult to deal with discrimination in situations where the law fails to categorize discrimination as an offense. Also, the co-existence of customary and religious laws that are not consistent with the legislative prohibitions could cloud the reasoning of judicial officers. The seemingly conflicting co-existence of customary, religious, and the formal Kenyan law was seriously critiqued in the hashtags #TotalShutDownKe, #HerLifeMatters, and #EndFemicideNow, especially in the cases of Winfred Mwende, Sharon Otieno, and Ivy Wangechi. The agreement among the tweets was that by homogenizing these deaths, it watered down the motive behind the many killings.

It appears that formal courts have taken judicial notice of the fact that the home (private sphere) has now become an unsafe haven for women. Therefore, any sentences passed must reflect the fact that offenses of this nature have pricked the judicial conscience. However, the three hashtags disagreed and accused judges of doublespeak, inconsistency, and laziness. Courts dealing with the offense of murder are allowed to exercise judicial discretion by considering any mitigating factors in sentencing an accused person charged with and found guilty of that offense. In applying the law governing femicide, the courts are likely to exercise their discretion judiciously, although in some cases, the courts may be too lenient on the accused persons. When the court is lenient on the accused, what results is an injustice to the woman, the victim of the femicide, as was seen in the cases of Sharon Otieno and Ivy Wangechi.

Do you, the judges, accept social media evidence in court when determining femicide cases? Judges argued that in the normal course of life or business, most people are likely to use their mobile phones: taking pictures, sending or receiving text messages, accessing the internet to send or receive an email, record a video, play music, and/or send or receive instant message service. This data is more often than not shared on social media. The data can be produced as primary evidence by the person who shared the data on social media. Section 106B (4)(d) of the Evidence Act provides for the admissibility of such evidence. Social media consequently becomes relevant in courts only where there is a person to authenticate the information shared on social media. This information is necessary, as it would help courts in decision-making.

Social media brings out femicide cases to the public. The unedited streams of videos that circulate present the event as it occurred with the unedited voices of the argument, if there was any. Here, the viewers become the jury, discussing the evidence produced and passing judgment. Of late, these discussions are specifically addressed to the necessary state apparatus like the DPP or the Inspector General of Police. The inclusion of social media in judging seems to have been brought forth by the continual instrumentalization of women's stories as part of the common public narrative in the formal courts. Additionally, social media strongly reflects underlying norms within Kenyan society. By sharing and calling for justice for the victims of GBV and femicide, social media persuades others to see the brunt of violence against women. Additionally, by sharing this information and discussing it, social media provides new information that influences individuals to accept it. Furthermore, it informs listeners about what others learn, thus facilitating coordination. This shows the shifting attitudes around GBV.

To this end, Winfred Mwende and David Nzomo's case would serve as an example. The incident, which captures extreme levels of brutality against a seemingly defenseless wife, woke the silent social media. Irate "netizens"[9] took to Twitter under the tagline #ArrestNzomo to demand justice following the ruthless attack. The video that sparked outrage among members of the public caught the attention of the DPP. The streams of videos that circulated on social media with captions #ArrestNzomo, and his eventual arrest and speedy prosecution and sentencing to 12 years, shows the centrality of social media in search of justice for women.

As already argued, the Kenyan formal courts have used opaqueness of some laws to deny women justice. It is also important to note that the Kenyan courts have in the past used the *sub judice* rule to deter people from debating on issues of the public interest but which were yet to be determined. The repealed Constitution of Kenya in section 79 (2) secured the common law position on *sub judice*. In recent times, however, and especially in this era of technological advancement, it has become clear that information about trials can be shared via social media. The *sub judice* rule is no longer an automatic bar to public discussion on matters pending before the court in Kenya. However, under the Constitution of Kenya, 2010, any limitation on the freedom of expression guaranteed under Article 33 must be justified. It is, thus, no longer enough to front *sub judice* as an automatic bar to public discussion on matters pending before the court.

When interrogating what #HerLifeMatters and #EndFemicide discussions have achieved, one repeated point of discussion which Kenyans belabor concerns miscarriage of justice in the formal courts. It would seem that social media shines light on the miscarriage of justice. Social media can shine light when existing redress mechanisms are corrupt or opaque. One case in point in Kenya involved the rape and killing of Sharon Otieno. One of the accused persons was an influential, wealthy politician, but because of the evidence provided in the social media, including recorded phone calls, the formal court had to detain the accused. However, the accused was later released on bail of 5 million Kenyan shillings.

In her incisive book *Digital Democracy, Analogue Politics: How the Internet Era Is Transforming Kenya,* Nanjala Nyabola explains how social media has "reinvigorated feminist discourse in Kenya." Nyabola describes how social media had cultivated a movement with the hashtag #MyDressMyChoice to call out a series of attacks on women in November 2014. The #MyDressMyChoice movement was created on the Facebook page of Kilimani Moms, a coalition of mothers from Nairobi who called for protests to support the right of women to dress as they wish. Following these protests, the Kenyan judiciary started to prosecute those caught molesting women, which as Nyabola suggests, is "the first time there had been a prosecution for this kind of behavior in recent memory" (2018, p.127).

Social media can be used to curb femicide in Kenya. Femicide is the ultimate form of violence against women and girls, often taking various forms and linked to gender power imbalance and historic gender-discriminatory practices, norms, and beliefs. For a case to be considered femicide, there must be an implied intention to carry out the murder and a demonstrated connection between the crime and the female gender of the victim (Kumari, 2013; Laurent et al., 2013). Femicide and gender-based violence are increasing all over the world, and this is exacerbated by the current global pandemic. Failure to comprehensively address femicide will signal to abusers that these actions are acceptable. The judiciary has a role in sending a signal that perpetrators will be punished for violating the fundamental human right to life of their victims.

Conclusion

To conclude this chapter, I briefly mention a subject elided in the argument so far—the downside of femicide and GBV cases playing out entirely on social media. Often, when this happens, there is the possible trolling of the survivors by supporters of the accused. This trolling may cause more harm to the victims. Therefore, as we embrace the changes brought about by online activism, we should also consider the impact of the "cancel culture" on both the accusers and the accused. However, through careful analysis, the chapter has established that social media in Kenya provides a powerful platform for the articulation of formally silenced voices, and therefore, its use has more advantages than its drawbacks. Indeed, it is helping victims get justice, because courts can no longer ignore these hashtags and also, judges are using social media artifacts to strengthen the evidence used to prosecute cases.

Judges can help in two ways. The first is through judicial support of social media evidence guided by acceptable legal norms, which will enable them to administer justice. The second is creating awareness about the legal implications of using social media wrongly. Through judicial activism, judges should participate in sensitization and creating awareness among the masses and disseminate existing norms on the rights of women and girls.

This chapter has shown that social media provides an alternative judicial forum that enables crafting an informed definition of femicide and its weight; it shines light on the miscarriage of justice in the judicial system through corruption and opaqueness of the Kenyan law on issues of femicide. Social media is feminized; both men and women are involved; the war against femicide involves both men and women in the social media; this is important, because the boy child also has to be emancipated to know that his sister, mother, and the child must also be respected. Through social media, WE CAN ALL BE FEMINISTS!

Notes

1 The term 'femicide' is used in this study to denote the killing of women because of their gender. In this sense, femicide is understood to be motivated by misogyny and prejudice against women. For a case to be considered femicide there must be an implied intention to carry out the crime and a demonstrated connection between the crime and the gender of the victim.

2 Here the term social media will be applied to describe the various forms of media content that are publicly available and created by end-users. Social Media is a group of Internet-based applications that build on the ideological and technological foundations of Web 2.0, and that allow the creation and exchange of User Generated Content.

3 This includes Radio and Television

4 Many femicide and GBV cases are perpetrated in the confines of the family/ home, by a close family member or a person known to the family. In most cases, these cases are left to be handled by the family, in a private arbitration or informal courts. In almost all cases, the girl/ woman cannot get justice because the family, the customary courts are punitively patriarchal. The figure of the father is the law by itself.

5 Watchman here refers to the formal Kenyan courts. Their mandate is to protect people from all sorts of violations, violence or any sort of harm.

6 Clark (2015) uses this phrase to stand for the photos, memes, quoted sayings, and original or curated commentary that is shared on social media. What is important is not just the photo, meme, or the quote itself; the item gains meaning because it was shared by someone known to the recipient. These artifacts therefore become imbued with meanings that are understood as actively lived and felt, yet are meanings that have not gained full expression but may lead to new starting points and new conclusions.

7 The sub judice rule is a common law principle that generally prohibits public discussion on matters pending before the court. It is a principle used in cases where there was genuine fear that lay jury members would be swayed by public opinion.

8 Kenya Law Cases Database, HCCRA NO.78 OF 2019; Julius Nzomo Daudi v Republic [2019] eKLR

9 A term coined in a 1992 by Michael Hauben to describe a person actively involved in online communities or the Internet in general.

References

Altinay A., & Pető, A. (2015). "Europe and the century of genocides: New directions in the feminist theorising of genocide." *European Journal of Women's Studies*, *22*(3), 379–385.

Arango, D., Morton M., Gennari, F., Kiplesund S., & Ellsberg, M. (2014). *Interventions to Prevent or Reduce Violence Against Women and Girls: a Systematic Review of Reviews.* Women's Voice and Agency Research Series, No.10.

Brock, A. (2012). "From the blackhand side: Twitter as a cultural conversation." *Journal of Broadcasting & Electronic Media*, 56(4): 529–549. https://doi.org/10.1080/08838151.2012.73214

Brock, A. (2018). "Critical technocultural discourse analysis." *New Media & Society*, *20*(3), 1012–1030. https://doi.org/doi:10.1177/146144481667753

Brown, R. (2020). 'Numbers don't lie': The team 'counting dead women' in Kenya." *The Christian Science Monitor*. ISSN 2573-3850 (online). https://www.csmonitor.com/

Chepkwony, V. (2016). *Factors Affecting Violence Against Women in Kenya: A Case of Live with Hope Non Governmental Organization, Kericho County, Kenya* [Published thesis]. University of Nairobi Press. http://erepository.uonbi.ac.ke/

Clark, L. (2015, May). Critical youth and media studies: Bringing youth voice into post-Ferguson law enforcement training. In Presentation at the International Communication Association, San Juan, Puerto Rico. Retrieved from http://www.slideshare.net/LynnSchofieldClark/civic-engagementypar

Farrell, J., & Rabin, M. (1996). "Cheap talk." *Journal of Economic Perspectives*, *10*(3), 103–118.

Feminist Collective (2019). *Stop Killing Us: On Femicide in Kenya.* Medium.com. https://medium.com/feminist-collective/stop-killing-us-on-femicide-in-kenya-25357bf430a2

Fiske, J. (1987). *Television Culture*. New York: Routledge.

Fraser, N. (1992). "Rethinking the public sphere: A contribution to the critique of actually existing democracy." In C. Calhoun (Ed.), *Habermas and the Public Sphere* (pp. 122–33). Cambridge, MA: MIT Press.

Gusse, J. (2016). "#BlackLivesMatter: How Social Media Became Social Justice." WRIT 201 http://mashable.com/2013/10/19/hijacked-hashtags/#9KPGa2gn7uq8

Heather, W., & McVey, J. (2016). "#BlackLivesMa<er as a case study in the politics of digital media: Algorithms, hashtag publics, and organizing protest online." *Teaching Media Quarterly*, 4(1). h<p://pubs.lib.umn.edu/tmq/vol4/iss1/5

International Development Law Organization (2020). *East, Horn and Southern African Regional Forum on Alternative Dispute Resolution & Customary and Informal Justice.* March 2nd–3rd 2020. Kenya: Safari Park Hotel Nairobi.

Jackson, S., & Banaszczyk, S. (2016). "Digital standpoints: Debating gendered violence and racial exclusions in the feminist counterpublic." *Journal of Communication Inquiry*, *40*(4), 391–407.

Kameri-Mbote, P. (2016). "The quest for equal gender representation in Kenya's Parliament: Past and present challenges." In J. Biegon (Ed.), *Gender and Political Processes in Kenya* (pp. 39–66). Nairobi: Strathmore University.

Kumari, R. (2013). "How do we fight femicide: Best practices and strategies." In C. Laurent, M. Platzer & M. Idomir (Eds.), *Femicide: A Global Issue that Demands Action* (pp. 37–41). Vienna: ACUNS. Available at http://acuns.org/femicidea-global-issue-that-demands-action/.

Liew, E., Vaithilingam, S., & Nair, M. (2014). "Facebook and socio-economic benefits in the developing world." *Behaviour & Information Technology*, *33*(4), 345–360.

Macharia, J. (2014). "Internet access is no longer a luxury." *Africa Renewal*, *28*(1), 18–19.

Mohammed, W. (2019). "Online activism: Centering marginalized voices in activist work." *Ada: A Journal of Gender, New Media, and Technology*, *15*. https://doi.org/10.5399/uo/ada.2019.15.2

Morrison, C. (2007), *Offending or Chastising? Towards Codifying Domestic Violence*. Boulder, CO: Lynne Rienner Publishers.

Mutune, M. (2019). "Femicide cases on the rise in Kenya." In *Akili Dada*. Nairobi, Kenya. http://akilidada.org/tag/femicide/

Napoli, P.M., & Obar, J.A. (2014). "The emerging mobile Internet underclass: A critique of mobile Internet access." *The Information Society*, 30(5), 323–334.

National Gender and Equality Commission (2016). *Gender-based Violence in Kenya: The Cost of Providing Services: A Projection Based on Selected Service Delivery Points*. Nairobi: HECTA Consulting Ltd., Edward Miller Printing.

Nissenbaum, A., & Shifman, L. (2017). "Internet memes as contested cultural capital: The case of 4chan's /b/ board." *New Media & Society*, 19(4), 483. https://doi.org/10.1177/146144481560931

Nyabola, N. (2018). *Digital Democracy, Analogue Politics: How the Internet Era is Transforming Politics in Kenya*. London: Zed Books.

Odhiambo, A. (2018). "Tackling the violence faced by women and girls in Kenya." *The Standard*, p. 12. https://www.hrw.org/news/2018/10/09/tackling-violence-faced-women-and-girls-kenya

Okoth-Ogendo, H. (1979). *On Customary Law*. Unpublished document, Faculty of Law, University of Nairobi.

Omondi, D. (2016). "The role of political parties in promoting women's political participation." In J. Biegon (Ed.), *Gender and Political Processes in Kenya* (pp. 91–114). Nairobi: Strathmore University.

Orlikowski, W., & Iacono, C. (2001) "Research commentary: Desperately seeking the "IT" in "IT" research: A call for theorising the IT artifact." *Information Systems Research*, *12*(2): 121–134.

Pacey, A. (1983). *The Culture of Technology*. Boston, MA: The MIT Press.

Papacharissi, Z. (2014). *Affective Publics: Sentiment, Technology, and Politics*. New York: Oxford University Press.

Pillay, S. (2016). "Silence is violence: (critical) psychology in an era of Rhodes must fall and fees must fall." *South African Journal of Psychology*, 46(2), 155–159. https://doi.org/10.1177/008124631663676

Roy, S. (2019). "Chip, but don't break walls of patriarchy." *The Mail & Guardian*. https://mg.co.za/article/2019-05-17-00-chip-but-dont-break-walls-of-patriarchy/

Sivi-Njonjo, K. (2016). "The path towards inclusive democracy in Kenya." In J. Biegon (Ed.), *Gender and Political Processes in Kenya* (pp. 67–90). Nairobi: Strathmore University.

Srinivasan, R. (2013). "Bridges between cultural and digital worlds in revolutionary Egypt." *Information Society*, 29(1), 49–60. https://doi.org/10.1080/01972243.2012.739594

Williams, R. (1977). "Structures of feeling." In *Marxism and Literature*. Oxford, UK: Oxford University Press.

World Bank. 2018. *Kenya Gender and Poverty Assessment 2015–2016 : Reflecting on a Decade of Progress and the Road Ahead*. Nairobi: World Bank © World Bank. https://openknowledge.worldbank.org/handle/10986/31285 License: CC BY 3.0 IGO."

6 Judging beyond gender

Maternal and infant mortality as an emerging gender-related issue in Ugandan courts

W. Naigaga Kyobiika

Introduction

The legal profession was historically fashioned as solely open to men. In the last couple of decades, however, women have joined the legal profession and, more specifically, the judiciary across Africa (Dawuni, 2016, p.1). As some of the chapters in this collection have demonstrated, judicial decisions from different parts of the continent indicate an increased jurisprudence on gender issues such as cyber sexual harassment, domestic violence, dissolution of marriage, and access to land. These changes have led to questions on the relationship between gender and judging, which have been advanced under two main schools of thought.

The first school consists of differential theorists with foundations in the works of Carol Gilligan, an American developmental psychologist best known for her work *In a different voice: Psychological theory and women's development*, where she studied the effects of gender on women's psychology and girls' development (Gilligan, 1982). The differential school of thought argues that women are naturally inclined to advance gender issues based on the inherent differences compared with men due to their sex and gender (Gilligan, 1982, p.1). Adopting this biological positioning, differential theorists argue that the increased jurisprudence on gender-related issues results from the increased number of women on the bench (Hunter, 2015, pp.123–125; Kenney, 2012, p.40; Rackley, 2012, pp.180, 186). However, other scholars note that not all women advance gender issues, and the differential theory does not explain feminist decisions written by men (Hunter, 2015, p.121; Kenney, 2019, p.416).

The second school of thought is the anti-essentialist theory, which helps explain some of the gaps that the differential theory does not cover. The anti-essentialist theory proposes that sex and gender are not the only factors that affect a person's decisions (Hunter, 2015, p.124; Kenney, 2009, pp.416–417). In the judiciary, judicial decisions result from a judge's lived experience, including experiences shaped by sex, gender, class, education, and other cutting axes of difference that ultimately create a person's identity. Under this theory, both men and women judges may or may not highlight gender-related issues based on their lived experiences (Albertyn & Bonthuys, 2016, pp.166–167; Kenney, 2012, pp.41–42; Kenney, 2019, pp.416–417; Rackey, 2012, pp.186–187).

DOI: 10.4324/9780429327865-8

Within the framework of these two theories, this chapter seeks to determine whether the gender of the judge might make a substantive difference to judicial reasoning and decision-making. In doing so, the chapter situates the gender-focused jurisprudence of maternal and infant mortality as an emerging issue in Ugandan courts within the existing literature on gender and judging. The chapter focuses on Uganda as a case study for a number of reasons. First, there is limited literature on gender and judging in African judiciaries. The paucity of scholarly knowledge and current data on the connections between gender and judging across Africa makes for an exciting scholarly project and one that promises to introduce a broader research agenda. Second, a Ugandan case decided under Justice Lydia Mugambe has been at the fore of internationally recognized recent jurisprudence on maternal and infant health (*CEHURD v. Executive Director*, 2013), making Uganda and its jurisprudence an ideal place to start the analysis.

The chapter is divided into five sections. The first section lays the theoretical framework on which the chapter is based by highlighting the differential and anti-essentialism theories and reviewing the existing scholarship on gender and judging. The second section discusses maternal and infant health as a human rights issue using the human rights legal framework as well as international and regional policy work. This section further examines the relationship between maternal and infant health and the legal principles of progressive realization and justiciability. The third section introduces Uganda as a case study by discussing the country's historical and legal background and considering the jurisprudence on maternal and infant health in the country. The fourth section investigates whether Ugandan women judges have had a singular effect on maternal and infant health in Uganda by analyzing court cases addressing maternal and infant health in Uganda. The fifth section concludes the chapter with recommendations for continuity in increasing the positive jurisprudence on gender-related issues and possibilities for more research.

A review of existing scholarship on gender and judging

The scholarship on gender and judging has been advanced under two main theories: the differential theory and the anti-essentialism theory. As introduced earlier, the differential theorists build on the works of Carol Gilligan. Her works suggest that men and women develop different perspectives about the world and different ways of thinking about themselves and their relationship to the world (Sherry, 1986, p.163; Hunter, 2015, p.125; Kenney, 2019, p.405). As individuals, "men see themselves as fundamentally autonomous and independent of others," but "women instead see themselves as fundamentally connected" to those around them (Sherry, 1986, p.163). Women perceive themselves as members of communities, while men perceive themselves as individuals who simply live in a community (Sherry, 1986, p.163; Bekker and van Assen, 2008, pp.540–541; Rackley, 2012, p. 139).

The differential theory further proposes that men tend to adhere to traditional values and beliefs about the nature of men and women and their proper roles in society (Rackley, 2012, p.160; Wikler, 1980, p.203). In the judicial context, differential theorists argue that women judges are responsible for influencing court outcomes by advancing gender issues that may otherwise be neglected by their male counterparts (Rackley, 2012, p.180; Ruiz, n.d.). Men judges tend to adhere to traditional rules of law and may not look deeply into a case's social circumstances. They may become anxious when a case tends to veer off course with a witness who gives more information beyond a simple "yes" or "no" (Wilson, 1990 pp.520–521).

Under the differential theory, women judges are focused on preserving relationships within communities. Their style of judging tends to take into account issues that broaden the context of the dispute that might solve a moral dilemma (Hunter, 2008, p.12; 2015, p.131; Kenney, 2012, pp.15–16). Judging is seen not only in terms of winning or losing but also with the goal "of achieving an optim[al] outcome for all individuals" (Wilson, 1990, p.520). The differential theory suggests that this style of difference is due to women judges' ability to "produce gender sensitive judgments that take into consideration the gendered factors that male judges may tend to overlook" (Dawuni, 2016, p.421).

Women judges have already made decisions that reflect the characteristics of the differential theory. Judge Navanethem Pillay helped broaden the definition of acts of genocide to include rape and other forms of sexual violence in *Prosecutor v. Akayesu* (1998) at the International Criminal Tribunal for Rwanda (Pillay, 2009, p.461). In Uganda, in 2018, Supreme Court Justice Lillian Ekirikubinza Tibatemwa put an end to the cautionary rule in sexual offenses, which required corroborative evidence in sexual assault cases beyond the victim's testimony (*Ntambala v. Uganda*, 2015, pp.2–3).[1] Justice Tibatemwa found that the cautionary rule "affects far more women than men" and therefore violated Uganda's constitutional guarantee of equality before the law (*Ntambala v. Uganda*, 2015, p.4). These women made judicial decisions to achieve optimal outcomes for all parties and considered factors that men would likely not have considered, therefore supporting the differential theory of judicial decision-making.

However, not all women advance gender issues. For example, even though Eleanor Roosevelt played a central role in drafting the Universal Declaration of Human Rights, her presence "did not generate a special recognition of gendered harms" (Kenney, 2019, pp.408–409). Further, when analyzing gender and judging under the differential theory, women judges "are highly likely to face motions to recuse and challenges as to their objectivity" (Kenney, 2019, p.408). For example, defense counsel objected to Judge Navanethem Pillay during the *Anto Furundzija* case in the International Criminal Tribunal for the former Yugoslavia because she had served on the U.N. Commission on the Status of Women (Kenney, 2019, p. 408). Additionally, the differential theory does not explain why men judges also advance gender issues (Hunter, 2015, p.121; Kenney, 2019, p.416).

This gap in the differential theory gives rise to the anti-essentialism theory. The anti-essentialism theory suggests that both men and women judges use their life experiences, including their social, economic, and political experiences, to make decisions, and not only their biological differences (Hunter, 2015, p.126; Kenney, 2012, p.175; Rackley, 2012, pp.144, 147; Wikler, 1980, pp. 207). The theory argues that the expectation that women judges will be more attentive to emotions or feelings through gender essentialism is gender stereotyping and is wrong (Kenney, 2019, p.419). While women judges may bring "experiences of pregnancy, child-birth, child-rearing, and juggling work and family responsibilities and gender discrimination to the bench" (Hunter, 2015, p.124), their gender is not the only thing that influences their judicial decision-making.

Neither men nor women judges are a homogeneous group (Olivier, 2013, p.452; Rackley, 2012, p.144). The anti-essentialism theorists propose that apart from gender, there are other cross-cutting axes of differences, such as race, class, education, "sexual orientation, rural origins, religious affiliation, and cultural heritage," that affect the life experiences and decisions of judges (Albertyn & Bonthuys, 2016, p.165). Under the anti-essentialism theory, all experiences and identities, and not sex or gender alone, may be responsible for advancing gender issues (Belcher, 2014, pp.423–424). Based on this tension between the differential and anti-essentialism theories, the scholarship is conflicted over whether the gender of a judge influences his or her decision. The case studies in the subsequent sections will help identify which theory best explains the jurisprudence in Uganda.

Maternal and infant health as a human rights issue

The World Health Organization (WHO) defines maternal death as "the death of a woman while pregnant or within 42 days of termination of pregnancy, irrespective of the duration and site of the pregnancy, from any cause related to or aggravated by the pregnancy or its management but not from accidental or incidental causes" (WHO et al., 2019, p.8). Maternal mortality is measured by the number of women dying of pregnancy-related causes out of 100,000 live births in a given year (WHO et al., 2019, p.9). Most maternal deaths are caused by "hemorrhage (severe bleeding) after childbirth, post-delivery infections, obstructed (difficult) labor, or blood pressure disorders during pregnancy" and other indirect causes that result from pre-existing medical conditions (Bohren et al., 2015; World Health Organization, n.d.b). Trained birth attendants and high-quality reproductive health services can help prevent these conditions (Bohren et al., 2015; WHO et al., 2018, pp.viii, 9–10). The infant mortality rate is measured by the number of infants who die below one year of age per 1,000 live births (World Health Organization, n.d.a). The causes of death in newborns range from "prematurity [to] intrapartum-related events such as birth asphyxia … birth trauma, and neonatal sepsis" (World Health Organization, 2019, p.2).

Maternal and infant health, as defined here, are pertinent issues at the heart of development. The United Nations adopted goals four and five of the Millennium Development Goals (MDGs) of 2000 as measures to reduce child mortality and improve maternal health (United Nations, n.d.). The Sustainable Development Goals (SDGs) followed in 2015 and adopted the third goal, to address maternal and infant health, by aiming to reduce the maternal mortality ratio to 70 per 100,000 live births and infant mortality to 12 per 1,000 live births (General Assembly, 2015, p.16).

The legal framework and barriers to quick implementation: Progressive realization and justiciability

Maternal and infant health have been regarded as a human rights issue within the broader right to health (General Assembly, 1948, Art. 25; OHCHR and WHO, 2008, pp.3–4). Several human rights instruments address the right to maternal and infant health and provide for the progressive realization of human rights rather than immediate or quick enactment. At the international level, the Universal Declaration of Human Rights (UDHR) recognizes the right to medical care and specifically provides that mothers and children are entitled to special care and assistance (General Assembly, 1948, Art. 25). The International Covenant on Economic, Social and Cultural Rights (ICESCR) further operationalized the right to health as recognized in the UDHR (General Assembly, 1966, Art. 12). The ICESCR enjoins States Parties to recognize the right of everyone to enjoy and attain the highest standard of physical and mental health, and especially demands that states take necessary steps to ensure the healthy development of the child and to reduce stillbirth and infant mortality rates (General Assembly, 1966, Art. 12 (2)(a)).

The Committee on Economic, Social and Cultural Rights emphasizes that the right to health contains both freedoms and entitlements (Economic and Social Council, 2000, Part I (8)). The freedoms include "the right to control one's health and body, including sexual and reproductive health, and the right to be free from interference, such as the right to be free from torture, non-consensual medical treatment, and experimentation" (Economic and Social Council, 2000, Part I (8)). The entitlements under the right to health "include the right to a system of health protection which provides equality of opportunity for people to enjoy the highest attainable level of health" (Economic and Social Council, 2000, Part I (8)). General Comment No. 14 interprets the essential elements of the freedoms and entitlements to mean that States Parties should take measures to improve child and maternal health services by making them available, accessible, acceptable, and of good quality (Economic and Social Council, 2000, Part I (12)(a-d)). Although General Comment No. 14 allows for the progressive realization of the rights, it "also imposes on States parties various obligations which are of immediate effect" and should not be interpreted as a way to remove the "meaningful effect" of the requirements (Economic and Social Council, 2000, Part II (30)).

The 1979 United Nations Convention on the Elimination of All Forms of Discrimination Against Women (CEDAW) was enacted to address the rights of women internationally. The treaty requires States Parties to ensure that women receive appropriate services in connection with "pregnancy ... and the post-natal period, granting free services where necessary, as well as adequate nutrition during pregnancy and lactation" (United Nations, 1979, Art. 12 (2)). The existence of a special treaty for women's rights is based on the understanding that women have a unique role in reproduction and thus require special social and legal protections to compensate for this biological difference (Twinomugisha, 2007, pp.285–287). Pregnancy and childbirth increase the risk of mortality, and women therefore have unique health concerns and a basic right to be protected (Twinomugisha, 2007, p.286). Finally, the Convention on the Rights of the Child addresses the right to health of children (United Nations, 1989). This treaty requires States Parties to take appropriate measures to diminish infant and child mortality and provide pre- and post-natal health care for mothers (United Nations, 1989, Art. 24(a).

At the regional level, in 2003, African states enacted the Protocol to the African Charter on Human and Peoples' Rights on the Rights of Women in Africa, commonly known as the Maputo Protocol (African Union, 2003). It mandates States Parties to take all appropriate measures to "establish and strengthen existing prenatal, delivery, and post-natal health and nutritional services for women during pregnancy and while they are breast-feeding" (African Union, 2003, Art. 14 (2). Despite this requirement, millions of women across the African continent are not fully enjoying their right to health.

In its decision in *Purohit and Moore v. The Gambia*, the African Commission on Human and Peoples' Rights (the "African Commission" or "Commission") recognized that "African countries are generally faced with the problem of poverty which renders them incapable of providing the necessary amenities, infrastructure and resources that facilitate the full enjoyment of this right" (African Commission on Human and Peoples' Rights, 2003, p.14). Maternal and infant health services require massive financial investments, which the states simply do not have (Twinomugisha, 2007, pp.291–292; UNICEF, 2018). Most African states, therefore, must at a minimum take steps to achieve the human rights as agreed to in the various international conventions. States then have a legal duty to take part in progressively realizing the agreed upon rights in light of available resources (International Covenant on Economic, Social and Cultural Rights, 1966, p.2).

This progressive realization of rights ensures that states fulfill their duties and responsibilities, as treaties may otherwise not invoke change on their own unless enforced by domestic governments. To help states implement these rights even with limited resources, the African Commission published guidelines on the implementation of economic, social, and cultural rights, showing that state parties have a duty "to respect, protect, promote and fulfill" all rights (African Commission on Human and Peoples' Rights, 2011, Part II (4)). The obligation to *respect* rights requires states "to take positive measures to ensure that all branches of government (legislative, executive and judicial) at all levels (national, regional and local), as well as all organs of state, do not violate economic, social and cultural rights" (African Commission on Human and Peoples' Rights, 2011, Part II (6)).

The obligation to *protect* rights requires that states regulate and monitor non-state actors to ensure they do not infringe on rights, along with implementing relevant legislation "to provide remedies for such violations" (African Commission on Human and Peoples' Rights, 2011, Part II (7)). The duty to *promote* rights requires states "to adopt measures to enhance people's awareness of their rights ... to provide accessible information relating to the programs and institutions adopted to realize [the rights, and] ... to promote the values and objectives of economic, social and cultural rights," such as through the training of the judiciary or administrative officials (African Commission on Human and Peoples' Rights, 2011, Part II (8–9)). Finally, the duty to *fulfill* rights mandates the states to take positive steps to advance the realization of the rights, with special attention to the rights of vulnerable and disadvantaged groups (African Commission on Human and Peoples' Rights, 2011, Part II (8–9)). Such measures should be "comprehensive, coordinated, and transparent, [with] clear goals, indicators, and benchmarks for measuring progress" (African Commission on Human and Peoples' Rights, 2011, Part II (10)).

As part of the guidelines for implementation of rights, the African Commission emphasized that "States must implement a reasonable and measurable plan, including set achievable benchmarks and timeframes, for the [realization] of economic, social, and cultural rights within the resources available to the state party" (African Commission on Human and Peoples' Rights, 2001, Part II (14)). On resources, the African Commission noted the variety of means through which states may raise the required finances, including through taxation and regional or international aid (African Commission on Human and Peoples' Rights, 2001, Part II (13, 15)). Because the African Commission suggested taxation as a form of raising finances, the Commission therefore "implies that there is an obligation on the State to institute an effective and fair taxation system and a budgeting process that ensures that economic, social and cultural rights are prioritized in the distribution of resources" (African Commission on Human and Peoples' Rights, 2001, Part II (15)).

The language of progressive realization from these guidelines has appeared in decisions by the African Commission. In *Purohit and Moore v. The Gambia*,[2] the Commission stated that there is an "obligation on part of States party to the African Charter to take concrete and targeted steps, while taking full advantage of available resources, to ensure that the right to health is fully realized in all its aspects without discrimination of any kind" (African Commission on Human and Peoples' Rights, 2003, para. 84). Therefore, the notion of progressive realization within available resources must not be viewed as an excuse to deny economic, social, and cultural rights, including the right to health. As verified by case law and Commission decisions, the guidelines provide concrete steps that states must take to ensure movement towards full realization of rights.

Apart from the principle of progressive realization, the principle of justiciability also acts as a barrier to the full realization of socio-economic rights. Justiciability is the legal standing (or *locus standi*) to bring a claim before the courts (Deshpande, 1971, p.156). Some theorists argue that socio-economic rights cannot be adjudicated upon by the courts due to the doctrine of separation of powers, whereby the implementation of those rights is left to the legislative and executive branches rather than the judicial (Twinomugisha, 2007, pp.292–293). Despite this challenge, there has been significant progress at the regional and domestic levels in the adjudication of socio-economic rights.[3]

Due to this growing adjudication, there are more possibilities now than ever before for bringing forward socio-economic rights claims in many different institutional contexts and different ways.[4] In *SERAP v. Nigeria*, for example, the ECOWAS court ruled that "it is also well established that the rights [which include the right to education under Article 17] guaranteed by the African Charter on Human and Peoples' Rights are justiciable before this Court" (*SERAP v. Federal Republic of Nigeria*, 2009, p.10). By holding the right to education justiciable, the court therefore rejected the government's contention that "the right to education is not justiciable as it falls within the directive principles of state policy" (*SERAP v. Federal Republic of Nigeria*, 2009, p.10). In noting the difference between human rights in domestic legal frameworks and the African Commission of Human and Peoples' Rights requirement, the court stated that it "clearly has jurisdiction to adjudicate on applications concerning the violation of human rights that occur in Member States of ECOWAS" (*SERAP v. Federal Republic of Nigeria*, 2009, p.6) and that it "has jurisdiction over human rights enshrined in the African Charter and the fact that these rights are domesticated in the municipal law of the Federal Republic of Nigeria, cannot oust the jurisdiction of the Court" (*SERAP v. Federal Republic of Nigeria*, 2009, pp.6–7).

From the foregoing, the principle of justiciability becomes especially important with issues such as maternal and infant health rights. If the court is unwilling to hear a dispute and leaves the legislative or executive bodies of government to address the problem, the grievance may not actually be addressed, since many human rights violations, including violations related to infant and maternal health rights, are a result of the executive's or legislative's failure to protect those rights. The case of *Centre for Health Human Rights and Development (CEHURD) v. Attorney General*, as will be discussed in the following section, highlights the importance of justiciability of maternal and infant health rights.

Despite the formal recognition of maternal health in the international and regional human rights regime, women continue to experience disrespectful and abusive treatment during pregnancy, childbirth, and post-partum. Research shows that complications related to childbirth and early motherhood have significant negative effects on women's health (Šimonović, Women & Secretary-General, 2019, pp.4–5; Yamin & Maine, 1999, p.566). The WHO has also gathered reports of disrespectful and abusive treatment, ranging from physical abuse to violations of confidentiality.[5] Such treatment violates a woman's and baby's right to the "highest attainable standard of health, which includes the right to dignified, respectful health care" (World Health Organization, 2015, p.1). This mistreatment also threatens the "rights to life, health, bodily integrity, and freedom from discrimination" (World Health Organization, 2015, p.1).

The U.N. has also identified a similar pattern. In 2006, the statement of the U.N. Special Rapporteur on the right of everyone to enjoy the highest attainable standard of physical and mental health stressed that no single cause of death and disability for men between the ages of 15 and 44 reaches the magnitude of maternal mortality and morbidity (Hunt, 2006, p.5). The statement detailed that "[f]or every woman who dies from obstetric complications, approximately 30 more suffer from injuries, infection, and disabilities" from those complications (Hunt, 2006, p.5). The statement argued that the availability of and access to maternal health services is a human right.

This section has shown that maternal and infant health falls within the human rights regime. Although the principles of progressive realization and justiciability hinder the quick and full realization of economic, social, and cultural rights, the African Commission and other international organizations have provided guidance on the best ways to implement these rights. Even with this guidance, however, access to health services remains difficult for many women and children.

Uganda's history and the rights-based legal framework

Beginning in 1894, the previously independent and diverse region of what is now Uganda was ruled as a protectorate by the British until 1962, when it regained its independence (Kanyeihamba, 2010, pp.1, 62–63). Uganda operates a common law system reflecting the legal structure left by the British colonial governance system.

The structure, powers, and functions of the judiciary are detailed in Uganda's constitution (1995), the Judicature Act (1996), Magistrates Courts Act (1971), and other legislative instruments and by-laws. Uganda's judicial system is two-tiered. At the top are the superior courts, consisting of the Supreme Court, the Court of Appeal, the High Court, and any tribunals that parliament establishes, such as the land tribunals (Adonyo, 2012, p.12). The lower courts, which form the second tier, consist of the Chief Magistrates' Courts, the Grade One and Grade Two Magistrates' Courts, the Local Council Courts (divided further into three levels), and any other such lower courts as parliament may establish by law (Adonyo, 2012, p.12).

In 1995, Uganda adopted a new constitution. The Ugandan constitution does not specifically mention maternal and infant health services, either within its human rights legal framework found in Chapter 4 or elsewhere in the constitution (Constitution, 1995). However, the rights can be read into the general social and economic objectives. Under General Objective XIV, the constitution provides that "the State shall endeavour to fulfill the fundamental rights of all Ugandans to social justice and economic development and shall, in particular, ensure that … (b) all Ugandans enjoy rights and opportunities and access to … health services" among others (Constitution, 1995). General Objective XV recognizes the "significant role that women play in society," though it does not elaborate on the meaning of women's roles (Constitution, 1995). Further, General Objective XX requires that Uganda as a state "shall take all practical measures to ensure the provision of basic medical services to the population" (Constitution, 1995). Several Articles of the constitution also suggest the right to maternal and infant health. Under Article 33 (3), labeled Rights of Women, the constitution mandates the state to "protect women and their rights, taking into account their unique status and natural maternal functions in society," while Article 24 provides that "no person shall be subjected to any form of torture or cruel, inhuman or degrading treatment or punishment" (Constitution, 1995).

Even though Uganda is a signatory of the 2001 Abuja Declaration,[6] which mandates signatories to spend at least 15% of their annual budget on the health sector, Uganda has not met that commitment (Organization of African Unity, 2001, p.5). As published in Uganda's National Budget Framework Paper, the country's Medium-Term Expenditure Framework allocated 7.9% of the budget to the health sector in the 2019/2020 fiscal year, but only 5.1% for the 2020/21 fiscal year (Ministry of Finance, 2019, p.xxxi).

Maternal and infant health and its jurisprudence in Uganda

Maternal and infant health data

Data from 2017 show that an estimated 66% of all maternal deaths occur in sub-Saharan Africa (WHO et al., 2019, p.xi). In 2017, Uganda registered a maternal mortality ratio, measured by the number of maternal deaths from pregnancy-related complications per 100,000 live births, of 375 (World Bank Data, 2019). Neighboring East African countries are equally in dire need of improvement. In 2017, Rwanda reported a maternal mortality ratio of 248, Kenya reported 342, Burundi reported 548, and Tanzania reported 524 (World Bank Data, 2019). In 2013, the UN estimated that 40% of pregnant women globally did not receive antenatal care (World Health Organization, 2018, p.5). Antenatal care "enables the early management of conditions which may adversely impact upon the pregnancy, thus potentially reducing the risk of complications for women and newborns during and after delivery" (World Health Organization, 2018, p.5). In the same study, the WHO revealed that fewer than half of all births in developing countries benefited from the presence of a trained midwife, doctor, or nurse (World Health Organization, 2018, p.5). A study in 2018 found that 3% of pregnant women in Uganda did not receive antenatal care, and 26% of women delivered without a skilled provider (Uganda Bureau of Statistics, 2018, p.141). The presence of a skilled provider is affected by the mother's geographic location, education, whether the birth was in a health facility, and the birth order (Uganda Bureau of Statistics, 2018, pp.145–146).

In 2017, the global infant mortality rate was reported at 29 per 1,000 live births (Infant mortality, n.d.). The WHO estimated that in 2017, 4.1 million infant deaths occurred within the first year of life globally; the Africa region had the highest infant mortality rate of 51 per 1,000 live births (Infant mortality, n.d.). In 2018, Uganda's infant mortality rate was estimated at 34 (World Bank Data, n.d.). The situation in other neighboring countries was also found to be wanting: Rwanda reported 27, Kenya reported 31, Tanzania reported 38, and Burundi 41 (World Bank Data, n.d.).

The right to maternal and infant health jurisprudence in Uganda

Maternal and infant health have not traditionally been litigated in the Ugandan court system. Nevertheless, cases of this nature have slowly found their way into Ugandan courts and successfully been determined by both male and female judges. *Joyce Nakacwa v. Attorney-General & Others* (2001) was one of the first cases that sought to advance maternal and infant health in Uganda. In this case, the petitioner was turned away from a medical facility while she was in labor, since she did not have money to pay at the hospital (*Joyce Nakacwa v. Attorney-General*, 2001, p. 3). Later, under suspicion of her having stolen the baby, her newborn was taken away from her and the petitioner was detained (*Joyce Nakacwa v. Attorney-General*, 2001, pp.4–6). She was released a week later only to find her baby dead (*Joyce Nakacwa v. Attorney-General*, 2001, p.7). The petitioner went to the Constitutional Court alleging that the denial of maternal care violated Article 33 (3), which obliges the state to "protect women and their rights, taking into account their unique status and natural maternal functions in society" (Constitution of the Republic of Uganda, 1995; *Joyce Nakacwa v. Attorney-General*, 2001, p.2). An objection was raised challenging the Constitutional Court's jurisdiction (*Joyce Nakacwa v. Attorney-General*, 2001, p.9). The Constitutional Court ruled that it had jurisdiction to interpret whether the alleged acts and omissions had contravened the petitioner's constitutionally guaranteed rights. Unfortunately, the court did not handle the petition on its merits as the petitioner died before the petition could be heard, leading to its abatement.

Centre for Health Human Rights and Development (CEHURD) v. Attorney General is a landmark case in Uganda's Constitutional Court jurisprudence on maternal and infant health. This public litigation case was brought after the deaths of two mothers, Sylvia Nalubowa and Anguko Jennifer (*CEHURD v. Attorney General*, 2011, p.2). Before the court heard the case, the court had to determine whether the provision of maternal and infant health services met the principle of justiciability, therefore warranting the plaintiffs' standing and the chance to have their issue adjudicated by the court.

The petitioners contended that the distressing numbers of maternal deaths in Uganda resulted from the government's failure to provide basic minimum maternal health care and the unethical behavior of health workers (*CEHURD v. Attorney General*, 2011, p.2–4). The Attorney General, represented by state attorney Ms. Mutesi Patricia, argued that provision of maternal and infant health services involves determining political questions, which in effect interferes with political discretion, which is considered a preserve of the executive and the legislative branches (*CEHURD v. Attorney General*, 2011, p. 8). The justices on the court consisted of two women and three men.[7] The justices unanimously agreed with the Attorney General and ruled that the concerns raised by the petitioner were not under the discretion of the court and should instead be left to the executive and legislative branches of government (*CEHURD v. Attorney General*, 2011, p.15). The case was summarily dismissed without hearing the merits (*CEHURD v. Attorney General*, 2011, p.15). With this ruling, the justices determined that maternal and infant health rights are not justiciable issues. Under a strict interpretation of the Constitutional Court's decision, all acts and omissions of the executive would be shielded from judicial scrutiny (*CEHURD v. Attorney General*, 2011, p. 30).

The ruling was appealed, presided over by a quorum of two women and five men justices in the Supreme Court (*CEHURD v. Attorney General*, 2013, p.1).[8] Ms. Patricia Mutesi again represented the Attorney General. The Supreme Court unanimously overturned the ruling of the Constitutional Court. In her lead judgment,[9] Honorable Lady Justice Kisaakye held that the Constitutional Court had erred in law when it abdicated its constitutional mandate to hear and determine the merits of the appellant's petition before reaching the decision of striking it out on the basis of the political question doctrine (*CEHURD v. Attorney General*, 2013, p. 31). While directing the Constitutional Court to hear the petition on its merit, Justice Kisaakye stated that the petition before the Constitutional Court had specified acts and omissions that were within the ambit of the powers vested in the Constitutional Court (*CEHURD v. Attorney General*, 2013, p.28). Justice Kisaakye further stated that the application of the political question doctrine had limited application in Uganda and should not be used to oust the court's jurisdiction (*CEHURD v. Attorney General*, 2013, p.31).

Justice Kisaakye added that the political question doctrine only extends to shielding both the executive arm of government and parliament from judicial scrutiny where either institution is properly exercising its mandate. Former Chief Justice Katureebe wrote in his concurring judgment that the petition before the Constitutional Court had created a significant opportunity in which the court could determine on the content and application of the right to life and health in Uganda (*CEHURD v. Attorney General*, 2013, p.2).

The Supreme Court decision is celebrated for paving the way for lower courts to deal with the political question doctrine and making it easier for courts to adjudicate on infant and maternal health (Nanima, 2018, p.15). The Constitutional Court heard *CEHURD v. Attorney General* on its merits and decided in 2020 after a long history moving through the courts, including the original dismissal at the Constitutional Court for lack of jurisdiction and the Supreme Court's reversal and remand back to the Constitutional Court. This time, when the case was heard with an all-male quorum[10] and an international human rights law lens that mandates a state to protect its citizens, the court found for the petitioners.

The lead judge, Justice Barishaki Cheborion, noted that the omission to adequately provide basic maternal health care services in public health facilities violates women's rights. He declared that the government's failure to adequately provide emergency obstetric care in public health facilities violates the right to health and life along with women's rights (*CEHURD v. Attorney General*, 2011, p.57). Those violations were inconsistent and in contravention of Articles 8(A), 22, 33 (1–3), 39, 45, and 287 as read together with objectives XIV and XX of the constitution (*CEHURD v. Attorney General*, 2011, p.57). He also found that the government's conduct subjects "women to inhuman and degrading treatment and is inconsistent with and in contravention of Article 24 and 44 (a) of the Constitution" (*CEHURD v. Attorney General*, 2011, pp.57–58).

Justice Barishaki called upon the state to henceforth prioritize and provide sufficient funds to improve maternal and infant health services in the country when making financial budgets (*CEHURD v. Attorney General*, 2011, p.58). The ruling mandated the Ministry of Health to ensure that "all the staff who provide maternal health care services in Uganda are fully trained and all health centers are equipped within the next [two] financial years (2020/2021 and 2021/2022)" (*CEHURD v. Attorney General*, 2011, p.58). The justice required the Minister of Health to compile and submit to parliament and the court an "audit report on the status of maternal health in Uganda at the end of each of the next two financial years (2020/2021 and 2021/2022)" (*CEHURD v. Attorney General*, 2011, p.58). The Attorney General was directed to submit a report at the end of the financial year 2020/2021 showing the progress and implementation of these orders (*CEHURD v. Attorney General*, 2011, p.58).

On an individual level, Justice Barishaki awarded two petitioners general damages for the psychological torture; violation of the rights to life and health; and cruel and degrading treatment of their loved ones (*CEHURD v. Attorney General*, 2011, p.58). They were further awarded exemplary damages for the loss suffered as a result of acts and omissions of the medical personnel at Mityana Hospital and Arua Regional Referral Hospital (*CEHURD v. Attorney General*, 2011, p.58).

The ruling in this case showed that on August 19, 2020, after a long nine-year wait, the rights to infant and maternal health care and emergency obstetric care were granted a place in Uganda's constitution.

Before *CEHURD v. Attorney General* was filed and determined by the Supreme Court in 2015 and the Constitutional Court determined the case on its merits in 2020, cases concerning infant and maternal health were being filed, heard, and determined by the High Court. It is praiseworthy to note that even without the decisions of the superior courts, the High Court was forging a path in uncharted waters and building its independent positive jurisprudence on maternal and infant health.

The case of *Watsemwa and anor v. Attorney General* (2006) is the first High Court case considered by this research. The case involved the baby David Goseltine, who suffered from asphyxia and was born by an emergency cesarean section after a cord prolapse during his birth (*Watsemwa and anor v. Attorney-General*, 2006, p.2). In 2015, Justice Elizabeth Musoke, a woman judge, found the hospital staff negligent. She held that "there is no doubt that the lapses at the ward caused by the nurses, which also led to delays in getting out the baby by caesarean as quickly as possible to get a normal baby; … caused that chain reaction of cord prolapse and asphyxia" (*Watsemwa and anor v. Attorney-General*, 2006, p. 18).

Justice Musoke further contributed to the infant and maternal health jurisprudence in her decision in *Kanyamugule and Another v. Attorney-General and 3 Others* (2011), which was decided later that same year. In this case, Namakula

Kate was admitted to Mulago Hospital for an emergency cesarean section, but the next day, before the surgery could be carried out, she had a stillbirth (*Kanyamugule and Another v. Attorney General and 3 Others*, 2011, p. 1). Justice Musoke once again found the hospital staff culpable in negligence, holding that "the defendants owed a duty of care to the [second] plaintiff and her unborn child the moment she was accepted and admitted into the hospital; they had a duty to exercise due caution and skill in ensuring her safety and the safety of the unborn child who had been confirmed to be alive … the doctors strayed beyond the bounds of what is expected of a reasonably skilled or competent doctor when they neglected to take the plaintiff to the theater within a reasonable time" (*Kanyamugule and Another v. Attorney General and 3 Others*, 2011, pp.5–6).

CEHURD v. Nakaseke District Local Administration (2012) was also decided in 2015. The case is centered on the passing of Irene Nanteza, who died of hemorrhage and a ruptured uterus after a nurse identified signs of obstructed labor and called the doctor on duty; the doctor did not arrive until eight hours later (*CEHURD v. Nakaseke District Local Administration*, 2012, pp.3, 8). The plaintiffs petitioned the Court for damages from violations to the right to life, the right to health, and inhuman and degrading treatment. After analyzing the health and human rights of Nanteza and her unborn child, Honorable Justice Benjamin Kabiito, a male judge, highlighted the negligence by the doctor and found the case for the plaintiffs (*CEHURD v. Nakaseke District Local Administration*, 2012, p.16). He also found that there had been a violation of the human and maternal rights of the deceased and the rights of her children and surviving spouse (*CEHURD v. Nakaseke District Local Administration*, 2012, p.17).

Judge Kabiito is also remembered for his contributions in *Hon. Bernard Mulengani v. Attorney General and 2 others* (2011). This case involved a suit to recover damages after the death of Gloria Kyesimire during childbirth due to a blood mismatch shortly after a transfusion (*Hon. Bernard Mulengani v. Attorney General and 2 others*, 2011). Judge Kabiito found for the petitioner and determined that the hospital staff's negligence was responsible for the death of the petitioner's wife (*Hon. Bernard Mulengani v. Attorney General and 2 others*, 2011).

In 2017, Uganda got another decision on maternal and infant health with the decision of *CEHURD v. The Executive Director, Mulago National Referral Hospital*. In this case, the plaintiff and her husband asserted she delivered two babies at the hospital, but she was discharged a day later with only one newborn (*CEHURD v. The Executive Director, Mulago National Referral Hospital*, 2013, p.1). The plaintiff and her husband demanded the hospital return the body of their second baby, but after biological testing, the government laboratory determined that the body that the hospital gave the couple had no biological relation to them (*CEHURD v. The Executive Director, Mulago National Referral Hospital*, 2013, p.2). Honorable Lady Justice Lydia Mugambe found negligence on the hospital's part for failing to account for the plaintiff couple's missing baby (*CEHURD v. The Executive Director, Mulago National Referral Hospital*, 2013, p.15). She determined that when the hospital denied the couple closure and burial rights for their child, the hospital subjected the parents to psychological torture as defined by Articles 24 and 44(a) of the Ugandan constitution (*CEHURD v. The Executive Director, Mulago National Referral Hospital*, 2013, pp.17, 19).

Even though Uganda's constitution does not explicitly refer to maternal and infant health protections, Justice Mugambe used both the international and the regional human rights legal framework to support her decision. She cited instruments such as General Comment 14 of the Committee on Economic, Social and Cultural Rights; General Comment No. 20 of the Committee on Civil and Political Rights; the African Commission on Human and Peoples' Rights Principles and Guidelines on the Implementation of Economic, Social and Cultural Rights in the African Charter on Human and Peoples Rights; and the Protocol to the African Charter on Human and Peoples Rights on the Rights of Women in Africa (*CEHURD v. The Executive Director, Mulago National Referral Hospital*, 2013, pp.6, 7, 16). Justice Mugambe held that the facts of the case pointed to a failed health system, implying that the state had failed to fulfill its obligation to ensure the right to health expected of it under the African Charter (with a particular emphasis on the failure to address the needs of rural women) (*CEHURD v. The Executive Director, Mulago National Referral Hospital*, 2013, p.16).

The maternal and infant health jurisprudence continued with the 2019 decision of *Kabiito Telesphorus v. Attorney General & 2 Others* (2012). The suit was brought after Katusabe Elizabeth died from an emergency cesarean section due to uncontrolled heavy bleeding (*Kabiito Telesphorus v. Attorney General & 2 Others*, 2012, p.3). The male Justice Musalu Musene found for the plaintiff. He held that "[Katusabe Elizabeth's] death was caused by the negligence of the [medical staff] … there was ultimately no proper medical attention towards the deceased who was in labour. Furthermore, there was failure by the Defendants' workers to provide lifesaving blood leaving the deceased to bleed without rescue and resulting into her death" (*Kabiito Telesphorus v. Attorney General & 2 Others*, 2012, p.7).

Apart from maternal and infant health, other notable emerging gender issues have received progressive judgments by both men and women judges. For example, Honorable Justice E.S. Lugayizi (a male judge) called out against the discriminatory nature of the cautionary rule in sexual offenses as regards evidence of a single identifying witness (*Uganda v. Kasumba Joseph*, 2002). As discussed in the previous section, Honorable Lady Justice Lillian Ekirikubinza Tibatemwa built on Justice Lugayizi's judgment and declared the cautionary rule unconstitutional (*Ntambala v. Uganda*, 2015). Justice Batema N.D.A. (a male judge) used the battered woman syndrome defense as a mitigating factor while sentencing an offender in a case involving continuous domestic violence (*Uganda v. Kamuhanda Emmanuel*, 2012, pp.6–7). Justice Musoke Kibuuka (a male judge) is also celebrated for interpreting Uganda's Penal Code Act under Section 123 not to include an exception for married people in rape charges and for using Article 31 of the Ugandan constitution on equality in marriage and Article 33 on women's equality to recognize marital rape as an offense, a rare occurrence in Ugandan courts (*Uganda v. Yiga Hamidu*, 2002, p.9).

The relationship between the gender of a judge and maternal and infant health jurisprudence in Uganda

As discussed previously, Uganda's legal profession has largely been a preserve of men until recently. The first woman to join the Ugandan bench was the former Deputy Chief Justice Laetitia Eulilia Mary Mukasa Kokonyongo, who joined as a Magistrate Grade One judge in 1971 (URN, 2017). She was followed by Justice Constance Byamugisha in 1976, who also joined as a Magistrate Grade One judge (Wekasa, 2013). Justice A.E.N. Mpagi-Bahigeine followed as the third woman in 1988 as a High Court judge (Women in Leadership Conference Award Bios, 2018). With the gradual growth of the economy (World Bank, 2020) and the introduction of human rights policies such as affirmative action as enshrined in the Ugandan constitution (Constitution, 1995), Uganda has seen more women attain law degrees and join the legal profession, which has greatly increased the number of women judges on the bench. The Ugandan judiciary currently boasts 45.8% women judicial officers on the bench (Judiciary, Republic of Uganda, 2020) (see Table 6.1).

With the case law examples and the data on the total number of women in the Ugandan judiciary, the remainder of this section will analyze whether more positive jurisprudence on gender-related issues is due to the increased number of women judges on the bench. The evidence found in maternal and infant health jurisprudence in Uganda as identified in the previous section suggests that there is no direct relationship between the increased number of women on the bench and the increase in maternal and infant health jurisprudence.

The court cases have demonstrated that gender essentialism, which is at the heart of the differential theory, does not fully explain the type of decision a judge will make concerning gender-related issues. The ruling in *CEHURD v. Attorney General* (2011) demonstrated both men and women judges failing to advance maternal and infant health issues. Two women judges, Justice A.E.N.

Table 6.1 Number of judicial officers as of January, 2020 as posted on the Ugandan Judiciary Website

Courts	*Number of women*	*% women*	*Number of men*	*% men*	*Total*
Supreme Court	5	41.6	7	58.3	12
Court of Appeal	5	35.7	9	64.3	14
High Court	27	45	33	55	60
Registrars	0	0	2	100	2
Deputy Registrars	14	58.3	10	41.6	24
Assistant Registrars	4	40	6	60	10
Chief Magistrates	24	51.1	23	48.9	47
Magistrates Grade 1	92	48.7	97	51.3	189
Magistrates Grade 2	8	25	24	75	32
Total	179	45.8	211	54.1	390

Mpagi-Bahigeine as lead judge and Justice C.K. Byamugisha, unanimously agreed with three men judges that maternal and infant health issues had no *locus standi* in court. When the ruling was appealed at the Supreme Court in *CEHURD v. Attorney General* (2013), with Lady Justice Esther Kisaakye as a lead judge and the author of the opinion in a court with a majority of men justices, the Court unanimously voted to do away with the political question with regard to maternal and infant health. When the case was heard on its merits, an all-male bench with Justice Barishaki Cheborion as lead judge and author of the opinion unanimously agreed to read the right to maternal and infant health care services in public health facilities into the human rights framework laid down in Chapter 4 of the Ugandan constitution.

The jurisprudence emanating from the High Court shows that Judge Musoke, Judge Kabiito, Judge Mugambe, and Judge Musene, judges of different sexes, found the various defendants culpable of negligence. Considering the numbers of male and female judges in the cases discussed earlier, this chapter's finding shows that women judges are not the sole bearers of the duty to advance gender-related issues (Albertyn & Bonthuys, 2016; Bauer & Ellett, 2016; Dawuni, 2016). The findings in this chapter have shown that men judges also have the ability to identify and address gender issues and have done so; however, the reasoning behind those decisions that may be classified as "gender-progressive" may differ between women and men. Therefore, the differential theory does not explain the increased positive jurisprudence on maternal and infant health in Uganda.

A further look at the decisions of Judge Musoke, Judge Kabiito, Judge Mugambe, and Judge Musene reveals that all judges agreed that the right to maternal and infant health exists and ruled for the petitioners. However, even though all these judges agreed on the outcome, Judge Mugambe's decision analyzed the issues further than the rest of her colleagues. Judge Musoke, Judge Kabiito, and Judge Musene found for the plaintiff only by focusing on the traditional factors of duty and negligence. Judge Kabiito decried the inadequate resources that the local governments (organs in charge of hospitals at the district level) had for their operations and management. Judge Musoke, Judge Kabiito, and Judge Musene fell short of reminding the state of its role in protecting the people by providing maternal and infant health services.

In contrast, Judge Mugambe looked not only at the factors of negligence but also at the psychological torture of the parents and the state's failure under international human rights law to provide reasonable maternal and infant health services. This analysis, however, does not mean that Judge Mugambe identified human rights violations because she is a woman. However, since Justice Mugambe is a woman and is aware that her judgment may raise issues as to her objectivity, she may have felt pressured to exercise judicial restraint or rule in a legally conservative manner. This pressure to exercise judicial restraint is supported in statements made in an interview conducted with Judge Mugambe[11] while writing this chapter. She stated that even though she advances gender issues, she does not see herself as an extremist in feminism who will rule in favor of women whenever gender-related issues arise in her court (L. Mugambe, personal communication, May 24, 2019). She further stated that she sees herself as a human rights judge, who objectively uses human rights lenses to give a balancing act to the law (L. Mugambe, personal communication, May 24, 2019). She was eager to point out that if she sees a wrong being done to a woman, she will not be held prisoner by the "gender card" (L. Mugambe, personal communication, May 24, 2019). Judge Mugambe opined that it is not only gender that dictates one's inclination to bring about social justice, but also education and training that contribute to an individual's appreciation of social wrongs (L. Mugambe, personal communication, May 24, 2019). Judge Mugambe's analysis, therefore, has more to do with her scholarly experience than with her gender and sex.

Other justices similarly emphasize the importance of experience. For example, Justice N.D.A. Batema[12] (a male judge) argues that even if men are not naturally inclined to advance gender issues, they can be educated to do so (Wamboga, 2019). He confesses that as a young judicial officer, he never considered gender issues while adjudicating; it was not until he was educated on human rights issues that his perspective changed and he began to analyze his cases with a gender perspective (Wamboga, 2019).

Despite the increase in women's representation in the judiciary in Uganda, judicial decisions in the cases reviewed in this section on infant and maternal health show that both men and women judges make decisions favorable to the protection of these rights. The variety of experiences in the judges making positive rights-based decisions, including but not limited to their sex and gender, highlights how different axes of experiences guide a judge's decisions.

The anti-essentialism theorists call us to look beyond sex and gender when determining whether a judge will contribute positively to gender-related issues. A review of the jurisprudence on maternal and infant health in Uganda shows that judicial decision-making is based on a multiplicity of factors, including the individual judge's experiences, judicial training, and awareness of the gendered nature of laws, and cannot be restricted to their sex or gender alone.

Conclusion

This chapter has demonstrated the need for continued studies to analyze whether there are gendered patterns in judicial decision-making across a broad spectrum of cases that come before the Ugandan courts. The cases and data analyzed in this chapter suggest that there is no gendered pattern to the decisions judges make regarding gender-related issues. Both men and women judges are capable of advancing issues relating to women as much as they are capable of discarding these issues. As discussed in this chapter, there is no discernable pattern to neatly categorize the voices of women and men judges. The difficulty to categorize does not mean that women should not be on the bench or that they are redundant additions. Women should be on the bench because they deserve to be there in their own right based on their own merit.

However, to increase positive jurisprudence on gender-related issues, the analyses of both men and women need to be developed to advance gender-related issues through education and training. As judiciaries plan and budget their resources, their training and education departments need to be adequately catered for, and these departments must prioritize themes around gender-related issues in their training manuals.

Because this study focuses on the jurisprudence on infant and maternal health in Uganda, the findings are limited to a particular subject, number of cases, and time period. Maternal and infant health jurisprudence is an emerging gender-related issue that this chapter has only been able to trace from the early 2000s. The findings are therefore limited and may change with more jurisprudence on the same subject matter or with consideration of other gender-related issues. Future research may address the changing landscape of maternal and infant health jurisprudence or include other gender-related issues that have been litigated.

Notes

1 In *Ntambala v. Uganda*, the appellant claimed that the evidence that the victim of the sexual assault provided was not corroborated (as the cautionary rule would require) and was therefore insufficient to uphold his conviction of 14 years in prison (2015, p.1). Justice Tibatemwa challenged the belief that sexual offenses required greater caution in establishing evidentiary rules by highlighting research that does not support claims that women falsify stories of sexual assault and showing the discriminatory nature with which the cautionary rule has been applied (*Ntambala v. Uganda*, 2015, p.3). She used Ugandan and international case law, international human rights instruments, and social science to uphold her point that the cautionary rule violated the equal protection guaranteed in the Ugandan constitution (*Ntambala v. Uganda*, 2015).

2 *Purohit and Moore v. The Gambia* concerned an investigation in the definition of the term "lunatic," the process of being found to be a "lunatic," and the treatment thereafter of those found to be "lunatics." The African Commission read into and interpreted its Article 16 concerning the right to health to determine the case (African Commission on Human and Peoples' Rights, 2003, Part II (14)).

3 One collection of developing jurisprudence can be found on the website for the International Network for Economic, Social, and Cultural Rights (ESCR-Net, n.d.).

4 See cases decided by the African Commission on Human Rights, e.g., *Purohit and Moore v. The Gambia*, which discussed the right to health of mentally ill patients (African Commission on Human and Peoples' Rights, 2003) and *SERAC and CESR v. Nigeria* discussing the implied rights to food and housing contained within the right to health (African Commission on Human and Peoples' Rights, 2001).

5 The WHO report specifies the forms of abusive treatment, including "physical abuse, … humiliation and verbal abuse, coercive or unconsented medical procedures (including sterilization), lack of confidentiality, failure to get fully informed consent, refusal to give pain medication, gross violations of privacy, refusal of admission to health facilities, [negligence of] women during childbirth to suffer life-threatening and avoidable complications, and detention of women and their newborns in facilities after childbirth due to an inability to pay" (World Health Organization, 2015, p.1).

6 The 2001 Abuja Declaration was a pledge made by members of the African Union at a conference in Abuja, Nigeria, where member nations pledged to increase their health

budget to at least 15% of the state's annual budget and also requested Western donor countries to increase their support (Organization of African Unity, 2001, p.6).

7 The justices on the Constitutional Court were Honorable Lady Justice C.K. Byamugisha; Honorable Lady Justice A.E.N. Mpagi-Bahigeine; Honorable Justice S.B.K. Kavuma; Honorable Justice A.S. Nshimye; and Honorable Justice Remmy Kasule (*CEHURD v. Attorney General*, 2011, p. 1).

8 The justices serving on the Supreme Court were Honorable Lady Justice Esther Kisaakye; Honorable Lady Justice C.N.B. Kitumba; Honorable Justice G.M. Okello; Honorable Justice J.W.N. Tsekooko; Honorable Justice B.J. Odoki (former Chief Justice); Honorable Justice Jotham Tumwesigye; and Honorable Justice Bart M. Katureebe (current Chief Justice) (*CEHURD v. Attorney General*, 2013, p.1).

9 A lead judgment is the opinion of the court on a particular matter before it. There are three ways in which a judge may author a lead judgment: (i) they can nominate themselves; (ii) they can be nominated by the head of the court, especially when they have expertise in the area of law relevant to the case; and (iii) through normal scheduling, where each judge gets an equal share of work load before the court (L. Tibatemwa Ekirikubinza, personal communication, October 19, 2020).

10 Justice Barishaki Cheborion (lead judge), Justice Alfonse Owiny Dollo (Chief Justice), Justice Kenneth Kakuru, Justice F.M.S. Egonda Ntende, and Justice Christopher Madrama (*CEHURD v. Attorney General*, 2011).

11 The judge has an LLM in Human Rights and Intellectual Property Rights Law from Lund University, Raoul Wallenberg Institute, Sweden, together with the World Intellectual Property Organisation (WIPO) and another LLM in Human Rights and Democratization in Africa from the University of Pretoria Centre for Human Rights, South Africa.

12 Judge David Batema has a Master of Laws in Women's Law from University of Zimbabwe; Justice Esther Kisaakye, the lead judge in the appeal of *CEHURD v. Attorney General*, has a Master of Arts in Women's Rights from Georgetown University, United States; and a Doctor of Juridical Science from American University, United States.

References

Adonyo, H. (2012). Structure and functions of the judiciary. *The Judiciary of Uganda*. Retrieved June 26, 2020, from http://judiciary.go.ug/files/downloads/Structure%20and%20Functions%20of%20the%20Judiciary%20-%20CR%202012.pdf.

African Commission on Human and Peoples' Rights. (2003). *Purohit and Moore v. The Gambia Decision*. Communication 241/2001. Retrieved June 26, 2020, from https://africanlii.org/sites/default/files/Purohit%20v.%20Gambia%2C%20Decision%2C%20241%20of%202001%20%28ACmHPR%2C%20May.%2029%2C%202003%29_0.pdf.

African Commission on Human and Peoples' Rights. (2011). Principles and guidelines on the implementation of economic, social and cultural rights in the African charter on human and peoples' rights. Retrieved June 26, 2020, from https://archives.au.int/bitstream/handle/123456789/2063/Nairobi%20Reporting%20Guidelines%20on%20ECOSOC_E.pdf?sequence=1&isAllowed=y.

African Union. (2003). *Protocol to the African charter on human and peoples' rights on the rights of women in Africa*. Retrieved May 22, 2020, from https://www.un.org/en/africa/osaa/pdf/au/protocol_rights_women_africa_2003.pdf.

Albertyn, C., & Bonthuys, E. (2016). South Africa: A Transformative Constitution and a Representative Judiciary. In G. Bauer & J. Dawuni (eds.), Gender and the Judiciary in Africa: From Obscurity to Parity (1st ed., pp. 49–66). New York: Routledge.

Bauer, G. and Ellet, R. (2016). *Botswana: Delayed Indigenization and Feminization of the Judiciary*. In G. Bauer, & J. Dawuni (Eds.), Gender and the Judiciary in Africa: From Obscurity to Parity (1st ed.). New York, US: Routledge.

Bekker, M. and van Assen, M. (2008). Autonomy-Connectedness and Gender. *Sex Roles*, (59), 532–544.

Belcher, R. D. (2014). The importance of women and the judiciary. *Journal of Gender, Race & Justice*, 17(3), 421–426.

Bohren, M., Vogel, J., Hunter, E., Sutsiv, O., Makh, S., Souza, J., Aguiar, C., Coneglian, F., Diniz, A., Tuncalp, O., Javadi, D., Oladapo, O., Khosla, R., Hindin, M., Gulmezoglu, A. (2015). The mistreatment of women during childbirth in health facilities globally: A mixed-methods systematic review. *Plos Medicine*. Retrieved June 25, 2020, from https://doi.org/10.1371/journal.pmed.1001847.

Centre for Health and Human Rights and Development (CEHURD) v. Attorney General. (2011). Constitutional Court Constitutional Petition No. 16.

Centre for Health and Human Rights and Development (CEHURD) v. Attorney General. (2013). Supreme Court Constitutional Appeal No. 01.

Centre for Health and Human Rights and Development (CEHURD) v. Executive Director, Mulago National Referral Hospital. (2013). High Court Civil Suit No. 212.

Centre for Health and Human Rights and Development (CEHURD) v. Nakaseke District Local Administration. (2012). High Court Civil Suit No. 111.

Dawuni, J. (2016). To "mother" or not to "mother": The representative roles of women judges in Ghana. *Journal of African Law*, 60(3), 419–440. doi: 10.1017/s0021855316000115.

Deshpande, V. (1971). Standing and justiciability. *Indian Law Institute*. *13*(2). 153–188. Retrieved from https://www-jstor-org.proxyau.wrlc.org/stable/pdf/43950266.pdf?refreqid=excelsior%3Aba02ed220aa39eee4afc7ac739c5662f.

Economic and Social Council. (2000). General comment no. 14. Retrieved June 26, 2020, from http://docstore.ohchr.org/SelfServices/FilesHandler.ashx?enc=4slQ6QSmlBEDzFEovLCuW1AVC1NkPsgUedPlF1vfPMJ2c7ey6PAz2qaojTzDJmC0y%2B9t%2BsAtGDNzdEqA6SuP2r0w%2F6sVBGTpvTSCbiOr4XVFTqhQY65auTFbQRPWNDxL#:~:text=1.,living%20a%20life%20in%20dignity.

General Assembly. (1948). Universal declaration of human rights. 71–79. Retrieved June 26, 2020, from https://www.un.org/en/ga/search/view:doc.asp?symbol=A/RES/217(III).

General Assembly. (1966). International covenant on economic, social and cultural rights. *Treaty Series*, 993 (3). Retrieved June 26, 2020, from https://treaties.un.org/doc/Treaties/1976/01/19760103%2009-57%20PM/Ch_IV_03.pdf.

General Assembly. (2015). Resolution adopted by the General Assembly on 25 September 2015. Retrieved June 25, 2020, from https://www.unfpa.org/sites/default/files/resource-pdf/Resolution_A_RES_70_1_EN.pdf.

Gilligan, C. (1982). *In a Different Voice: Psychological Theory and Women's Development*. Cambridge, MA: Harvard University Press.

Hon. Bernard Mulengani v. Attorney-General and 2 others. (2011). UG High Court Civil Suit No. 29.

Hunt, P. (2006). Report of the Special Rapporteur on the right of everyone to the enjoyment of the highest attainable standard of physical and mental health. Retrieved June 26, 2020, from https://www.un.org/en/ga/search/view:doc.asp?symbol=A/61/338

Hunter, R. (2008). Can feminist judges make difference. *International Journal of the Legal Profession*, *15*(1–2), 7–36.

Hunter, R. (2015). More than just a different face? Judicial diversity and decision-making. *Current Legal Problems*, 68(1), 119–141. doi: 10.1093/clp/cuv001

Judiciary, Republic of Uganda. (2018). Women in leadership conference award bios. Retrieved.

Judiciary, Republic of Uganda. (2020). *Judicial officers*. Retrieved June 22, 2020, from http://www.judiciary.go.ug/data/smenu/91/1/Judicial%20Officers.html.

Joyce Nakacwa v. Attorney-General and Others. (2001). UG Constitutional Court Constitutional Petition No. 2.

Kabiito Telesphorus v. Attorney-General and 2 Others. (2012). UG High Court Civil Suit No. 26.

Kanyeihamba, G. (2010). Constitutional and Political History of Uganda: From 1894 to Present. Law Africa Publishing.

Kanyamugule and Another v. Attorney-General and 3 Others. (2011). UG High Court Civil Suit No. 285.

Kenney, S. (2009). Which Judicial Selection Systems Generate the Most Women Judges? Lessons from the United States. *SSRN Electronic Journal*. doi:10.2139/ssrn.3324661.

Kenney, S. (2012). Gender and justice: Why women in the judiciary really matter. Retrieved July 17, 2020, from http://ebookcentral.proquest.com.

Kenney, S. (2019). Towards a less essentialist, more intersectional, and institutional approach to gender and judging. *Connecticut Journal of International Law*, *34*(3), 401–419.

Magistrates Courts Act Chapter 16.

Ministry of Finance, Planning and Economic Development. (2019). National Budget Framework Paper FY 2020/21–FY 2024/25. Retrieved July 9, 2020, from https://budget.go.ug/sites/default/files/National%20Budget%20docs/National%20Budget%20Framework%20Paper%20FY%202020-21_0.pdf.

Nanima, R. D. (2018). Using the 'Political Question Doctrine' in Adjudicating the Right to Health: A Review of Centre for Health Human Rights & Development and 3 Others v Attorney General (2011). *ESR* Review, *19*(3), 15–19.

Ntambala v. Uganda. (2015). Supreme Court of Uganda Criminal Appeal No. 34.

OHCHR and WHO. (2008). The Right to Health: Factsheet No. 31. Retrieved July 17, 2020, from https://www.ohchr.org/Documents/Publications/Factsheet31.pdf.

Olivier, M. (2013). A perspective on gender transformation of the South African judiciary. *South African Law Journal*, 130(3), 448–464

Organization of African Unity. (2001). Abuja declaration on HIV/AIDS, tuberculosis and other related infectious diseases. OAU/SPS/ABUJA/3. Retrieved June 26, 2020, from https://au.int/sites/default/files/pages/32894-file-2001-abuja-declaration.pdf.

Pillay, N. (2009). Sexual violence: Standing by the victim. *Case Western Reserve Journal of International Law*, *42*(1), 459–467.

Prosecutor v. Akayesu. (1998). ICTR-96–4-T, Judgment, 1 598, 37 I.L.M. 1399.

Rackley, E. (2012). Women, judging and the judiciary: From difference to diversity. Retrieved July 17, 2020, from http://ebookcentral.proquest.com

Ruiz, V. (n.d.). The role of women judges and a gender perspective in ensuring judicial independence and integrity. Retrieved June 24, 2020, from https://www.unodc.org/dohadeclaration/en/news/2019/01/the-role-of-women-judges-and-a-gender-perspective-in-ensuring-judicial-independence-and-integrity.html.

SERAP v. Federal Republic of Nigeria and the Universal Basic Education Commission. (2009). Community Court of Justice, ECOWAS No. ECW/CCJ/APP/0808.

Sherry, S. (1986). The Gender of Judges. Retrieved 15 July 2021, from http://scholarship.law.umn.edu/lawineq/vol4/iss1/13

Simonovic, D., Women, U., & Secretary-General, U. (2019). A human rights-based approach to mistreatment and violence against women in reproductive health services with a focus on childbirth and obstetric violence :. Retrieved 15 July 2021, from https://digitallibrary.un.org/record/3823698?ln=en

Twinomugisha, B. (2007). Exploring judicial strategies to protect the right of access to emergency obstetric care in Uganda. *African Human Rights Law Journal*, *7*(2), 283–306.

Uganda. (1995). *The Constitution of the Republic of Uganda*. Kampala: Republic of Uganda.

Uganda Bureau of Statistics. (2018). Uganda demographic and health survey. Retrieved June 25, 2020, from https://dhsprogram.com/pubs/pdf/FR333/FR333.pdf.

Uganda v. Kamuhanda Emmanuel. (2012). High Court Criminal Session Case No. 24.

Uganda v. Kasumba Joseph (2002). High Court Criminal Session Case No. 08.

Uganda v. Yiga Hamidu. (2002). High court Criminal Session Case No. 05.

United Nations. (1979). Convention on the elimination of all forms of discrimination against women. *Treaty Series*, *1249*, 13. Retrieved June 26, 2020, from https://www.ohchr.org/Documents/ProfessionalInterest/cedaw.pdf.

United Nations. (1989). Convention on the Rights of the Child. *Treaty Series*, *1577*, 3. Retrieved June 26, 2020, from https://www.ohchr.org/Documents/ProfessionalInterest/crc.pdf.

United Nations. (n.d.). News on millennium development goals. Retrieved June 25, 2020, from https://www.un.org/millenniumgoals/.

URN. (2017). Justice Leticia Kikonyogo dies aged 77. *The Observer*. Retrieved June 26, 2020, from https://observer.ug/news/headlines/56114-justice-leticia-kikonyogo-dies-aged-77.html.

Wamboga, S. (2019). Meet the male judge fondly known as sister Batema. *Daily Monitor*. Retrieved from https://www.monitor.co.ug/Magazines/Life/Meet-the-male-judge-fondly-known-Sister-Batema/689856-5099870-8bqabbz/index.html.

Watsemwa and anor v. Attorney-General. (2006). UG High Court Civil Suit No. 675.

Wekasa, A. (2013). Judiciary mourns Byamugisha. *Daily Monitor*. Retrieved June 26, 2020, from https://www.monitor.co.ug/News/National/Judiciary-mourns-Byamugisha/688334-1727072-108a2ys/index.html.

WHO, UNFPA, UNICEF, ICM, ICN, FIGO, and IPA. (2018). Defining competent maternal and newborn health professionals. Retrieved June 25, 2020, from https://apps.who.int/iris/handle/10665/272817.

WHO, UNICEF, UNFPA, World Bank Group and United Nations Population Division (2019). Trends in maternal mortality: 2000-2017. Retrieved July 9, 2020, from https://www.unfpa.org/sites/default/files/pub-pdf/Maternal_mortality_report.pdf.

Wikler, N. (1980). On the judicial agenda for the 80s: Equal treatment for men and women in the courts. *Judicature*, 64(5), 202–209.

Wilson, B. (1990). Will women judges really make difference. *Osgoode Hall Law Journal*, 28(3), 507–522.

Women in Leadership Conference Award Bios. (2018). Retrieved 12 July 2021, from http://judiciary.go.ug/data/news/507/200/Women%20in%20Leadership%20Conference%20Award%20Bios.html

World Bank. (2020). The World Bank in Uganda. Retrieved June 26, 2020, from https://www.worldbank.org/en/country/uganda/overview.

World Bank Data. (2019). Maternal mortality ratio (modeled estimate, per 100,000 live births). Retrieved June 25, 2020, from https://data.worldbank.org/indicator/SH.STA.MMRT.

World Bank Data. (n.d.). Morality rate, infant (per 1,000 live births). Retrieved June 25, 2020, from https://data.worldbank.org/indicator/SP.DYN.IMRT.IN.

World Health Organization. (2015). The prevention and elimination of disrespect and abuse during facility-based childbirth. Retrieved June 26, 2020, from https://apps.who.int/iris/bitstream/handle/10665/134588/WHO_RHR_14.23_eng.pdf;jsessionid=EDB1FFABA1EE3AA9E4487615D54B2774?sequence=1.

World Health Organization. (n.d.a). Definitions: Emergencies. Retrieved June 25, 2020, from https://www.who.int/hac/about/definitions/en.

World Health Organization. (n.d.b). Infant mortality. Retrieved June 25, 2020, from https://www.who.int/gho/child_health/mortality/neonatal_infant_text/en.

World Health Organization. (n.d.c). Maternal mortality ratio (per 100 000 live births). Retrieved June 26, 2020, from https://www.who.int/healthinfo/statistics/indmaternalmortality/en.

Yamin, A., & Maine, D. P. (1999). Maternal morality as human rights issue: Measuring compliance with international treaty obligations. *Human Rights Quarterly*, *21*(3), 563–607.

7 Revenge pornography as a form of sexual and gender-based violence in Ghana

Emerging judicial issues

Maame Efua Addadzi-Koom

Introduction

Technological advancements in the 21st century have greatly influenced the dynamics of social life, particularly intimate relationships. Digital intimacy has been culturally embraced, leading to an alarming increase in "sexting" (Burris, 2014; Bates, 2015; Chisala-Tempelhoff & Kirya, 2016; Ngo et al., 2017).[1] However, this cultural endorsement of digital intimacy runs a risk of destructive and enduring consequences for those whose sexually explicit images end up on the internet.

One morning in January 2018, Ghanaians woke up to a leaked sex video that made waves on social media. The infamous "kitchen stool" sex video featured the headmaster (school principal) of Adumanu D/A Basic School, Robert Sepey, and his former student girlfriend having sex on a kitchen stool (*My Newsgh*, 2018).[2] The 4-minute, 16-second video, which went viral, was said to have been recorded a year prior to the leakage. The recording was made at a time when the headmaster and his former student were in the prime of their romantic relationship. The lovers voluntarily agreed to record this intimate sexual act, which they intended to watch at a later time in admiration of their sexual prowess. Unfortunately for the two, the video landed in the hands of the wrong persons, leading to the scandal.[3] Preliminary investigations conducted by the Ghana Education Service (GES) revealed that the young lady's brother's friends were behind the leakage as payback for her refusing their love proposals (*My joy online*, 2018).

In the past, heart-broken and rejected lovers simply wallowed in self-pity or discarded all memories, including photos of their beloved. Today, through technology, there is a more pernicious payback option: revenge porn. Revenge porn simply means non-consensual, involuntary pornography (Burris, 2014). Unfortunately, the "kitchen stool" sex scandal is just one example of the increasing spread of non-consensual pornography over the internet in Ghana. There are at least three revenge porn posts on social media every day, a majority of the victims being women and girls (*News Ghana*, 2017).

Shortly after the release of the "kitchen stool" sex video, there was parliamentary debate as to whether rigorous legislation was necessary to deal with the menace. The then majority leader of parliament, Osei Kyei Mensah Bonsu, was

DOI: 10.4324/9780429327865-9

of the view that appropriate legislation was needed to combat revenge porn and its related activities. He advocated that criminalizing revenge porn and related activities would protect the constitutional right to privacy of all Ghanaians. On the other hand, the then minority leader, Haruna Iddrisu, disagreed with a legislative approach to addressing revenge porn and relied on self-discipline as the key to overcoming the menace. To him, "the best way to avoid this scandal is self-discipline. Privacy must be respected and protected, but I am afraid legislation may not be able to resolve it. We must ensure conscious use of the mobile phone and stop the continuous abuse of these gadgets" (Parliament of Ghana, pp.455–446).

This discussion on the floor of parliament reflects the ongoing debates surrounding the classification of revenge porn: that is, whether revenge porn is simply a matter of user naivety calling for self-discipline or a form of violence requiring legislation (Chisala-Tempelhoff & Kirya, 2016).

This chapter looks at revenge porn from a gender perspective and makes a case for considering it as a women's rights issue and a form of gender-based violence. The chapter argues that framing revenge porn as a women's rights issue will positively impact the course of any future legislation to protect women, who comprise the bulk of revenge porn victims in Ghana. The role of the courts in contributing to this gendered perspective of revenge porn matters is examined. The chapter offers suggestions to address the issues raised.

The chapter progresses in four parts. The first part explains the concept of revenge porn by defining it and exploring the nature of "consent" as it pertains to revenge porn, and looks at the gendered context of revenge porn. The second part focuses on revenge porn in Ghana. It gives a brief background on the revenge porn spree in Ghana and assesses the socio-legal consequences of revenge porn. The third part contains an overview of the existing legal framework, that is, the judicial response and legislative framework relating to revenge porn in Ghana, and exposes the inadequacies in addressing the problem. The fourth part discusses the critical role of the court in addressing revenge porn–related issues, particularly through a gender-conscious lens. The discussion in this part is set against the backdrop of inadequate legislation on the matter. The fifth part concludes the chapter.

The concept of revenge porn

Defining revenge porn

Revenge porn has been defined as "non-consensual, involuntary pornography" (Burris, 2014, p.2327) or "sexually explicit images disclosed without consent and for no legitimate purpose" (Franks, 2015). Usually, some personal information accompanies the images, such as the name, address, and social media profiles of the victim (Arimoro, 2015; Poole, 2014).

Revenge porn is considered a form of cyber-harassment (Arimoro, 2015, p.76; Dickson, 2016)[4] because the sexually explicit images are disclosed to an audience other than the intended private audience (Burris, 2014). The images may have been originally created or obtained with or without the consent of the subject (Citron & Franks, 2014; Kitchen, 2015).

Although the most common form of revenge porn is that induced by failed intimate relationships and scorned ex-lovers, there are other forms of involuntary porn not triggered by revenge per se (Chisala-Tempelhoff & Kirya, 2016; Martinez, 2014; Quiles, 2016). The sexually explicit images may be "acquired through hacking, theft by repair people, or false personal ads" (Martinez, 2014). Perpetrators may engage in non-consensual pornography for earning, notoriety, or sheer amusement (Chisala-Tempelhoff & Kirya, 2016). Its distribution may also result from negligence, recklessness, or inadvertence (Burris, 2014).

There have also been recent variants of non-consensual pornography such as "parasite porn"—where harmless images of victims are copied without their consent and uploaded onto pornographic sites—and "morph porn" or edited portrayals—where the victim's face, without consent, is cropped from a harmless picture and pasted onto the body of another person engaging in sexual activity (Dickson, 2016; Goudsmit, 2017; *My joy online*, 2017; *GhanaWeb*, 2014).[5]

In light of the broad and evolving meaning of "revenge porn," some scholars prefer to use the term "non-consensual pornography" instead of "revenge porn," as the latter is considered to be misleading (Chisala-Tempelhoff & Kirya, 2016; Dickson, 2016, p.46; Goudsmit, 2017, pp.26–27; Quiles, 2016).[6]

This chapter, however, uses the terms interchangeably, as "revenge porn" is now a generic term for all forms of non-consensual pornography regardless of the fact that the act may not have been purely motivated by revenge (Burris, 2014; Citron & Franks, 2014).

Revenge porn in a gendered context

Women and girls are the primary targets of non-consensual pornography (Citron & Franks, 2014). Thus, in African societies where there are strong traditional patriarchal attitudes that hold women to a higher standard of sexual morality than men, female revenge porn victims are vilified. They are slut-shamed, sternly criticized, condemned, and mocked in the court of public opinion. It is this unsympathetic attitude toward the autonomy of women that pushes back at any attempt to frame non-consensual pornography as gender-based violence (GBV). However, given the increasing use of technology and the internet to facilitate harassment against women, and the resultant gender inequality in cyberspace, revenge porn can be nothing short of GBV (Chisala-Tempelhoff & Kirya, 2016).

Gender-based violence refers to abuse or harm directed against a person or group of persons that is associated with the normative perception of their gender.[7] Accordingly, gender-based violence is experienced by both men and women, although women are the mainstream victims of gender-based violence, especially where the violence is sexual in nature. Gender-based violence is engrained in gender inequalities, which are tolerated by society, in that men often use violence as a means of asserting their authority or chastising the alleged transgressions of gender roles (Bott, Morrison, and Ellsberg, 2005). The United Nations General Assembly in 1993 defined violence against women as "any act of gender-based violence that results in, or is likely to result in physical, sexual, or psychological harm or suffering to women, including threats of such acts, coercion or arbitrary deprivations of liberty, whether occurring in public or private life" (UN, 1993). As a form of sexual violence against women in the cyberworld, revenge porn cannot be recognized apart from the societal normative understanding of gender roles that affects women's vulnerability to violence. It should therefore be classified as a form of gender-based violence.

Throughout history, women have had to fight for their rights to be acknowledged and their sexual boundaries respected. Yet, the apathy toward women's rights and sexuality still persists. The apathy extends to revenge porn, which affects more women than men (Citron & Franks, 2014). It is this apathy that influences the decision to classify revenge porn as a consequence of user naivety rather than a gendered issue. However, such an assumption in itself is a form of discrimination against women, because it shames women when their sexual activities are made public. When it comes to sexual activities, men are acclaimed, but women are judged; men are "studs," but women are "sluts." It takes a legal intervention, such as laws against revenge porn, to gradually address and deal with such discriminatory attitudes toward women's sexuality (Poole, 2014).

The threat of revenge porn is consistently being used as a tool to perpetrate cyber-stalking and cyber-rape against women. The threat of revenge porn is also used by sex offenders such as rapists, who record their rape episodes in order to silence their victims from reporting them to the police. Sex traffickers also use the threat of revenge porn to compel reluctant persons to engage in the sex trade (Chisala-Tempelhoff & Kirya, 2016; Burris, 2014).

Revenge porn is also a form of domestic violence, as intimate male partners often silence and coerce their female partners through the threat of public distribution of intimate images. Often, the images are coercively obtained by the abuser. As a result of such threats, women are unable to report abuses, leave the abusive relationship, or fight for the custody of their children. Where the abused partner musters the courage to break out, the abuser makes good his threats (Chisala-Tempelhoff & Kirya, 2016; Citron & Franks, 2014).

Irrespective of the moral position one may take on revenge porn, the fact that people, especially young women, are being subjected to severe and lasting harm is real (Martinez, 2014). It is essential, therefore, that revenge porn is viewed as a form of gender-based violence that denies women their capacity to fully control their bodies and guard their reputation, with the ultimate effect of ruining their lives (Chisala-Tempelhoff & Kirya, 2016; Burris, 2014). With this in mind, judicial processes should be sensitive to the pressing need to protect women's rights in order to lead to positive judicial outcomes that will advance justice to female victims of revenge porn, and influence future legislation.

Revenge porn in Ghana

The revenge porn spree in Ghana

In Ghana, there are at least three revenge porn posts on social media every day, the majority of the victims being women and girls. There are also records of female revenge porn victims in Ghana committing suicide. There are over 20 revenge porn sites currently operating in Ghana (*News Ghana*, 2017; Mensah & Donkor, 2017).

The rising spree of revenge porn in Ghana can be managed by introducing specific laws to address the nuances of the phenomenon. Prior to and immediately after the infamous "kitchen stool" sex video referenced earlier, there have been increased records of non-consensual pornography.

For example, in 2013, one Henry Alibah, a student, uploaded nude photos of his ex-girlfriend on Facebook (*Citifmonline*, 2014).[8] In 2016, a young lady committed suicide after her boyfriend leaked her sex video on the internet (*News Ghana*, 2017). In the first quarter of 2017, two young men were arrested for posting nude pictures of a young girl on Facebook after she broke up with one of them, who was her ex-boyfriend (*My joy online*, 2017).[9] Later that year, in December, a video showing 7 teenage boys gang-raping an 18-year-old girl at Bantama in Kumasi was circulated on social media platforms (Mensah & Donkor, 2017).

In all these cases, the reactions of government and law enforcement personnel have been ad hoc, leading to inconsistencies while the unresolved issues remain. In order to completely stamp out the growing plague of revenge porn and provide the needed support to its victims, judicial intervention and comprehensive legislation are essential.

The damaging consequences of revenge porn

The damaging consequences of revenge porn are numerous. They transcend the digital world into real life, making it even more difficult for revenge porn victims to cope. Chief among them is public humiliation and embarrassment. The distribution of sexually explicit images of revenge porn victims "converts unwilling citizens into sexual commodities" who are vilified. Revenge porn victims, particularly female victims, are slut-shamed and are featured in false prostitution ads on the internet, which further deepens the humiliation. They are also exposed to rape, cyber-stalking, sexual harassment, and domestic violence (Burris, 2014; Citron & Franks, 2014; Chisala-Tempelhoff & Kirya, 2016; Dickson, 2016; Martinez, 2014; Scheller, 2015, p.553).

Revenge porn does not only denigrate its victims sexually; it also denigrates them professionally and domestically. Some victims have lost educational opportunities. In some cases, the humiliation is extended to the victim's close family relations, friends, and employers. It comes as no surprise, therefore, that revenge porn victims are often either dismissed by their employers or coerced to resign from their jobs. Relationships are broken and friendships lost (Burris, 2014; Citron & Franks, 2014; Dickson, 2016).

For the most part, sexually explicit images, once they hit the internet, cannot be blotted out. The harm caused to victims is perpetual. To end the humiliation, therefore, some revenge porn victims have been forced to take on a new identity and re-locate. In extreme cases, others have contemplated suicide, while some have actually committed suicide to end it all (Burris, 2014; Dickson, 2016; Martinez, 2014).

Aside from these personal consequences for the victims, the betrayal implicit in non-consensual pornography imperils societal values such as human intimacy, gender equality, and privacy (Burris, 2014).

These consequences may be even more damaging in closely communal societies. In Ghana, for example, the communal residential arrangements, the extended family systems, as well as the religious environment mean that revenge porn information will spread not only to strangers but to family, friends, co-tenants, neighbors, and religious group members that the victim encounters on a regular basis. Public humiliation and embarrassment are likely not to be borne by the victim alone but by the victim's entire family, friends, and other close relations. In very traditional settings, the embarrassment and humiliation may eventually lead to the victim's family being negatively tagged, and they may be cut off from participating in certain communal activities and public appearances. In religious organizations, revenge porn could lead to the loss of members, as many of them would not want to be associated with an organization that is named and shamed. Conversely, revenge porn victims may also suffer a more brutal backlash from among their closest family and religious members of the community, who may dissociate themselves from and shun victims, pushing the victims further away into a lonely space.

These adverse effects hardwired into non-consensual pornography warrant the need for active judicial intervention and revenge porn–specific legislation.

The judiciary and the application of existing Ghanaian laws on revenge porn

In Ghana, some parts of the existing law loosely apply to revenge porn, such as the constitutional provisions on privacy and dignity as well as the traditional criminal laws against obscenity. Tort, copyright, and family law also offer some civil remedies to revenge porn victims, although not in all cases. The consequence is that judicial intervention in revenge porn cases can only go as far as these existing laws permit. The changing legal complexities of non-consensual pornography cannot be fully addressed by the current existing pieces of law—the reason why a comprehensive and specific legislation is necessary to enable the judiciary to be more effective in adjudicating cases involving revenge porn. This part offers an overview of the existing Ghanaian laws as they could be applied to revenge porn while pointing out the inadequacies. It also assesses how the judiciary has applied these laws in its decisions where applicable.

Constitutional law

Article 18 (2) of the 1992 Constitution of Ghana protects the right to privacy: "[n]o person shall be subjected to interference with the privacy of his home, property, correspondence or communication except in accordance with law as may be necessary in a free and democratic society." By this constitutional provision, sexually explicit images taken by a revenge porn victim are protected, since the images are her property. Likewise, nude pictures that are exchanged between lovers are also protected, since their distribution amounts to interference with the privacy of the victim's correspondence or communication.

The protection of privacy under the constitution of 1992 is, however, limited. For example, where the sexual images were not taken by the victim and so are not the victim's property, or where the images were inadvertently posted on a public platform by the victim, the distribution will technically not be an interference of the victim's privacy of property or communication. In these instances, a victim may rely on the constitutional right to dignity, which is inviolable (1992 constitution, Art. 15 (1)).[10] Additionally, a victim may make a case for violation of her rights based on the importation clause under Article 33 (5) of the constitution, which imports all other rights not specifically mentioned in the constitution that are "inherent in democracy and intended to secure the freedom and dignity of man." Thus, failing any domestic laws to protect, a victim may look to international human rights law for protection, including such rights as the right to be forgotten[11] (Fiedler, 2014).

While these constitutional protections are remarkable, their application, interpretation, and enforcement require judicial intervention. However, the judiciary may sometimes grapple with understanding the mechanics of the conduct that may give rise to revenge porn (Citron & Franks, 2014), and so the judiciary will need the assistance of specific legislative intervention to clear any ambiguities and ensure uniformity in judicial decisions.

Criminal law

The criminal laws of Ghana are limited in addressing revenge porn. The current criminal law tackles revenge porn only to the extent that it falls within the scope of the conventional laws against obscenity and indecency or where revenge porn is carried out for the purposes of extortion. Section 278 of the Criminal Offences Act 1960 (Act 29) makes it a misdemeanor to publicly and willfully engage in a grossly indecent act. A misdemeanor is punishable by a term of imprisonment not exceeding three years. Sections 280 and 281 also criminalize the publication, sale, distribution, advertising, importation, or exportation of obscene materials. Section 101A (1) of Act 29 (as amended) makes it an offense to sexually exploit a person.[12] Sexual exploitation has been defined to mean the use of a person for sexual activity that causes or is likely to cause serious physical and emotional injury or in prostitution or pornography (Act 29, s. 101A (1)).

From this law, it is evident that so far as revenge porn results in pornography or distribution of obscene images leads to, or is likely to lead to, physical or emotional harm, a perpetrator may be criminally liable under the criminal laws of Ghana. Such a scenario was seen in 2017, when it was reported that two persons had been arrested by the Somanya District Police Command for circulating nude pictures of a young lady. The young lady lodged a complaint with the police concerning her nude pictures, which were circulating on Facebook. She reported that her ex-boyfriend and another were responsible for the circulation. The police arrested the duo and charged them with circulation of obscene material and abetment of crime, and they were arraigned before the Somanya circuit court (*My joy online*, 2017). All the same, the inadequacies of the criminal laws on obscenity and indecency are exposed by other aspects of non-consensual pornography, which are not covered by the criminal laws. Take, for example, the distribution of sexually explicit images that are not intended to cause harm but for entertainment, or cases of "morph porn." In such situations, the criminal laws of Ghana on obscenity and indecency fall short in addressing these possibilities (Rackley & McGlynn, 2018).

The criminal laws on extortion may also be applicable to revenge porn where a perpetrator threatens to distribute nude photos or videos of a person for purposes of extorting property from the victim. Section 151 of Act 29 provides that a person who extorts property from any other person by means of threat commits a second-degree felony. A person convicted of second-degree felony is liable to a term of imprisonment not exceeding ten years. The challenge with this extortion law in relation to revenge porn is that it excludes liability where threats of criminal assault or bodily harm to the person threatened is used; thus, it limits the acceptable forms of threats in cases of revenge porn to only threat of distribution and not threat of harm (Act 29, s. 151 (2)). This state of the law on extortion is principally because extortion as mentioned in s. 151 of Act 29 is closely linked with robbery under s. 150 of Act 29, such that the use of threat of violence to obtain property such as money is considered as robbery and not extortion.

Also, under the Electronic Transactions Act, 2008 (Act 772), s. 136 on child pornography could be applied to revenge porn cases where the victim is a child, that is, a person below 18 years. Child pornography includes, among other things, materials that visually depict a child engaged in sexually explicit conduct or images representing a child in such a manner and unauthorized images of nude children. A person who intentionally publishes, produces, procures, or possesses child pornography in a computer system or electronic record storage medium is liable to a fine or a term of imprisonment of not more than ten years or both.

Aside from the challenges mentioned earlier, the current state of the laws that could possibly impose criminal liability are also limited because they do not specifically categorize non-consensual pornography as a sexual offense. The lack of express law that classifies non-consensual pornography as a sexual offense makes victims more vulnerable, as they do not have any form of anonymity in open court, which is often available in sexual offense cases. Although the criminal sanctions that the current criminal laws impose on perpetrators are moderate, the criminal justice system alone cannot offer complete satisfaction to revenge porn victims. Consider, for instance, a 60-day imprisonment for a revenge porn perpetrator[13] as opposed to a lifetime of humiliation, tarnished reputation, and loss of educational and employment opportunities. These loopholes therefore signal the need to consider the viability of civil law remedies as well.

Civil law

Moving away from criminal law, which focuses predominantly on perpetrators, I now turn to assess the adequacy or otherwise of Ghanaian civil laws, particularly tort, copyright, and family law, which are more victim oriented.

Tort law

For a revenge porn victim, tort law may allow reliefs for physical injury, economic injury, emotional distress, and possibly invasion of privacy and damage to reputation. Civil remedies for physical and economic injury resulting from revenge porn are often non-contentious, as they are relatively easier to prove. However, remedies in tort law for emotional distress, invasion of privacy, and damage to reputation are not easily forthcoming due to the nature of such injuries. These remedies will be the focus of this part.

Emotional distress to a revenge porn victim must be intentionally inflicted and calculated to cause harm in order to warrant a remedy under tort law (Bermingham & Brennan, 2010; *Wilkinson v. Downton*, 1897). Thus, where emotional distress was not intentionally inflicted, such as where the distribution of the intimate photos or videos was inadvertent or negligent, there will be no remedy for the victim. Additionally, in common law, conduct that is calculated to cause distress and inflicts emotional distress without more is not tortious (Bermingham & Brennan, 2010; *Wainwright v. Home Office*, 2003). This means that a revenge porn victim who suffers emotional distress or humiliation alone is unlikely to successfully establish liability of the perpetrator. Hence, no remedy.

Although in some common law jurisdictions there is an incremental development toward a tort of privacy invasion,[14] it is alien under traditional common law, which forms part of the common law of Ghana. In *Wainwright*, the absence of a tort of privacy under the common law was made clear by the House of Lords.

Instead of a tort of privacy, English courts have adapted the equitable action for breach of confidence, which allows persons to be held liable for publicly disclosing information which they "knew or ought to have known that there was a reasonable expectation that the information would be kept confidential or private" (Applegarth, 2009). It seems to be the case that while a revenge porn victim may claim infringement of privacy under the Ghanaian constitution, she cannot do so under the law of torts, though the equitable remedy for breach of confidence is attainable.

A revenge porn victim may initiate a defamation action for damage to her reputation. The chances of such an action succeeding are, however, slim, since in most cases, the image or video involved depicts the truth; the truth being that the victim is the one engaging in the sexual act in the photograph or video. Truth is a complete defense to a claim of defamation (Bermingham & Brennan, 2010; Quiles, 2016). That notwithstanding, a defamation action is more likely to be successful in instances of "morph" porn, which involves false images.

Copyright law

The possible reliefs under copyright law for non-consensual pornography are narrow at best. Generally, a person may bring an action for copyright claims where that person is the author, co-author, or joint author of the work in question (Copyright Act 690, s.1). Thus, where a revenge porn victim did not take the nude images or record the sex video either singularly or jointly with another, the victim has no remedy under copyright laws (Burris, 2014; Citron & Franks, 2014).

Revenge porn images and videos fall under artistic works and/or audio-visual works under the copyright laws of Ghana (Copyright Act 690, s.1 (1)). Artistic works include photographs "not comprised in an audio-visual film" (Copyright Act 690, s.76), meaning that a still image from a film is not a photograph and cannot be the subject matter of a copyright action. In this regard, a perpetrator who takes still nude images from an audio-visual work[15] created by a revenge porn victim cannot be held liable under the copyright laws of Ghana.

Another downside of applying copyright laws to revenge porn is that it reduces gender-based violence to a battle of property rights. It shifts the focus from the gendered issues of cyber-violence to the ownership of images that victims are not proud of. Copyright law, in revenge porn matters, will undoubtedly be a good servant but a bad master. Its place should be supplementary at best (Citron & Franks, 2014; Levendowski, 2014).[16]

Family law

Revenge porn victims also stand the chance of bringing claims against perpetrators with whom they had or continue to have a domestic relationship.[17] Section 1 of the Domestic Violence Act, 2007 (Act 732) criminalizes acts, or threats to commit acts, likely to result in physical abuse, emotional abuse, verbal abuse, or psychological abuse. Thus, where the threat of publicizing nude photos or sex videos is used as a basis for domestic violence, it is possible for the perpetrator to be found guilty of committing a criminal offense (Act 732 s. 3(2)). Protection orders may also be made against the perpetrator (Act 732, ss. 11–22).

Civil claims are available in addition to criminal actions. A finding of domestic violence can be made whether the act or threat of non-consensual pornography is a single act or repeated acts (Act 732, s. 5).

In February 2014, the Accra circuit court relied on the combined effect of sections 1 and 3 (2) of the Domestic Violence Act to sentence 21-year-old Henry Alibah to six months' imprisonment for uploading nude photos of his ex-girlfriend in a Facebook post that portrayed her as a prostitute. The post was a result of the victim ending the romantic relationship with the accused. The presiding judge, Ms. Ellen Vivian Amoah, found the accused guilty on the grounds of causing emotional, verbal, or psychological abuse under the Domestic Violence Act. Justice Amoah also relied on a number of foreign legal authorities from other Commonwealth jurisdictions and the United States of America in arriving at her decision. The heavy reliance on foreign authorities that have a persuasive effect in Ghanaian courts is a glaring sign of the inadequate Ghanaian authorities, both legislation and case law, relating to non-consensual pornography.

Clearly, there is limited protection for revenge porn victims under the existing Ghanaian legal framework and equally limited judicial intervention. So far, revenge porn liability has been shoehorned into existing laws by the Ghanaian courts where cases have been brought before them, but a lot of the details remain unaddressed. It is the responsibility of the state to "cultivate among all Ghanaians respect for fundamental human rights and freedoms and the dignity of the human person" (1992 constitution, Art. 35 (4)). To effectively discharge this constitutional responsibility in relation to victims of non-consensual pornography, the judiciary has a key role to play, failing comprehensive legislation. The nature and extent of this role is discussed in the next section.

The role of the court in addressing revenge porn

"The prophecies of what the courts will do in fact and nothing more pretentious are what I mean by the law." This legendary quote by Oliver Wendell Holmes Jr.[18] captures the role of the courts in addressing revenge porn. As a common law country, Ghanaian courts have a significant role to play in shaping the legal regime concerning revenge porn and related offenses both pre- and post-specific legislation.

In the absence of specific revenge porn laws, there is the need for a lot more judicial activism. The courts will have to extrapolate prohibitions of revenge porn and related offenses from the existing legal framework. For example, the courts will have to broadly and purposively interpret the constitutional right to privacy under Article 18 and the importation clause under Article 33 (5) of the 1992 constitution in order to offer some form of protection and assistance to revenge porn victims. The constitution is the supreme law of the land, and if applied appropriately by the courts, its provisions will serve as a great tool for dealing with issues of non-consensual pornography.

Additionally, the courts will have to work with the traditional criminal provisions on obscenity, indecency, and extortion to sanction revenge porn perpetrators. In construing these provisions, the courts under section 4 (1) of Act 29 are required not to do so strictly but to construe them amply and beneficially for giving effect to the purposes of the Act. In extremely challenging revenge porn cases where ample and beneficial construction of Act 29 would be impracticable, the courts may possibly use their judicial decisions as a conduit to alert parliament to the inadequacies of the existing law and the need for legislation on the subject.

It is believed that by the courts adding their voice in this way, parliament may eventually have its attention drawn once again to the urgent need for legislation and may act accordingly.

Laws are hardly sufficient on their own to cause change. Thus, once laws on revenge porn and related offenses are passed in the future, more activism from the bench will be necessary to facilitate the implementation of the law. The application of and interpretation given by the courts to the letter of the law will enhance clarity. It is also of utmost importance that decisions that are brought before the courts are delivered promptly. Swift delivery of judgment will not only help with closure for victims but will also add to the body of judicial precedent on the subject, which will lead to greater certainty and predictability of the law.

In performing their judicial functions, both pre- and post-specific legislation, the courts will have to be gender conscious. Due to the fact that the majority of revenge porn victims are female, it is essential that judges exercise sensitivity to the peculiar needs of the female gender. It is recommended that there should be awareness, education, and training of judges on gender-based stereotypes and attitudes. Regardless of the high standard of fairness that judges must adhere to, they are still part of society and have consciously or unconsciously imbibed certain gender-based attitudes from society's structure and cultural norms. Therefore, in order to overcome the influences of these overt and indirect gender-based stereotypes and attitudes that they may have taken in, creating awareness about these gender attitudes is important to ensure fair delivery and administration of justice. While the gender attitudes education and training should be for all judges, attention should be given to creating awareness for male judges as well as female judges who are not gender sensitive (Dawuni, 2016; Huhtanen & Halilović, 2014).

In pre-trial stages, for example, judges could consider asking victims about their fears and the basis for their fears, being mindful of the fact that some female victims may not be as expressive due to several factors, including the extent of trauma or fear and cultural barriers. Where there has been an application for bail, judges could notify victims of the bail application and the implications it may have for their safety if granted. They may also ask female victims about their opinion on the likelihood that the perpetrator would adhere to the release conditions. Rather than offering women protection in a paternalistic manner, these measures afford female victims an outlet to effectively engage with and build trust in the justice system while preparing them to confidently participate in the trial itself (UNODC, 2019).

Judges, by virtue of their position, have the ability to take measures to protect and ensure the safe engagement of female victims of revenge porn during trial by issuing protection orders as seen in the Domestic Violence Act against perpetrators. Again, immediate judicial orders requiring perpetrators and service providers to take down and desist from distributing revenge porn images or videos is relevant in protecting female victims and empowering them to fully cooperate with the justice system. The judicial orientation in matters of non-consensual pornography must be that of affirmative action—seeking to correct past and present discriminations and biases against women and girls. Doing so will bring about holistic justice.

As Ghana is a common law country, the courts should take advantage of the vast case law resources in other advanced common law jurisdictions in deciding revenge porn cases. Although foreign cases have only a persuasive effect, they have the potential of guiding the judiciary's decision-making process especially in an area such as non-consensual pornography, where the Ghanaian law is limited.

Also, preserving the anonymity of female victims in revenge porn cases throughout the trial process is essential. Judges can ensure this by making orders that will prohibit the media, for example, from publishing the names and other details that may expose the identity of victims in news reports on such cases while pending in court (UNODC, 2019). Female victims may also be allowed to use aliases throughout the trial. Such anonymity is important to encourage victims to develop trust in the formal justice system, and also goes a long way toward presenting the police and the courts to victims as a welcoming and safe platform for reporting their cases.

Furthermore, the courts should also allow a multi-jurisdictional approach to handling revenge porn cases, that is, there should be room for civil actions in addition to criminal ones. A hybrid approach by the courts is essential for the following reasons. Criminal actions serve as a deterrent by imposing stringent sanctions on perpetrators that stay on their record for life (Burris 2014; Citron & Franks, 2014). It sends a message that demands respect for the sexuality of persons, particularly women, and condemns objectifying them. Yet, it is not victim oriented. It focuses on the perpetrator to the detriment of the victim, who perhaps only needs an apology.

Civil actions, on the other hand, are more victim oriented[19] and offer a wider range of remedies, yet these remedies are modest and do not serve as a deterrent to perpetrators, unlike criminal penalties. They also come at a high cost, which most victims cannot afford, because they may have lost their jobs as a result of the distribution of their explicit photos. Civil actions also rob victims of their anonymity, as they will have to pursue the case with their real names (Burris, 2014; Citron & Franks, 2014). Thus, a hybrid approach will better address the identified complexities of adjudicating revenge porn cases. The court would exercise its judicial discretion in determining which approach to use.

Where revenge porn cases are less aggravated, the courts could direct that such cases should be resolved through alternative dispute resolution mechanisms such as negotiation, mediation, and arbitration. In the absence of comprehensive legislation, determining which revenge porn cases are aggravated and which are not is a matter that would be largely left to the discretion of the judiciary. In Ghanaian law, however, the term "aggravated" and its terms of reference are not novel. In the Domestic Violence Act, for example, the term "aggravated" is used to describe offenses that are punishable by more than three years' imprisonment. On this basis, it can be deduced, for example, that revenge porn liabilities that could be premised on the offenses of obscenity and indecency under s. 278 of Act 29 could be classified as non-aggravated because they are punishable by not more than three years' imprisonment, while those premised on extortion under s. 151 of Act 29 could be classified as aggravated.

Judges should be guided by this existing standard to determine the level of aggravation of revenge porn cases. Also, the 1992 Constitution of Ghana provides guidelines for exercising discretionary powers, which include a duty to be fair and candid; avoidance of arbitrary, capricious, or biased exercise of discretionary power due to either resentment, prejudice, or dislike; and adherence to due process. It is believed that these constitutional guidelines will also check the adverse use of judicial discretion against victims.

Despite the significance of the court in tackling revenge porn, there is a fundamental limitation. The performance of the courts is dependent on persons submitting cases to it. There will be no cases to decide unless victims and/or prosecutors institute actions. For instance, in the case of the "kitchen stool" scandal, although the headmaster, Mr. Sepey, was eventually dismissed by the GES for breaching its Code of Professional Conduct, there is no record of a court action instituted against the distributors of the video. To offset this challenge, it is recommended that the courts liaise with both government institutions such as the police (particularly, the cyber-crime unit of the Criminal Investigation Department (CID)) as well as civil society organizations to ensure first, that cases are reported, and second, that those cases reported at these institutions and organizations find their way into the courtroom.

In less severe cases, court-connected settlements can be used. The judiciary, working together with the institutions mentioned, for example, could send out notices to the general public through various media outlets about their renewed commitment to take on reported revenge porn cases seriously, and handle them sensitively by guaranteeing anonymity, respecting privacy, waiving filing fees, and waiving other court fees on an as-needed basis. These assurances will go a long way toward persuading more victims to report their cases and pursue them through the court system. Engaging in such collaborations will ultimately enhance the courts' role in addressing issues of non-consensual pornography.

Another challenge is that the few revenge porn cases that have found their way into the courtroom have been decided by lower courts, that is, circuit courts and district courts, which in Ghana are not courts of record. The implication is that the decisions made by these courts do not have an extensive reach and may often fade out with time. It is necessary that actions involving non-consensual pornography are filed at superior courts of records, particularly the High Court, as its decisions have a binding effect on lower courts and will remain in the judicial archives for posterity. The High Court is a court of general jurisdiction in both civil and criminal matters. It also has jurisdiction to enforce fundamental human rights and freedoms (1992 constitution, Art. 140: courts Act, s. 15). As a result, the High Court is a welcoming forum for filing revenge porn claims, be they criminal, civil, or constitutional. While in some cases, revenge porn claims may be filed at the district or circuit court due to territorial jurisdiction, it is submitted that the judicial service of Ghana should encourage prosecutors as well as litigants and their lawyers to file revenge porn cases at the High Court, which has original jurisdiction in all matters, or better still, frame their claims in terms of fundamental human rights, such as the right to privacy, since such cases can be filed at the High Court. Filing revenge porn cases in human rights terms could be set as a judicial agenda for a period, say two years, with the sole aim of promoting and increasing the number of judicial decisions by courts of record regarding revenge porn.

Conclusion

Revenge porn constitutes a "disturbing niche of the vast and untamed world of amateur erotica" that has damaging and enduring consequences, especially for women and girls (Calvert, 2015, pp.676–677). That the scourge of revenge porn has finally caught the attention of the Ghanaian courts and parliament is a sign of hope that the crime will be addressed through judicial and legislative means. This chapter has made a case for revenge porn to be framed as gender-based violence, since women are the primary targets. The chapter has also highlighted the shortcomings of the existing laws in addressing revenge porn and the role of the Ghanaian courts in addressing revenge porn, which is critical, especially within the current limited legislative milieu. A cursory call for specific legislation was also made. Legislation is only a first step toward the fight against revenge porn. More importantly, effective law enforcement and support systems need to be in place and running in order to give life to the law. Otherwise, the law will only be protecting revenge porn victims in theory. The courts stand to play important roles both prior to specific laws being passed and after such laws are passed. Taking into account the measures outlined earlier, the courts can play a critical role in alleviating the malaise of revenge porn in Ghana.

Postscript

While the book was in press, Ghana passed the Cybersecurity Act 2020 (Act 1038) which contains some express provisions, in sections 67 and 68, on non-consensual pornography. The said provisions share in some of the limitations of existing laws discussed earlier including restraining revenge porn to distribution of intimate images with the intent to cause serious emotional distress only (excluding to the exclusion of entertainment intents or "morph porn" cases), and the absence of civil remedies. The chapter should therefore be read with this recent development in mind.

Notes

1 These authors define "sexting" as a portmanteau of "sex" and "texting," which involves sending, receiving, or posting sexually explicit images or sexually suggestive messages via cell phone or other forms of electronic communication.
2 A kitchen stool is a portable wooden low bench usually used as a seat in the kitchen.
3 The video was on the young lady's cell phone. Her brother saw it when he took the lady's phone to transfer songs. Her brother's friends then saw the video and leaked it.
4 Some scholars advocate for calling "revenge porn" "image-based sexual exploitation" or "image-based sexual abuse." Arimoro (2015) explains that revenge porn can take

place both online (on the internet) and offline (by showing the hardcopy or electronic copy to another person).

5 In 2017, one Desmond Attipoe was arrested in Kumasi for engaging in edited portrayals of women following a report to the police by one of his female targets. In 2013, former President John Dramani Mahama fell victim to morph porn when Mr. Omari Wadie, a member of the New Patriotic Party, a political party then in opposition, posted a nude photo of a man having sex with a woman in an office edited to depict the former president as the man in the picture. Mr. Wadie admitted on Radio Gold on May 22, 2013 to posting the picture on Facebook but added that he was not the creator of the photograph.

6 Goudsmit (2017) explains that the term "non-consensual pornography" also has its flaws in that it waters down the distinct nature of "revenge porn," eliminates "revenge," and lumps it in with other forms of non-consensual pornography. Thus, all concepts under non-consensual pornography must be clearly defined so that they are distinguished from each other.

7 Gender refers to the roles assigned to men and women by the socio-cultural demands of society.

8 He was sentenced to six months' imprisonment by the Accra circuit court in February 2014.

9 The two young men were charged with circulating obscene materials and abetment of crime.

10 In April 2014, a circuit court in Accra sentenced a 24-year-old laborer to 60 days' imprisonment for posting nude pictures of his ex-girlfriend on Facebook. The circuit court indicated that the publication of the nude photos was a gross violation of the victim's right to privacy and dignity. He was charged with causing emotional, verbal, and psychological abuse to the victim

11 This right allows a person to start afresh by wiping out any digital dirt or humiliating information. The right prevents others from associating a person with her past.

12 The offense is punishable by a minimum of 5 years' and a maximum of 25 years' imprisonment if the victim is not a child. The minimum sentence is seven years if the victim is a child.

13 See note 9.

14 The United States, New Zealand, and the Province of Ontario, Canada are some common law jurisdictions building on a tort of privacy. Under Australian law, a tort of privacy was introduced by the decision in *Jane Doe v. Australian Broadcasting Corporation* [2007] VCC 281.

15 An audio-visual work is "a work that consists of a series of related images which impart the impression of motion, with or without accompanying sounds, susceptible of being made visible, and where accompanied by sounds susceptible of being made audible."

16 Conversely, Levendowski (2014) argues that copyright law provides all the desirable remedies revenge porn victims seek, such as takedowns, civil liability for perpetrators, and money damages. In short, copyright can combat revenge porn.

17 Section 2 of Act 732 defines domestic relationship broadly to include not only familial or marital relations but also other intimate or romantic ties as well as live-in house helps.

18 Oliver Wendell Holmes Jr. was an American jurist and former Associate Justice of the Supreme Court of the United States from 1902 to 1932.

19 Dunlap (2016) argues that in civil courts victims have much more control, since they appear for themselves and not as mere witnesses as is the case in criminal courts.

Laws and statutes

Constitution of the Republic of Ghana of 1992.
Copyright Act of 2005, Act 690.

Courts Act of 1993 (as amended), Act 459.
Criminal Offences Act of 1960, Act 29.
Criminal Offences (Amendment) Act of 2012, Act 849.
Domestic Violence Act of 200, Act 732.

Cases

Jane Doe v. Australian Broadcasting Corporation [2007] VCC 281.
Wainwright v. Home Office (2003) UKHL 53.
Wilkinson v. Downton (1897) 2 QB 57.

Books

Bermingham, V., & Brennan, C. (2010). *Tort Law: Directions*. Oxford: Oxford University Press.

Tamale, S. (2018) *When Hens Begin to Grow: Gender and Parliamentary Politics in Uganda*. New York: Routledge.

United National Office on Drugs and Crime (2019). *Handbook for the Judiciary on Effective Criminal Justice Responses to Gender-based Violence against Women and Girls*. Vienna: English, Publishing and Library Section.

Articles, Monographs and Other Scholarly Works

Applegarth, P. (2009). The tort of privacy invasion in Australia after Jane Doe. Supreme Court of Queensland Library. Retrieved from http://www5.austlii.edu.au/au/journals/QldJSchol/2009/9.pdf.

Arimoro, A. (2015). Applying the law to tackle the menace of revenge porn in Nigeria: Lessons from the United Kingdom. *Journal of Humanities and Social Science*, 20, 75–80.

Bates, S. (2015). *"Stripped": An Analysis of Revenge Porn Victims' Lives after Victimization* (Masters dissertation). Retrieved from http://summit.sfu.ca/system/files/iritems1/15668/etd9124_SBates.pdf

Bloom, S. (2014). No vengeance for 'revenge porn' victims: Unraveling why this latest female-centric, intimate-partner offense is still legal, and why we should criminalize it. *Fordham Urban Law Journal*, 42, 233–289.

Bott, S., Morrison, A., & Ellsberg, M. (2005). *Preventing and Responding to Gender-based Violence in Middle and Low-Income Countries: A Global Review and Analysis*. World Bank Policy Research Working Paper No. 3618. Retrieved from https://ssrn.com/abstract=754927.

Burris, A. (2014). Hell hath no fury like a woman porned: Revenge porn and the need for a federal nonconsensual pornography statute. *Florida Law Review*, 66, 2325–2359.

Calvert, C. (2015). Revenge porn and freedom of expression: Legislative pushback to an online weapon of emotional and reputational destruction. *Fordham Intellectual Property, Media and Entertainment Law Journal*, 24(3), 673 –702.

Chisala-Tempelhoff, S., & Kirya, M.T. (2016). Gender, law and revenge porn in Africa: A review of Malawi and Uganda. *Palgrave Communications*, 2, 1–9. http://dx.doi.org/10.1057/palcomms.2016.69

Citron, D. K., & Franks, M. A. (2014). Criminalizing revenge porn. *Wake Forest Law Review*, 49, 345–391.

Dawuni, J.J. (2016). To "mother" or not to "mother": The representative roles of women judges in Ghana. *Journal of African Law, 60*(3), 419–440. Doi:10.1017/S0021855316000115.

Dickson, A. (2016). "Revenge porn": A victim-focused response. *UniSA Student Law Review, 2*, 42–69.

Fiedler, L. (2014). Public shaming in the digital age: Are criminal laws the most effective means to regulate revenge porn? *Loyola of Los Angeles Entertainment Law Review, 34*(2), 155–192 http://digitalcommons.lmu.edu/elr/vol34/iss2/2.

Franks, M.A. (2015). Drafting an effective "revenge porn" law: A guide for legislators. *SSRN*. Retrieved from http://dx.doi.org/10.2139/ssrn.2468823.

Giliker, P. (2015). A common law tort of privacy? The challenges of developing a human rights tort. *Singapore Academy of Law Journal, 27*, 761 –788.

Goudsmit, M. (2017). *Revenge pornography: A conceptual analysis: Undressing a crime of disclosure* (Master's dissertation). Retrieved from https://openaccess.leidenuniv.nl/bitstream/handle/1887/47472/20170127%20MG%20Revenge%20pornography%20a%20conceptual%20analysis_Redacted.pdf?sequence=4.

Holmes, O.W. (1897). The path of the law. *Harvard Law Review, 10*, 457.

Huhtanen, H., & Halilović, M. (2014). Gender stereotypes and attitudes within the judiciary of Bosnia and Herzegovina: A case for increased awareness and education. *International Journal of the Legal Profession, 21*(3), 319–331. doi: 10.1080/09695958.2015.1047841

Kirchengast, T. (2016). The limits of criminal law and justice: 'Revenge porn' criminalisation, hybrid responses and the ideal victim. *UniSA Law Review, 2*, 96–101.

Kitchen, A.N. (2015). The need to criminalize revenge porn: How a law protecting victims can avoid running afoul of the first amendment. *Chicago-Kent Law Review, 90*, 247–299. http://scholarship.kentlaw.iit.edu/cklawreview/vol90/iss1/11.

Levendowski, A. (2014). Using copyright to combat revenge porn. *New York University Journal of Intellectual Property and Entertainment Law, 3*, 422–446.

Martinez, C. (2014). An argument for states to outlaw 'revenge porn' and for congress to amend 47 U.S.C. 230: How our current laws do little to protect victims. *Journal of Technology Law and Policy, 14*, 236–252.

Ngo, F., Jaishankar., K., & Agustina, J.R. (2017). Sexting: Current research gaps and legislative issues. *International Journal of Cyber Criminology, 11*, 161–168.

Poole, E. (2014). Fighting back against non-consensual pornography. *University of San Francisco Law Review, 49*, 181–214.

Quiles, A. (2016). *Revenge porn* (Dissertation) Retrieved from, http://scholarship.shu.edu/student_scholarship/832

Scheller, S.H. (2015). A picture is worth a thousand words: The legal implications of revenge porn. *North Carolina Law Review, 93*, 551–595.

United Nations (1993). *Declaration on the Elimination of Violence Against Women*. New York: United Nations Department of Public Information.

Internet sources

10 facts about the headmaster and student: 'Kitchen stool' sex scandal. (2018). *My Newsgh*. Retrieved from https://mynewsgh.com/10-facts-about-the-headmaster-and-student-kitchen-stool-sex-scandal/

Dunlap, B. (2016). 3 ways revenge porn is already illegal. *Rolling Stone*. Retrieved from https://www.rollingstone.com/culture/culture-news/3-ways-revenge-porn-is-already-illegal-113689/

Entamoty media to launch campaign against revenge porn in Ghana. (2017). *News Ghana*. Retrieved from https://www.newsghana.com.gh/entamoty-media-to-launch-campaign-against-revenge-porn-in-ghana/

GES begins probe into viral 'kitchen stool sex tape'. (2018). *My Joy Online*. Retrieved from https://www.myjoyonline.com/news/2018/january-24th/ges-begins-probe-into-viral-kitchen-stool-sex-tape.php

Man jailed for posting ex-girlfriend's nude photos on Facebook. (2014). *My Joy Online*. Retrieved from https://www.myjoyonline.com/news/2014/April-12th/man-jailed-for-posting-ex-girlfriends-nude-photos-on-facebook,php

Man jailed for posting ex-girlfriend's nude pictures. (2014). *Citifmonline*. Retrieved from citifimonline.com/2014/02/18/man-jailed-for-posting-ex-girlfriends-nude-pictures

Mensah, M., & Donkor, B. (2017). Police arrest 3 teenagers involved in gang-rape. *Graphic Online*. Retrieved from https://www.graphic.com.gh/news/general-news/police-confirm-arrest-of-3-members-of-gang-rapists.html

Nude picture scammer busted. (2017). *My Joy Online*. Retrieved from http://m.myjoyonline.com/marticles/news/nude-picture-scammer-busted

Parliament to ban nudes, revenge porn and secret recordings. (2018). *GhanaWeb*. Retrieved from https://www.ghanaweb.com/GhanaHomePage/NewsArchive/Parliament-to-ban-nudes-revenge-porn-and-secret-recordings-622883

Pastor's wife who sent her nudes on church Whatsapp platform attempts suicide. (2018). *Ghanaweb*. Retrieved from https://mobile.ghanaweb.com/GhanaHomePage/NewsArchive/Pastor-s-wife-who-sent-her-nudes-on-Church-WhatsApp-platform-attempts-suicide-621960

Rackley, E., & McGlynn, C. (2018). 'Upskirting' and 'revenge porn': The need for a comprehensive law. *The Conversation*. Retrieved from https://theconversation.com/uoskiting-and-revenge-porn-the-need-for-a-comprehensive-law-98403

The intersection of communication and law: Revisiting Wadie v. The Republic of Ghana through the lens of American jurisprudence. (2014). *GhanaWeb*. Retrieved from https://mobile.ghanaweb.com/GhanaHomePage/NewsArchive/The-Intersection-of-Communication-and-Law-299329

Two arrested for circulating nude photos of SHS graduate. (2017). *My Joy Online*. Retrieved from https://www.myjoyonline.com/news/2017/april-26th/two-arrested-for-circulating-nude-photos-of-shs-graduate.php

Other sources

Parliament of Ghana. (2018). Parliamentary debates: Official report. Retrieved from https://www.parliament.gh/epanel/docs/pb/1%20Feb%20%202018.pdf#viewer.action=download

8 Litigating gender discrimination cases before the ECOWAS Community Court of Justice and the African Court on Human and Peoples' Rights

Osai Ojigho

Introduction

The African regional courts have decided on hundreds of human rights claims, but very few cases on women's human rights and gender discrimination have been litigated before the courts. The courts may only adjudicate on matters brought before them. If persons who have faced gender discrimination do not bring cases, the court will be limited in its ability to decide on them. This chapter examines the few cases before the ECOWAS Community Court of Justice (CCJ) and the African Court on Human and Peoples' Rights (African Court) initiated by women or brought on their behalf. The goal is to critically evaluate how both courts[1] have interpreted the rights of women enshrined in human rights laws and the facts presented before them.

The chapter examines five cases. The first four are from the CCJ, while the fifth case analyzed is from the African Court. By December 2019, *Aminata Diantou Diane (represented by APDF & IHRDA) v Mali*;[2] *Hadijatou Mani v Niger*;[3] *Dorothy Njemanze & 3 Ors. v. Nigeria*[4]; and *Mary Sunday v Nigeria*[5] were the only cases decided by the CCJ where women alleged violations of their rights and discrimination based on their gender. The chapter interrogates the reasoning supporting the decisions of the CCJ, which found violations of several human rights in all four cases but failed to recognize gender discrimination in all the situations under review except in one case, *Dorothy Njemanze & 3 Ors v Nigeria*. In comparison, the African Court in its first women's human rights case, *Association Pour le Progrès et la Défense des Droits des Femmes Maliennes (APDF) and The Institute for Human Rights and Development in Africa (IHRDA) v. Republic of Mali*,[6] found a violation of gender discrimination against the state.

This chapter analyzes the extent to which legal, socio-political, or cultural norms influence how African regional courts judge gender and in particular, how this limits the impact of the decisions for the greater good of women in the society. In light of this discussion, the chapter concludes with the opportunities within the regional human rights system to strengthen the protection of women's human rights in Africa. The decisions in these cases may yet have an

DOI: 10.4324/9780429327865-10

impact in encouraging other complainants to come forward or in the interim, provide knowledge for complainants, lawyers, and advocacy groups to improve approaches, litigation strategies, and tactics when seeking justice before the regional courts.

Background: Economic Community of West African States (ECOWAS) Community Court of Justice

ECOWAS, established in 1975,[7] currently comprises 15 countries in West Africa: Benin, Burkina Faso, Cape Verde, Côte d'Ivoire, The Gambia, Ghana, Guinea, Guinea Bissau, Liberia, Mali, Niger, Nigeria, Senegal, Sierra Leone, and Togo.[8] From the beginning, ECOWAS envisaged a court or tribunal,[9] but none was created. It was only in 1991 that a protocol[10] establishing the CCJ was adopted by the ECOWAS Authority of Heads of State and Government. The CCJ's primary function is to observe law and justice in the interpretation and application of the provisions of the treaty and other legal instruments. It is also responsible for settling disputes among member states.[11] ECOWAS retained the scope of the CCJ in the ECOWAS Revised Treaty of 1993,[12] when the ECOWAS member states revised the 1975 treaty to strengthen their processes to benefit from international and regional developments. The Revised Treaty also identified the CCJ as the final arbiter for settling disputes under the treaty.[13]

The CCJ has the competence to ensure respect for law and equity in the interpretation and application of the ECOWAS Treaty.[14] The CCJ could deal with matters referred to it by member states or the Authority of Heads of State and Government in ECOWAS concerning disputes between member states or by one or more member states and an ECOWAS institution on the interpretation and application of the ECOWAS treaty.[15] In situations involving nationals of member states, the 1991 Protocol envisaged that after attempts at amicable settlements have failed, a member state of the concerned nationals may institute proceedings against another member state or ECOWAS institution.[16] The 1991 Protocol, therefore, did not grant non-state actors direct access to the CCJ. Although ECOWAS set up the CCJ in 1991, it only became operational in 2001 on the swearing-in of the first set of judges on January 30, 2001, in Bamako, Mali.[17]

In 2005, ECOWAS adopted the Supplementary Protocol,[18] which effectively granted access to individuals to bring cases, including on human rights matters, before the CCJ. ECOWAS amended Article 9 of the 1991 Protocol to expand the jurisdiction and competence of the court to accommodate such human rights claims,[19] and a new Article 10 on access to the court[20] was inserted that expressly provided for ECOWAS member states, its Executive Secretary, its Council of Ministers, individuals, and corporate bodies to bring disputes before the court, as relevant. Individuals may bring human rights applications to the court provided that they are not anonymous and not before another international court.[21] Moreover, there is no need for applicants to exhaust local remedies before approaching the CCJ.[22]

The expansion of the human rights mandate of the CCJ was welcomed and opened possibilities for victims of human rights violations to plead any human rights treaty ratified by the state concerned (Ebobrah, 2010). As of October 2017, the CCJ had delivered 249 verdicts.[23] In the 2018/2019 legal year, the court delivered 28 judgments and 8 rulings,[24] and currently, over 130 decisions are published on its website.[25] Of the total number of cases heard and rulings delivered, only five decisions have ruled on gender.[26]

Background: African Court on Human and Peoples' Rights

The Organisation of African Unity (OAU), the predecessor of the African Union (AU), created the African Court in 1998 when it adopted the Protocol to the African Charter on Human and Peoples' Rights on the Establishment of an African Court on Human and Peoples' Rights.[27] The African Court's mandate was to protect human rights as provided for in the African Charter on Human and Peoples' Rights (African Charter) and other human rights treaties ratified by the state concerned.[28] In carrying out its role, it complements the protective mandate of the African Commission on Human and Peoples' Rights (ACHPR).[29] The ACHPR suffers weak enforcement of its recommendations by member states (Udombana, 2000).

The African Court's reach potentially covers all the 55 member states of the AU that are parties to the African Charter.[30] However, it may only adjudicate cases involving states that have ratified the African Court's constitutive Protocol.[31] The African Court may receive petitions from the ACHPR, States Parties, or African inter-governmental organizations.[32] Individuals and non-governmental organizations (NGOs) cannot directly bring cases before it except where ratifying states have made a declaration accepting the competence of the African Court to receive such cases from these kinds of actors.[33] At the time of writing, nine countries, Burkina Faso, Benin, Ghana, The Gambia, Côte d'Ivoire, Mali, Malawi, Tanzania, and Tunisia, have made this declaration.[34]

The African Court shared similar set-up challenges with the CCJ. It became operational in 2006 when the first judges were elected.[35] It also took some time before it received cases.[36] However, by July 2020, the African Court had received 285 cases and finalized 100,[37] of which only 1 case is on gender discrimination. As long as cases in this area are not filed, there will be fewer decisions.

Analyses of five cases before the CCJ and the African Court

The following analysis focuses on four cases from the CCJ and one from the African Court where the complaints alleged gender discrimination.

Gender discrimination and the Dorothy Njemanze case

Dorothy Njemanze and 3 Others v Nigeria (2017) was the first time a regional court interpreted women's rights contained in the Protocol to the African

Charter on Human and Peoples' Rights on the Rights of Women in Africa (the Maputo Protocol), and this was lauded as a ground-breaking judgment (Ojigho, 2017). Dorothy Njemanze and three other women, Edu Oroko, Justina Etim, and Amarachi Jessyford, had separately been picked up by the Nigerian security agents (including the police) and agents of the Abuja Environmental Protection Board (AEPB) in Abuja, the federal capital city in Nigeria. These state agents would carry out raids claiming that in keeping the Abuja environment clean, they also had to remove prostitutes. They forcibly took any woman they saw on the streets at night, labeling them prostitutes and putting them in buses to convey them to detention centers. Many women, including the petitioners, experienced beatings, verbal abuse, sexual assault, and threats during the raids and subsequently, in detention. Some made complaints to the police and other state institutions. However, none of the Nigerian authorities investigated the allegations or held anyone responsible for the violations the women had experienced.

The petitioners in *Dorothy Njemanze's case* argued that the raids were discriminatory, as they targeted women. No men were abducted or harassed during the raids by the state agents. The CCJ analyzed the evidence before it and concluded that the

> whole hug [*sic*] of the operation was targeted against women. This systematic sting operation directed against only the female gender furnishes evidence of discrimination. There is an obligation placed on State Parties to the Convention on Elimination of All Forms of Discrimination against Women (CEDAW) to adopt laws, administrative, and Policy measures to prevent gender-based discrimination. Prostitution is claimed to be a crime in the laws of the Defendant [Nigeria]. However, it takes two persons to engage in such criminal activity. There is no law that suggest that when women are seen on the streets at midnight or anytime thereafter, they are necessarily idle persons or prostitutes. If it were so, it ought to apply to all persons irrespective of sex.[38]

The CCJ held, therefore, that the treatment the petitioners experienced by agents of the AEPB and the security forces constituted gender-based discriminatory treatment contrary to Articles 2, 3, and 18(3) of the African Charter, Articles 2 and 8 of the Maputo Protocol, Articles 2, 3, and 15 (1) of CEDAW, Articles 2 (1), 3, and 26 of the International Covenant on Civil and Political Rights, and Articles 2 and 7 of the Universal Declaration of Human Rights.

The defendant state, Nigeria, did not dispute that the perpetrators of these violations against the women were its agents. It followed, therefore, that Nigeria was responsible for the actions of its agents under international law.[39] Moreover, the failure and refusal of the Nigerian authorities to investigate allegations of violations against its agents, despite the formal complaints made, constituted a breach of the defendant states' duty under international law. Nigeria had failed to recognize, promote, and protect the rights of the women in the case. Furthermore, failure by Nigeria to take measures to give effect to their rights amounted to multiple violations of Articles 2, 3, 4 (1) and (2), 5, 8, and 25 of the Maputo Protocol, Articles 1, 2, 3, 5, and 18(3) of the African Charter, Articles 2, 3, 5(a) and 15 (1) of CEDAW, and other relevant international treaties. The CCJ held that the women experienced cruel, inhumane, and degrading treatment, which violated Articles 3 and 4 (1) of the Maputo Protocol on the dignity of person and rights to life, integrity, and security of person.

The CCJ awarded six million Naira (approximately US$16,500) as damages to each complainant except one, Edu Oroko. Under Article 9 (3) of the Supplementary Protocol, an alleged violation must be brought to the CCJ within three years. However, Edu Oroko's violation had occurred much earlier, and the CCJ dismissed it as outside the time limit and barred by the statute.

In many respects, the decision in *Dorothy Njemanze's case* reflects a challenge posed by traditional perceptions about women's behavior and gender stereotypes. The state's defense rested on the notion that women found at night are "prostitutes"; therefore, they are immoral, and violence against them is justified.

The CCJ did not interrogate intensely the cultural and social beliefs and practices that contribute to gender discrimination or how this contravenes international human rights laws. But the case did give an opening to challenge so-called vagrancy laws and archaic prostitution laws that discriminate against marginalized and vulnerable groups and sex workers (Chakaya, 2017). A rule that marks and victimizes one gender over another and labels persons based on social status or perceptions creates a dangerous tool that enables an environment where human rights violations can persist.

O'Connell criticized the CCJ for missing an opportunity to analyze the impact of such discriminatory laws and their application on sex workers (O'Connell, 2019). The CCJ did not provide a thorough analysis of each of the rights claimed by the women, e.g., rights to dignity, life, integrity, and security of the person, and to access justice and equal protection before the law. If it had done so, then the logical conclusion would be that every person, regardless of their social status, is entitled to these rights (O'Connell, 2019). Moreover, the fact that the violence the applicants faced was linked to their alleged "business of commercial sex work" leaves the issue open for abuse by creating the impression that violence against sex workers is permissible (O'Connell, 2019).

Dorothy and the other women were not sex workers, and the thrust of their case was to address gender-based violence and gender discrimination exacerbated by cultural, religious, and traditional views about the role of women in society. While the case would have benefited from a comprehensive interpretation of the rights in the Maputo Protocol and other international human rights instruments, particularly within the African context, it remains, for now, the lone case at the CCJ that has pronounced against gender discrimination.

Slavery and equality in the Hadijatou Mani Koraou case

In *Hadijatou Mani Koraou v Niger*,[40] a woman named Hadijatou, who had been sold as a slave for 240,000 CFA in 1996 when she was a 12-year-old girl, brought a suit against the Republic of Niger, alleging violations of her human rights and seeking compensation. She endured many years of hard labor, sexual harassment, and rape by her master, El Hadj Souleymane Naroua. On August 18, 2005, her master gave her a freedom certificate, stamped by a village chief, which meant she was no longer a slave. However, the master denied Hadijatou the right to leave and insisted that she remained in his household as a wife. When she got the opportunity to visit her mother, Hadijatou left and did not return. In February 2006, Hadijatou filed a suit in the local courts for a declaration that a marriage had never happened between Naroua and herself. The court at the first instance held that they were never properly married. Naroua contested the suit, and it was overturned on appeal at the High Court. On further appeal to the Supreme Court, Hadijatou invoked a violation of Niger's law on "slavery and slavery-related practices" in her suit. While the Supreme Court quashed the High Court decision, it only referred for the issue of slavery re-examination.

While waiting for the final decision, Hadijatou moved on with her life and met Ladan Rabo, whom she married. Naroua was displeased and accused Hadijatou of bigamy, leading to the police arresting her, her husband, and her brother, Koraou Mani. The High Court found them guilty and sentenced them to six months' imprisonment and a fine. While in detention, Hadijatou, through her lawyers, filed a complaint, which led the state prosecutor to bring a criminal charge of slavery against Naroua at the High Court's criminal division. The same High Court in its civil division held that Hadijatou was "divorced" from Naroua. He challenged this by seeking an annulment of the decision. Eventually, the Court of Appeal provisionally released Hadijatou and her brother on appeal. The Court of Appeal also revoked the arrest warrant of Ladan Rabo.

On September 14, 2007, Hadijatou filed a case against Niger at the CCJ, alleging that her experience of slavery violated her human rights and was discriminatory, in contravention of Articles 1, 2, 3, 5, 6, and 18 (3) of the African Charter. She argued that Niger failed to take appropriate measures to protect and enforce human rights, and violated its laws and the constitution, which ensures equal protection before the law without distinction and punishes torture and cruel, inhuman, or degrading treatment. She further demanded that the court direct Niger to enact laws that protect women against discriminatory customs relating to marriage and divorce as well as abolish harmful customs and practices that discriminate against women.

The CCJ stated that its core mandate was hearing human rights violation cases and declined to review the laws of Niger, suggesting, rather, that there are many monitoring bodies, such as the ACHPR, which play this role.[41] The court found that it was undeniable that Hadijatou was a victim of slavery. Despite the legal prohibition of the practice in Niger, she had not been able to get justice in the legal system. Therefore, the Republic of Niger was liable for the inaction of its administrative and judicial authorities. In compensation for the harms she had suffered, the CCJ ordered the state to pay her 10 million CFA francs (approximately US$20,000).

On whether Hadijatou had suffered gender discrimination, the CCJ curiously declared that the discrimination she suffered is not attributable to the Republic of Niger. Hadijatou was sold under the practice of *Wahiya*, where a girl slave works as a servant and a concubine. Such female slaves are referred to as *Sadaka*, or fifth wife, denoting a concubine, since they are not part of the four legal wives recognized under Islam. Hadijatou had argued that because only females were affected by the kind of slavery she endured; this was gender discrimination. The CCJ held that Hadijatou was discriminated only in relation to the other wives of her former master, and that the Republic of Niger did not cause the discrimination but, rather, her former master, who was not a party to the case before it.[42] It is hard to understand the court's rationale for taking this position. States have international obligations to protect, respect, and fulfill human rights. The CCJ should have probed the state's actions or inaction (in this case) and reviewed how this contributed to the continued discrimination faced by women due to the institution of customary practices like the *Wahiya*. The court, therefore, missed an opportunity to pronounce strongly on gender discrimination and in the process, leaves us with a judgment that is in certain aspects inconsistent with international law and practice (Duffy, 2008).

Domestic violence in the Mary Sunday case

In *Mary Sunday v Nigeria*,[43] the CCJ was presented with facts of a violent incident on August 24, 2012, between the applicant, Mary Sunday, and her fiancé Corporal Isaac Gbanwuan, which resulted in Mary sustaining severe burns all over her body. Mary's fiancé allegedly kicked and dragged her on the floor, and to escape him, Mary ran to a neighbor's kitchen. It is reported that he was so angry he broke the kitchen door and then carried the neighbor's cooking stove with hot oil on it and poured the contents on Mary. In the process, the stove exploded and set her body on fire. Mary's family reported the incident to the police. The police claimed that they investigated the matter but concluded that it was Mary who accidentally burned herself while attempting to pour the contents on her fiancé. While following up on her complaint, a Ministry of Justice official informed Mary that the police had referred the matter to a court. Unfortunately, the police prosecutor handling the case died, and her case file was missing.

Mary, with the support of two NGOs, applied to the CCJ for justice in August 2015. In her application, she claimed that the failure of the state to conduct an independent and diligent investigation and prosecution of the perpetrator (her fiancé) was a violation of her human rights to an effective remedy and freedom from gender-based violence and discrimination against women. She also argued that Nigeria violated her right to health by the state's failure to provide adequate medical services and to protect her from domestic violence, and that the inability of the state to treat her injuries inhibited her rehabilitation, thereby violating her right to work.

The CCJ, as in *Hadijatou's case*, found no difficulty in holding the Nigerian government in the *Mary Sunday case* responsible for failing to provide an effective remedy for the applicant, thereby violating her right to access to justice. It was clear to the judges that the fact that the Nigerian police did not carry out an investigation observing minimum standards to establish the truth or to facilitate an independent prosecution, especially in this case where the allegations of violence involved a police officer, was a failure on the part of the state. The fact that the applicant's case file went missing at the state judiciary was held to constitute a "blatant disregard for the right of access of a litigant to a judge in a court of law."[44] The CCJ awarded Mary 15 million Naira (approximately US$41,500), in compensation for all the harms she had suffered against the Federal Republic of Nigeria.

The CCJ established the state's failure to provide an effective remedy by linking the steps taken and the seriousness of Mary's injuries. The CCJ concluded that it was safe to infer that running to a neighbor's kitchen meant that Mary feared for her life as a result of the violence she experienced. As Mary was present in court during the hearings, the judges saw the extent of her wounds. They reprimanded the state agents for failing to consider them grave enough to warrant a proper investigation. The CCJ rejected the state's position that the incident between Mary and her fiancé was a private matter, stating that the issue is not the incident or perpetrators at stake but whether the steps available to a complainant lead to access to justice. The court also firmly reasoned that if states could use the defense that they would not meddle in private matters, then impunity could arise in the case of certain violations committed in families. The CCJ further reasoned that the progressive view is for the state to find ways to combat violence, including in homes, and the influence of the law does not stop on the "doorsteps of the homes of married couples."[45]

However, in examining whether Mary suffered gender discrimination, the CCJ restricted itself to a definition of exclusion that affects a "generality" of the gender in question, and those acts must show a "systematic" feature to determine that discrimination is at stake. It found that Mary's situation fell within the private domain, in the family, and did not show a "general" or "systematic" feature, and that the facts applied only to one person and not to all persons of the female gender. The court further noted that intimate partner violence does not directly or indirectly implicate the state. The fact that Mary's fiancé was a police officer and therefore, an agent of the state is irrelevant, as the violence occurred in the home, and even if he were acting in the performance of his duties, any acts committed would be considered assault. In all cases, the actions which Mary complained about are the acts of an individual who can be brought before a national court for justice. The CCJ, therefore, dismissed the allegation of gender-based discrimination. The CCJ did not see the link between the failure of the state to investigate Mary's wounds and the endemic tolerance of violence against women in society, which leads to such complaints being treated as a less severe violation by the state.

According to the World Bank, gender-based violence is a global pandemic affecting one in three women in their lifetime. About 35% of women worldwide have experienced either physical or sexual intimate partner violence or non-partner sexual violence, and globally, 38% of murders of women are committed by an intimate partner (World Bank, 2019). In Nigeria, an analysis of the 2013 Demographic and Health Survey showed that about one-fourth of Nigerian women had experienced some form of intimate partner violence (Benebo et al., 2018).

The shocking statistic is the reality faced by many women, and the resistance of the courts against holding states responsible for failing to protect victims of domestic violence under the pretext that it is in the private sphere is a crushing blow to women everywhere who run to the courts for protection.

Women and family life in the Aminata Diantou Diane case

In *Aminata Diantou Diane v Mali*,[46] the applicant was in dispute with her sick husband's brothers over the management of his property. Aminata was married to Mahamadou Samassa, and they had five children together. He became very ill, leading to him being bed-ridden even though the family took him abroad for medical treatment. As his illness persisted, his brothers sought to hold his property in trust, excluding the wife and putting her and her children at risk. One of Aminata's brothers-in-law, Cheickna Hamalla Samassa, presented a document allegedly giving him power of attorney to administer the properties. Aminata contested this and the takeover of her husband's properties in the Malian court. At the time of writing, no hearing had taken place in the Malian courts on the contested power of attorney. Similarly, another brother-in-law, Sekou Samassa, a judge, filed an application in court for the trusteeship of his brother's properties, which the court granted. Aminata appealed this decision. The Malian Court of Appeal, ruling in her favor, relied on the Malian Code on Persons and Families, which provides that where a man's wife is alive and of sound mind, the trusteeship of a married man shall not be granted to another person.[47] The Supreme Court dismissed Sekou Samassa's subsequent appeal. Despite the court's decision, the brothers-in-law continued to contest access to the properties and accused Aminata of attempting to kidnap their brother. Aminata decided to file a separate suit before the Malian court accusing them of forgery, assault and battery, illegal confinement, and abetment. Eventually, in June 2015, the brothers took Mahamadou Samassa to an unknown place. Aminata brought a case seeking redress against her brothers-in-law and the police officers for violence against her and kidnapping her husband. As the cases stalled, Aminata decided to approach the CCJ in August 2017.

The CCJ, in examining the facts before it, took into cognizance several relevant provisions of international treaties, such as Article 18 of the African Charter, Articles 2 and 26 of CEDAW, Articles 4, 5, and 18 of African Charter on the Rights and Welfare of the Child (ACERWC), and Articles 2, 3, 4, 6, and 8 of the Maputo Protocol. These provisions collectively address rights to dignity and freedom from discrimination, and urge States Parties to combat all forms of violence against women and children and eliminate harmful practices. Aminata argued that the state failed to protect her against the violations by her in-laws, and that the customs her in-laws used to dispossess her of her husband's properties legitimized discrimination against women. She also decried the long delays in getting the Malian courts to investigate and prosecute and alleged that this violated the enjoyment of her rights. The Mali government reiterated the position of the applicant's brothers-in-law by claiming that the applicant was on a mission to hasten the death of her husband so that together with her children, she could enjoy his properties as an inheritance exclusively. They admitted, though, that the applicant had filed four complaints, which were still pending.

The CCJ in interpreting Article 18 of the African Charter stated that the obligation to protect the family, particularly women and children, is binding on the state and it is the state's responsibility to ensure that women and children are not exposed to threats and prosecution as a result of their vulnerability. The CCJ held, therefore, that Mali had violated Aminata's and her children's right to protection. The CCJ also found that her right to fair hearing in a reasonable time had been violated and ordered the government of Mali to pay her 15 million CFA francs (approximately $US27,000) in reparation for the suffering she had endured. The court also ordered Mali to take all necessary steps to find Mahamadou Samassa but dismissed all the applicant's other requests.

Once more, the CCJ avoided a clear pronouncement on gender discrimination, preferring to rely only on Article 18 of the African Charter without delving into the applicant's complaints that her rights under the relevant provisions of the Maputo Protocol, which Mali had ratified,[48] had been violated. Strangely, the court did not avail itself of the progressive provisions in the Maputo Protocol, which directed states to eliminate harmful cultural practices and take steps to enforce equal rights in marriage and women's freedom from discrimination and violence. But like the national courts, it appears that the CCJ is avoiding this Pan-African women's treaty. While resistance is expected, it is disheartening that the CCJ appears to favor a narrow and strict focus in interpreting gender discrimination even where the applicants plead violations of the Maputo Protocol.

Equal rights in marriage and inheritance in the APDF and IHRDA V Mali case

So far, only one case has been decided on gender discrimination at the African Court. In *APDF and IHRDA v Mali*,[49] two NGOs, a Malian women's rights organization and a Pan-African human rights organization based in The Gambia, alleged that the Republic of Mali's Family Code of 2011 violated some provisions of key human rights treaties. The Family Code reduced the minimum age of marriage for girls, limited the rights to consent to a marriage and inheritance for women and natural children, and the state's obligation to eliminate practices or traditions against women and children. Mali had ratified many human rights treaties, including the African Charter, the Maputo Protocol, the ACERWC, and CEDAW.

In 2009, the Malian authorities concluded a reform process to update Mali's marriage and family laws by proposing a new Family Code. While this law offered much promise, it faced opposition by many religious bodies, which protested strongly that the law conflicted with some Islamic practices. Mali, a predominantly Muslim country, was keen to have broad acceptance of the draft law and proceeded to amend it. On December 30, 2011, the government enacted the Family Code, which in many aspects, imposed differences in treatment for girls compared with boys. While the minimum age of marriage for boys was set at 18 years old, in conformity with international human rights minimum standards, the minimum age of marriage for girls was set at 16 years old. The law further provides for approvals through a special exemption for marriage at 15 years old, provided for a boy, his mother's or father's consent is obtained, while for a girl, only the father's consent is required. The African Court found that the obligation to guarantee compliance with the minimum age of marriage and the right to non-discrimination lies with the state, and it had failed to do so in this instance, in violation of Article 6(b) of the Maputo Protocol and Articles 2, 4 (1), and 21 of ACERWC.

The African Court also found that the Family Code statutorily made Islamic law applicable as one of the options for determining inheritance. Islamic law does not give women equal inheritance rights, and children born out of wedlock are not accorded an inheritance by right but only as a discretionary favor. Therefore, the African Court decided that these practices were not in conformity with international human rights standards. Overall, the African Court found that by including discriminatory practices against women and children in the Family Code, Mali had violated its international commitments.[50]

The African Court granted all the prayers of the applicants, holding Mali in violation of several provisions of international treaties. Besides, it held that Mali had violated the right to non-discrimination of women and children as guaranteed by Article 2 of the Maputo Protocol, Articles 3 and 4 of ACERWC, and Article 16 (1) of CEDAW. This decision clarifies that acts or inactions of a state that affect women can lead to or condone gender-based discrimination. By being ordered to amend the Family Code and harmonize its laws, the state needed to ensure that its laws and customary practices do not constitute discrimination against the principles of equality and freedom from discrimination, which it is obligated to promote, respect, and fulfill.

While there are challenges in lumping women and children together, which can feed into stereotypes about women's capacity and agency (Davis, 2017), it is significant in this judgment because it focused on the rights of women and the girl-child, who are most affected by negative or harmful traditional and religious practices regarding rights in marriage and family life (Goonesekere & De Silva-De Alwis, 2005). However, regarding the rights of inheritance for children born out of wedlock, all children, regardless of gender, are affected. It was important to the court that discrimination on social status and the circumstances of one's birth needed to be addressed.

It is worth noting that during the proceedings, Mali recognized that the Family Code it enacted was not perfect. The state raised the huge threat and pushback it had faced from religious bodies, which had led to the passing of the compromised law. The state had argued that it had to balance social-cultural realities in Mali to prevent a situation where it could not implement the law.[51] In the same proceedings, the state argued that, fully aware of the resistance, it had embarked on raising public awareness and sensitization on the rights of women and children.[52] Therefore, Mali should not have much difficulty in complying with the African Court's decision to inform and educate its people on freedoms and rights as provided in Article 25 of the African Charter. The state was also ordered to submit a report on measures it had taken to comply with the decisions of the African Court within two years from the date of the judgment.[53] The judgment was delivered on May 11, 2018.

Mali is one of the countries where child marriage, often girls married to much older men, is rampant.[54] Several studies exist on the health risks to child brides and the impact of child marriage on girls' education, sexual and reproductive health of women and girls, women's economic empowerment, and poverty alleviation (Girls Not Brides, 2015). The state, therefore, in compliance with international human rights laws, can amend the Family Code to eliminate harmful practices to improve the lives of all girls and women.

Conclusion

Across Africa, women face challenges in enforcing their human rights. Conservative social attitudes, gender norms, customary law, and cultural practices are some of the difficulties encountered in implementing women's rights (IPPF Africa Region, 2018). In analyzing the five cases so far on women's rights, it appears that regional courts are willing to find a case of gender discrimination against a state if state agents are involved and if the issues in the case affect more than one woman. It can be inferred that the number of applicants in *Dorothy Njemanze's case* may have helped to show a pattern of human rights violations. In that case, one of the women had her case struck out for being out of time, but there was a high likelihood that their chances of success were higher because this was a joint petition. Each woman's case helped to strengthen the others. There is no doubt that the involvement of state agents shows that the state can be held responsible for the actions of its agents, provided they are working in their professional capacity. In Mary Sunday, the alleged perpetrator, the survivor's fiancé, was a policeman—an agent of the state. Yet, the court did not think it was key, because this was a personal matter, and he was not working when the violent incident happened.

In all cases, the state in question must have ratified the relevant international treaties. In *Hadijatou's case*, Niger had ratified CEDAW but not ratified the Maputo Protocol at that time. Perhaps the claimant could have benefited from provisions of the Maputo Protocol on the elimination of harmful practices against women in Africa if it had been ratified by Niger. And the decision, in that case, could have been different, since she would have claimed that the slavery she experienced was a harmful traditional practice against women and girls. The CCJ has also made it clear in *SERAP v Nigeria*[55] and several cases since that it will give precedence to international treaties over a state's national laws. Therefore, a practice of studying international treaties and applying them to local contexts would be a strong tool in the hands of an advocate for gender equality. Similarly, affected communities and groups must act as of necessity, working with advocacy groups and the relevant United Nations and AU bodies to ensure that African states ratify treaties to ensure access of the population in the continent to justice based on international standards and norms.

However, the CCJ appears to hesitate in linking violations committed in the family to failings of the state. Unlike the *Dorothy Njemanze case*, the three other cases before the CCJ analyzed in this chapter were decided differently. While the CCJ in each of these cases found that the women had suffered various human rights violations, the CCJ refrained from declaring any of the violations as constituting gender discrimination. In *Aminata's case*, the brothers of her husband were abusive and had used their influence in public life to harass and attack her. Yet, the court felt this was a family matter. Similarly, in the cases of *Mary Sunday* and *Hadijatou*, the participation of family members or close relatives in the commission of the acts seem to give the court leeway to distinguish the discriminatory acts the women experienced as social vices rather than gender discrimination. The CCJ chose to narrow the state's obligation to respect, protect, and fulfill the rights of women and missed the chance to impose stronger state interventions for preventing and punishing gender discrimination.

The African Court, in its first case on gender discrimination, was quite progressive. The time for the Malian government to report on the implementation of the decision against it lapsed in May 2020. At the time of writing, information was not available to confirm whether a report had been submitted. The implementation report would have offered an opportunity to evaluate the effectiveness of the court and for the Malian government to show, at the minimum, steps taken to educate the populace about gender equality and any progress made since the judgment. Such a review would contribute to advancing the status of women in the continent.

The CCJ offers tremendous opportunities for human rights litigation in West Africa. The unique characteristic of dispensing with the requirement that litigants first exhaust domestic remedies makes it a court of the first instance and increases access for individuals and NGOs. It continues to strengthen its jurisprudence. In February 2018, the CCJ finally put to rest the issue of the time limit for bringing actions before the court, which had previously affected one of the women in *Dorothy Njemanze's case*, by holding in *FAJ v The Gambia*[56] that there are no time limits for bringing human rights cases before it and overruled its previous decisions stating otherwise.

Both the CCJ and the African Court will, of course, need to update their understanding and evolution of women's human rights jurisprudence. The court will benefit from the expertise of African gender experts and experiences from other international jurisdictions and the United Nations Treaty bodies in taking a progressive and comprehensive approach to addressing historical gender discrimination cases in Africa.

Notes

1 There are other African regional courts, such as the East African Court of Justice (EACJ) and the Southern African Development Community (SADC) Tribunal, which are not examined because the focus is on courts that have received cases on gender discrimination. There are also challenges with the human rights jurisdiction of the EACJ, and the SADC Tribunal remains suspended. More information on the status of these courts is available at Luambano, T.R. (2018). Litigating human rights through the East African Court of Justice: Overview and challenges. *Journal of Law, Policy, and Globalization*, (71), 76–90; Swart, M. (2018, April). *A house of justice for Africa: Resurrecting the SADC Tribunal* [Weblog post]. Retrieved from https://www.brookings.edu/blog/africa-in-focus/2018/04/02/a-house-of-justice-for-africa-resurrecting-the-sadc-tribunal/
2 (2018) ECW/CCJ/JUD/14/18.
3 (2008) ECW/CCJ/JUD/06/08.
4 (2017) ECW/CCJ/JUD/08/17.
5 (2018) ECW/CCJ/JUD/11/18.
6 (2018) Application No. 046/2016.
7 Treaty of the Economic Community of West African States (ECOWAS) 1975. Reproduced in the United Nations Treaty Series (1976), *1010*(14843), 17. Hereafter referred to as the 1975 Treaty: https://treaties.un.org/doc/Publication/UNTS/Volume%201010/v1010.pdf
8 The original members were 16 until Mauritania withdrew its membership in 2000. News24 Archives (2000, December 28). *Mauritania out of ECOWAS*. Retrieved from https://www.news24.com/xArchive/Archive/Mauritania-out-of-ECOWAS-20001228
9 Arts. 4, 11 of the 1975 Treaty.
10 Protocol A/P.I./7/91 on the Community Court of Justice. Hereafter the 1991 Protocol.
11 Arts. 11, 56 1975 Treaty; Preamble to 1991 Protocol.
12 Economic Community of West African States (ECOWAS) Revised Treaty 1993. Adopted in Cotonou on July 24, 1993. Hereafter referred to as the Revised Treaty. https://www.ecowas.int/wp-content/uploads/2015/01/Revised-treaty.pdf
13 Art. 76, 6 (1)(e), 15 ECOWAS Revised Treaty 1993.
14 Art 9 (1) 1991 Protocol.
15 Art 9 (2) 1991 Protocol.
16 Art 9 (3) 1991 Protocol.
17 ECOWAS CCJ Annual Report (2002) para 9. Retrieved from http://prod.courtecowas.org/annual-reports-2/
18 Supplementary Protocol A/SP.1/01/05. Hereafter the 2005 Protocol.
19 Art. 3, 2005 Protocol
20 Art. 4, 2005 Protocol
21 Art. 10(d) in Art. 4, 2005 Protocol.
22 Valentine Ayika v. Republic of Liberia (2012) ECW/CCJ/AAP/07/11.
23 See Agency report (2017, October 9). ECOWAS Court delivers 249 verdicts in 16 years. *Premium Times*. Retrieved from https://www.premiumtimesng.com/foreign/west-africa-foreign/245545-ecowas-court-delivers-249-verdicts-16-years.html
24 See NAN (2019, July 12). ECOWAS court records highest number of judgment, ruling in 2018/19. *The Guardian*. Retrieved from https://guardian.ng/news/ecowas-court-records-highest-number-of-judgment-ruling-in-2018-2019/
25 http://prod.courtecowas.org/decisions-3/
26 Four of the cases are analyzed in this chapter. The fifth gender ruling is the case of Women Against Violence and Exploitation in Society (WAVES) v Sierra Leone (2019) ECW/CCJ/APP/22/18, which was decided after the selection of the cases for this chapter.
27 Hereafter, African Court Protocol. It was adopted at the 34th ordinary session of the OAU Assembly, held June 8–10, 1998 in Ouagadougou, Burkina Faso, and entered

into force on January 25, 2004 upon deposit of 15 ratification instruments. Full text available at the African Union website: https://au.int/en/treaties/1164

28 Article 3, African Court Protocol.

29 (ACHPR). Article 2, African Court Protocol.

30 Art 3, African Court Protocol. Note that all member states of the AU except Morocco have ratified the African Charter. For status of ratification: https://au.int/en/treaties/1164

31 Art 34, African Court Protocol.

32 Art 5 (1), African Court Protocol.

33 Arts 5 (3), 34 (6), African Court Protocol.

34 Tanzania, in November 2019, wrote to the African Union of its intention to withdraw its declaration; if all advocacy fails, it will become the second country to do so following Rwanda's withdrawal in 2016. See Afrimechanisms hub (2019, Dec 2) [Tweet]. Retrieved from https://twitter.com/AfrimechsHub/status/1201572103176302592. Rwanda Ministry of Justice Press Release. Retrieved from https://minijust.gov.rw/fileadmin/Documents/Photo_News_2016/Clarification2.pdf; Benin and Côte d'Ivoire, in reaction to judgments of the court in March and April, 2020, respectively, have now indicated their intention to withdraw their declaration. See International Justice Resource Centre (2020, May 6). Retrieved from https://ijrcenter.org/2020/05/06/benin-and-cote-divoire-to-withdraw-individual-access-to-african-court/. See also Adjolohoun, S. (2020). A crisis of design and judicial practice? Curbing state disengagement from the African Court on Human and Peoples' Rights. *African Human Rights Law Journal*, (*20*)(1), 1–40. Retrieved from https://www.ahrlj.up.ac.za/adjolohoun-s-h.This means that direct access to the African Court will be greatly reduced going forward.

35 The decision on the election of judges of the African Court on Human and Peoples' Rights (2006) EX.CL/Dec.261 (VIII), Eighth Ordinary Session of the Executive Council of the African Union, Retrieved from https://au.int/sites/default/files/decisions/9639-ex_cl_dec_236_-_277_viii_e.pdf

36 Its first case, Yogogombaye v Senegal (2008) Application No. 001/2008, was dismissed for lack of jurisdiction.

37 African Court statistical information. Retrieved from https://www.african-court.org/en/index.php/cases/2016-10-17-16-18-21

38 Per Justice Friday Chijoke Nwoke, at 38 Dorothy Njemanze's case.

39 See Velasquez Rodrigues v. Honduras (1988), Series C, No. 4, paras. 170 referred to in Dorothy Njemanze's case at 39.

40 (2008) ECW/CCJ/JUD/06/08.

41 Paragraphs 60 and 61, Hadijatou's case.

42 Paragraphs 70 and 71 of Hadijatou's case.

43 Women Advocates Research and Documentation Center and Institute for Human Rights and Development in Africa (On behalf of Mary Sunday) v The Federal Republic of Nigeria. (2018). ECW/CCJ/JUD/11/18. Retrieved from http://prod.courtecowas.org/wp-content/uploads/2019/02/ECW_CCJ_JUG_11_18.pdf. After this, referred to as Mary Sunday's case.

44 Mary Sunday's case, the official English translation of the case [Translator: Emmanuel Nkansah] at 10.

45 Ibid at 8, 9.

46 ECW/CCJ/JUD/14/18. After this, Aminata's case. http://prod.courtecowas.org/wp-content/uploads/2019/02/ECW_CCJ_JUG_14_18.pdf

47 Paragraph 6, at 4 in Aminata's case, official English translation from the court's registry.

48 Mali ratified the Maputo Protocol in January, 2005. See Status of Maputo Protocol on African Union's website. https://au.int/en/treaties

49 Association Pour le Progrès et la Défense des Droits des Femmes Maliennes (APDF) and The Institute for Human Rights and Development in Africa (IHRDA) v Republic

of Mali (2018). Retrieved from http://www.african-court.org/en/index.php/56-pendi ng-cases-details/942-app-no-046-2016-apdf-ihrda-v-republic-of-mali-details
50 Paragraphs 124, APDF v Mali case.
51 Paragraphs 63–66, APDF v Mali case.
52 Paragraph 119, APDF v Mali.
53 Paragraph 135 (xiii), APDF v Mali .
54 See Paragraph 61, APDF v Mali, where applicants in their petition presented World Bank statistics showing that between 2012 and 2013, 59.9% of Malian women 18–22 years old were married before their 18th birthday.
55 SERAP v. the Federal Republic of Nigeria and the Universal Basic Education Commission (2010). ECW/CCJ/JUD/07/10.
56 Federation of African Journalists & 4 Ors v The Republic of The Gambia (2018). ECW/CCJ/JUD/04/18. http://prod.courtecowas.org/wp-content/uploads/2019/02/ECW_CCJ_JUD_04_18.pdf

Constitutions and legislation

African Charter on Human and Peoples' Rights
African Charter on the Rights and Welfare of the Child (ACERWC)
Convention on Elimination of All Forms of Discrimination against Women (CEDAW)
ECOWAS Revised Treaty 1993
Protocol A/P.I./7/91 on the Community Court of Justice of ECOWAS
Protocol to the African Charter on Human and Peoples' Rights on the Establishment of an African Court on Human and Peoples' Rights
Supplementary Protocol A/SP.1/01/05 of ECOWAS
Treaty of the ECOWAS 1975

Case law

Aminata Diantou Diane (represented by APDF & IHRDA) v Mali (2018) ECW/CCJ/JUD/14/18
Association Pour le Progrès et la Défense des Droits des Femmes Maliennes (APDF) and The Institute for Human Rights and Development in Africa (IHRDA) v Republic of Mali (2018) Application No. 046/2016
Yogogombaye v Senegal (2008) Application No. 001/2008
SERAP v. the Federal Republic of Nigeria and the Universal Basic Education Commission (2010) ECW/CCJ/JUD/07/10
Federation of African Journalists & 4 Ors v The Republic of The Gambia (2018) ECW/CCJ/JUD/04/18
Hadijatou Mani v Niger (2008) ECW/CCJ/JUD/06/08
Dorothy Njemanze & 3 Ors. v Nigeria (2017) ECW/CCJ/JUD/08/17
Mary Sunday v Nigeria (2018) ECW/CCJ/JUD/11/18
Valentine Ayika v Republic of Liberia (2012) ECW/CCJ/AAP/07/11

References

Adjolohoun, S (2020) A crisis of design and judicial practice? Curbing state disengagement from the African Court on Human and Peoples' Rights. *African Human Rights Law Journal*, 20(1), 1–40 https://www.ahrlj.up.ac.za/adjolohoun-s-h

Agency Report (2017, October 9). ECOWAS Court delivers 249 verdicts in 16 years. *Premium Times*. Retrieved from https://www.premiumtimesng.com/foreign/west-africa-foreign/245545-ecowas-court-delivers-249-verdicts-16-years.html

Benebo, F. Schumann, B., & Vaezghasemi, M. (2018) Intimate partner violence against women in Nigeria: a multilevel study investigating the effect of women's status and community norms. *BMC Women's Health, 18*(136), 1–17 at 9. https://bmcwomenshealth.biomedcentral.com/articles/10.1186/s12905-018-0628-7

Chakaya, B. (2017, November 30). Africa (Nigeria): ECOWAS court challenges vagrancy laws that target women. *Reprohealthlaw Blog*. Retrieved from https://reprohealthlaw.wordpress.com/2017/11/30/africa-nigeria-ecowas-court-challenges-vagrancy-laws-that-target-women/

Davis, R. (2017, November 29). SA's government should stop grouping women and children together. [Weblog] *Daily Maverick*. Retrieved from https://www.dailymaverick.co.za/opinionista/2017-11-29-sas-government-should-stop-grouping-women-and-children-together/

Duffy, H. (2008). Hadijatou Mani Koroua v Niger: Slavery unveiled by the ECOWAS court. *Human Rights Law Review*, 9(1), 151–171 at 14.

Ebobrah, S. (2010). Critical issues in the human rights mandate of the ECOWAS court of justice. *Journal of African Law*, 54(1), 1–25.

Girls Not Brides (2015) *Ending Child Marriage in Africa*. Retrieved from https://www.girlsnotbrides.org/wp-content/uploads/2015/02/Child-marriage-in-Africa-A-brief-by-Girls-Not-Brides1.pdf

Goonesekere, S., & De Silva-De Alwis, R. (2005) *Women's and Children's Rights in A Human Rights-Based Approach to Development*. New York: United Nations Children's Fund (UNICEF). Retrieved from https://www.unicef.org/gender/files/WomensAndChildrensRightsInAHumanRightsBasedApproach.pdf

IPPF Africa Region (2018). *The State of African Women Report*, 99. Retrieved from https://www.ippfar.org/resource/state-african-women-report

NAN (2019, July 12). ECOWAS court records highest number of Judgment, ruling in 2018/19. *The Guardian*. Retrieved from https://guardian.ng/news/ecowas-court-records-highest-number-of-judgment-ruling-in-2018-2019/

News24 Archives. (2000, December 28). Mauritania Out of ECOWAS. *News24 Archives*. Retrieved from https://www.news24.com/xArchive/Archive/Mauritania-out-of-ECOWAS-20001228

O'Connell, C. (2019). Reconceptualising the first African women's protocol case to work for all women. *African Human Rights Law Journal, 19*, 510–533 at 520, 526–530. http://dx.doi.org/10.17159/1996-2096/2019/v19n1a24

Ojigho, O (2017, October). Finally, justice for women. [Weblog post]. *Human Rights Post*. Retrieved from https://rightspost.wordpress.com/2017/10/18/finally-justice-for-women/

Udombana, N. (2000). Toward the African court on human and peoples' rights: Better late than never. *Yale Human Rights and Development Law Journal, 3*(1), 45 at 66–69.

World Bank (2019, April 2). Gender-based violence (violence against women and girls) *World Bank Brief*. https://www.worldbank.org/en/topic/socialdevelopment/brief/violence-against-women-and-girls

Part III

Judicial appointments and gender representation in regional bodies and national courts

9 The feminine face of the African Commission on Human and Peoples' Rights

Reine Alapini-Gansou

Introduction

The African Commission on Human and Peoples' Rights (hereafter African Commission or ACHPR) was established on May 28, 1987,[1] after the African Charter on Human and Peoples' Rights (hereafter African Charter) entered into force in 1986 (African Charter, 1981). This Charter, together with its implementation mechanism (i.e., the African Commission), remains, at the African continental level, a symbol of the need to regionalize the promotion and protection of human rights systems as advocated during the 1980s by doctrine, emerging civil society,[2] and political actors. The African Commission is intended to be an extension and strengthening of the universal human rights system on the African continent and in line with other regional systems.[3]

In this respect, the African regional system has often been compared to other regional systems, particularly the European and Inter-American regional systems. The Asian regional system is gradually being established and has not yet reached the level of consolidation required.[4] Like the United Nations Charter, which promotes the basic principles for promoting and respecting human rights, the African Charter contains 68 provisions (African Charter, 1981). Civil and political rights are embodied in the first generation; the economic, social, and cultural rights are found in the second generation; and solidarity rights are in the third generation. However, unlike other international treaties, the third generation of rights has not been adequately enumerated in the Charter.[5]

The African Commission, the first African human rights treaty body, was established under Articles 30–36 of the African Charter and is composed of 11 members chosen from among African personalities of the highest reputation (African Charter, 1981). The Assembly of Heads of State and Government elects the members, who serve six-year terms.[6] Members are chosen for their "high morality, integrity, impartiality and competence in matters of human and peoples' rights; particular consideration being given to persons having legal experience" (African Charter, 1981, Art. 31). Further, the members "serve in their personal capacity" (African Charter, 1981, Art. 31). Under Article 45 of the African Charter, the African Commission has the mandate to promote and protect human and peoples' rights under conditions described by the Charter

DOI: 10.4324/9780429327865-12

(African Charter, 1981). The Commission is also charged with interpreting the provisions of the Charter at the request of States Parties or recognized African institutions and organizations (African Charter, 1981, Art. 45). Furthermore, it performs any other tasks entrusted by the Assembly of Heads of State and Government (African Charter, 1981).

As a body whose mission is to promote and monitor human rights across the African continent, the ACHPR must set an example by rigorously applying the rules and respecting stakeholders' wishes. Indeed, the logic of political actors is often different from those of human rights experts and technicians, even when states commit themselves under international legal instruments to promote equal rights. Thus, from the perspective of the right to non-discrimination provided in Article 2 of the African Charter and to hold the Commission to a high standard, non-governmental organizations (NGOs) and civil society organizations (CSOs) quickly raised the issue of the equitable representation of women within the African Commission. These civil society groups include Solidarity for African Women's Rights (SOAWR), the African Women's Development and Communication Network (FEMNET), and Femmes Africa Solidarité, which were, and still are, active in lobbying the African Commission on gender issues (Open Society Initiative, 2009). The lobbying efforts by these actors were essential for achieving the equitable representation of women both in political decision-making bodies and in the states' judicial positions.

This chapter aims to analyze the trajectory of the African Commission in terms of women's representation and how women members of this human rights institution have progressively fulfilled its several mandates. This focus considers the fact that the African Commission as a quasi-judicial body remains the oldest model of the African human rights system.

This chapter outlines the steadily increasing trend of women's representation in the African Commission and the reasons for such changes. The first part analyzes this trend and the representation of women within the ACHPR, noting that initially this representation was non-existent in terms of effective participation and that, progressively, the trend changed. In addition, it further examines the importance of women's representation as a way of advancing human rights in the region. The second part then highlights some striking examples of the role that elected women of the African Commission have played over time. These examples include two essential mechanisms with mandates that have been constantly held by women and are concrete demonstrations of the valuable work women representatives have carried out and developed within the system: the Special Rapporteur on the Rights of Women in Africa and the Special Rapporteur on Human Rights Defenders in Africa. Finally, the chapter argues that although much has been achieved in terms of representation, work must be done to continue and expand upon this representation. Thus, some strategies for ensuring the continuation of the upward trend in women's representation are briefly discussed.

The present chapter aims to present a critical conceptual overview of the African Commission based on a legal analysis of the available literature on the topic, including documents, reports, articles, and papers from diverse human rights bodies and their actors. Furthermore, it draws from this writer's experiences as a human rights actor with a personal and professional background in the African human rights systems. The chapter highlights some ways that the Commission has implemented its objective of expanding women's participation within the system and the region, including gender-balanced representation requirements for the election of its commissioners; civil society participation in the work of the Commission, especially those segments that advocate for gender equality; the adoption of the Protocol to the African Charter on Human and Peoples' Rights on the Rights of Women in Africa (the Maputo Protocol); and the creation of a special procedure (the Special Rapporteur on Human Rights Defenders in Africa) to specifically address women's rights in the region. Each of these channels is further discussed throughout the text.

The representation of women within the ACHPR: An almost successful challenge

The African Commission: A short history

At the time of its creation in May 1987, the African Commission was marked by the same shortcoming as that of other institutions that predated it—namely, the absence of women in the spheres of professional life. As a result, the African Commission initially suffered from an absence of women among its commissioners. Despite changes that will be discussed, the secular struggle of feminists to change preconceived ideas about women's role in professional life continues, and women activists are still working tirelessly on these topics. The Beijing Conference[7] and its aftermath are also relevant to this matter, given how the conference positioned women's issues on a global platform.

After the first elections of the African Commission members in 1987, the institution was led by two men: the late Commissioner Isaac Nguema, first chairperson of the African Commission, and its vice-chairperson, Commissioner Ibrahim Ali Badahoui el Cheikh (African Commission, n.d.a). The African Commission's first activity report in 1988 did not include any women (African Commission, n.d.b). It was in June 1993, during the 29th Summit of the Assembly of Heads of State and Government of the Organisation of African Unity, that Mrs. Vera Valentina De Melo Martins Duarte was elected as a member of the African Commission, becoming the first woman in the institution alongside her male peers (Organisation of African Unity, 1994).

During the internal election that followed, as set out by Article 42 of the Charter, Commissioner Duarte became the vice-chairperson of the African Commission, alongside Chairperson Mr. Youssoupha Ndiaye, from 1997 through 1999 (African Commission, n.d.b).[8] Mrs. Duarte's expertise in human rights and international law, coupled with her role as a Supreme Court judge in Cabo Verde and being the first woman elected to the African Commission, was determinant in her earning this position (Lima-Neves, n.d.).[9] Two years later, Mrs. Duarte was joined by Mrs. Julienne Ondziel-Gnelenga, a Congolese lawyer and seasoned women's rights activist who worked as a member of the Women, Peace, and Security Network Africa (Gutto, 2001). Mrs. Ondziel-Gnelenga was elected for a six-year term in June 1995 in accordance with the term guidelines in Article 36 of the African Charter (Malmstrom & Oberleitner, 1996).

In April 1998, during the 23rd session of the African Commission at Banjul in The Gambia, Mrs. Ondziel-Gnelenga was announced as the Special Rapporteur on the Rights of Women in Africa (African Commission, n.d.b). Her functions as Special Rapporteur on the Rights of Women in Africa were confirmed by Resolution 38 (XXV)99, adopted during the 25th Ordinary Session of the African Commission held in Bujumbura, Burundi, in 1999 (African Commission, n.d.b). She served as vice-chairperson of the African Commission under the chairmanship of Commissioner Mr. E. V. O. Dankwa of Ghana from November 1999 until October 2000 (African Commission, n.d.b). Thus, from 1995 to 2000, Commissioners Duarte and Ondziel-Gnelenga were the only two women at the African Commission. These developments show that the Beijing recommendations and the various resolutions regarding the adoption of a gender approach were not fully implemented without difficulty.[10]

After Commissioner Duarte's election in 1993, women's representation on the Commission slowly increased. In 2002, 4 out of 11 members of the African Commission were women;[11] this number increased to 5 in 2003.[12] In 2005, there were still five women on the Commission, as two women and two men were elected to replace the commissioners whose terms of office were expiring.[13] During the elections held during the 2007 African Union (AU) Summit and because of lobbying pressure by NGOs and CSOs, African member states proposed a number of women candidates,[14] a wake-up call for gender equality on the Commission. As a result, in 2007, there was a surge in women's representation on the African Commission: Women represented a strong majority of the membership—seven women to four men.[15]

In 2009, Angela Melo was elected for a three-year term.[16] In 2011, after the resignation of Commissioner Fayek, three women and two men were elected;[17] then, in 2013, two women and two men were elected.[18] In 2015, two women and one man were elected,[19] and in 2017, the election resulted in two women and two men being on the Commission.[20] Table 9.1 shows the shifting gender composition of the Commission.

The African Union now takes into account the principles of equitable geographical distribution and balanced representation of men and women in the election of commissioners (African Commission, n.d.a; African Union, 2016a). From 2011 to 2020, of the 11 members of the African Commission, at least 6 positions have been filled by women. The women currently on the Commission are Jamesina Essie L. King from Sierra Leone, Lucy Asuagbor from Cameroon, Maria Teresa Manuela from Angola, Maya Sahli-Fadel of Algeria, Soyata Maiga from Mali, and Sylvie Zainabu Kayitesi from Rwanda (African Commission, n.d.b).

Looking at Table 9.2, it is important to recall how the members of the ACHPR have since made a judicious application of the African Charter concerning the

Table 9.1 Gender composition of the African Commission 1987–2019*

Year	*Women*	*Men*
1987	0	11
1989	0	11
1991	0	11
1993	1	10
1995	2	9
1997	2	9
1999	4	7
2001	4	7
2003	5	6
2005	5	6
2007	7	4
2009	5	6
2011	7	4
2013	6	5
2015	7	4
2017	6	5
2019	6	5

* Gender composition measured after elections from the second ordinary session of that year.

Table 9.2 Women in chairperson positions: Consecutive years of leadership in the ACHPR

Year	*Chairperson*	*Vice-Chairperson*
2003–2005	Salimata Sawadogo	Yassir Sid Ahmed El Hassan
2005–2007	Salimata Sawadogo	Yassir Sid Ahmed El Hassan
2007–2009	Sanji Monageng	Angela Melo
2009–2011	Reine Alapini-Gansou	Mumba Malila
2011–2013	Catherine Dupe Atoki	Sylvie Zainabu Kayitesi
2013–2015	Sylvie Kayitesi Zainabo	Mohamed Bechir Khalfallah
2015–2017	Faith Pansy Tlakula	Soyata Maiga
2017–2019	Soyata Maiga	Lawrence Mute

election of the members of the Bureau. According to Article 42 of the Charter, "the board members shall be elected for a renewable term of two years" (African Charter, 1981). However, members assume that no one should lead the African Commission *ad vitam aeternam*,[21] even if Article 42 of the Charter does not prescribe any limitation of mandates. Except for Commissioners Sawadogo and Ahmed El Hassan, who both served two consecutive terms because, in the exceptional circumstances, no election was held, all board members have served a non-renewable two-year term since 2007. This is an important example of the democratic alternation that the members of the African Commission should continue to apply.

Mechanisms and strategies that contributed to increasing women's participation and representation in the African Commission

This change in trends and the increase in women's participation cannot be attributed to only one or a few mechanisms. They are due to a combination of complex acts taken by the Commission with the participation of several actors. For the purpose of this chapter, three of these instruments deserve emphasis.

The first point is the adoption of legal requirements with gender specifications. Since the creation of the African Commission, states have adopted two possible attitudes toward the representation of women: States either comply with their national laws, reinforced by African Union rules on gender compliance in elections, or take strict account of vacancy notices that now clearly indicate the number of candidates by gender for each region of the continent. The second approach is an obligation under the African Union system to ensure that candidates are diverse by gender and by region.

As a human rights body entrusted to implement the Maputo Protocol, the African Commission, alongside other actors like the Special Rapporteur on the Rights of Women in Africa, lobbies for and monitors several female candidates to ensure that women are represented in the African Commission.[22] During each African Union summit, the chairperson of the Commission, previously Commissioner Soyata Maiga, followed by Commissioner Lucy Asuagbor, is present for the record beside African women institutions and women activists to ensure that gender issues are discussed at the summits. The fact that women occupy these positions helps to encourage gender-related discussion. The African Union system requires details on the number of candidates by gender and region. For example, the Maputo Protocol requires in Articles 8 and 9 "that women are represented equally in the judiciary and law enforcement organs" and that "women are represented equally at all levels with men in all electoral processes" (African Union, 2003). Further, the African Union Gender Policy explicitly calls for equal gender representation in decision-making through the AU Parity Principle (African Union, 2009, pp. 13–16).[23]

Failure to achieve a fair representation of female and male judges risks the possible postponement of the elections; today, we observe that this right, which belongs to female candidates, is being undermined.[24] Even if implementation is slow, these gender inclusion requirements represent efforts at the level of the African Union that must be encouraged and strengthened to ensure equity and justice.

Another tool that contributed to the increase of women's participation was the Maputo Protocol and the several activities related to its implementation.[25] The Maputo Protocol, which entered into force on November 25, 2005, echoes many of the same provisions contained in the United Nations Convention on the Elimination of All Forms of Discrimination against Women (CEDAW), but it has further developed the mechanisms for the protection of women and takes into account issues unique to the region, such as child marriage and female genital mutilation (FGM) (African Union, 2003). The Protocol addresses the effects that culture and tradition have on women's rights (African Union, 2003). In sum, the Protocol is a strong framework for ensuring the rights of women in the African continent.

The Protocol is a treaty body in the African context and establishes obligations toward states that intersect with obligations established in other international documents, such as CEDAW and the Convention on the Rights of the Child (CRC), for instance. Therefore, it expands and reinforces the regional level states' obligations toward women and reinforces states' accountability for specific women's rights violations. The Commission is responsible for supervising states' implementation of the Maputo Protocol and offers guidance on the interpretation and application of rights. Article 26, for instance, obliges states to submit reports every two years on the domestic steps taken to implement and give effect to the Protocol (African Union, 2003).

By addressing gender-based discrimination, reducing the gap between men and women in access and enjoyment of rights, and creating mechanisms to hold states accountable for violations, the Maputo Protocol restated the importance of equality between men and women in the African region. It opened the path to higher professional positions for women. It also reaffirmed the importance of women's rights for the Commission and as a central point to be promoted among the states. Since women's rights are important to the Commission, an increase in women's representation on the Commission is also important. Thus, the Maputo Protocol is both the result of and the reason for the expansion of women's presence on the African Commission.

In addition, perhaps one of the most effective and relevant mechanisms for ensuring women's representation on the Commission and other organs is the participation of human rights defenders, civil society actors, NGOs, and gender equality activists. These actors played and continue to play an important role in the implementation of the Commission's mandate and of the values enshrined in the African Charter. Human rights are the result of people's suffering and the struggle to resist oppression and discrimination. Therefore, civil society is essential for pressuring political actors and institutions to change practices and attitudes toward a more equal and justice world.

For instance, the International Commission of Jurists[26] was alongside the African Commission from the beginning of its mandate and provided technical support.[27] Many other civil society actors were also present on the Commission, and their work gradually crystallized around the public sessions of the African Commission.[28] The Commission resolved to allow NGOs to seek and obtain observer status, which bolstered them in encouraging women's participation and representation in the Commission.[29] To date, the results of the various NGO forums that have been held in the lead-up to each session of the African Commission are commendable. The constant and sustained presence of women in the African Commission results from this civil society pressure and lobbying, which resonated to the African Union summit. Civil society actors secured their places in the African Union Commission by obtaining observer accreditation for the African Union summit.[30] Indeed, the very creation of the Maputo Protocol resulted from civil society pressure aligned with the activism of the Special Rapporteur on the Rights of Women in Africa (African Union, 2016b).

There is no one exclusive feature that made it possible for the Commission to increase women's participation. It was a process shaped by political articulation, struggle, achievement of rights, and participation by multiple groups. Certainly, the election of the first woman, Vera Duarte, exemplifies this combination. Her election opened the path for more women to engage in the work of the Commission. While still a commissioner, Duarte organized a seminar in Togo, where she proposed that the African Charter should have a complementary document to address women's rights (Nos Genti, 2012). Her proposal was accepted and adopted by the African Commission. Subsequently, a commission was created that included different human rights actors and organizations, such as the International Commission of Jurists, responsible for working on the project of this document. Finally, it resulted in the creation and eventual approval of the Maputo Protocol (Nos Genti, 2012). This example shows how those mechanisms act together and how representation created a circle of empowerment. The fruits of Duarte's election and of her prioritization of women's rights on the agenda of the Commission were the protection of and respect for women's rights, the emancipation and empowerment of other women, and consequently, more women's representation.

Women's representation in the African Commission: A human rights achievement

The women elected to the African Commission have outstanding personal and intellectual skills combined with a notable set of experiences. The members of the African Commission do not hold a permanent position and therefore continue their professions in their home countries while serving the Commission,[31] which highlights the level of commitment and responsibility to the human rights causes that these professionals have. Women members of the African Commission, who work full-time in their countries, come from strongly intellectual backgrounds. While maintaining their own careers, as members of the African Commission the women must properly apply and implement the Charter and Article 45 through human rights promotion and protection activities (African Charter, 1981), which they must report upon to each ordinary session under Rule 72 of the Rules of Procedure of the African Commission (African Commission, 2010).

Beyond their legal expertise, most women elected to the African Commission are highly competent in specific human rights issues. For example, they have expertise in the rights of Indigenous peoples, the rights of people living with HIV, the rights of people in detention related to police action, the rights of people of African descent, the rights of people living with disabilities, and the rights of older persons.[32] Further, these varied issue-based human rights foci are used to implement economic, social, and cultural rights regarding extractive industries, the death penalty in Africa, and many other discrete issues facing the continent.

Therefore, the Commission now profits from these valuable professionals, who were once excluded from this field. The African Commission is composed of women sitting judges; women from the prosecutor's office; and lawyers with extensive expertise in all areas of human rights law, international law, and women's rights in particular. Some are also academics with expertise in criminal law, criminal procedure, and human rights trials.[33] All these women bring their professional acumen and can apply their experiences and knowledge to the work of the Commission.

Women commissioners certainly offer a wider range of highly qualified professionals to the Commission, but most importantly, they diversify points of view, help to expand the topics of issues approached, and offer new inputs and problem-resolution methods throughout their representation, without which it is impossible to build human rights for all. As in many other discriminatory dynamics, gender-based discrimination is systemic and present in the whole society and political structure. Therefore, gender-based discrimination has consequences for the law as well. For decades, men's views, experiences, and ideas have dominated the legal-judicial work and led to a system designed by and for men. This design becomes per se exclusive of and blind to women's problems, perspectives, and needs (Olsen, 1990). A system created, articulated, and operated mainly by and for men will never represent and properly address issues uniquely faced by women.

To address this discrimination, human rights systems, either international or regional, were created to achieve equality among people and to be applied universally. Therefore, those rights should be created, applied, and operated with the presence and representation of as great a diversity of experiences, especially regarding gender, as is possible. This representation is the only means by which the rights of all, including women, will be preserved and protected equally.

When women start to participate more actively in developing human rights bodies such as the African Commission, not only do those professionals gain from their participation, but the whole system gains. Women's presence guarantees that issues related to women's experience and needs will receive due attention and consideration. For instance, matters that affect women specifically in more oppressive ways, such as child marriage, FGM, human trafficking for sexual exploitation, absence of reproductive rights like safe abortion and forced sterilization, and sexual abuse are included in the agenda of the Commission more vehemently. Similarly, even though the African Union has addressed the fact that issues such as housing, access to decent work, and education, for example, affect all, women and girls are still affected more negatively than men (African Union, 2018). For instance, in the context of armed conflicts, women tend to suffer greater deprivations (African Union, 2018). In many cases, women face multiple and intersectional discrimination based on other grounds, such as their health condition, language abilities, or geographic location, along with gender discrimination.

Further, women's presence is important for initiating changes in sexist practices and harmful gender-based stereotypes embedded within the culture, costumes, practices, political context of states, and political actors and is thus equally reproduced in international bodies. Women's presence in the Commission through the decision-making and political articulation processes, for instance, is essential for challenging the tendency of discriminatory practices to pass as elements of culture, religion, or normality. In addition, women become the protagonists of their own history and advance their own rights rather than depending on the benevolence of those in charge. Further, women's presence on the Commission sends a message to all women of the continent: They are represented by people who know their struggle and understand their needs. The representation is a source of inspiration to young girls, who now see themselves occupying those important positions and can feel motivated to seek the same path. Representation is a process that leads to empowerment.

As a human rights body, the African Commission is most efficient when all the rights enshrined in the Charter are realized equally. An essential part of that means guaranteeing to women and girls, who have many of their rights violated for reasons of gender-based discrimination or experience harsher violations, the achievement of the full enjoyment of rights free of discrimination. This cannot be accomplished solely by men in the Commission and in the institutions that are supposed to secure this cause. In sum, although women's presence in the African Commission is in itself a concrete result of the struggle for equality, those women put their skills at the service of African populations on a daily basis in the fight to continue to advance human rights. Their action has enabled the African Commission to achieve a more diverse, inclusive, and representative board, thereby varying the ways to realize many of its objectives. In this way, many of the Commission's special procedures to implement these objectives have been led by women. In this regard, the following section will highlight two of these special procedures[34] that have reinforced the female face of the African Commission.

Model of the female face of the African Commission: Rights of women and rights of human rights defenders in Africa

As demonstrated earlier, for several years after its establishment in 1987, the African Commission suffered from the total absence of women in its membership; but in 1993, the trend began to change. The women who were subsequently elected put their expertise, sense of initiative, and skills at the service of the African populations and of the African Commission itself. Due partly to the work of these women, the African Commission has achieved visibility as a leading human rights body within Africa. Women lead many of the special mechanisms currently evolving within the African Commission, including areas addressing rights of women, prisoners, people with disabilities, people with HIV, environmental protections, and advocacy against the death penalty.[35] However, only two special mechanisms will be highlighted in this section. The Special Rapporteur on Rights of Women in Africa will first be examined because of its precedence in establishing the African Commission's special procedures. The Special Rapporteur on Human Rights Defenders in Africa will then be examined because of its importance in the world generally and specifically in Africa, as those called human rights defenders are people on the front line of danger and fight courageously against political actors and other perpetrators of human rights violations. Since their creation, these mandates have been occupied mostly by women.

In addition to the mechanism of the Special Rapporteur on Rights of Women in Africa led by Lucy Asuagbor (at the time of writing), the following special mechanisms are all ones for which women hold the mandates: the Special Rapporteur on Detention and Prisons in Africa led by Maria Teresa Manuela; the Working Group on Death Penalty in Africa led by Zainabo Sylvie Kayitesi; the Special Rapporteur on Refugees, Asylum Seekers, and Internally Displaced Persons in Africa led by Sahil-Fadel; the Working Group on Human Rights and HIV in Africa led by Soyata Maiga; the Working Group on Indigenous Populations and Communities in Africa, also led by Soyata Maiga; the Special Rapporteur on Freedom of Expression and Access to Information led by Faith Pansy Tlakula; and the Working Group on Economic, Social and Cultural Rights led by Jamesina Eddie L. King (African Commission, n.d.c).[36] Thus, the representation of women, in terms of both number and intellectual qualification, in addition to meeting regional and international gender requirements and standards, has shown itself successful in face of the work provided in each of these mechanisms.[37]

Special Rapporteur's mechanism on the rights of women in Africa: A successful model of women's activism

As one of the oldest mechanisms of the African Commission, the Special Rapporteur's Mechanism on the Rights of Women in Africa was adopted at its 23rd Ordinary Session in Banjul, in 1998 (African Commission, n.d.c). The mandate of the Special Rapporteur on the Rights of Women in Africa is to assist African governments in the implementation of the Maputo Protocol through national mechanisms and legislation; undertake promotion and protection missions throughout the continent and report back to the African Commission; initiate and develop tools and studies on the situation of women's rights in Africa; and keep contacts with similar mechanisms around the world (African Commission, n.d.c).[38] This resolution has been renewed several times to respond to changing needs and improve the effectiveness of the mechanism.[39] This renewal process applies to all the special procedures created within the African Commission, although this mechanism was one of the first to be renewed and is one of the oldest special procedures in Africa.[40]

The initiative to create the mandate coincided with the preparations for the 1995 Beijing Conference, whose action plan, recommendations, and lobbying surrounding the implementation of the United Nations CEDAW[41] subsequently promoted the adoption of the Protocol to the African Charter on the Rights of Women in Africa. The mechanism of the Special Rapporteur on the Rights of Women in Africa, led by Mrs. Julienne Onziel-Gnelenga in 1998, promoted the adoption of the Maputo Protocol[42] with the support of African civil society

(African Commission, n.d.c). The effective implementation of the Protocol has been carried out gradually under the African Commission's supervision pursuant to Article 26 of the Protocol.[43] Since its creation, this mechanism has been carried out by women.

At the completion of Julienne Onziel-Gnelenga's term with the Commission, the mandate for the Special Rapporteur on Rights of Women in Africa was carried out from 2001 to 2007 by Commissioner Angela Melo.[44] The mechanism then made significant progress under the leadership of Commissioner Soyata Maiga from 2007 through 2015 (Durojaye, 2018), particularly with her initiatives developing General Comments on many provisions of the Maputo Protocol.[45] She also pushed for significant reform of the African Commission resolution on reporting within Article 62 of the Charter and Article 26 of the Maputo Protocol while she was working for the full implementation of the Protocol (Durojaye, 2018). Thanks to her efforts and the adoption of General Comments, the States Parties have specific direction on how to implement and apply various articles in the Maputo Protocol. Commissioner Lucy Asuagbor has been in office as Special Rapporteur on Rights of Women in Africa since 2015 (African Commission, n.d.c).

Increasingly, the presence of the Special Rapporteur on Rights of Women in Africa at all African Union summits has influenced the African Union by raising gender issues at the summits. The Special Rapporteur has involved women's associations, such as Women in Law and Development in Africa (WiLDAF), to work alongside the African Commission (Wandia, 2004). This participation has also led to an increasing number of women joining other bodies of the African Union, a presence that has been felt in reforms since the African Union's creation. The increased presence of women was also made possible by the Gender Is My Agenda Campaign, which lobbied political actors before and during the elections of African Commission members.[46]

While advocating for African integration through development, the heads of state and governments within the African Union system have not overshadowed the necessary resolution of the gender issue. The proactive role that the Special Rapporteur plays helps ensure that gender issues remain at the forefront of the African Union's policies and discussions. Without gender representation in the African Union system, development efforts in other instances would undoubtedly be undermined. For example, the Commission of the African Union, as the African Union's secretariat in accordance with the Constitutive Act, considers equitable geographical distribution. Additionally, it now considers a balanced representation of men and women in all technical and political bodies of the Union regarding elected members (African Union, 2016a). This shift to inclusion was in response to instructions from the African Union Assembly in an Executive Council decision in 2016 (African Union, 2016a).

These principles of geographic distribution and gender representation also apply to the election of commissioners and the judicial bodies.[47] In support of this initiative, the Executive Council suspended the election of a judge for the African Court on Human and Peoples' Rights for lack of female candidates for the Southern

African region after the legal counsel of the African Union Commission[48] highlighted the lack of balanced gender nominations. As a result of this challenge, Mrs Tujilane Rose Chizumla from Malawi was subsequently elected in January 2017. Mrs Imani Daud Aboud from Tanzania was similarly elected in July 2018 after the balanced gender condition was applied (African Court, 2018).

The Special Rapporteur's mechanism on human rights defenders in Africa: A new era

The mechanism of the Special Rapporteur on Human Rights Defenders in Africa remains one of the best examples of the work of the African Commission from a woman's perspective, since most of the time the mandate has been carried out by women. Its creation is based on two important factors. The first is linked to the many cases of serious violations of the rights of individuals who have chosen, individually or in association, to promote or protect human rights through advocacy and dialogue with stakeholders. These violations are found both in States Parties to the African Charter during times of conflict and in States Parties where there is relative peace. The second factor is the impetus provided by the creation of the United Nations Special Rapporteur on Human Rights Defenders, whose main objective was to effectively implement the United Nations Declaration on Human Rights Defenders (UNDHRD).[49]

The success of this United Nations mechanism depended on the joint efforts of all human rights defenders around the world, including those in Africa. Civil society actors organized the Johannesburg International Conference in 1998 as a first response to the implementation at the African regional level of the UNDHRD (Amnesty International, 1998). They created the Johannesburg Declaration and recommended to the African Commission that a special mechanism for African human rights defenders (HRDs) be established (Amnesty International, 1998). The Grand Baie Declaration followed in 1999,[50] and African HRDs subsequently benefited from the Kigali Declaration in 2003.[51] After the establishment of the focal point on HRDs in 2003, the special mechanism of the Special Rapporteur on Human Rights Defenders in Africa was established in June 2004 and adopted at the 35th Ordinary Session of the African Commission held in Banjul, Gambia (African Commission, n.d.b). The mandate of the Special Rapporteur on Human Rights Defenders in Africa includes an obligation to

> seek, receive, examine, and act on information related to the situation of human rights defenders in Africa; submit … [periodic] report[s] on the situation of human rights defenders in Africa; establish collaboration and dialogue with States Parties to the charter, national human rights institutions, human rights defenders, and other partners; develop and recommend strategies to better protect human rights defenders and follow up on these recommendations; and promote and raise awareness about the implementation of the Declaration of Human Rights Defenders in Africa.
>
> (African Commission, n.d.b)

The first Special Rapporteur on Human Rights Defenders in Africa position, established in 2004, was held by a woman—Commissioner Jainaba Johm.[52] Appointments for the Special Rapporteur are made according to the will and the availability of the commissioners during internal consultations. Since this mechanism was created in June 2004, it took some time to explore options for successors for Commissioner Jainaba Johm, whose term in the Commission was ending in 2005. The second mandate holder was also a woman—Commissioner Reine Alapini-Gansou, who held the position from 2005 to 2009 (International Service, 2011). Commissioner Alapini-Gansou transitioned to lead the African Commission as chairperson in 2009, and Commissioner Mohamed Khalfallah acted as Special Rapporteur in 2010 (International Service, 2011). The position was then taken over by Commissioner Lucy Asuagbor from 2010 to 2011 and again by Commissioner Alapini-Gansou from 2012 through 2017 (International Service, 2011). The current Special Rapporteur is Commissioner Rémy Ngoy Lumbu (African Commission, n.d.b). The achievements of the mechanism under the gender approach in this case, and the different challenges it has faced during these periods, were especially visible to the African Union community.

From 2005 to 2009, Commissioner Reine Alapini-Gansou carried out her mandate under the campaign *Synergy with Stakeholders*, which led to the creation of the Pan-African Network of Human Rights Defenders (HRDs) and the strengthening and establishment of regional networks of HRDs.[53] Because of this continental networking, the actions of HRDs are increasingly effective, especially concerning the rights and protections of HRDs at risk. HRDs are often in conflict with state actors given the nature of their work, and their work is often subject to attacks and reprisals. These conflicts and attacks justified the extension of the mechanism's mandate to include issues related to reprisals under the terms of Resolution 273 adopted at the 55th Ordinary Session of the African Commission in 2014 in Luanda, Angola (African Commission, n.d.b).

The mechanism of the Special Rapporteur on Human Rights Defenders has been active since its creation. It has promoted communication through press releases; it has created urgent appeals procedures on allegations of rights violations of human rights defenders and has created a newsletter as an information tool for stakeholders. Strong resolutions have been adopted under pressure from the mechanism on reprisals against HRDs and the right to freedom of sexual orientation. As of today, about 30 resolutions have been created on behalf of the mechanism.[54]

While maintaining its overall mission to promote and protect the rights of HRDs, the mechanism has undertaken several studies in various fields on behalf of HRDs in Africa. Examples include studies on freedom of association, the situation of women HRDs in Africa, the guidelines and principles of human rights and terrorism in Africa, and the guidelines on freedom of association and assembly in Africa.[55] Due to the mechanism's efforts, HRDs are recognized for their work and are increasingly called upon in the context of serious and massive human rights violations resulting from conflicts between States Parties and the African Charter. These activists are now deployed as part of human rights monitoring systems. The mechanism has supported a model law for recognizing HRDs in Africa for the benefit of States Parties to the African Charter.[56]

By carrying out their mandate with responsibility and commitment, the Special Rapporteurs have established the necessary collaboration between regional human rights bodies across Africa, Asia, Europe, and the Americas and the universal United Nations mechanism by launching periodic meetings now called "inter-mechanism meetings."[57] These meetings aim to strengthen all human rights mandates of HRDs through joint activities meant to promote and protect human rights.

Looking back at the African Commission's past and current situation with regard to women's representation in the body, the mechanisms have achieved success in sensitive areas like human rights, especially improving the protection of women's rights (Pretoria University, 2016). The two examples provided earlier concretely show how women can assume their responsibilities, meet their commitments, demonstrate their sense of duty, and assume their roles as leaders. These skills are also demonstrated in other cases of women's participation in the work of the Commission. Moreover, as of this writing, the African Commission is the first body within the African Union system to include more women and has best met the African Union's gender strategy.

Other bodies, like the African Court on Human and Peoples' Rights[58] and the African Committee of Experts on the Rights and Welfare of the Child,[59] are also improving with regard to women's representation.[60] The high level of expertise required in international human rights law and in international justice may be one of the reasons why women's representation is improving in these various mechanisms, as with the active agenda for gender equality, women have better conditions and chances to seek professional qualification and thus are encouraged to build on their professional portfolios. Because women were denied those rights and spaces for so long, they now can see moving forward professionally as a valuable achievement. Building up a career for most women is not only a professional act but also an act of resistance and transformation taken with great enthusiasm. Further, the sense of sacrifice and the knowledge that the Special Rapporteur's function is temporary requires that the members of the ACHPR give the best of their time to serve human rights across the African continent. The women who have occupied these Rapporteur positions have had to make sacrifices while juggling their primary professional careers in their home countries and their personal obligations, often as caregivers of their immediate and extended families.

Conclusion

The foregoing discussion shows that the efforts to ensure women's presence in the African Commission are worthy of analysis, even if the risk faced by all human rights actors, including experts, activists, and HRDs, is very high. Implementation of international human rights law is not easy, especially when it is women who must help to achieve such an objective. Women embark on such tasks, often encouraged by their peers and States Parties in some respects; they are to be commended for crossing both socio-cultural and material barriers. Just because women are encouraged to take on these tasks does not mean that women's rights have been achieved; we do not have to accept the *status quo* knowing that the recognition of gender disparities underlying the concern for human rights always remains an ideal to strive for, like human rights themselves. Women's representation in the African Commission should be maintained and used as an example to achieve gender parity within all AU organs and within the institutions of domestic States Parties. More women are working hard to achieve their goals through their ambition to push for equality.

Things are changing, but there is still a lot to be done. As highlighted previously, the African Commission is currently composed of five men and six women. Women should continue to work together with their male colleagues to achieve the goals of the Commission and promote human rights across Africa. But much remains to be done to achieve the much-needed strengthening of women's substantive representation in the African Commission. As a recent victory, this representation is always subject to resistance from cultural traditions, for instance, but also from political interests; however, this resistance is a normal process. Social and political changes, especially those of high magnitude, pass through a moment of adaptation and face opposition on different levels exactly because those changes challenge the conventional power relations and privileged positions. For this reason, even if women's representation within the African Commission shows remarkable progress toward gender parity from when the Commission first started, it is necessary to strengthen and continue this progress to guarantee the continued and effective participation of women in the Commission's work and in mainstreaming the rights of women in Africa, thereby avoiding a regress in terms of the achievements already conquered. The three recommendations presented in the following sections reflect on that risk.

The institutionalization of the gender question

If gender equality is to be mainstreamed, this agenda must be reflected in political and judicial institutions. For example, as part of its action plan, the African Union has institutionalized gender equity in elections within the African system, thereby marking a progressive implementation of its gender equality plan. Further, on the African Union level, there are some mechanisms in place to institutionalize gender equity, such as the 2004 African Union Solemn Declaration on Gender Equality in Africa (SDGEA), where all the AU member states agreed to ratify the Maputo Protocol and to internalize the provisions of that document; and the Directorate of Women, Gender and Development (WGDD), which works within the AU to ensure that states are complying with the SDGEA and are promoting gender equality in the region (African Union, 2016b). The AU Strategy for Gender Equality and Women's Empowerment 2018–2028 has also been adopted to implement this policy (African Union, 2018). The African Union has also established the African Union Specialized Technical Committee on Gender Equality and Women's Empowerment in 2006 (African Union,

2016b). It is an organization composed of African women (chosen based on representative criteria) and intended to serve as an advisory committee to the chairperson of the African Union Commission on women's rights–related issues (African Union, 2016b). These initiatives are essential in institutional terms, and they are important for maintaining the current trends to avoid the possibility that the progress will be slowed or stopped.

Political actors have to ensure gender equality, especially on the domestic level, since the strengthening of women's rights within the states reflects on the regional bodies such as the Commission and the African Union. Therefore, state leaders would do well to implement the gender agenda within their government plan by integrating gender perspectives in the ministries and in the national human rights institutions (the Maputo Protocol). For this integration, qualified women with backgrounds in human rights and experts in gender studies in these ministries are essential. Further, states can create ministries or government agencies specializing in women's rights and gender discrimination, such as the "Ministry of Equality" (Ministerio de Igualdad) created in Spain. This could be an effective way of incorporating these equality objectives into government actions and creating effective policies focused on women and girls. These are measures that could result in an irrevocable institutionalization of gender parity within the African system.

Toward the necessary eradication of sociological fear

Africa continues to carry the weight of certain cultural and social practices that infringe on women's rights. Among other things, the family and community environment in which women live and the gender-based expectations they face, such as the duty to serve at home and to be caregivers, are social and cultural barriers to women's advancement and contribute to their reservations when women are deciding whether to pursue leadership positions. States should act to overcome these stereotypes that are built into the culture and society. States may pass laws criminalizing acts of gender-based violence and other culturally harmful practices such as forced marriage and FGM while following up with effective investigation and prosecution. Additionally, it is important to repeal existing laws that make it difficult for women to exercise their reproductive rights and laws that hinder access to the right to property and inheritance for women.

It is impossible to discuss effective cultural changes without including education. Thus, it is essential to have an education system free of discriminatory ideologies that do not reinforce gender roles for young girls and boys. Instead, children can grow up learning that women and men should develop their lives in partnership and with equality. In this respect, girls should have access to schools and universities and be encouraged to attend at the same level as boys. It is essential to empower them with an emancipatory education. They will learn that they can and should lead their lives and make their own choices, including regarding when, how, or whether they want to constitute a family.

At the nuclear and the extended family levels, men, husbands, fathers, and brothers reinforce particular roles for women through their daily behavior. Men's role in this system of discrimination highlights why any action addressing women and gender issues should involve men. Because many relationships between men and women are interdependent, men must act as women's allies. In this respect, continuous awareness-raising of men's duties, through campaigns and educational programs focused on men, will help reduce women's sociological fear and build a world in which the relationship between men and women can be based on collaboration rather than on exploitation and oppression. As the cause of women's representation in formal institutions progresses, male representatives and authorities should also see themselves as part of this cause to open the dialogue within the male community and with their partners about the need for equality. Men, therefore, support women in empowerment and in carrying the burden of their own liberation.

The shadow of human rights—Creating a political culture of human rights

Human rights remain the channel through which adversity—and often, violence by political actors—must be addressed. Because of this, making the choice to work in the field of human rights is difficult and fraught. Outside the academic and professional curriculum, African HRD women must make the difficult choice of bearing the actions of governments and political actors whose development agendas still disregard the need for human rights. The persistence of human rights violations, which is evident through conflicts in many States Parties to the African Charter, does not allow us to give up. Human rights violations in the context of African conflicts affect the population generally, but not equally. In these contexts, women and children are normally affected more intensely. The conflicts normally stress and worsen previous forms of gender-discriminatory patterns and create new forms of dangers to women and girls, such as sexual and physical abuse (African Union, 2016b). Because of this, women have historically had the most at stake and many reasons to participate in conflict resolution for peace through justice and reconciliation programs. It is important to comprehend the differences between the effects of these conflicts on women and on men to also address more appropriate solutions. Every transitional justice process must involve women. It is necessary to equip legal and political institutions with women to bring women's needs and perspectives to decision-making processes in states that are experiencing political transformation.

The scale of sexual crimes or crimes committed by minors and children in the context of armed conflicts is yet another factor necessitating women's participation in any justice and human rights processes. In this context, the involvement of female judges and commissioners would give a chance to the many women victims of sexual crimes, and of other serious and massive human rights violations, to make their voices heard. Special juries composed exclusively or predominantly of women are one interesting example that some human rights defenders have advocated for. Systemic discrimination that occurs within the justice institutions themselves, which are permeated with gender stereotypes and gender-discriminatory views regarding women, is a big challenge to guaranteeing accountability for sexual crimes.

As the majority of the victims of sexual violence, women face several challenges in the justice systems. Their statements are often treated as suspicious, and those responsible for the investigation and prosecution of cases tend not to believe women entirely or to ascribe less credibility to women's words, not uncommonly even blaming the victims themselves for the crime. Individuals tend to reproduce their prejudice in the analysis of the cases. Having lost confidence in the justice system, victims may end up not taking the crime to the legal field for fear of being misunderstood and humiliated. One way to address this issue in a credible and effective way would be to have a panel of women jury members, which would make victims feel more protected and provide the necessary compassion and sensitivity that such cases require. Moreover, a panel of women would, at least theoretically, be less inclined to misjudge victims of those crimes, and the result would be an institution more committed to the fair administration of justice.

The African Commission has been called upon to deal with a number of cases of serious human rights violations in recent years, including cases on gender-based discrimination and violence.[61] In this regard, the trend toward greater representation of women in the African Commission should be maintained so that these sorts of cases can be better addressed. In fact, as demonstrated in this chapter, it is impossible to talk about universalism in human rights without proper representation of human diversity; to achieve diversity, gender representation is essential because of the historical exclusion and oppression women have suffered. If we also recognize the vital role played by women in the African system, considering their work as commissioners of the African Human Rights Commission and as Special Rapporteurs, in addition to their participation in peace and security agendas, their presence in human rights bodies at the level of the African Commission should be a given.

Notes

1 Temporarily based in Addis Ababa, Ethiopia in November, 1987, the headquarters moved to Banjul, The Gambia in 1989 (African Commission, n.d.a). The African Commission is established under Article 30 of the African Charter (African Charter, 1981).

2 The International Commission of Jurists worked hard for the establishment of the African Commission and has remained an active NGO (African Commission, n.d.a).

3 These other regional human rights systems and documents include the 1950 European Convention on Human Rights and Fundamental Freedoms (Council of Europe, 1950); the Inter-American human rights system with the 1969 American Convention on Human Rights (Organization of American States, 1969); and the Asian system with the 1988 Asian Convention on Human Rights (Asian Human Rights, 1998).

4 Read *La défense internationale des droits de l'homme* by Jean-Luc Mathieu for more information (1998).

5 The Charter contains 68 provisions addressing civil, political, economic, social, and cultural rights along with rights of solidarity (African Charter, 1981). The Charter is not structured in the same way as the Universal Declaration of Human Rights of 1948 (Universal Nations, 1948) or as the twin covenants of the International Covenant on Civil and Political Rights and the International Covenant on Economic, Social and Cultural Rights developed in 1966 (United Nations, 1966a, b) in that the third generation of community rights and solidarity is not specifically enumerated in the Charter.

6 See Articles 33 and 36 of the Charter (African Charter, 1981).

7 As part of its series of women's conferences, the United Nations 1995 Fourth World Conference on Women in Beijing was the final conference of the series (UN Women, n.d.c). Notably, the Beijing Conference produced the Beijing Declaration and Platform for Action, which was adopted by 189 different countries (UN Women, n.d.c). The documents serve as an "agenda for women's empowerment and [are] considered the key global policy document[s] on gender equality" (UN Women, n.d.c). Further, the follow-up activities to the Beijing Conference include reviews and appraisals every five years of the Platform for Action (UN Women, n.d.c). The most recent review was scheduled for March 2020, but aside from a procedural meeting that included adoption of the draft Political Declaration, all substantive debate and activities were postponed because of the COVID-19 pandemic (UN Women, n.d.b).

8 Article 42 of the African Charter sets out that the chairperson and vice-chairperson are elected for a two-year period and are eligible for re-election (African Charter, 1981).

9 Mrs. Duarte's expertise was recognized in 1995 when she was awarded the Council of Europe's North-South Prize for her "commitment to human rights, democracy and rule of law" (Council of Europe, n.d.b, c).

10 The Beijing Declaration and Platform for Action created policy recommendations to ensure equality for women. Notably, those documents identified women's under-representation in decision-making positions in all fields, including legal and diplomatic positions, and called on States Parties to work for better women's representation (United Nations, 1995). Since the African Commission was lacking in women's representation in its early years, it was slow to implement the Beijing recommendations.

11 Women representatives included Commissioners Angela Melo of Mozambique, Vera M. Chirwa of Malawi, Jainaba Johm of The Gambia, and Salamata Sawadogo of Burkina Faso (African Commission, n.d.b).

12 Female members from the 2002 session remained the same, with the addition of Sanji Monageng of Botswana, who first attended an ACHPR session in November 2003 (African Commission, n.d.b).

13 Commissioners Sawadogo, Melo, and Monageng remained, and Reine Alapini-Gansou of Benin and Faith Pansy Tlakula of South Africa were added (African Commission, n.d.b).

14 Little information is available about the national processes for nominating candidates to the African Commission, and the Executive Council noted in 2011 that only nine candidates were nominated for five positions; since then, the Commission has recommended that each region nominate candidates in surplus of the number of available positions (Murray, 2019).

15 This majority was represented by new members Soyata Maiga of Mali, Zainabo Sylvie Kayitesi of Rwanda, and Catherine Dupe Atoki of Nigeria, along with returning Commissioners Alapini-Gansou, Monageng, Tlakula, and Melo (African Commission, n.d.b).

16 Commissioner Angela Melo was elected following Article 39 of the African Charter (African Charter, 1981).

17 In 2011, Commissioners Alapini-Gansou and Tlakula were re-elected, and Commissioners Maya Sahil-Fadel, Med S. K. Kaggwa, and Pacifique Manirakiza were elected as new members (African Commission, n.d.b).
18 In 2013, Commissioners Yuen, Soyata Maiga, and Lucy Asuagbor were re-elected, and Commissioner Lawrence Murugu Mute was newly elected (African Commission, n.d.b).
19 Commissioner Kayitesi was re-elected, and Commissioners Jamesina E. L. King and Solomon A. Dersso were newly elected in 2015 (African Commission, n.d.b).
20 The newly elected members in 2017 included Commissioners Hatem Essaiem, Rémy Ngoy Lumbu, and Maria Teresa Manuela with Commissioner Maya Sahil-Fadel re-elected (African Commission, n.d.b).
21 Meaning "everlasting life," or, in this case, to serve a life term (Decock, 2013, pp.159–160).
22 Read Article 25 of the Maputo Protocol, which requires that states have a duty to provide remedies to women whose rights or freedoms have been violated (African Union, 2003). It follows, therefore, that if female candidates were not given the opportunity to run for elected positions, the states would have to provide a remedy.
23 Other international treaty bodies have encouraged equal representation. For example, the Rome Statute for the International Criminal Court in Article 36(8)(a) provides:

> "The States Parties shall, in the selection of judges, take into account the need, within the membership of the Court, for:
> (i) The representation of the principal legal systems of the world;
> (ii) Equitable geographical representation; and
> (iii) A fair representation of female and male judges" (International Criminal Court, 1998).

24 For example, in the case of the Maputo Protocol, 16 countries have signed but not ratified; even though the right to better gender representation is enshrined in this protocol, women's rights are being undermined by a lack of political will (Ayeni, 2016, p.309). States often have interests to share and negotiate, sometimes to the detriment of texts.
25 The Maputo Protocol has been described by the African Union Commission's Women, Gender and Development Directorate as "one of the most progressive legal instruments providing a comprehensive set of human rights for African women" (Women, Gender and Development, 2016, p.1). Articles in the Protocol point to equal representation of women during electoral processes and in the judicial and law enforcement arms of government (African Union, 2003).
26 The International Commission of Jurists (ICJ) is a human rights NGO created in 1952 (International Commission of Jurists, n.d.a) and currently has up to 60 prominent figures in the legal world, such as judges, lawyers, and law professors (International Commission of Jurists, n.d.b). Mary Robinson, the former president of Ireland and former United Nations High Commissioner for Human Rights, served as the ICJ president from 2008 until her successor took over at the end of January 2011 (International Commission of Jurists, 2011). The ICJ has consultative status with the Economic and Social Council of the United Nations (Economic and Social Council, 2018), the United Nations Educational, Scientific, and Cultural Organization (UNESCO, n.d.), the Council of Europe (Council of Europe, n.d.a), and the Organization of African Unity (Murray, 2007).
27 The technical support was especially prevalent in the context of the African Charter's redaction and the adoption of the African Commission's first Rules of Procedure in 1995 (Tolley, 2003).
28 See the list of participating NGOs in the prelude to the sessions of the African Commission (Network, 2020). The Open Society Initiative subsequently took over on many issues.

29 As of 2021, the African Commission has granted observer status to NGOs that so desire from all over the world (African Commission, n.d.a). See resolution on Cooperation between the African Commission on Human and Peoples' Rights and NGOs having Observer Status with it—ACHPR/Res.30 (XXIV) 98 (African Commission, n.d.b). Although NGOs play an important role as observers with the African Commission, their power to bring suit against states in the African Court has recently been diminished. Rwanda, Tanzania, Côte d'Ivoire, and Benin have all withdrawn from Article 30(f) of the Protocol on the Statute of the African Court of Justice and Human Rights, leaving only six states that allow NGOs this access to the court (International Justice Resource Center, 2020).

30 Today, NGOs such as the International Federation for Human Rights (FIDH, 2019) or the Open Society Initiative can be found advocating at the African Union summits and African Commission sessions.

31 Article 38 of the ACHPR requires Commissioners to make an oath or "declaration to discharge their duties impartially and faithfully" (African Charter, 1981). This does not, however, require the members to discontinue their individual professions.

32 Many of these areas of expertise reflect the various Special Rapporteur and Working Group positions that many women commissioners have led or been a part of.

33 For example, Commissioner and Chairperson Reine Alapini-Gansou litigated constitutional cases in Benin and served as a lecturer researcher in criminal law and criminal procedure at the Benin National University of Abomey (International Criminal Court, 2015), and Commissioner and Chairperson Catherine Dupe Atoki similarly worked as a lawyer in private practice and as a senior lecturer at the State Polytechnic Kaduna in Nigeria (African Commission, n.d.a). Both these women also led extensive careers in human rights in addition to working with the African Commission and fulfilling their other responsibilities.

34 The Commission's Rules of Procedure specifically give the Commission the power to create any subsidiary mechanisms, such as Special Rapporteurs, Committees, and Working Groups, in Rule 23 (African Commission, 2010).

35 As of 2021, there are 13 special mechanisms: Special Rapporteur on Prisons and Conditions of Detention in Africa, 20th Ordinary Session (Kampala; September, 1996); Special Rapporteur on Rights of Women in Africa, 23rd Ordinary Session (Banjul; April, 1998); Working Group on Indigenous Populations/Communities in Africa, 28th Ordinary Session (Cotonou; November, 2000); Resolution on Guidelines and Measures to Prohibit and Prevent Torture and Sentences or Cruel, Inhuman or Degrading Treatment or Punishment in Africa, 32nd Ordinary Session (Banjul; October, 2002); Protection of Human Rights Defenders in Africa, 35th Ordinary Session (Banjul; May–June, 2004); Special Rapporteur on Freedom of Expression in Africa, 36th Ordinary Session (Dakar; November–December, 2004); Special Rapporteur on Refugees, Asylum Seekers and Displaced Persons in Africa, 35th Ordinary Session (Dakar; November–December, 2004); Economic, Social and Cultural Rights in Africa, 36th Ordinary Session (Dakar; November–December, 2004); Working Group on the Death Penalty and Extrajudicial, Summary or Arbitrary Executions in Africa, 38th Ordinary Session (Banjul; November–December, 2005); Working Group on Rights of Older Persons and People with Disabilities in Africa, 42nd Ordinary Session (Brazzaville; November, 2007); Working Group on Extractive Industries, Environment and Human Rights Violations in Africa, 46th Ordinary Session (Banjul; November, 2009); and Committee on the Protection of the Rights of People Living with HIV (PLHIV) and Those at Risk, Vulnerable to and Affected by HIV, 47th Ordinary Session (Banjul; May, 2010) (African Commission, n.d.c).

36 Recent resolutions by these special mechanisms can be found on the website of the African Commission (African Commission, n.d.c).

37 For example, in Article 9.2, the Maputo Protocol encourages "increased and effective representation and participation of women at all levels of decision-making" as an international gender requirement (African Union, 2003).
38 See the compilation of documents drafted by the various mechanisms during the celebration of the 25th anniversary of the African Commission (African Commission, n.d.b).
39 The mandate has been renewed four times, the last time being in Resolution 154 of the 46th Ordinary Session (African Commission, n.d.c).
40 The Special Rapporteur on Prisons, Conditions of Detention and Policing in Africa is the oldest, created in 1996 (African Commission, n.d.c).
41 United Nations CEDAW was adopted in 1979; its implementation is evaluated annually by the Commission on Status of Women in connection with the committee of experts on the Committee on the Elimination of Discrimination against Women (United Nations Human Rights, n.d.; UN Women, n.d.a).
42 The Maputo Protocol was adopted pursuant to Article 66 of the African Charter, which allows for special protocols or agreements to supplement the African Charter (African Charter, 1981).
43 According to Article 26 of the Protocol to the African Charter on Human and Peoples' Rights on the Rights of Women in Africa, "States shall ensure the implementation of this Protocol at the national level, and in their periodic reports submitted in accordance with Article 62 of the African Charter, indicate the … measures undertaken for the full realisation of the rights herein recognised" (African Union, 2003).
44 Commissioner Melo was first appointed at the 30th Ordinary Session of the African Commission in 2001 (African Commission, n.d.b) and was renewed at the 34th Session in 2003 (African Commission, n.d.b) and at the 38th Session in 2005 (African Commission, n.d.b).
45 Under Commissioner Soyata Maiga, two General Comments were adopted on Article 14 related to the right to health, including more specific steps for governments to implement regarding HIV prevention measures and access to reproductive care, including abortions (Durojaye, 2018). Commissioner Maiga also worked on drafting two additional General Comments before the end of her mandate, including one on the "equal sharing of property between husband and wife upon divorce" according to Article 7(d) and another jointly with the African Committee of Experts on the Rights and Welfare of the Child on child marriage related to Article 6(b) of the Protocol (Durojaye, 2018, p.5).
46 The Gender is My Agenda Campaign (GIMAC) has been active in organizing gender initiatives and convening the Pre-Summit Civil Society Organizations Consultative Meetings before the African Union summits, most recently in February 2020 (African Union, 2020).
47 Similar language is present throughout the protocols. For example, the Protocol on the Statute of the African Court of Justice and Human Rights requires "equitable gender representation in the [judicial] nomination process" in Article 5 and equitable gender representation in election of Judges in Article 7 (African Union, 2008). Article 14 in the Protocol establishing the African Court on Human and Peoples' Rights requires that during elections the Assembly shall "ensure that there is adequate gender representation" (African Union, 1998).
48 Josephine Dawuni notes that "the postponement of the election … appears to have been a deliberate action on the part of the AU to make good on its gender parity promise" according to Articles 12 (2) and 14 (3) for the Protocol establishing the Court (Dawuni, 2017, para. 1).
49 Ms. Hina Jilani of Pakistan was the first appointed United Nations Special Representative on this issue following the 1998 adoption of the Declaration on the Right and Responsibility of Individuals, Groups and Organs of Society to Promote and Protect

Universally Recognized Human Rights and Fundamental Freedoms; commonly called the United Nations Declaration on Human Rights Defenders (United Nations, 2000).
50 The Grand Baie Declaration and Plan of Action of 1999 was adopted during the First OAU Ministerial Conference on Human Rights (African Commission, 1999).
51 The Kigali Declaration of 2003 was adopted at the First African Union Ministerial Conference on Human Rights in Africa, held in Kigali, Rwanda (African Commission, 2003).
52 Commissioner Jainaba Johm was the focal point of this mechanism in 2003 before being appointed Special Rapporteur on Human Rights Defenders in 2004, but her term on the Commission ended soon after in 2005 (African Commission, n.d.b).
53 Currently, five subregional networks are members of the Pan-African Human Rights Defenders Network: Réseau Ouest Africain des Défenseurs des Droits Humains; DefendDefenders—East and Horn of Africa Human Rights Defenders Network; Réseau des Défenseurs des Droits Humains en Afrique Centrale; Cairo Institute for Human Rights Studies; and Southern African Human Rights Defenders Network (African Defenders, n.d.).
54 See the conclusions of the 63rd session of the African Commission, 20th anniversary of the 1998 UN Declaration on Human Rights Defenders.
55 See Compendium on the Legal Protection of Human Rights Defenders in Africa (Lumbu, 2018).
56 With the initiative of the International Human Rights Service.
57 For a reference to these meetings, see the report by Commissioner Alapini-Gansou (Alapini-Gansou, 2012) covering the 52nd Ordinary Session.
58 The Protocol establishing the Court was adopted in 1998 and entered into force in 2004; the first judges were sworn in during 2006. (African Court, 2020).
59 The Protocol establishing the Charter on the Rights and Welfare of the Child was adopted in 1990, came into force in November, 1990, and formed in 2001 (African Union, n.d.a).
60 To date, six women and five men are sitting judges at the African Court on Human and Peoples' Rights (African Court, 2020). Seven women also hold Special Rapporteur positions on the African Committee of Experts on the Rights and Welfare of the Child (ACERWC, n.d.).
61 For example, in *Egyptian Initiative for Personal Rights and Interights, et al. v. Egypt*, the African Commission used language from the African Charter to show that women who were sexually assaulted during a demonstration in 2005 had their rights to non-discrimination as women violated (FIDH, 2019).

Bibliography

African Commission on Human and Peoples' Rights. (n.d.a). Home. https://www.achpr.org/home

African Commission on Human and Peoples' Rights. (n.d.b). Sessions. https://www.achpr.org/sessions

African Commission on Human and Peoples' Rights. (n.d.c). Special mechanisms. https://www.achpr.org/specialmechanisms

African [Banjul] Charter on Human and Peoples' Rights. (1982). Adopted June 27, 1981, OAU Doc. CAB/LEG/67/3 rev. 5, 21 I.L.M. 58, *entered into force* October 21, 1986.

African Commission on Human and Peoples' Rights. (1999). Grand Bay (Mauritius) declaration and plan of action, 1999. https://www.achpr.org/legalinstruments/detail?id=44

African Commission on Human and Peoples' Rights. (2003). Kigali Declaration, 2003. https://www.achpr.org/legalinstruments/detail?id=39

African Commission on Human and Peoples' Rights. (2010). *Rules of Procedure of the African Commission on Human and Peoples' Rights.* https://www.achpr.org/public/Document/file/English/Rules_of_Procedure_of_the_African_Commission_on_Human_and_PeoplesRightsof2010_%20Legal%20Instruments%20_%20ACHPR.pdf

African Committee of Experts on the Rights and Welfare of the Child. (n.d.). Experts. https://reporting.acerwc.africa/CommitteeExperts

African Court on Human and Peoples' Rights. (2018, July 17). Three new judges elected to the African court on human and peoples' rights: VP Justice Ben Kioko re-elected for second terms [Press release]. http://www.african-court.org/en/index.php/news/press-releases/item/245-three-new-judges-elected-to-the-african-court-on-human-and-peoples-rights-vp-justice-ben-kioko-re-elected-for-second-term

African Court on Human and Peoples' Rights. (2020). Current judges. https://en.african-court.org/index.php/judges/current-judges

African defenders. (n.d.). Member networks. https://africandefenders.org/members/

African Union. (n.d.a). *African Charter on the Rights and Welfare of the Child.* https://au.int/en/treaties/african-charter-rights-and-welfare-child

African Union. (n.d.b). Constitutive act. https://au.int/en/constitutive-act

African Union. (1998). *Protocol to the African Charter on Human and Peoples' Rights on the Establishment of an African Court on Human and Peoples' Rights.* https://au.int/sites/default/files/treaties/36393-treaty-0019_-_protocol_to_the_african_charter_on_human_and_peoplesrights_on_the_establishment_of_an_african_court_on_human_and_peoples_rights_e.pdf

African Union. (2000). *Constitutive Act of the African Union.* https://au.int/sites/default/files/pages/34873-file-constitutiveact_en.pdf

African Union. (2003). *Protocol to the African Charter on Human and Peoples' Rights on the Rights of Women in Africa.* https://www.un.org/en/africa/osaa/pdf/au/protocol_rights_women_africa_2003.pdf

African Union. (2004). *Solemn Declaration on Gender Equality in Africa.* https://www.un.org/en/africa/osaa/pdf/au/declaration_gender_equality_2004.pdf

African Union. (2008). *Protocol on the Statute of the African Court of Justice and Human Rights.* https://www.african-court.org/en/images/Basic%20Documents/ACJHR_Protocol.pdf

African Union. (2009). AU gender policy. *African Union.* https://www.un.org/en/africa/osaa/pdf/au/gender_policy_2009.pdf

African Union. (2016a). *Executive Council Twenty-Eighth Ordinary Session: Decisions.* https://au.int/sites/default/files/decisions/29513-ex_cl_dec_898_-_918_xxviii_e.pdf

African Union. (2016b). *Women's Rights in Africa.* https://www.ohchr.org/Documents/Issues/Women/WRGS/WomensRightsinAfrica_singlepages.pdf

African Union. (2018). *AU Strategy for Gender Equality and Women's Empowerment: 2018–2028.* https://au.int/sites/default/files/documents/36195-doc-au_strategy_for_gender_equality_womens_empowerment_2018-2028_report.pdf

African Union. (2020, February 3). 35th gender is my agenda campaign (GIMAC) civil society gender pre-summit. https://au.int/en/newsevents/20200203/35th-gender-my-agenda-campaign-gimac-civil-society-gender-pre-summit

Alapini-Gansou, R. (2012). Report on the implementation of the mandate of the special rapporteur on human rights defenders in Africa of the African Commission on Human and Peoples' Rights. *African Union.* https://www.achpr.org/sessions/intersession?id=140

Amnesty International. (1998). *All Africa Human Rights Defenders' Conference.* https://www.amnesty.org/download/Documents/148000/afr010101998en.pdf

Asian Human Rights Commission. (1998). *Asian Human Rights Charter*. https://www.refworld.org/pdfid/452678304.pdf
Ayeni, V.O. (2016). *The Impact of the African Charter and the Maputo Protocol in Selected African States*. Pretoria University Law Press (PULP).
Council of Europe. (n.d.a). Conference of INGOs. http://coe-ngo.org/#/Ingos
Council of Europe. (n.d.b). FAQ. https://www.coe.int/en/web/north-south-centre/faq#{%2227718377%22:[9]}
Council of Europe. (n.d.c). Previous laureates of the North-South prize. https://www.coe.int/en/web/north-south-centre/previous-laureates-of-the-north-south-prize#27717772_27724221_True
Council of Europe, European Court of Human Rights. (1950). European convention on human rights. https://www.echr.coe.int/Pages/home.aspx?p=basictexts&c
Dawuni, J. (2017, March 13). African women judges and gender parity on the African Court on Human and Peoples' Rights. *LSE*. https://blogs.lse.ac.uk/africaatlse/2017/03/13/african-women-judges-and-gender-parity-on-the-african-court-on-human-and-peoples-rights/
Decock, W. (2013). *Theologians and Contract Law: The Moral Transformation of the Ius Commune (ca. 1500–1650)*. Nijhoff
Durojaye, E. (2018). The special rapporteur on the rights of women in Africa (SRRWA) 2007–2015. *Gender & Behaviour*, *16*(1), 10700–10709.
Economic and Social Council. (2018). *List of Non-Governmental Organizations in Consultative Status with the Economic and Social Council as of 1 September 2018*. https://undocs.org/E/2018/INF/5
Genti, Nos. (2012, September). *Vera Duarte, por grandes causas, pela vida, pelas pessoas*. http://nosgenti.com/vera-duarte-por-grandes-causas-pela-vida-e-pelas-pessoas
Gutto, S. (2001). The reform and renewal of the African regional human and peoples' rights system. *African Human Rights Law Journal*, *1*(2), 175–184.
International Commission of Jurists. (n.d.a). Part one: 1952–1970. https://www.icj.org/history/part-one-1952-1970/
International Commission of Jurists. (n.d.b). The commission. https://www.icj.org/commission/
International Commission of Jurists. (2011, January 27). Pedro Nikken elected new ICJ president. https://www.icj.org/january-2011-pedro-nikken-is-elected-new-icj-president/
International Criminal Court. (1998). *Rome Statute of the International Criminal Court*. https://www.icc-cpi.int/resource-library/documents/rs-eng.pdf
International Criminal Court. (2015). *Alapini Gansou, Reine (Benin): Curriculum Vitae*. https://asp.icc-cpi.int/iccdocs/asp_docs/Elections/EJ2017/ICC-ASP-EJ2017-BEN-CV-ENG.pdf
International Federation for Human Rights. (n.d.). African Union. https://www.fidh.org/en/international-advocacy/african-union
International Federation for Human Rights. (2019). *The Impact of Litigation on Combating Sexual Violence and Its Consequences in Africa: Sharing Experience and Practical Advice*. https://reliefweb.int/sites/reliefweb.int/files/resources/436237467-The-Impact-of-Litigation-on-Combating-Sexual-Violence-and-its-Consequences-in-Africa.pdf
International Justice Resource Center. (2020, May 6). Benin and Côte d'Ivoire to withdraw individual access to African court. https://ijrcenter.org/2020/05/06/benin-and-cote-divoire-to-withdraw-individual-access-to-african-court/
International Service for Human Rights. (2011, February 17). Special rapporteurs. https://www.ishr.ch/news/special-rapporteurs

Lima-Neves, T.S. (n.d.). Duarte, Vera. *Oxford African American Studies*. https://doi.org/10.1093/acref/9780195301731.013.50507

Lumbu, N. (2018). *Compendium on the Legal Protection of Human Rights Defenders in Africa*. Pretoria University Law Press. https://www.achpr.org/public/Document/file/English/english_chrd.pdf

Malmstrom, S. & Oberleitner, G.. (1996). Africa. *Netherlands Quarterly of Human Rights*, *14*(1), 92–96.

Mathieu, J. (1998). *La défense internationale des droits de l'homme*. Presses universitaires de France

Murray, R. (2007). *Human Rights in Africa: From the OAU to the African Union*. Cambridge University Press.

Murray, R. (2019). *The African Charter on Human and Peoples' Rights: A Commentary*. Oxford University Press.

Olsen, F. (1990). El sexo del derecho. In: D. Kairys (Ed.) & Santoro, M. & Courtis, C. (Trans.). *The Politics of Law* (pp. 452–467). Pantheon.

Open Society Initiative for Southern Africa (OSISA) and Oxfam. (2009). *Strengthening Popular Participation in the African Union: A Guide to AU Structures and Processes*. https://oi-files-d8-prod.s3.eu-west-2.amazonaws.com/s3fs-public/file_attachments/au-guide-eng.pdf

Organisation of African Unity. (1994). *Chapter Seven Seventh Annual Activity Report of the African Commission 1993–1994*. https://archives.au.int/bitstream/handle/123456789/5365/7e%20Rapport%20Annuel_E.pdf?sequence=1&isAllowed=y

Organization of American States. (1969). *American Convention on Human Rights*. http://www.oas.org/dil/treaties_B-32_American_Convention_on_Human_Rights.pdf

Pretoria University Law Press. (2016). *A Guide to the African Human Rights System*. https://www.corteidh.or.cr/tablas/31712.pdf

Tolley, H. (2003). *The International Commission of Jurists: Global Advocates for Human Rights*. University of Pennsylvania Press.

UN Women. (n.d.a). A brief history of the commission on the status of women. https://www.unwomen.org/en/csw/brief-history

UN Women. (n.d.b). CSW64/Beijing+25 (2020). https://www.unwomen.org/en/csw/csw64-2020

UN Women. (n.d.c). World conferences on women. https://www.unwomen.org/en/how-we-work/intergovernmental-support/world-conferences-on-women

UNESCO. (n.d.). *List of NGOs in Official Partnership with UNESCO within the Framework of the Directives Concerning UNESCO's Partnership with Non-Governmental Organizations (36C/Res. 108)*. https://en.unesco.org/sites/default/files/list_of_ngos_in_official_partnership_with_unesco_-_liste_des_ong_en_partenariat_officiel_avec_lunesco_-_feb_2020_0.pdf

United Nations. (1948). *Universal Declaration of Human Rights*. https://www.ohchr.org/EN/UDHR/Documents/UDHR_Translations/eng.pdf

United Nations. (1966a). *International Covenant on Civil and Political Rights*. https://www.ohchr.org/Documents/ProfessionalInterest/ccpr.pdf

United Nations. (1966b). *International Covenant on Economic, Social and Cultural Rights*. https://www.ohchr.org/Documents/ProfessionalInterest/cescr.pdf

United Nations. (1995). *Beijing Declaration and Platform for Action*. https://www.un.org/en/events/pastevents/pdfs/Beijing_Declaration_and_Platform_for_Action.pdf

United Nations. (2000, August 18). Secretary-General names Hina Jilani, Pakistan, as special representative on human rights defenders [Press release]. https://www.un.org/press/en/2000/20000818.sga743.doc.html

United Nations Human Rights Office of the High Commissioner. (n.d.). Committee on the elimination of discrimination against women. https://www.ohchr.org/en/hrbodies/cedaw/pages/cedawindex.aspx

Wandia, M. (2004, June 3). Rights of women in Africa: Launch of petition to the African Union. *Pambazuka News*. https://www.pambazuka.org/gender-minorities/rights-women-africa-launch-petition-african-union

Women & Gender and Development Directorate. (2016). *Maputo Protocol on Women's Rights: A Living Document for Women's Human Rights in Africa*. https://au.int/sites/default/files/documents/31520-doc-maputo_protocol_on_womens_rights_a_living_document_for_womens_human_rights_in_africa_submitted_by_the_women_gender_and_development_directorate_wgdd_of_the_african_union_commission.pdf

10 Pursuing gender equality through the courts

The role of South Africa's women judges

Penelope Andrews

Introduction

This chapter will focus on the contribution of female judges to the transformation of the judiciary in South Africa and specifically the pursuit of gender equality. It is a limited project that will explore the impacts of women judges on constitutional jurisprudence and how the influence of women judges has interacted with the broader transformation of the judicial and political system in South Africa after apartheid.[1] In examining the impact of women judges on constitutional jurisprudence with respect to gender equality, I explore whether women judges have, in their judgments, conscripted and interpreted the constitution to highlight and guarantee its transformative potential and possibilities.

The focus of my research project is partial, since it is based on a small number of judgments of the Constitutional Court, the highest court in South Africa. The very nature of the work of the Constitutional Court, the venue of last judicial resort, renders it an arcane institution vis-à-vis the rest of the judicial system. It was only established in 1995 in the wake of democracy and therefore occupies a rarefied place in the court structure. Most people in South Africa experience justice, or at least have their legal disputes adjudicated, in the lower courts, especially the Magistrates' Courts, as well as Indigenous courts. Since the decisions of these courts are not published, a study of their decisions would require resources, time, and particularized expertise—which is outside the scope of this chapter. A study of judgments of the Constitutional Court, however, does provide a mechanism to investigate constitutional interpretation early on in the South African democratic project. These judgments do provide an indication of the jurisprudential direction of the country—and how lower courts might in turn implement and interpret the constitution.

A curtain-raiser

Although their cohabitation was never formalized, they had lived together for over two decades as a married couple and were perceived as such by the outside world. One of the few legal avenues available to her to claim some access to the property they had accumulated over the course of their relationship was to

DOI: 10.4324/9780429327865-13

prove that a universal partnership existed between them. The law provided limited relief by analogizing the universal partnership rules for commercial transactions to the private situation of cohabitation. Several criteria needed to be satisfied, and an important factor for the court in its deliberations was her tangible contribution as well as the notion that the partnership existed for profit. He claimed that no universal partnership existed and that her claim should be thrown out for failure to demonstrate the evidence needed to establish such a partnership.

The judge, who had researched and written extensively on women's rights and gender equality, considered both the tangible (monetary) resources brought to the partnership by the plaintiff and her intangible (non-monetary) contributions of domestic labor, care, and nurturing of the family. The couple had no children, but she had shared child-caring duties with him when his children from a previous marriage stayed periodically. The judge was familiar with the research that demonstrated how women historically had contributed to the household with unpaid labor—and how such labor was often not included in monetary settlements at the dissolution of a long-term relationship. The judge concluded that in fact, the plaintiff had shown sufficient evidence to establish a universal partnership, which permitted the plaintiff to survive a motion to dismiss her claim.

Could an argument be made that without these insights of a female judge, many women in South Africa would be bereft of an equitable distribution of property if they happen to have cohabited with a man for a considerable period without entering into a marriage or concluding a written contract? And would these insights be restricted to only female judges, who are assumed to be more "feminist" in their worldview than men? Coontz and others have suggested that a male judge may not express the insights highlighted because of the discrete experiences of women (Coontz, 2000; Wilson, 1990). No doubt, some male judges *do* bring an empathetic gendered perspective to their judgments, as I highlight later, but because of the lingering sexist attitudes and lived experiences of male and female judges in contemporary South Africa, the philosophical default for female judges may, on average, lean more contextually, and therefore more empathetically, toward the experience of female litigants.[2]

This minor example and the questions raised here to go to the heart of the discussion of why it is important that women judges be appointed and what women judges add to the bench, as well as the development of jurisprudence that speaks to the lived realities of women. Are their perspectives different, and are women judges more committed to an "ethic of care" (Gilligan 1982)? Is there a feminist judicial methodology? These are in many ways hackneyed questions that form part of the wider conversation regarding the feminization of the legal profession and the increasing presence of larger numbers of women in law schools and in the legal profession (Schultz & Shaw, 2013; Norgren, 2018; Li et al., 2020). These questions have been part of an ongoing discussion among scholars, legal practitioners, and feminist activists for some time and have generated substantial research questions and analyses. What the research so far has demonstrated is the importance of a diverse judiciary for a range of reasons, including legitimacy, representation, competence, cultural competence, and empathy (Mossman, 2005; Hunter, 2008; Dixon, 2010; Durojaye & Oluduro, 2016; Coontz, 2000).

In late 2018, I had the opportunity to serve as an acting judge of the North Gauteng High Court in Pretoria, a court of first instance as well as an appeal court. I presided over a range of cases: criminal appeals, civil trials, motion court, and admission of attorneys and advocates. The decision regarding universal partnerships mentioned earlier was one of the judgments that I delivered during the course of my term. As a longstanding law professor, the judicial experience was probably the most exhilarating and challenging of my career, engaging with the law from a hitherto unfamiliar vantage point. It helped me to consider up close some questions that I had raised before in relation to the judiciary, namely, how one's racial and gender identity impacts upon our decisions, as well as how we are perceived by lawyers who appear before us and the litigants that they represent (Andrews 2010) The experience confirmed my scholarly insights about how women and people of color (previously excluded from the judiciary) may be particularly attuned to a range of non-legal factors that impact the legal controversies that they adjudicate. The experience also confirmed for me the challenges that female judges, as voices of authority in the courtroom, continue to confront in the face of the male bias in the law (Dawuni & Kuenyehia, 2018). As a former Judge-President of the Supreme Court of Appeal noted, "the advent of the liberating and empowering provisions of the constitution did not act, as might have been expected like the flick of an attitudinal switch."[3]

The question of whether women judges make a difference remains relevant, with different conclusions reached by different studies (Dawuni & Bauer, 2016; Irving, 2017). In this chapter, I put that question to the test by investigating the contribution of South Africa's Constitutional Court judges, through their written judgments, to the pursuit of constitutional rights that reinforce gender equality. I have chosen to focus only on the Constitutional Court judges, since that court is the apex court in the country.

Historical exclusion of women judges in South Africa

The first woman to practice law in South Africa was only admitted in 1923, and up until the 1980s, the number of female legal practitioners, particularly black female practitioners, was very small. Colonialism and apartheid excluded black South Africans, male and female, from serving as judges on the High Courts, although black males, and to a lesser extent black females, served as magistrates in the lower courts. Gender discrimination excluded white women from serving as judges, although some managed to be appointed as magistrates (Masengu 2016, 2019).

Since 1994, with the adoption of a new constitution and the establishment of a democracy in South Africa, women have been appointed as judges. Their appointment in the past two decades raises many questions that go beyond the need for greater numbers and greater gender representation. As I have written elsewhere, consideration of racial and gender diversity, and to a lesser extent disability and sexual orientation diversity, has propelled the transformation of the judiciary in South Africa (Andrews 2008). This consideration is underpinned by the assumption, both stated and unstated, that a majority white and male judiciary is unable to serve and deliver justice to a majority black and female population. The project of constitutional democracy is contingent on a bench that reflects the racial and gender diversity of the society (Andrews 2010).

A recognition of and the reflection of diversity generate a further set of considerations as they pertain to women judges. In addition to the questions raised earlier, the issue of women's judicial authority and its interface with implicit bias is pertinent. So too are the notions of judicial neutrality and objectivity and their intersection with the subjective perspectives that women may bring, which are based on women's discrete experiences, particularly in the workplace. Some of these issues have been systematically addressed in the research in other jurisdictions as well as in various research projects globally (Mossman, 2005; Hunter, 2008; Dawuni, 2016; Dixon, 2010; Banks, 2017; Graycar, 2009; Coontz, 2000). A few comprehensive volumes have recently been published that have highlighted and analyzed the key questions relating to the role of women judges globally, focusing on the history of women in the judiciary; women serving on international tribunals; quotas, diversity, and representation; judicial training; judicial selection processes; the career paths of women judges; the difference in perspective between female and male judges; feminist adjudication; and women's place and impact in the judiciary (Schultz & Shaw, 2013; Kenney, 2013; Hunter et al., 2010; Dawuni & Bauer, 2016; Stanchi et al., 2016; Helen Irving, 2017; Dawuni & Kuenyehia, 2018).

These questions are increasingly being addressed by scholars in South Africa and beyond. A range of feminist scholars have explored judicial transformation in South Africa, including the obstacles facing females for appointment to the judiciary, especially the pervasive discrimination against women in the legal profession and the wider society, the legal and political context of the judicial appointments process, and the impact of female judges on the bench and on constitutional jurisprudence (Masengu, 2016; Albertyn & Bonthuys, 2016; Bauer & Dawuni, 2016; Cowan, 2006; Phooko & Radebe, 2016).

A perennial concern of research of this kind relates to gender essentialism, the notion of conflating women judges with feminist judges. The research, however, suggests that despite concerns of gender essentialism, there are concrete examples to demonstrate that women judges in fact make a difference (Wilson, 1990; Malleson, 2003; Coontz, 2000). But the difference is located in experience and not biology, with judges bringing not just legal knowledge and skill but also a "set of values, experiences and assumptions that are thoroughly embedded."[4]

Transformation of the legal and judicial system

Since 1994, the legal system in South Africa has moved from one premised on racism, sexism, and authoritarianism to one that strives to provide human rights for all South Africans; from a culture of authoritarianism to a culture of justification

(Mureinik, 1994). Most significantly, the political transition in South Africa has seen a shift from a system of parliamentary supremacy to one of constitutional democracy. These were legal tectonic shifts affecting all branches of government, including the judiciary. These changes required a fundamental rethinking and restructuring, especially regarding the demographic make-up of the judges, judicial processes, judicial interpretation, judicial training, judicial appointments, and judicial tenure. These proposed shifts were comprehensively included and outlined in the constitution in a section devoted to the judicial system.

After the establishment of the first democratic system of government in South Africa in 1994, the judicial system was substantially overhauled, including the creation of a Constitutional Court. As the chart at the end of this chapter shows, at the apex of the court structure is the Constitutional Court as the final court of appeal. The Constitutional Court is solely mandated to decide disputes between organs of state and review the constitutionality of amendments to the constitution as well as provincial constitutions and legislation passed by all levels of government. Below the Constitutional Court sits a range of lower courts, some replicating the court structure under apartheid, albeit with a name change. The apex court under apartheid, the Appellate Division, was renamed the Supreme Court of Appeal. The Supreme Courts were renamed High Courts, and below them were the Magistrates' Courts. New courts were especially created to accommodate this transformative vision of the constitution, including the Land Claims Courts, the Equality Courts, the Electoral Court, and the Sexual Offences Courts. In addition, a nod to the emerging globally integrated economy at the end of apartheid was the establishment of the Competition Appeals Court and the Tax Court.

The constitution mandated a reimagining of the legal system to be more representative, accountable, accessible, and capable of providing justice to all South Africans irrespective of race, gender, and ethnicity. The appointment of judges was seen to be reflective of these values in their make-up, demographics, commitment, and philosophy. The issue of diversity and equity in the judiciary cannot seriously be confronted without addressing the context of ubiquitous patriarchy and sexism in South Africa—and especially within the legal profession. As I have argued elsewhere (Andrews, 2008), the legal profession in South Africa has always been dominated by white males, has generated a peculiarly masculinist culture, and is therefore not amenable to attracting huge numbers of female practitioners.[5]

I have also written elsewhere about the deeply patriarchal and masculinist cultural attitudes and odious sexist practices that still pervade South Africa despite a Bill of Rights that is unequivocally committed to the principle of equality (Andrews, 1998, 2001). Moreover, South African society evinces one of the highest statistics in the world regarding violence against women.[6] The appointment of women judges, therefore, has to be examined within the context of a constitutional commitment to gender equality, on the one hand, and on the other hand, countervailing persistent negative attitudes and stereotypes of women, which prove very resistant to transformation.

As a legacy of the British legal system, the profession is divided between advocates (barristers) and attorneys (solicitors), with only advocates mandated to appear before the higher courts in the country and attorneys relegated to practice in the lower Magistrates' Courts.[7] Before 1994, admission as an advocate required an undergraduate and a law degree with passage in the then official languages, English and Afrikaans, as well as a course in Latin. Those admitted as attorneys required only an undergraduate law degree. It is not a stretch to imagine that overcoming these stringent academic requirements was a significant obstacle for black South Africans (for whom English and Afrikaans were second or third languages). In an adversarial system, and with only advocates traditionally having the right of appearance in the higher courts, advocates have historically attracted among their ranks individuals, overwhelmingly male, who are more predisposed to trial work. This is so for many reasons, including a greater sense of confidence that white males experience in a racially hierarchical society, more contacts with attorneys who may brief them, and the ability to work the long and erratic hours that trials sometimes require. These factors have resulted in fewer women practicing as advocates.[8] Since the pool of judges has historically come from the ranks of advocates, who are seen as having relevant trial experience, this has therefore resulted in a limited pool of women available for appointment to the bench.

Because the transformation of the judiciary is mandated in the constitution, the situation has changed in South Africa, and judges are no longer chosen only from the ranks of advocates. As mentioned earlier, the numbers of women, especially black women, practicing as advocates was minimal in 1994—and to effect transformation, candidates from the ranks of attorneys (and to a lesser extent, academics and the civil service), had to be considered for appointment to the bench. In addition, the Legal Practice Act in South Africa, which was adopted in 2014 and came into force in late 2018, intends, among others, to streamline and regulate the legal profession and remove the traditional barriers between advocates and attorneys. The Act is clear about its intended goals, stating that it aims

> [t]o provide a legislative framework for the transformation and restructuring of the legal profession in line with constitutional imperatives so as to facilitate and enhance an independent legal profession that broadly reflects the diversity and demographics of the Republic.[9]

This development is a significant one and should go some way toward removing some of the obstacles that women judges, especially black women judges, have experienced in gaining access to judicial appointments. However, since the provision has been in effect for less than two years, it is hard to evaluate its overall impact at this stage.

Judicial diversity

In South Africa, the issue of judicial diversity, and especially the appointment of female judges, is unique in two respects. The first is that the appointment of female judges emerged as part of the entire project of transformative constitutionalism, the purpose of which was to upend apartheid laws and policies in all their manifestations as well as to facilitate a fundamental shift in the unequal social, political, and economic relations that prevail in South Africa. Their historical exclusion from the bench and therefore, the absence of their perspectives meant that appointing female judges fell squarely within the project of transformative constitutionalism. In other words, new perspectives were brought into the process of adjudication.

The second unique aspect regarding judicial diversity in South Africa is that built into the project of constitutionalism is the idea that the jurisprudence itself would be transformative and therefore feminist.[10] In other words, the South African constitution and Bill of Rights is designed to achieve certain ends, including racial justice, gender equality, and a broad range of social justice and human rights goals. The Preamble to the constitution states the need to "establish a society based on democratic values, social justice and fundamental human rights" and to "improve the quality of life of all citizens and free the potential of each person."[11]

Therefore, the constitutional imperative or mandate for all South African judges is a commitment to eradicating or minimizing the systemic inequality, repression, and subjugation that were the defining features of the apartheid legal order—and it is against this backdrop that the impact of female judges is to be evaluated. At least as a formal proposition, the judges had to be feminist in their jurisprudence[12]—and the following discussion on the constitutional jurisprudence of the Constitutional Court in fact demonstrates such a commitment on the part of the overwhelming number of judges. Justice Sachs has noted that

> certainly, all the judges on the Constitutional Court recognized the need for major transformations in society, not only the ugliness and unfairness and injustice of apartheid dreadfulness, but the fact that it had left quite deeply entrenched patterns of inequality and disparity.[13]

But the apparent ubiquity of the transformative constitutional vision does not render the issue of whether female judges make a difference an irrelevant or even a moot question. My point here is that following the establishment of the Constitutional Court in the wake of democracy in South Africa, a philosophical litmus test for its founding judges was introduced. They were handpicked and appointed to be the standard bearers for this new transformative jurisprudence. The selection of the first set of Constitutional Court judges was also symbolic, with all the judges having a pedigree of anti-apartheid credentials, including the first President of the court, a noted public interest lawyer. As noted by Justice Kriegler, one of the first judges appointed to the Constitutional Court by President Mandela, "the court has been painfully aware of its role as a constitutional trailblazer," signaling to South Africa and the world the radical jurisprudential shift from apartheid to democracy.[14]

As the terms of office of the initial cohort of judges come to an end (because of term limits), as the constitutional and other courts evolve, and as the commitment to transformation becomes more contested, it is not a given that those individuals who are appointed as judges will show the same heightened appreciation of gender equality as their female counterparts. Indeed, it is arguable that the decade-long incumbency of President Jacob Zuma, who was charged and acquitted of rape, has set back the formal commitment to gender equality (Gqola, 2015).

Appointment of female judges

In the dying days of apartheid, except for a black male and two females, the judiciary was comprised entirely of white men. In its final report, the Truth and Reconciliation Commission recommended that imbalances in the racial and gender composition of judges be urgently addressed and a fast-track judicial training program be introduced for black and women advocates, attorneys, or academics who aspire to judicial appointment.[15] The drafters of South Africa's first post-apartheid constitution, in keeping with the principles of transparency and accountability, completely revamped the system of appointing judges. Under the apartheid system, the appointment of judges had been at the discretion of the President on the recommendation of the Minister of Justice, without formal input from the judiciary, the legal profession, or members of civil society—and certainly without public scrutiny (Dugard, 1978).

The Judicial Services Commission (JSC), comprising membership of the judiciary, government, the legal profession, and civil society, is empowered under the constitution to make recommendations to the President on the appointment of judges—after screening and interviewing "any appropriately qualified woman or man who is a fit and proper person" (as stated in the constitution). A transparent public process, with great scrutiny from the media and civil society organizations, the JSC was initially seen as a step toward greater transparency and inclusivity and a break from the secretive and exclusive approach adopted by prior apartheid and colonial administrations (Albertyn & Bonthuys, 2016). And with the constitutional imperative that the judiciary reflect the South African racial and gender demographics, the appointments process is vital to achieving the goal of gender inclusivity and diversity.

Since 1994, the racial and gender make-up of the South African judiciary has been dramatically altered. In 1994, South Africa's 200 judges were overwhelmingly white and male, including only 2 black and 2 female judges. In 2018, the number of female judges has increased, and women now make up one-third of the judiciary. The Judge-President of the Supreme Court of Appeal, the second highest court, is female, and the acting head of the Land Claims Court is a woman. The Constitutional Court, however, has failed to appoint more than three females at any given time—and that court is still overwhelmingly male (Baines, 2017). Overall, the number of female judges, who make up only 36% of the judiciary, falls far short of the goal of a diverse and representative judiciary. This is in contrast to the racial transformation of the judiciary, where in 2017 it was recorded that white judges comprise only 34% of the judiciary. The judiciary has been transformed from being overwhelmingly white and male in 1994 to being overwhelming black and male today.[16]

Several reasons account for this deficit, including the legacy of apartheid and its exclusion of black women, the career paths in law that women choose (which may not always be congruent with judicial ambitions), the lack of support for women with judicial aspirations as well as confidence among women lawyers to make themselves available for judicial appointments, and the work–life balance and other issues that women, and indeed all professionals, constantly have to juggle. All these reasons are located in the rampant sexist and patriarchal attitudes that pervade South African society, including in the legal profession as well as the judicial appointment processes. The last factor, namely the judicial appointments process, has been a serious obstacle to the goals of gender equality in the judiciary.[17]

The JSC has shown a lack of commitment to appointing women judges and has on occasion demonstrated outright hostility to qualified female candidates during the JSC hearings. For example, in April 2019, a highly respected female judge was described as "overbearing" during her JSC interview.[18] When I was interviewed by the JSC for an appointment to the Constitutional Court in 2005, one JSC member pondered aloud whether "a boyfriend" would encourage my return to South Africa. Another female candidate for promotion to Deputy Judge-President, who is openly gay, was asked whether her gay lifestyle might not make her colleagues uncomfortable.[19] What was alarming about this exchange—visible to the public—was that despite the fact that the questions raised were inappropriate and also unconstitutional (at least regarding the lifestyle of the gay judge), not one member of the JSC, including the Chief Justice, intervened to stop such a line of questioning. That room mirrored the attitudes prevalent in the wider South African society. Only a fundamental rethink of the make-up, operation, and processes of the JSC, with the stated goals of gender equality, will satisfy the constitutional mandate of inclusivity and equality in the judiciary (Johnson, 2014; Malleson, 1999).

Jurisprudence on equality

In this section, I explore the question of the difference that women judges make and what impact women judges have on constitutional jurisprudence with respect to gender equality.

As mentioned earlier in this chapter, the constitution sets out a particularized transformative vision of rights, a hegemonic interpretive endeavor embedded within a tacit societal agreement as to specific outcomes (Johnson, 2014). Part of that vision and purported outcomes relates to the capability and commitment of those who will review and adjudicate those rights. In short, who are the most appropriate judges to bring about the transformative outcomes? It may be worth noting a few unique features of South African constitutionalism to demonstrate its transformative potential, particularly regarding gender equality, as Karl Klare and others have noted (Klare, 1998; Johnson, 2014; Moseneke, 2002). The first is the horizontal and vertical nature of the constitution, applying to relationships between the state and citizens as well as to relationships between citizen and citizen. This approach to constitutionalism recognizes that discrimination is often shielded by and embedded in private as well as public relationships (McKinnon, 2012). The drafters of the constitution recognized that constitutional interpretation occurs within a universe of structural disadvantage, subordination, and discrimination, which are embedded in South Africa's political, economic, social, and legal system. The imperative is for courts, in their interpretation of the constitution, to derogate from the *status quo* to redress these structural impediments to equality (Liebenberg, 2005).

The constitution provides not just for a range of negative proscriptions on government conduct but also for a range of positive actions that need to be taken to address the unequal social and economic realities of South Africa. Therefore, a range of social and economic rights are made as fully justiciable as political and civil rights (Wilson & Dugard, 2011; Liebenberg, 2005). The constitution also mandates that courts must consider international law and may consider foreign law in their deliberations, thereby creating the discursive space for jurisprudential innovation and creativity alongside global and comparative developments (Andrews, 2008).

The jurisprudence of the Constitutional Court suggests a clear break from the apartheid legal past to one forged on principles of dignity, equality, and non-discrimination, with the goal of eradicating the legacies of subordination and discrimination against members of previously disadvantaged communities, including women. Women judges have, in their judgments, conscripted and interpreted the constitution to highlight and guarantee its transformative potential and possibilities. The judgments of the Constitutional Court, particularly in the first decade of its operation, elucidate a rich and compelling jurisprudence that has been heralded by constitutional and human rights scholars globally (Kende, 2009). The cases discussed later demonstrate a thoughtful articulation by the justices, especially the female justices, of the Constitutional Court for the need to eradicate the vestiges of discrimination against women.

On the issue of gender equality, the Court has for the most part articulated a comprehensive approach to equality, eschewing narrow formalistic approaches in favor of methodologies that adopt a more substantive version. Particularly in the first decade of the Court, the judges consistently underscored the primacy of equality as a foundational constitutional value. This approach has been accentuated in a range of early cases, including those involving the workplace rights of HIV-positive persons not to be discriminated against;[20] the right of prisoners to vote;[21] the rights of unmarried fathers in relation to adoption of their children;[22] the employment rights of permanent residents not to be treated unfairly in comparison to citizens;[23] the rights of homosexuals to engage in consensual sexual conduct;[24] and the rights of African girls and women not to be discriminated against under Indigenous customary law.[25]

In one of its most notable early decisions and emblematic of its jurisprudential trajectory on equality, the Constitutional Court considered the constitutionality of an executive order signed by President Nelson Mandela.[26] The President had sought to pardon "all mothers in prison on 10 May 1994, with minor children under the age of 12 years." In a gender equality challenge by a male prisoner, the Constitutional Court first considered the nature of the power granted to the President to pardon individuals or groups and concluded that the presidential power to pardon is guided by the principle of equality as articulated in the constitution.

In a lengthy multi-authored opinion, the court first found that the presidential pardon discriminated against the complainant, which triggered the presumption of unfairness and shifting the burden to the President to establish that the discrimination was fair. The court turned to an examination of the rationale that motivated the pardon in allowing the special remission for mothers of minor children. With empirical evidence from social welfare, psychiatric, and other experts to highlight the distinctive role that mothers play in the rearing of their children, the court highlighted the contradiction between the constitutional dictate that everyone be treated equally and the contextual reality that mothers bear the greatest burden of childrearing.

The majority noted that it could not be blind to the contemporary reality in South Africa, namely, the idealized situation in which fathers and mothers equally share childrearing tasks and the reality of the unequal burden of childrearing borne by mothers. The court noted that historically, stereotypes about women bearing the greater responsibility of childrearing were used to discriminate against women, whereas this stereotype was justified, since it resulted not in a burden to women but in an opportunity. Moreover, children would benefit substantially from the presidential pardon.

The Constitutional Court also considered what the likely outcome would be if equal treatment were applied, namely, the release of all prisoners, male and female, with children under the age of 12. It concluded that no public benefit would be gained by releasing fathers, because they were not the primary caretakers of children. Noting that the Presidential Act provides for the individual application for remission of sentences by male prisoners where special circumstances can be shown, the court therefore found the discrimination to be fair. The dissent took issue with the rationale that women were the primary caregivers of young children, stating that this generalization was "a root cause of women's inequality" and that the rationale for majority decision would operate as a "detriment to all South African women who must continue to labor under the social view that their place is in the home."

As one of the two female justices on the Court, Justice O'Regan's concurring opinion is particularly noteworthy. She noted that the determination of whether the discrimination was unfair required a recognition that the ultimate constitutional goal is equal treatment, but that "equal treatment in circumstances of established inequality may well result in the entrenchment of that inequality." Justice O'Regan observed that despite the primacy of equality in the constitution, the factual reality in South Africa was that women did carry, and would continue to carry in the foreseeable future, the greater burden of childrearing.

She considered this a crucial fact in looking at discrimination and determining the unfairness of the distinction made. Referring to the dissent's proposition that there would be a profound disadvantage for women in perpetuating the stereotype through the distinction, Justice O'Regan pointed out that the profound disadvantage did not result from the presidential pardon but from the inequality that was part of the social fabric of South African society. She disagreed with the dissent that this presidential pardon harmed women.

Justice O'Regan and the majority exemplify the broad contours of equality that the Constitutional Court was prepared to embrace from the outset. The court was concerned not just with formal equality (equal treatment), which can at times lead to inequality, but also with substantive equality, which contextualizes the actual experiences and reality of women within the formal impediments to equality. In a similar vein, another early case on gender equality involved a challenge by an unmarried father to the provisions of the Child Care Act, which allowed the adoption of children born out of wedlock without the consent of the father.[27] For children born in wedlock, the consent of both parents was required. The father successfully challenged the law, and it was declared unconstitutional. Adopting a contextual approach reflecting the social reality of South Africa, the court, in a unanimous judgment, stated that a mother's "biological relationship with the child," nurtured during pregnancy and breastfeeding, is a special one. The court also noted that a mother gives "succor and support" to a child that is "very direct and not comparable to that of a father." In its analysis, the court surveyed several systems of marriage in South Africa, including some that were not formal, resulting in children being rendered illegitimate and disposing of the father's permission for adoption. For the court, the core issue was the relationship between the father and the child, and it found that the statute was too broad and therefore discriminatory in its blanket exclusion of the need for an unmarried father's permission for adoption of his child.

In 1996, the Constitutional Court considered another significant challenge to the equality provision in the constitution.[28] It is in this case that we see the alternative perspectives that women judges bring, even when they are relegated to the dissent. A sex worker, along with the brothel owner, was charged under South Africa's Sexual Offences Act, which criminalizes sex for reward and brothel-keeping. The two charged brought a challenge to the constitutionality of the statute, claiming that it violated their right to human dignity, freedom of person, privacy, and economic activity. All the justices agreed that the prostitution provision does not infringe on the rights to human dignity and economic activity and that if it does limit the right to privacy, such limitation is justifiable. They also all agreed that the regulation of prostitution is primarily a matter for the legislature. An argument was made that the statute criminalizes the conduct of the sex worker but not the customer, and that targeting only the former was discriminatory based on gender. Disagreeing with this argument, the majority in the Constitutional Court upheld the law as gender neutral. They further held that in targeting the sex worker, the state is selecting an effective way to curb prostitution and that customers may be prosecuted under other criminal statutes.

In her dissenting judgment (which she co-wrote with Justice Albie Sachs), Justice Kate O'Regan found the impugned provision discriminatory against women. Regarding the statute's designation of the prostitute as the "primary offender" and the customer as an accomplice, she noted that although the difference between a primary offender and an accomplice may have little impact as a matter of legality, the social stigma and impact is prejudicial to women and "runs along the fault lines of archetypal presuppositions about male and female behavior," thereby reinforcing gender inequality.

In addition, she also referred to the sexual double standards inherent in the distinction, observing that the discrimination in the distinction in the criminal statute has the "potential to impair the fundamental human dignity and personhood of women." Disagreeing with the majority that the stigma attaching to prostitutes arises not from the law but from social attitudes, she found the discrimination to be unfair. In her view, by primarily criminalizing the prostitute, the law reinforces and perpetuates sexual stereotypes, while it degrades the prostitute and the client escapes stigma. Justice O'Regan concluded that although the criminal statute appears, on the face of it, neutral, its substance undermines the value of the constitution and is therefore unconstitutional, violating a woman's right to dignity, equality, privacy, and freedom of the person. It is clear from the majority (male) judgment that issues of morality loomed large, positing the woman as someone making a choice to engage in immoral activity. For the dissenting justices, this was an issue of female subordination and outright discrimination.[29]

To further illustrate their different perspectives, in another case involving discrimination against a woman in a life partnership without a marriage contract, the two female justices gave a thoughtful dissenting judgment.[30] The applicant here was in a cohabiting relationship for 16 years before the death of her partner. They chose not to get married. Her lawsuit emerged when she was denied a claim of maintenance against the estate of the deceased, since she was not deemed a "survivor" entitled to maintenance under the relevant statute. The lower court found the exclusion of permanent life partners from maintenance to be in violation of the constitutional right to equality and dignity, since the relationship seemed to all appearances akin to a marriage. On appeal to the Constitutional Court, the executor of the estate argued that the basis of the relevant statute was to protect surviving spouses who were married, not those who were in life partnerships. The majority of the court agreed with the executor, holding that the statute is intended to deal with the rights and obligations of marriage, especially in relation to maintenance payments. They held that the reciprocity regarding the duty of support between married people did not extend to unmarried couples. They believed that the discrimination was not unfair and that to expand the meaning of the statute to include life partners who were not married was to impose a duty upon death which did not exist during the lifetime of the deceased. In the words of the majority, such an imposition would be "incongruous, unfair, irrational and untenable."

The two female dissenting justices thought that the discrimination on the grounds of marital status was unfair. The justices noted that discrimination against cohabiting partners is not equal to racial or gender discrimination, but that such partners have suffered legal exclusion and are vulnerable members of society, especially regarding financial need. Many are subject to stigma and disapproval within society, even though such attitudes are on the wane. In the absence of comprehensive legal remedies that may ameliorate the situation of the surviving cohabitant upon the death of a partner, even where the relationship has been one of considerable length, she will be particularly vulnerable. The two dissenting justices acknowledged the importance of marriage as a social institution and in their decision, they explored the many ways that the law justifiably makes distinctions between married and unmarried persons. Emphasizing that the constitution prohibits unfair discrimination on the ground of marital status and that the discrimination cannot be justified, the justices noted that cohabiting relationships serve a similar social function to marriage.

It is notable that the two female justices of the court found the discrimination between married and unmarried couples unfair. To some extent, this case parallels the position of the majority in the prostitution case (mentioned earlier) where the male justices appear to be motivated by a sense of morality and a particular vision of a society, one that arguably is gendered. In contrast, the female judges are motivated by a sense of social justice, women's empowerment, and women's dignity.

Do women judges make a difference?

In this chapter, I have attempted to outline some of the challenges to attaining gender diversity in the judiciary in South Africa in line with the transformative vision of the constitution. I have also attempted to grapple with the question of whether female judges make a difference, especially regarding the outcome of cases. There are several factors to demonstrate that in fact, in South Africa, women judges have made and do make a difference. First, their historical exclusion on the basis of gender and also race ensures that female presence in the judiciary enables perspectives that were previously absent. (Cowan, 2006; Masengu, 2016). Indeed, many of the first wave of female judges, especially the female black judges, had grown up and been educated in the racist and authoritarian apartheid system, and many were activists against that system.[31] Some were prominent public interest and human rights lawyers. Their perspectives were crucial in shaping the emerging constitutional jurisprudence, as witnessed, for example, in the development of substantive equality.

Second is the issue of representation, which goes to the core of the standing and credibility of the judiciary. The absence of female judges is not tolerable in a society committed to the constitutional goals of equality and dignity for all its citizens. In fact, as Ruth Cowan has shown in her film *Courting Justice*, by their very presence, they have added legitimacy to the judiciary (Cowan, 2006). Third, women judges are very important role models, and they create the real and imagined space for girls in South Africa to aspire to a judicial appointment. Women judges occupy previously held "men only" spaces, and their presence reinforces the normality of women in black robes as part of the judiciary, a characteristic that Dawuni refers to as the direct and indirect representative roles of women judges (Dawuni & Bauer, 2016) Fourth, the presence of women judges may create a more inclusive courtroom space for lawyers, especially female lawyers (Kenney, 2013; Rackley, 2012). A former female Canadian Supreme Court Justice has observed that it is easier for women lawyers to appear as counsel before a woman judge, noting that the "difference is that the female judge is perceived as normal, with shared experiences and a shared reality that removes the need to 'translate' the submissions into 'man talk' or a context that a male judge will understand" (Wilson, 1990, at 518).

Fifth, women judges collaborating with their male judges in a visionary constitutional transformative project provides an important blueprint for other democracies. Just as the non-racial project in South Africa involves the support of whites, the project of gender equality requires males to demonstrate a fundamental commitment to the project. This is particularly crucial in South Africa, where the struggle for gender equality has been sorely tested, as noted by the alarming statistics on violence against women as well as the statistics on female poverty and employment equity. Finally, the presence of women judges in the room where deliberations are being conducted regarding the outcome of cases makes a difference (Peresie, 2005). Research has shown, for example, that the presence of female judges affects collegial decision-making and that in cases involving females as plaintiffs, male judges are more likely to be influenced by the perspectives of female judges (Choi, 2011).

Conclusion

The appointment of female judges in South Africa is part of the transformative project envisaged in the constitution. The presence of women in the judiciary is not merely symbolic but a substantive commitment to ensuring that the judiciary has credibility and legitimacy among the population and that the discrete experiences, competence, and legal skills of women are embraced to satisfy the constitutional mandate. Although limiting my examination to the female judges and jurisprudence of the Constitutional Court, I have pointed out that despite some overlap between the opinions of the female and male judges, the opinions of the female judges differ in some significant ways from their male counterparts. This difference is located in the distinct way that female judges have framed the legal issues, for example, formal versus substantive equality in the case of mothers, choice versus subordination in the case of unwed cohabitees, or morality versus subordination in the context of sex workers. The chapter has pointed out that considerable institutional obstacles continue to impede women's appointment to the judiciary, but once on the bench, they really make a difference.

Notes

1 This question implicitly revives the earlier sameness/difference debate among feminists. See Williams, J.C. (1991). Dissolving the sameness/difference debate: A postmodern path beyond essentialism in feminist and critical race theory. *Duke Law*

Journal, 296 and Scott, J.W. (1988). Deconstructing equality-versus-difference: Or, the uses of poststructuralist theory for feminism. *Feminist Studies*, *14*, Spring 32. My intention here is not to revive that debate, since I am using the question here in the normative sense, namely, that women make a difference not because they bring perspectives based on their essential gendered characteristics but because of their lived experiences as women. As noted by Madam Justice Bertha Wilson of the Canadian Supreme Court, "If women lawyer and women judges through their differing perspectives on life can bring a new humanity to bear on the decision-making process, perhaps they will make a difference. Perhaps they will succeed in infusing the law with an understanding of what it means to be fully human," Wilson, B. (1990). Will women judges really make a difference? *Osgoode Hall Law Journal*, *28*, 507, 522. Sally Kenney also explores this question in her research. Kenney, S.J. (2013). *Gender and justice: Why women in the judiciary really matter* (p.6). Routledge.

2 Cowan, R.B. Women's representation on the courts in the republic of South Africa. (2006). *University of Maryland Law Journal of Race, Religion, Gender and Class*, 6, 291, 304 (quoting female judges in South Africa reflecting on disrespectful and disparate treatment by their male counterparts).

3 Ibid., 302 (citing comments from Judge Howie in a lecture given in 2005).

4 Abella, R.S. (1987) The dynamic nature of equality. In S. Martin & K. Mahoney (Eds) *Equality and judicial neutrality* (pp.8–9). Carswell, Toronto.

5 See *Discussion Document on Gender Transformation in the Judiciary and the Legal Sector, Commission for Gender Equality* (7/13/2018). Retrieved from https://www.justice.gov.za/legislation/notices/2018/20180713-gg41766_gen394-CGE-GenderTransformationJudiciary.pdf

6 *Report of the Special Rapporteur on Violence Against Women, its Causes and Consequences on her Mission to South Africa* (2016). United Nations Human Rights Council.

7 In this chapter, I have not included a discussion of the Indigenous courts, which exist throughout the country to serve Indigenous communities in the implementation of customary law. As I have stated elsewhere, Indigenous law and Indigenous courts were always relegated to a secondary place in the racist colonial and apartheid structure. See Andrews, P.E. (2009).Who's afraid of polygamy? Exploring the boundaries of family, equality and custom in South Africa. 209 *University of Utah Law Review*, *2*, 351. The seminal work on this subject has been the research of Martin Chanock. See Chanock, C. (2001). *The making of South African legal culture 1902–1936: Fear, favour and prejudice*. Cambridge.

8 *Discussion Document on Gender Transformation in the Judiciary and the Legal Sector* at Note v.

9 Legal Practice Act 28 of 2014.

10 Although the constitution does not use the term "feminist," I am suggesting that transformation and feminism are synonymous in this context, since feminism is committed to the project of the transformation of gendered structures, hierarchies, and relationships.

11 Constitution of The Republic of South Africa Act 1996. The human rights scholar, Makau Mutua, has noted: "The construction of the post-apartheid state represents the first deliberate and calculated effort in history to craft a human rights state—a polity that is primarily animated by human rights norms. South Africa was the first state to be reborn after the universal acceptance, at least rhetorically, of human rights ideals by states of all the major cultural and political traditions." Makau wa Mutua (1997). Hope and despair for a New South Africa: The limits of rights discourse. *Harvard Human Rights Law Journal 10*, 63, 65.

12 I am using the word "feminist" here in the same sense as I did earlier, namely, that the transformative vision of the constitution mandates a transformative approach. I use the term to analogize feminism with transformation—beyond formal gender

equality. For example, in the following discussion of the *Hugo* case, I examine the Constitutional Court's elaboration of a substantive equality.

13 *Assessment of the Impact of Decisions of the Constitutional Court and Supreme Court of Appeal on the Transformation of Society*.(2017). Department of Justice and Constitutional Development. Retrieved from http://www.justice.gov.za/reportfiles/2017-CJPreport-Nov2015-Final.pdf
14 Justice Johan Kriegler (2002). The Constitutional Court of South Africa. *Cornell International Law Journal* 36, 361, 364.
15 *Report of the Truth and Reconciliation Commission*, 5, 326. Retrieved from http://www.justice.gov.za/trc/report/finalreport/Volume5.pdf
16 *Discussion Document on Gender Transformation in the Judiciary and the Legal Sector* at Note 5.
17 Tilley, A. and Masengu, T. (2013). How the JSC fails gender test. *Sunday Independent* at: https://www.iol.co.za/sundayindependent/how-the-jsc-fails-gender-test-1503769
18 Rabkin, F. (2019). Constitutional Court interviews turn he-said-she-said. *Weekly Mail and Guardian*. Retrieved from https://mg.co.za/article/2019-04-05-00-constitutional-court-interviews-turn-he-said-she-said/
19 Rickard, C. (2005). Judging women harshly. *Sunday Times*, October 23, 2005. Retrieved from https://allafrica.com/stories/200510240207.html
20 *Hoffmann v South African Airways* 2001 (1) SA 1.
21 *August and Another v Electoral Commission and Others* 1999 (3) SA 1 (CC).
22 *Fraser v Naude & Another* 1998 (11) BCLR 1357 (CC).
23 *Larbi-Odam and Others v Member of the Executive Council for Education (North-West Province) and Another* 1998 (1) SA 745 (CC).
24 *National Coalition for Gay and Lesbian Equality and Others v Minister of Home Affairs and Others* 2000 (2) SA 1 (CC).
25 *Bhe & Others v Magistrate, Khayelitsha, & Others* 2005 (1) SA 580 (CC).
26 *President of the Republic of South Africa (and Another) v Hugo* 1997 (4) SA 1.
27 *Fraser v Children's Court Pretoria North and Others* 1997 (2) SA 261 (CC).
28 *S v Jordan and Others* 2002 (6) SA 642.
29 The other female justice, Justice Mokgoro, took no part in the deliberation. Justice O'Regan's dissent was joined by Justice Ackermann, Langa, and Goldstone.
30 *Volks NO v Robinson and Others* 2005 (5) BCLR 446 (CC).
31 A perusal of the biographies of the female justices of the Constitutional Court highlights their involvement in the struggle against apartheid and for social justice. See https://www.concourt.org.za/index.php/judges/former-judges

Bibliography

Abella, R.S. (1987). The Dynamic Nature of Equality. In Martin, S. & Mahoney, K. (Eds.), *Equality and Judicial Neutrality*, 3, 8–9. Carswell.

Albertyn, C., & Bonthuys, E. (2016). South Africa: A Transformative Constitution and a Representative Judiciary. In Bauer, G. & Dawuni, J. (Eds.), *Gender and the Judiciary in Africa: From Obscurity to Parity?* 49. Routledge.

Andrews, P. (2010). The Judiciary in South Africa: Independence or Illusion? In Dodek, A. & Sossin, L. (Eds.), *Judicial Independence in Context* 466. Toronto, ON: Irwin Law.

Andrews, P. (2010). Without Fear, Favor or Prejudice: Judicial Transformation and the Independence of the Judiciary in South Africa. In: Cummings, S. (Ed.), *Law and Social Movements* 197. Routledge.

Andrews, P.E. (1998). Striking the Rock: Confronting Gender Equality in South Africa. *Michigan Journal of Race and Law*, 3, 307.

Andrews, P.E. (2001). The Step-Child of National Liberation: Women and Rights in the New South Africa. In Andrews, P.E. and Ellmann, S. (Eds.). *The Post-Apartheid Constitutions: Reflections on South Africa's Basic Law* 326. Ohio University Press.

Andrews, P.E. (2008). Incorporating International Human Rights Law in National Constitutions: The South African Experience. In: Bratspies, R. & Miller, R. (Eds.), *Progress in International Organizations* 837. Martinus Nijhof.

Andrews, P.E. (2009). Who's Afraid of Polygamy? Exploring the Boundaries of Family, Equality and Custom in South Africa. *University of Utah Law Review*, *2*, 351.

Baines, B. (2017). Women Judges on Constitutional Courts: Why Not Nine Women? In: Irving, H. (Ed.), *Constitutions and Gender*. Edward Elgar.

Banks, T.L. (2017). President Obama and the Supremes: Obama's Legacy: The Rise of Women's Voices on the Courts. *Drake Law Review*, 65, 912.

Bauer, G. and Dawuni, J. (Eds.) (2016). *Gender and the Judiciary in Africa: From Obscurity to Parity?* Routledge.

Chanock, M. (2001). *The Making of South African Legal Culture 1902–1936: Fear, Favour and Prejudice*. Cambridge University Press.

Choi, S.J. et al. (2011). Judging Women. *Journal of Empirical Legal Studies*, 8(3), 504.

Coontz, P. (2000). Gender and Judicial Decisions: Do Female Judges Decide Cases Differently than Male Judges? *Gender Issues 18*, 59.

Cowan, R. (2006). Women's Representation on the Courts in the Republic of South Africa. *University of Maryland Law Journal of Race Religion Gender* 6, 291.

Dawuni, J. (2016). To "Mother" or Not to "Mother": The Representative Roles of Women Judges in Ghana. *Journal of African Law*, 60, 419.

Dawuni, J. and Kuenyehia, A. (Eds.) (2018). *International Courts and the African Woman Judge: Unveiled Narratives*. Routledge.

Department of Justice and Constitutional Development, *Assessment of the Impact of Decisions of the Constitutional Court and Supreme Court of Appeal on the Transformation of Society* (2017). at: http://www.justice.gov.za/reportfiles/2017-CJPreport-Nov2015-Final.pdf

Dixon, R. (2010). Female Justices, Feminism, and the Politics of Judicial Appointment: A Re-Examination. *Yale Journal of Law and Feminism*, 21, 297.

Dugard, J. (1978). *Human Rights and the South African Legal Order*. Princeton University Press.

Durojaye, E. and Olubayo, O. (2016). The African Commission on Human and People's Rights and the Woman Question. *Feminist Legal Studies*, *24*, 315.

Former Judges, Constitutional Court at: https://www.concourt.org.za/index.php/judges/former-judges

Gilligan, C. (1982). *In A Different Voice: Psychological Theory and Women's Development*. Harvard.

Gqola, P. (2015). *Rape: A South African Nightmare*. Jacana.

Graycar, R. (2008). Gender, Race, Bias and Perspective: Or, How Otherness Colours Your Judgment. *International Journal of the Legal Profession*, *15*, 73.

Hunter, R. (2008). Can Feminist Judges Make a Difference? *International Journal of the Legal Profession*, *15*, 7.

Hunter, R., McGlynn, C., & Rackley, E. (Eds.) (2010). *Feminist Judgements: From Theory to Practice*. Hart.

Irving, I. (Ed.) (2017). *Constitutions and Gender*. Edward Elgar.

Johnson, R.E. (2014). Women as a Sign of the New: Appointments to South Africa's Constitutional Court Since 1994. *Politics and Gender*, *10*(4), 595.

Kende, M. (2009). *Constitutional Rights in Two Worlds: South Africa and the United States*. Cambridge University Press.

Kenney, S.J. (2013). *Gender and Justice: Why Women in the Judiciary Really Matter*. Routledge.

Klare, K. (1998). Legal Culture and Transformative Constitutionalism. *South African Journal on Human Rights*, 146–188.

Kriegler, J. (2002). The Constitutional Court of South Africa. *Cornell International Law Journal*, *36*, 361.

Lack of Transformation of the Judiciary, *Commission for Gender Equality* (2016). at: https://genderjustice.org.za/publication/lack-gender-transformation-judiciary/

Li, M. et al. (2020). Who's Going to Law School? Trends in Law School Enrolment since the Great Recession. *U.C. Davis Law Review* 54. forthcoming at: file:///C:/Users/penel/Downloads/SSRN-id3559213.pdf

Liebenberg, S. (2005). *Needs, Rights and Social Transformation: Adjudicating Social Rights*. Center for Human Rights and Global Justice Working Paper, Economic and Social Rights Series 8.

Mackinnon, C.A. (2012). Gender in Constitutions. In: Rosenfeld, M. and Sajo, A. (Eds.). *Oxford Handbook of Comparative Constitutional Law*. Oxford University Press..

Malleson, K. (1999). Assessing the Performance of the Judicial Services Commission. *South African Law Journal* 116, 36.

Malleson, K. (2003). Justifying Gender Equality on the Bench: Why Difference Won't Do. *Feminist Legal Studies*, *11*, 1.

Masengu, T. (2016). It's a Man's World: Barriers to Gender Transformation in the South African Judiciary. Perspectives from Women Advocates and Attorneys. *International Journal of the Legal Profession*, *23*, 305–319.

Masengu, T. (2019). The Judicial Service Commission and the Appointment of Women: More to It than Meets the Eye. *International Journal of the Legal Profession*.

Mckinnon, C.A. (2011). Substantive Equality: A Perspective. *Minnesota Law Review*, 96, 1.

Moseneke, D. (2002). Transformative Adjudication. *South African Journal of Human Rights*, *18*, 309.

Mossman, M.J. (2005). Defining Moments for Women as Lawyers: Reflections on Numerical Gender Equality. *Canadian Journal of Women and the Law*, *17*, 15.

Mureinik, E. (1994). A Bridge to Where? Introducing the Interim Bill of Rights. *South African Journal of Human Rights*, *10*, 31.

Mutua, M. (1997). Hope and Despair for a New South Africa: The Limits of Rights Discourse. *Harvard Human Rights Law Journal*, *10*, 63.

Norgren, J. (2018). *Stories from Trailblazing Women Lawyers: Lives in the Law*. NYU Press.

Peresie, J.L. (2005). Female Judges Matter: Gender and Collegial Decisionmaking in the Federal Appellate Courts. *Yale Law Journal*, *114*, 1759.

Phooko, M.R. and Radebe, S.B. (2016). Twenty-Three Years of Gender Transformation in the Constitutional Court of South Africa: Progress or Regression. *Constitutional Court Review*, 8, 306.

Rabkin, F. (2019). Constitutional Court Interviews Turn He-Said-She-Said. *Weekly Mail and Guardian* at: https://mg.co.za/article/2019-04-05-00-constitutional-court-interviews-turn-he-said-she-said/

Rackley, E. (2012). Why Feminist Legal Scholars Should Write Judgments: Reflections on the Feminist Judgments Project in England and Wales. *Canadian Journal of Women and the Law*, *24*, 389.

Report of the Special Rapporteur on Violence Against Women, Its Causes and Consequences on Her Mission to South Africa (2016). United Nations Human Rights Council.

Report of the Truth and Reconciliation Commission, Volume 5 at: http://www.justice.gov.za/trc/report/finalreport/Volume5.pdf

Rickard, C. (2005). Judging Women Harshly. *Sunday Times*, October 23, 2005 at https://allafrica.com/stories/200510240207.html

Schultz, U. and Shaw, G. (2003). *Women in the World's Legal Profession*. Hart Publishers.

Schultz, U. and Shaw, G. (eds.) (2013). *Gender and Judging*. Hart Publishers.

Scott, J.W. (1988). Deconstructing Equality-versus-Difference: Or, the Uses of Poststructuralist Theory for Feminism. *Feminist Studies*, *14*(1) 32.

Stanchi, K.M., Berger, L.L. and Crawford, B.J., (Eds.) (2016). *Feminist Judgments: Rewritten Opinions of the United States Supreme Court*. Cambridge.

Tilley, A. and Masengu, T. (2013). How the JSC Fails Gender Test. *Sunday Independent* at: https://www.iol.co.za/sundayindependent/how-the-jsc-fails-gender-test-1503769

Williams, J.C. (1991). Dissolving the Sameness/Difference Debate: A Post-Modern Path Beyond Essentialism in Feminist and Critical Race Theory. *Duke Law Journal*, *1991*, 296.

Wilson, B. (1990). Will Women Judges Really Make a Difference? *Osgoode Hall Law Journal*, *24*, 507.

Wilson, S. and Dugard, J. (2011). Taking Poverty Seriously: The South African Constitutional Court and Socio-Economic Rights. *Stellenbosch Law Review*, *22*, 664.

Case law

August and Another v Electoral Commission and Others [1999] 3 SA 1 (CC)

Bhe & Others v Magistrate, Khayelitsha, & Others [2005] 1 SA 580 (CC)

Fraser v Naude & Another [1998] 11 BCLR 1357 (CC)

Larbi-Odam and Others v Member of the Executive Council for Education (North-West Province) and Another [1998] 1 SA 745 (CC)

National Coalition for Gay and Lesbian Equality and Others v Minister of Home Affairs and Others [2000] 2 SA 1 (CC)

President of the Republic of South Africa (and Another) v Hugo [1997] 4 SA 1 (CC)

S v Jordan and Others [2002] 6 SA 642 (CC)

Volks NO v Robinson and Others [2005] 5 BCLR 446 (CC).

Legislation

Constitution of the Republic of South Africa Act 1996

Legal Practice Act 28 of 2014

11 One sauce for the goose, another for the gander

Zambian women judges and perceptions of illegitimacy

Tabeth Masengu, PhD

Introduction

As of late 2018, 53% of judges in the Zambian Superior Courts were women, which is uncommon even in Scandinavian countries considered as beacons of gender equality.[1] If one compares women's statistics in the three arms of government, the judiciary is an outlier on statistical terms alone. As of 2018, only 18.8% of members of parliament are women, and only 30% of cabinet ministers are women.[2] A judiciary with 53% of women judges evokes suspicion, as it is considered "abnormal" in comparison to other branches of government. Consequently, there have been questions about whether these judges are deserving of their appointments. This chapter examines these questions and explores the content of this skepticism. It argues that in Zambia, current doubt regarding women judges is partially attributable to historical legitimacy perceptions. These perceptions view men as the "right" candidates for authoritative positions. This perception is worth examining, because illegitimacy perceptions of women can harm judicial governance for three reasons. Firstly, democratic values such as transparency, accountability, participation, and representativeness are essential for a court's legitimacy (Grossman, 2012). Therefore, negative views of women's roles have the potential to impede the value of representativeness, because they could dissuade judicial selectors from selecting more women judges. The reluctance to pick women judges would invariably also affect the value of participation, because equal participation of genders in decision-making bodies is a critical aspect of good governance.

Secondly, one of the justifications advanced for gender diversity is that it enhances the legitimacy of the judiciary and improves public trust in the courts (Mokgoro, 2010). Citizens are more likely to have a favorable experience with the justice system if they believe that the courts are trustworthy. However, illegitimacy perceptions can affect the legitimacy justification for gender diversity, because the legitimacy rationale for diversifying the courts is probably based more on perception than on the actual outcome (Albertyn, 2014). Therefore, negative perceptions of women have the potential to undermine the legitimacy of the judiciary and judicial governance as a whole.

DOI: 10.4324/9780429327865-14

Thirdly, illegitimacy perceptions also have symbolic ramifications for the quest to diversify judiciaries. Judges have a symbolic and substantively powerful duty—that of interpreting and defending constitutional values (Arrington et al., 2017). In adjudication, the presence of women signals equality of opportunity for women not just as subjects of the law but as actors in the critical task of breathing life into constitutional values. Negative perceptions devalue the symbolic value of women judges in the constitutional project, thereby questioning the ability of women to be actors and changemakers in a time when constitutional jurisprudence is needed.

The analysis provided in this discussion draws upon 23 interviews conducted in Zambia from November 2016 to August 2018.[3] The interview participants were women judges, legal professionals, members of the Judicial Service Commission (the body that selects judges), and civil society members. I triangulate these accounts by referring to the work of Alice Evans (2014, 2016), who has conducted empirical research in Zambia, and media statements by influential Zambian women on the challenges they have faced. I commence with a discussion of the judicial role in contemporary times before highlighting the status of Zambia's Superior Courts. The next section considers how women are regarded as outsiders because of historical experiences as illegitimate power holders. This chapter then makes specific reference to the situation of Zambian women in positions of power.

Consequently, the chapter outlines the criteria to be a judge in Zambia to provide context to the discussions that follow regarding skepticism in respect of women judges. Accordingly, I examine the interview responses to reveal how these perceptions of illegitimacy work and why they are invariably a result of the perceived incongruence between the ideas of womanhood and the role of a judge. I conclude by suggesting that further research on judicial performance would help negate these perceptions of illegitimacy.

The judicial role in contemporary times

The role of the judge on the African continent has taken on different meanings since the 1990s. Before this period, judges were mostly confined to criminal, civil, and labor law adjudication; now, judges adjudicate core human rights cases, public policy questions, and political controversies. These are questions of mega politics—political controversies that define the boundaries of the collective or cut through the heart of entire nations (Hirschl, 2008). Accordingly, the legitimacy of courts and the public's confidence in the role of courts to address these controversies are determined by many factors, among them the diversity of the court (Solanke, 2008). Importantly, gender-diverse courts are more likely to make better decisions, because they infuse the perspectives of different judges from different backgrounds (O'Regan, 2012). Devlin et al. have also argued that the equality argument for diversity means that there should be equal opportunities for those who apply the law, and this is absent when one group (men) dominate the adjudication of law (Devlin, MacKay, & Kim, 2000). Article 12 of the

Southern African Development Cooperation (SADC) Protocol on Gender and Development (SADC, 2008) and the United Nations Sustainable Development Goal (SDG) 5 both call for, among others, "women's full and effective participation and equal opportunities for leadership at all levels of decision-making" (Sustainable Development Solutions Network, 2020). The judicial role is a public decision-making role. Thus, it falls squarely under these guidelines, placing states under an obligation to ensure that more women are appointed as judicial officers.

The Commonwealth Latimer House Principles recognize the importance of gender diversity. They state that the appointment process should ensure equal opportunities for eligible persons, that appointment should be based on merit, and that attention should be given to the need for progressive attainment of gender equality (Commonwealth, 2003). The first judicial appointment guidelines issued by the Southern African Chief Justices Forum (SACJF) also identify gender as an appropriate ground on which to actively prioritize the recruitment of appointable candidates (Southern African Chief Justices Forum, 2018). Amidst these developments, it is worth remembering that the role of a judge comes with heavy responsibilities and sometimes, even expectations that judges will be superhuman. Green (2014) counters this expectation by reminding us that judges are humans who need to calculate, who need to use languages, and who need to conform to moral principles. He goes on to add that the judicial role consists of three main families of obligations: first, law-applying obligations, which include correct findings of fact and knowledge of the law and how to apply it; second, law-improving obligations, which means clarifying where necessary and resolving conflicts in law; third, law-protecting obligations, which occur when judges are regulating their own process and protecting the rule of law and the integrity of the jurisdiction from attack (Green, 2014, pp.19–20). Also, judges are required to adhere to a particular type of conduct that corresponds to the judicial office. In this regard, the Bangalore Principles on Judicial Conduct also provide guidance.

The Bangalore Principles identify six fundamental values that "afford the judiciary a framework for regulating judicial conduct" (Strengthening Judicial Integrity, 2002). These values are independence, impartiality, integrity, propriety, equality, competence, and diligence. The Principles are said to give expression to the highest traditions relating to the judicial function as visualized in all cultures and legal systems, and many states have modeled their principles of judicial conduct on them (Commentary on The Bangalore Principles of Judicial Conduct, 2007). Cowen has also highlighted that potential judges need to have forensic abilities, an appreciation of the practical workings of court procedure, a thorough knowledge of the law, an appreciation of ethical duties, and independent-mindedness (Cowen, 2013). The obligations described here, and the abilities and conduct expected of judges, as outlined by the Bangalore Principles and Cowen, are not only inherent in men. This has been proven over the decades, as the legal profession has gradually embraced women. Consequently, women have proven their capabilities and competence by ascending to the judiciary.

Table 11.1 Gender breakdown of the courts as of 2018[4]

Court	*Total # of judges*	Female (%)	Male (%)
Constitutional Court	7	4 (57%)	3 (43%)
Supreme Court of Appeal	13	4 (31%)	9 (69%)
Court of Appeal	12	7 (58%)	5 (42%)
Specialized High Court Divisions	40	23 (57.5%)	17 (43.5%)
Overall Composition	72	38 (53%)	34 (47%)

Data obtained from the website of the Zambian Judiciary

Therefore, Zambia is to be commended in this regard, because it has achieved gender equity on the Superior Courts, as presented in Table 11.1.

Cook (1984) describes two primary patterns regarding the distributive representation of women in the judiciary, which are useful in assessing the figures presented earlier: namely, the pyramid pattern and the inverted bell pattern. In terms of the pyramid pattern, women have greater access to entering courts that are at the bottom of the pyramid (ordinary High Courts) than courts at the top (Appellate Courts). In terms of the inverted bell pattern, women have access as token representatives to the top and bottom court levels but not at significant trial court levels. Pointedly, the Zambian data outlined here follows neither of these patterns. In the Zambian scenario, women are represented well in the Constitutional Court and Court of Appeal in addition to the High Courts. This was not the case in 2011, when Ndulo (2011) lamented the scarcity of women in the apex courts in Zambia. To assist with the paucity of women in the judiciary at the time, he suggested a fast-tracking of women candidates, whereby preference would be given to a woman candidate if she was meritorious. Seven years later, the composition is admirable without the creation of a fast-tracking program, but this does not mean that societal discrimination is absent.

Women's experience in the judicial and legal realm

When women are outsiders on the bench

Traditionally, women have been characterized as agents of reproduction, which has resulted in women's confinement to the private sphere of home and family. In contrast, the public sphere of politics and work has been considered as the male sphere of endeavor (Thornton, 1985). Despite the image of Lady Justice, the judge is invariably masculinized. Women, people of color, and those who do not fit the dominant male narrative are marked as "other," which taints the adjudicative role and renders the delivery of justice problematic (Thornton, 2007). As Malleson argues, "almost without exception, official expressions of support for proactive measures to encourage diversity have been qualified by a statement of commitment to a strict application of the merit principle" (2006, p.131). Mcloughlin points out that "when eminent men are appointed judges, little is said on the matter as it is taken for granted that they are appointed on the basis of merit, and yet merit is determined in the context of power" (McLoughlin 2015, p.168.). Inevitably, those who are outside the dominant group culturally and economically (or who have not managed the skill to mimic the attributes and attitudes of the culturally and economically dominant group) are often dismissed as not possessing the requisite "merit" to be appointed to higher positions (de Vos, 2013).

Those who are considered meritorious are men who have been in dominant positions of power for so long that they are the standard for who is worthy of being a judge. Even when women have proved themselves as fit to be appointed, they still face challenges on the bench. According to Rackley (2007), a growing collection of tales show women as "remote beacons in hostile environments, whose presence deviates from the judicial norm and disrupts homogeneity on the bench" (p.76). This reveals the unavoidable, yet mostly unacknowledged, gender dimensions to traditional understandings of adjudication (Rackley, 2007). In other instances, "women have to work harder and extra just to be acknowledged," because appointment to the bench does not mean that their capabilities will stop being undermined and questioned (Mocumie, 2017, p.7). In Brazil, empirical research on the Supreme Court revealed that justices on the court are more likely to dissent when the leading judgment was written by a woman, and women judgment writers attracted more dissenting opinions than male justices (Carvalho, 2018). The researchers attribute this to the view that male justices are more likely to view their women counterparts as less competent, knowledgeable, or reliable, and they are less likely to be worried about a strain on the collegiality between colleagues.

World-renowned jurist Justice Florence Mumba was the first woman judge appointed to the Zambian High Court in 1980, four decades ago. She wrote about what she refers to as her "first test of the prejudice" when she initially started presiding in trials at the International Criminal Tribunal for the former Yugoslavia (Mumba, 2018). Some interpreters at the tribunal refused to commence trial at the mandated time of 8:30 am. Upon making enquiries, she learned that the interpreters started trial at 8:30 am for her male colleagues, and she realized that they had refused to do so for her because she was a woman. She decided that she had to assert her authority as a judge like everybody else, which meant "no soft robes." This meant that she had to put her foot down and demand the same respect afforded to male judges. Thus, even when women are finally appointed to the bench, they still face a hostile environment.

Women as illegitimate holders of power

Andre Vial et al. (2016) use a model centered on legitimacy to explain the persistence of the gender gap in leadership positions. They describe legitimacy as the sense of obligation or duty to comply freely with the decisions and directions of authorities (Vial, Napier, & Brescoll, 2016). They posit that the difficulties that female leaders face often stem from low legitimacy perceptions. That is, powerful women (those with the means to make a societal impact), relative to powerful men, are less likely to be perceived as legitimate authorities. Other theories account for the difficulties that women face by positing women as norm violators.

In contrast, Vial et al. examine the questions that emerge when bias against female leaders is thought of as a particular case of bias against an illegitimate leader (Vial et al. 2016, p.401). In essence, the focus is not on the women as "disruptors" and unusual power holders, which results in bias, but rather, on the perspective that the women are undeserving of the authority that they wield. Within this, power, status, and legitimacy are distinct but intimately related constructs. Power comes attached to the leadership role, but legitimacy is a state in which a leader's power over others is seen as deserved and justified (Vial et al., 2016). People who occupy a low-level status are more likely to face negative presumptions about their competence and trustworthiness. Hence, when they assume leadership positions, they are viewed as illegitimate power holders.

The experience of women in positions of power in Zambia

Historically, women in Zambia have mainly been stereotyped as housewives, while men tended to present themselves as masters of their households. Public leadership has also been male-dominated: women's prescribed role has been to support men's endeavors (Evans, 2014). According to Evans (2014), the few women elected to public office endured tremendous scrutiny regarding their sexuality and morality; they were mocked if too timid, chastised if overly aggressive, and generally denied respect. Widely perceived as deviating from prescriptive gender stereotypes, female leaders might at best be accepted as "honorary men" (Evans, 2014, pp.981–982). Evans has theorized that in the Zambian political arena, "the limited supply of women candidates for public office may not be due to their gendered self-perceptions or internalized stereotypes." Instead, it is because of the anticipated penalties incurred by transgressing (or even openly questioning) cultural expectations (Evans, 2016, p.392). Even in a constitutional process that has long been an Achilles heel in Zambian history, women were repeatedly under-represented in constitutional reform bodies and the National Constitutional Conference in 2017 (Masengu, 2015). The research on the constitutional process found that the poor representation of women was not as a result of any passivity on the part of the women. Instead, it was an expression of the patriarchal nature of Zambian society, which affects all spheres, including law (Masengu, 2015).

The conservative nature of Zambian society, which is deeply religious, further endorses gender status beliefs. These beliefs assume that men are more suited to and deserving of positions of influence and esteem in a broad range of social and economic domains (Evans, 2016). Nonetheless, Evans' studies on women in politics in the north of the country showed that incrementally, Zambian women are being recognized and supported as independent actors and increasingly stepping into historically male-dominated and socially valued domains (Evans, 2016). Since the Patriotic Front (PF) came into government in 2011, there has been a concerted political will to include more women in top decision-making positions. There is limited data available to explain what prompted this decision, and there is insufficient data available to suggest that it could be because more women were qualifying with the requisite experience. An interview participant alluded to the SADC gender quotas or possibly the need to gratify donors as the reason why the PF sought to promote women, but this was unsubstantiated information. What is known is that former President Michael Sata appointed several women into various decision-making positions in all sectors. This included the appointment of the first ever woman Inspector General of Police, an acting woman Chief Justice, and a woman Deputy Chief Justice at the same time.[5] His successor Edgar Lungu continued this commitment by selecting a woman Vice President, appointing the first ever permanent Chief Justice, Irene Mambilima, and the first woman Director of Public Prosecution (DPP).[6] Despite these appointments, women still face an extra layer of judgment, which would not apply to men.

In an article about how Zambian women have "failed" the country, Richard W epitomizes the nature of the sexist judgment that women have often had to face (W, 2018). He accuses particular Zambian women, including former Chief Justice Irene Mambilima, Vice President, and DPP, of not being vigilant enough. He argues that they have "sunk into the political sofas, sipping coffee, and chatting about which part of Dubai they can find nice heels and wigs" (W, 2018). He urges women to qualify and earn their positions through competence and not motherliness and to avoid falling into the male trap of normalizing corruption and political manipulation. Ironically, he encourages women to fight sexism. Yet in the same breath, he admits in passing that his article does not seek to overlook the many contributions the said women have made (W, 2018). The writer expresses disappointment in "these" women while accepting the frailties of the male species. He expects these women to be without blame, thereby demonstrating the skewed framework facing women in influential positions. This asymmetric framework is exemplified further in a discussion later, focusing on appointments to the Constitutional Court.

Due to the scarcity of literature on gender and judging in Zambia, I cannot draw on previous studies in the judiciary attesting to the odd situation that women face. Therefore, reliance is placed on my interview data as a source of Zambian women's experience on the bench. However, the inaugural woman president of the Zambian Law Association (LAZ), Linda Kasonde, has spoken openly about the challenges she faced as a leader in the profession. In her article calling for more women in leadership, she states:

> I cannot do that without talking about how insidious unconscious bias is. As a female leader in the public eye, you must be prepared for a lot of criticism, sexual objectification, and even threats to your personal safety. Women leaders also experience very personal attacks on social media. That is why we need to build a critical mass of women in leadership. Not only will it allow men and women to see women in leadership as a normal thing, but it will also create a bigger support network for women in leadership.
>
> (Kasonde, 2018)

Ms. Mbikusita-Lewanika, a seasoned politician and the first woman to ever run for the Zambian presidency in 2001, has also highlighted the difficulty of women in leadership. In her comments, she said, "when you have young children, you have to rush home while your male counterparts carry on with discussions in the bars or the chambers of parliament" (Mutame, 2012). Consequently, she opined that if a woman wanted to pursue politics in addition to being a wife and a mother, it would be necessary to have support from her husband. This example highlights both the role of primary caregiver that men do not often have and the tension between the private and the public sphere.

Backing the wrong horse? Do women meet the requirements for judicial office?

The appointment process and criteria to be a judge

The Judicial Service Commission (JSC) is responsible for appointing judges in Zambia. The JSC has proved to be an ally for women, as it has actively engaged in the promotion of women to the bench in Zambia, unlike in some other countries, where JSCs are stumbling blocks to women's appointment to the bench (Dawuni & Masengu, 2019). The JSC sends out communications about vacancies to the LAZ, the internal judiciary mailing system, and government and parastatal companies (Masengu, 2017a). Candidates apply, and the JSC interviews the shortlisted ones. Names of selected candidates are sent to the President for appointment, subject to ratification by the National Assembly as per section 140 of the Constitution of Zambia Amendment Act 2016 (hereafter the constitution). A parliamentary select committee further interviews the candidates before the names are sent to the main house in the National Assembly for a vote.

I asked the interview participants to comment on the criteria to be a good judge. All the participants referred to the constitutional criteria as the starting point for judicial office. These criteria are what I refer to as constitutional requirements for judicial office, which are found in section 141 of the constitution. It states that:

(1) A person qualifies for appointment as a judge if that person is of proven integrity and has been a legal practitioner, in the case of the—
  (a) Supreme Court, for at least fifteen years;
  (b) Constitutional Court, for at least fifteen years and has specialized training or experience in human rights or constitutional law;
  (c) Court of Appeal, for at least twelve years; or
  (d) High Court, for at least ten years.

(2) A person appointed as judge to a specialized court shall have the relevant expertise, as prescribed.

In addition to the constitutional requirements, when the JSC is assessing a candidate in privately conducted interviews, it refers to additional criteria. Here, the focus is on professional qualifications and character traits. The guiding philosophy of the JSC is that candidates should have extensive experience in legal work acquired either from private practice, from the bench, or from public service (Zambian Judicial Service Commission, 1993). The criteria also state that a record of competence must be established through recommendations or references, and they must have a lengthy post-call period of legal experience before an appointment.[7] Unquestionable integrity, suitable temperament, patience, and impartial disposition, objectivity, and courage are also essential. The criteria particularly mention the desire for candidates without strong business interests, since strong business interests are considered as a potential area where conflict could arise if one is on the bench.[8]

There were varying views from interview participants concerning what is required from candidates aspiring for judicial office. The top three identified character criteria for good judges were integrity, competence, and experience. Regarding integrity, former JSC Commissioner Mr. Fraser Chishimba submitted that integrity is not a moral question but instead, it is about professional reputation.[9] This was disputed by the current Chair of the JSC, former Chief Justice Mathew Ngulube, who averred that despite how brilliant they may be, a person with integrity could not be "morally bankrupt." Another former commissioner emphasized the need for candidates to be of sound character and have no "skeletons" in their closet.[10] When describing competence, participants emphasized the importance of an ability to write clear and precise judgments, prepare for trials, and have an understanding of the judicial role. The relevant experience was highlighted as a mandatory requirement, because previously, people were appointed when they had not been in roles that actively engaged with the law.[11] Thus, experience as a legal practitioner with related responsibilities over the years was discussed as the best way to gauge knowledge.[12]

Other additional requirements included honesty, efficiency, expertise, intellectual capacity, ability to be non-partisan, and commitment to the judicial role. There was a unanimous view that this criterion was not exclusive to men and that women could and did possess these qualities. Thus, how meritorious a candidate is, is independent of their gender. We are made to believe that the definition of merit is neutral because merit is the quality of excellence and great worth (Davis & Williams, 2003). Yet, "the best person to occupy a position of authority has tended to be unproblematically defined in masculinist terms that reflect the values of the public sphere" (Davis & Williams, 2003, 831; Olivier, 2013; Malleson, 2006). The values of the public sphere and the perceptions of who is deserving of influential roles are evident in the skepticism toward women judges in Zambia.

Skepticism about the appointment of women judges

None of the JSC members I interviewed expressed any concern about the performance or capabilities of women judges. There were, however, four views from the legal professionals and Non-Governmental Organization (NGO) members that relayed skepticism about the competence and capability of women judges.

The first view was that there were better-qualified men who should have been appointed in the same period.[13] This view was expressed by two men. One is a registrar, who is possibly in the pipeline for future judgeship himself and the other a resident magistrate. A second view was submitted by Advocate Sangwa SC, a well-known and highly respected senior advocate. His view was that there were more women on the bench because they had failed to succeed in private practice.[14] He posited that in his many years of legal practice, he had witnessed a fall in jurisprudential standards and an increase in delayed judgments. Thirdly, it was argued that there was a certain threshold one could reach in public service. This was opined by a qualified advocate currently in a position of responsibility in academia. She pointed out that since there were more women in public service, judicial appointments were a tool to "move officers around and to get desired political appointees in specific public offices."[15] Mr. Mweenge, a senior member of the local branch of an international NGO, however, offered a different and final assertion relating to women judges. He argued that while women were being appointed to high positions, they did not have the autonomy to work independently. "An invisible hand" that made them more likely to "play out some favors" impeded their independence.[16] Effectively, the judges would not be individually independent, because they would owe allegiance to others.

Establishing the validity of the skepticism regarding women judges

In respect of the first claim, there is no indication that the "better-qualified" men referred to by the Registrar and Magistrate did apply for and were rejected for judicial positions. Nevertheless, a few participants used the Constitutional Court judgment in *Hakainde Hichilema & Others v Edgar Lungu & Others* as evidence that women lack the required competencies.[17] In this matter, the newly established Constitutional Court had refused to hear a much-anticipated election petition that challenged the re-election of Edgar Lungu and Inonge Wina as President and Vice President of the Republic of Zambia, respectively, due to fraud.[18] The court found that the petition failed on a technicality and not because there was no substantive case to be heard. This decision was made despite an earlier assurance that the court would listen to substantive arguments.[19] At the time, the court was comprised of two men and four women, although only five members heard the election petition case (three of them were women). Further, two participants also referred to a public memorandum written by Advocate John Sangwa SC, mentioned earlier. Advocate Sangwa had expressed dissatisfaction with the initial selection of the Constitutional Court judges, and decision in this Constitutional Court case was advanced as proof of Advocate Sangwa's warning.

The warning was in the form of a lengthy and scathing document. The document commenced with a historical overview of why the Constitutional Court was established. It was then submitted that all six candidates did not have the requisite number of years of actively practicing law and were all unqualified for the position. Sangwa alleged that the selected judges lacked working experience in prosecuting constitutional or human rights–related cases (Sangwa, 2016). Notwithstanding this, it is suggested that using the Constitutional Court judgments as a means of appraising women's competency and capabilities is flawed for the following reasons. One woman justice and two male justices wrote the majority judgment, which was roundly criticized. Women wrote both dissenting opinions, which held that the petition should have been heard. Therefore, by apportioning blame to the women justices, these critics absolved the men who co-wrote that majority judgment of any responsibility. Secondly, the assessment by Advocate Sangwa that the Constitutional Court judges were unqualified applied to all the judges, not just the women. Therefore, using the said assessment as evidence of women's failings is discriminatory, because it is being applied to women and not to men. This discrepancy in treatment led an interview participant to opine that the Constitutional Court is not respected simply because the majority of its justices are women.[20]

Further, it is essential to consider the role that informal political networks play in supporting women leaders and the effect of an absence of such political networks. Research has shown that the formation of a successful unified women's movement was pivotal in supporting the rise of women legislators in Rwanda, South Africa, and Uganda (Conner, 2008). A vibrant and strong legacy of civil society movements and strong international women's rights networks helped women navigate spheres of legislative power previously dominated by men (Bauer & Burnet, 2013). These social movements have the possibility of supporting and defending women when citizens wrongly criticize them. However, Zambian women judges are not privy to networks that can defend against false allegations of incompetence. Unlike legislators, judges have to maintain a certain distance from the public to avoid impropriety and to prevent claims of bias if any supporting movement comes to court. Women judges are natural targets because they lack women's support systems and the long-established support structures formed by the "old boys club" of lawyers and judges.

The second claim for the skepticism centered on a high attrition of women from private practice to the bench. Yet, there was no specific evidence of more women having left private practice to join the bench, and Advocate Sangwa did concede that the problem could apply to both men and women. Further on in my research, I also discovered that a fair number of judges had come from the public service and the judiciary itself and not private practice. The women concerned deliberately chose to pursue their legal careers outside public practice. There is insufficient data available to tabulate the exact numbers of women versus men who have come from private practice service in a particular period (in comparison to men). However, a perusal of the biographies of the justices of the Supreme Court showed that both men and women justices worked in public service before appointment to the bench.[21] This refutes the argument that the women who came to the bench were "failures" in private practice. Also, the view that women may have failed in private practice is indicative of the archaic notion that the best judges must be litigators. There is no evidence to show that this is the case. If one considers the issue of delayed judgments, in the period 2013–2017, there was only one reported investigation probing judicial misconduct arising from delayed judgments.

In September 2013, then President Michael Sata suspended High Court judges Emelia Sunkutu and Timothy Katanekwa and instituted a tribunal to probe them for professional misconduct.[22] One judge was a woman, and one was a man. They were eventually cleared of the charges, and their suspension was lifted. The tribunal held that they were not at fault, as the delays in judgments were occasioned by the fact that they were transferred continuously from one town to another.

I was unable to collect sufficient data to test the third claim, that women were moved around in public service. This theory could be confirmed or disproved by examining the number of women judges who have come from the public service in a particular period (in comparison to men). A perusal of the biographies of the justices of the Supreme Court, however, showed that there were a number of both men and women justices who worked in public service before appointment to the bench.[23] This is not uncommon. The Chairperson of the JSC informed me that historically, judges were chosen from within the judiciary—from registrars and magistrates.[24] It is only in the last two decades that candidates from private practice have been considered. What is ironic is that this move to include a previously neglected pool of candidates has resulted in the belief that that pool has a monopoly on the requisite judicial criteria.

I submit that the final claim expressed by Mr. Mweenge regarding the lack of independence among women judges is informed by one instance—the tenure of one particular woman justice. It is therefore necessary to explore this circumstance in more detail.

Justice Lombe Chibesakunda's tenure as Acting Chief Justice

Justice Lombe Chibesakunda was the first woman lawyer admitted to the Bar in Zambia in 1969 (Mumba, 2018). She served as a justice of the Supreme Court of Zambia until June 2012, when she was appointed as Acting Chief Justice by then President Michael Sata. At the time of her appointment, Chibesakunda had already reached the stipulated retirement age of 65. Still, the President relied on Article 93 (6) of the 1996 constitution, which stated that "a person may act as the Chief Justice, Deputy Chief Justice or a Supreme Court judge notwithstanding that they had attained the age prescribed by article 98" (The Government of Zambia, 1996). There were allegations that Sata appointed her because she was his cousin, (Munshya, 2013). The proposal to ratify did not proceed to the main parliamentary house after it failed before the Select Committee and it was eventually withdrawn. However, President Sata ignored the non-ratification and other legal challenges, and Chibesakunda's term only came to an end in 2015 when a new President was elected.[25] What is considered more alarming to critics was the politicization of the judiciary during Chibesakunda's reign as Acting Chief Justice.

In the controversial case of *Mutuna & Others v. Attorney General*[26] on May 12, 2012, the President unilaterally suspended three judges without following due process as prescribed under the Judicial Code of Conduct Act No. 13 of 1999. The three judges were granted an *ex parte* order for leave to apply for judicial review and a stay of the President's decision on May 14. The Attorney General appealed to the Supreme Court after a bid to discharge the leave failed; the Supreme Court of Appeal by a majority of 4 to 3, with Chibesakunda delivering the majority judgment, found that there was no condition precedent to the President's exercising the powers vested in him under Articles 98(2), (3), and (5).[27] This decision was widely criticized,[28] with renowned academic Muna Ndulo stating that Article 98 had not been drafted to become the conduit of executive influence over the judiciary. He went on to state that removing judges from the bench on spurious grounds was the greatest threat to judicial independence (Ndulo, 2016). Some considered Chibesakunda's decision in this case as a move to curry favor with Sata and ensure that she would be permanently appointed as Chief Justice (Munshya 2013). This is despite the fact that it was a unanimous court decision and other justices could have dissented if they thought the main judgment was incorrect.

In addition, during her tenure, the Supreme Court nullified several parliamentary seats that were the subject of a petition by the ruling party. Some election petitions were alleged to have been decided in favor of the ruling PF, as most of the subsequent by-elections resulted in the vacant seat falling to the ruling party (Freedom House, 2014). However, once again, it is difficult to prove any undue influence exerted by the former Chief Justice. All the discussions of the justices of the Supreme Court were in camera, and the decisions were passed by a majority bench. Thus, it was arguable whether Justice Chibesakunda's period as Acting Chief Justice was tainted because of alleged judgments in favor of the ruling party. Her refusal to step down even when the National Assembly refused to ratify her, however, indicates bad judgment on her part. Nonetheless, it would be unfair to judge women based on Chibesakunda's acting tenure, because succeeding male leaders have not been judged based on their predecessors' actions. Before her extended tenure as Acting Chief Justice, Chibesakunda had distinguished herself well on the Supreme Court.

Secondly, in 2002, a male Chief Justice, Mathew Ngulube, stepped down after allegations of corruption after he was alleged to have received large amounts of money from previous President Frederick Chiluba (Daily Nation, 2015). Justice Ngulube was eventually cleared because he did not know that the source of the gift was government funds, and he paid back the money to the government. However, a critic could argue that the fact that he accepted a monetary gift from the then sitting President was also an instance of bad judgment. No reference was made to this and other indiscretions of male judges, which begs the question: "Why is the lack of judicial independence a reason for skepticism concerning women and not men?" I submit that this is because of the differentiation made between male judges and women judges; more precisely, the view that women judges are considered as illegitimate holders of power.

Hence, we see that historical perceptions of women have not disappeared as women have entered politics, governance, and other professions. Instead, they have morphed into prejudice and illegitimacy perceptions of women in respect of women leaders. Studies suggest that traditional sex-role stereotypes are imperative for understanding the dynamics and expectations for women and men in leadership (Adebayo & Udegbe, 2004). In the Zambian scenario, the majority of interview participants perceive women judges as illegitimate holders of power because they assume that these women lack the required competencies and capabilities. The low legitimacy perceptions of women mean that even though they have the authority to preside, opinions are that their power is unjustified and undeserved.

The effects of perceptions of illegitimacy

Prejudice toward women judges

The perceived mismatch or lack of fit between the traits seen as typical behaviors of leaders and those considered to be characteristic of women drives expectations that women will be less competent than men with identical credentials (Vial et al., 2016, p.403). This mismatch between the behavior of "typical" leaders and women results in prejudice. This is known as the role congruity theory. Eagly and Karau suggest that in general, prejudice toward female leaders follows from the incongruity that many people perceive between the characteristics of women and the requirements of leadership roles (Eagly & Karau, 2002). The potential for prejudice against women leaders that is inherent in the female gender role follows from its dissimilarity to the expectations that people typically have about leaders. Prejudice can arise when perceivers judge women as actual or potential occupants of leadership roles. The judgment stems from the inconsistency between the predominantly communal qualities that perceivers associate with women and the predominantly agentic attributes they believe are required to succeed as a leader (Eagly & Karau, 2002, p.575). In short, because women are not ordinarily considered as convincing, authoritative, independent, and assertive actors, any role that affirms these qualities activates prejudice.

As mentioned earlier, women in Zambia have previously played a supporting role and are latecomers to governance and politics. This subordinate role is contrary to positions of authority such as judging, and an interview participant, Mr. Habasonda, aptly explains this:

> The women participating on the bench are also informed in the traditional lenses that we find in the society that we are anchored in. The fact that those women are not necessarily able to resolve conflict within society. I think that our chiefdoms are in such a way that men take the lead, even in situations where the woman is the chief; it is the men surrounding her that make the decision.[29]

Thus, the idea of a woman taking the lead is historically incongruent with what is expected of her; worse yet for the role of a judge, which requires a woman to take charge of a courtroom and decide matters, sometimes matters of life and death, and to admonish lawyers when necessary. The reference to the Constitutional Court decision as proof of women's failures is a fitting example. The male justices who signed on to the majority judgment were not criticized, nor were their actions considered as proof of their incapabilities. The role of men as justices is uncontested, or rather, it does not violate any expectations, because they are expected to be holders of this power. The women, on the other hand, are singled out as proof that women are not up to the task, even though there is no empirical evidence to support this argument. Three legal professionals suggested that though there has been a drop in standards regarding quality of judgments, this was across the board. One legal professional expressed concern about placing the blame for "falling" standards on women, and she wondered whether the judgments were better than they currently are when the bench was male-dominated.[30] When asked why there was a perception that women were to blame for the challenges of the judiciary, some participants alluded to societal attitudes of women and general sexism as reasons why women continued to be judged unkindly.

One legal professional mentioned that men are more prominent or reported more in the media than women lawyers.[31] Thus, because women were less prominent lawyers, they were less likely to be perceived as the ideal judge in comparison to men. Invariably, this means that they are less likely to be perceived as deserving of the judicial power that is accorded to judges, thereby invoking perceptions of illegitimacy. These societal perceptions of women are a result of the incongruence of the role of the judge and women's role in society. It is suggested that they also result from a belief that there has been a violation of the standard mode of operation, where men are expected to dominate every sphere of society—including the judiciary. The statistics in the judiciary point to how this belief has been disrupted, but they also fuel the need to explain why the feminization of the judiciary is not justified. These explanations come in the form of suggestions that jurisprudential standards are falling, that women judges lack autonomy, or even that women perceive the bench as a more relaxed environment than private practice. Irrespective of which argument is tendered, it originates from the same source—low perceptions of women's legitimacy.

The effect of these perceptions on women and judicial governance

Legitimacy occurs when the power of those who have it is seen as deserved and justified. The perceptions of legitimacy concerning judges affect the overall legitimacy of the courts. In the introduction, I listed three reasons for how the overall legitimacy of the courts is affected. However, there are also consequences for the individual women judges, because women judges have the power to adjudicate. The perceptions that this power is not justified can affect their work. Through my interviews with the women judges and women legal professionals, I found empirical evidence that the occupation of a high-rank position by a person belonging to a group that occupies a subordinate role in society did lead to negative reception. The consequence of this amongst the judges I interviewed was that they felt that they had to prove themselves and to justify their positions. For example, one justice mentioned that there are higher expectations of women judges in comparison to men. She said:

> [t]hey said at the workshop that the women judges were not performing as expected. And yet there had been men for many years who were

> underperforming, and they had made many mistakes, and now it was interesting that because it was women judges, suddenly there was a problem.[32]

She noted that women are often placed under a microscope. The focus on women judges at the workshop in question was also without merit, as no factual evidence led to showing that women were not performing as expected. It was a general statement that cast aspersions on all women judges, which, another judge submitted, are because of cultural constructs. She posited that "if a woman fails to perform, they will attack her more" than they would a man.[33] Thus, in addition to working hard, being diligent and consistent were perceived as the only other ways to mitigate the effect of these negative perceptions.

This is not unusual. Studies have shown that women are evaluated less favorably, even when performing precisely the same leadership roles as men (Ryan et al., 2016). Further, women candidates for high positions are more likely to receive more negative media coverage (Brenner & Knake, 2012). They are more likely to be judged on dressing, their gender is more likely to be mentioned, and their family life is mentioned more frequently than men's (Brenner & Knake, 2012). Societal perceptions of gender roles are also present in interviews for the selection of judges, and I obtained empirical data supporting this. One former JSC commissioner spoke of her surprise at how candidates were treated differently in interviews. She noticed that only women were asked questions about what would happen if their husband was transferred to another town or if they had to be moved.[34] She stated that she found these questions problematic because they were not asked of male candidates. These questions placed the women in the traditional and private sphere of wife and homemaker. The implication here was that their desire to be in positions of power is incompatible with their expected gender role, while for men, this disjuncture is absent; hence the ease with which they are considered legitimate power holders.

The women judges I interviewed in Zambia did acknowledge the challenges of having to balance their family roles and their work. They concluded that the capabilities and competencies required to be a judge or the qualities of a good judge were not the stumbling blocks in their career. Rather, it was the strain of balancing family responsibilities and burdens (which are expected of women in Zambia) that sometimes put them at a disadvantage in relation to their male colleagues.

Illegitimacy perceptions that result in women having to prove themselves can also have a detrimental effect on the women judges themselves. I submit that in trying to prove themselves, they may take on more cases than they should, leaving them exhausted from carrying a heavier workload. There is another possible effect of illegitimacy perceptions evidenced in other studies. When women prove that they are as competent as their male colleagues, either by having a firm hand in court proceedings or by being assertive with lawyers, they will face backlash for "acting like men." Godsil et al. (2016) refer to this as penalizing women for not meeting gendered expectations of female friendliness and gentleness. It is important to remember that attaining the role of a judicial officer is not a menial exercise. Unlike the legislature or executive, where members do not necessarily have to hold professional qualifications to attain positions, the judiciary is a different arena.

While character traits such as honesty, integrity, equality, and propriety can be found in a large number of people, competence in legal matters, university qualifications, and subsequent further legal training cannot. One has to have reached a certain professional level to meet the constitutional requirements mentioned in the first part of this chapter and the additional criteria required by the JSC. Current and former commissioners interviewed stated that women are more likely to have higher postgraduate qualifications than men. In the last two years, they have performed better in JSC interviews than men have. If women have more impressive qualifications and interviews at the JSC than men, and they pass scrutiny at the National Assembly, is it fair that they are perceived as illegitimate merely because they are perceived as the "second" sex?

Conclusion

In this chapter, I have argued that despite the commendable equitable representation of women in the Zambian judiciary, women still face skepticism primarily based on perceptions of illegitimacy. I have located these perceptions within the perceived incongruence between women's characteristics or traditional roles in society and a leader's qualities. I use the argument that women are perceived as unjustified power holders, as opposed to norm violators, because of data I gathered during my interviews, which are corroborated by existing research. Increasingly, the majority of law school students and graduates are women, so it is not a field with a lack of women. It is the role of the judge, with power, privilege, and responsibilities, that is considered by some as "too much" for many women to have. I acknowledge that the judiciary in Zambia is unique in that women occupy high positions, which is both unusual and different, especially compared with other branches of government. However, this particular situation does not merit the view that women are undeserving of being the majority and serving as leaders in the judiciary. It is undeniable that the illegitimacy perceptions discussed in this essay are buttressed by cultural and social constructs of womanhood in Zambia. There is no evidence to suggest that women judges are performing worse than men are or are bringing the judiciary into disrepute. A research project on court efficiency and justice is currently underway by a reputable research institution, which seeks to provide policymaking, research capacity, and governance.[35] While preliminary results indicate that there are some issues with performance and case mismanagement, there is no evidence as yet that this is attributable to the feminization of the judiciary.[36]

Notes

1 Norway, Sweden, and Finland have long been lauded for their gender-equitable parliaments.
2 Statistics obtained from http://www.parliament.gov.zm/members/gender and http://www.parliament.gov.zm/ministers/cabinet.
3 Most of these interviews were conducted in the capital city Lusaka, with a few from Kitwe, the second largest city in the country.

4 The statistics were obtained from the website of the Judiciary of Zambia in April, 2018. See http://www.judiciaryzambia.com.
5 Justices Lombe Chibesa-Kunda and Florence Mumba, respectively.
6 Vice President Inonge Wina is serving her second term in office, while DPP Lillian Fulata Shawa-Siyuni was appointed in 2016.
7 The call period is the training at the Zambian Institute of Advanced Legal Studies and admission as an Advocate.
8 Interview with Deputy Chief Justice (DCJ) Marvin Mwanamwambwa on December 1, 2016 in Lusaka, Zambia.
9 Interview on April 12, 2017 in Lusaka, Zambia.
10 Interview with Commissioner 1, April 21, 2017, Lusaka, Zambia.
11 An example of the appointment of a previous Registrar of Companies was cited here.
12 Interview with Judge 4, April 18, 2017, Lusaka, Zambia.
13 Interview with Legal Professional 1, August 15, 2017, Kitwe, Zambia.
14 Interview with Legal Professional 3, August 14, 2017.
15 Interview with Legal Professional 2, April 19, 2017, Lusaka, Zambia.
16 Interview with Mr. Mweenge, April 18, 2017, Lusaka, Zambia.
17 (*Hakainde Hichilema & Others v Edgar Lungu & Others*, 2016.)
18 President Edgar Lungu garnered 1,860,877 votes against the opposition United Party for National Development (UPND) Hakainde Hichilema's 1,760,347 votes.
19 For a detailed explanation, see Owiso, R. *Zambia: The 2016 Zambia Presidential election petition: How not to handle election petitions*. Retrieved from https://www.lusakatimes.com/2016/09/20/2016-zambia-presidential-election-petition-not-handle-election-petitions
20 Interview with Commissioner 1.
21 The website for the Zambian judiciary only contains short biographies of the judges of the Supreme Court.
22 Interview with Mr. Frederick Mudenda.
23 The website for the Zambian judiciary only contains short biographies of the judges of the Supreme Court.
24 Interview with former Chief Justice Mathew Ngulube.
25 The Law Association of Zambia mounted an unsuccessful legal challenge against Justice Chibesakunda's continued stay in office.
26 Appeal No. 088/2012 [2013] ZMSC 38 (9 May 2013); SCZ/8/185/2012.
27 Appeal No. 088/2012 [2013] ZMSC 38 (9 May 2013); SCZ/8/185/2012.
28 See Elias Munshya wa Munshya. With forked tongues: Why Chibesakunda's majority ruling in Attorney-General v. Mutuna & Others is flawed. Retrieved from https://eliasmunshya.org/2013/07/01/with-forked-tongues-why-chibesakundas-majority-ruling-in-attorney-general-v-mutuna-others-is-flawed
29 Interview with Mr. Habasonda, April 19, 2017, Lusaka, Zambia.
30 Interview with Legal Professional 2, April 19, 2017.
31 Interview with Legal Professional 5, April 20, 2017.
32 Interview with Justice 2, April 18, 2017.
33 Interview with Judge 3, November 26, 2016.
34 At note 9.
35 I am unable to identify the organization, as it would compromise the anonymity of the interview participant working on this project.
36 Interview with Legal Professional 6.

References

Adebayo, D.O., & Udegbe, I.B. (2004). Gender in the Boss-Subordinate Relationship: A Nigerian Study. *Journal of Organizational Behavior*, *25*(4), 515–525. https://doi.org/10.1002/job.255

Albertyn, C. (2014). Judicial Diversity. In Cora Hoexter & Morné Olivier (Eds.), *The Judiciary in South Africa* (pp. 245–287). Cape Town: JUTA.

Arrington, N., Bass, L., Glynn, A., Staton, J.K., Delgado, B., & Lindberg, S.I. (2017). Gender Diversity on High Courts. *Working Paper Series*, 54. https://www.researchgate.net/publication/320657176_Gender_Diversity_on_High_Courts

Bauer, G., & Burnet, J.E. (2013). Gender Quotas, Democracy, and 'Women's Representation in Africa: Some Insights from Democratic Botswana and Autocratic Rwanda. '*Women's Studies International Forum*, *41*, 103–112. https://doi.org/10.1016/j.wsif.2013.05.012

Brenner, H., & Knake, R.N. (2012). Rethinking Gender Equality in the Legal 'Profession's Pipeline to Power: A Study on Media Coverage of Supreme Court Nominees. *Temple Law Review*, *84*(2), 325–384. Retrieved from https://www.scopus.com/inward/record.uri?eid=2-s2.0-84861493752&partnerID=40&md5=9915447401171ed106b9d2c0341165dd

Carvalho, R. (2018). "They 'don't let us speak": Gender relations and judicial decision-making in the Brazilian Supreme Court. *Women, Gender & the Law Ejournal*, *14*(10). Retrieved from https://papers.ssrn.com/sol3/papers.cfm?abstract_id=3116338

Commentary on the Bangalore Principles of Judicial Conduct (2007). Vienna. Retrieved from https://www.icj.org/wp-content/uploads/2014/10/Commentary-bangalore-principles.pdf

Commonwealth. (2003). Commonwealth (Latimer House) Principles on the Three Branches of Government. Retrieved from http://www.cmja.org/downloads/latimerhouse/commprinthreearms.pdf

Conner, B. (2008). You Made a Mistake-You Selected Women: The Implementation of Political Gender Quotas in Postconflict African Nations. *Tulane Journal of International and Comparative Law*, *17*, 1–26. Retrieved from http://heinonlinebackup.com/hol-cgi-bin/get_pdf.cgi?handle=hein.journals/tulicl17&section=11

Cook, B.B. (1984). Women Judges: A Preface to Their History. *Golden Gate University Law Review*, *14*(3), 1–38.

Cowen, S. (2013). *Judicial Selection in South Africa* (First). Cape town: Democratic Governance and Rights Unit.

Daily Nation (2015). Justice Ngulube Cleared. Retrieved March 25, 2019, from https://www.zambiadailynation.com/2015/04/09/justice-ngulube-cleared/

Davis, R., & Williams, G. (2003). A Century of Appointments but Only One Woman. *Alternative Law Journal*, *28*(2), 54–58.

Dawuni, J.J., & Masengu, T. (2019). Judicial Service Commissions and the Appointment of Women to High Courts in Nigeria and Zambia. In S. Sterett & L.D. Walker (Eds.), *Research Handbook on Law and Courts* (pp. 213–230). Northampton: Edward Elgar Publishing.

Devlin, R., MacKay, A.W., & Kim, N. (2000). Reducing the Democratic Deficit: Representation, Diversity and the Canadian Judiciary, or towards a Triple P Judiciary. *Alberta Law Review*, *38*, 734–865. Retrieved from http://heinonline.org/HOL/Page?handle=hein.journals/alblr38&id=746&div=34&collection=journals

Eagly, A.H., & Karau, S.J. (2002). Role Congruity Theory of Prejudice Toward Female Leaders. *Psychological Review*, *109*(3), 573–598. https://doi.org/10.1037//0033-295X.109.3.573

Evans, A. (2014). "Women Can Do What Men Can Do": The Causes and Consequences of Growing Flexibility in Gender Divisions of Labour in Kitwe. 'Women Can Do What Men Can Do': The Causes and Consequences of Growing Flexibility in Gender Divisions of Labour in Kitwe, Zambia. *Journal of Southern African Studies*, 40(5), 981–998. https://doi.org/10.1080/03057070.2014.946214

Evans, A. (2016). "'For the Elections. We Want Women'!": Closing the Gender Gap in Zambian Politics. *Development and Change*, *47*(2), 388–411. https://doi.org/10.1111/dech.12224

Freedom House (2014). Zambia | Freedom House. Retrieved March 25, 2019, from https://freedomhouse.org/report/freedom-world/2014/zambia

Godsil, R.D., Tropp, L.R., Atiba, G.P., Jay, J., Powell, J., & MacFarlane, J. (2016). The Effects of Gender Roles, Implicit Bias, and Stereotype Threat on the Lives of Women and Girls. *Science of Equality*, *2*, 1–88.

Green, L. (2014). *Law and the Role of a Judge* (Legal Research Paper Series No. 47). Oxford. Retrieved from https://papers.ssrn.com/sol3/papers.cfm?abstract_id=2495953

Grossman, N. (2012). Sex on the Bench: Do Women Judges Matter to the Legitimacy of International Courts? *Chicago Journal of International Law*, *12*, 647–682. https://doi.org/10.2139/ssrn.1773015

Hakainde Hichilema & Others v Lungu & Others (2016). (2016/CC/0031) ZMCC 4 (5 September 2016). https://zambialii.org/node/12445

Hirschl, R. (2008). The Judicialization of Mega-Politics and the Rise of Political Courts. *Annual Review of Political Science*, *11*(1), 93–118. https://doi.org/10.1093/oxfordhb/9780199208425.003.0008

Kasonde, L. (2018). Why We Need More Women in Leadership. Retrieved May 28, 2018, from https://diggers.news/guest-diggers/2018/03/07/why-we-need-more-women-in-leadership/

Malleson, K. (2006). Rethinking the Merit Principle in Judicial Selection. *Journal of Law and in Society*, *33*(1), 126–140. https://doi.org/10.1111/j.1467-6478.2006.00351.x

Masengu, T. (2015). Standing on the Sidelines Watching: Women and 'Zambia's Constitutional Processes. In *Constitution Building in Africa* (pp. 48–74). Baden-Baden: Nomos.

Masengu, T. (2017a). *Research Report on the Zambian Judicial Appointment System*. Cape Town: Democratic Governance and Rights Unit.

Masengu, T. (2017b). The Vulnerability of Judges in Contemporary Africa: Alarming Trends Author(S). *Africa Today*, *63*(4), 3–19.

McLoughlin, K. (2015). The Politics of Gender Diversity on the High Court of Australia. *Alternative Law Journal*, *40*(3), 166–170. Retrieved from http://heinonline.org/HOL/Page?handle=hein.journals/alterlj40&id=170&div=46&collection=journals

Mocumie, C.B. (2020, Forthcoming). *Gender Transformation of the Judiciary in South Africa through the Eyes of a Woman Judge*. Lanham: Lexington Books.

Mokgoro, Y. (2010). Judicial Appointments. *Advocate*, *23*(3), 43–48.

Mumba, F.N.M. (2018). The Quest for Equal Opportunities. In J. Dawuni & A. Kuenheyia (Eds.), *International Courts and the African Woman Judge: Unveiled Narratives* (pp. 27–35). New York: Routledge.

Munshya, E. (2013). *Kuya Bebele: Why Lombe Chibesakunda Should Vacate the Office of Chief Justice | Elias Munshya, LL.M, MBA, M.DIV*. Retrieved February 5, 2019, from https://eliasmunshya.org/2013/09/11/kuya-bebele-why-lombe-chibesakunda-should-vacate-the-office-of-chief-justice/

Mutame, G. (2012). African Women Are Ready to Lead. Retrieved May 28, 2018, from https://www.un.org/africarenewal/magazine/special-edition-women-2012/african-women-are-ready-lead

Ndulo, M. (2011). Judicial Reform, Constitutionalism and the Rule of Law in Zambia: From a Justice System to a Just System. *Zambia Social Science Journal*, *2*(1), 1–26. Retrieved from http://scholarship.law.cornell.edu/zssj

Ndulo, M. (2016). Professor Muna Ndulo on Judicial Independence and Supreme 'Court's Decision in Matter of Three Judge. Retrieved April 20, 2016, from http://www.zambiawatchdog.com/professor-muna-ndulo-on-judicial-independence-and-supreme-courts-decision-in-matter-of-three-judges/

O' Regan, K. (2012). A Pillar of Democracy: Reflections on the Role and Work of the Constitutional Court of South Africa. *Fordham Law Review*, *81*, 1169–1186

Olivier, M. (2013). A Perspective on Gender Transformation in the South African Judiciary. *South African Law Journal*, *13*(3), 449–464

Owiso, R. (2016). Zambia : The 2016 Zambia Presidential Election Petition: How Not to Handle Election Petitions. Retrieved March 12, 2018, from https://www.lusakatimes.com/2016/09/20/2016-zambia-presidential-election-petition-not-handle-election-petitions/

Rackley, E. (2007). Judicial Diversity, the Woman Judge and Fairy Tale Endings. *Legal Studies*, *27*(1), 74–94.

Ryan, M.K., Haslam, S.A., Morgenroth, T., Stoker, J., Peters, K., Heilman, M., Peters, K., & Ryan, M.K. (2016). Getting on top of the Glass Cliff: Reviewing a Decade of Evidence, Explanations, and Impact. *The Leadership Quarterly*, *27*(3), 446–455. https://doi.org/10.1016/j.leaqua.2015.10.008

Sangwa, S.J. (2016). *Brief to the President of the Republic of Zambia on the Constitutional Court Appointments*. Lusaka: Advocate John Sangwa

Solanke, I. (2008). Diversity and Independence in the European Court of Justice. *Columbia Journal of European Law*, *15*, 89–121. Retrieved from https://www.copyright.com/ccc/basicSearch.do?

Southern African Chief 'Justices' Forum (2018). *Lilongwe Principles and Guidelines on the Selection and Appointment of Judicial Officers*. Lilongwe. Retrieved from https://www.unodc.org/ji/

Southern African Development Community (2008). *SADC Protocol on Gender and Development*. Johannesburg: SADC. Retrieved from https://www.sadc.int/files/8713/5292/8364/Protocol_on_Gender_and_Development_2008.pdf

Strengthening Judicial Integrity, J. G. (2002). *The Bangalore Principles of Judicial Conduct*. The Hague. Retrieved from http://www.unodc.org/pdf/crime/corruption/judicial_group/Bangalore_principles.pdf

Sustainable Development Solutions Network. (2020). *Launching a data revolution for the Sustainable Development Goals*. Retrieved from https://indicators.report/targets/5-5/.

The Government of the Republic of Zambia. (1996). *Constitution of Zambia Act 18 of 1996*.

Thornton, M. (1985). Affirmative Action, Merit and the Liberal State. *Australian Journal of Law and Society*, *2*(2), 28–39.

Thornton, M. (2007). "Otherness" on the Bench: How Merit is Gendered. *Sydney Law Review*, *29*, 391–413.

Vial, A.C., Napier, J.L., & Brescoll, V.L. (2016). A Bed of Thorns: Female Leaders and the Self-Reinforcing Cycle of Illegitimacy. *The Leadership Quarterly*, *27*(3), 400–414. https://doi.org/10.1016/j.leaqua.2015.12.004

Vos de, P. (2013). The JSC Must Redefine Merit to Advance Judicial Transformation. *Constitutionally Speaking*. Retrieved May 8, 2018, from https://constitutionallyspeaking.co.za/the-jsc-must-redefine-merit-to-advance-judicial-transformation/

W, R (2018). Have the Women Failed US? A Verdict on Zambian Women in Leadership. Retrieved May 28, 2018, from https://www.zambianobserver.com/have-the-women-failed-us-a-verdict-on-zambian-women-in-leadership/

Zambian Judicial Service Commission (1993). *JSC Criteria for Appointing Judges*. Lusaka: Judicial Service Commission

Part IV

Judicial training and gender

12 Unlocking gender inequality through judicial training

Insights from Tanzania

Juliana Masabo, PhD

Introduction

The pursuit of gender equality is an intrinsic component of international and national justice systems. In Tanzania, the Judiciary of Tanzania (JoT) is the ultimate authority for dispensation of justice under the constitution (United Republic of Tanzania, 1977).[1] It is inevitably the guardian of laws and societal integrity and therefore critical in the advancement of substantive equality between men and women. In this regard, the JoT's vision and mission as stipulated under its Five-Year Strategic Plan (2015/2016–2019/2020) points to the need to promote equal justice for all. The JoT's Strategic Plan has three pillars, namely, Governance, Accountability, and Management of Resources; Access to justice and Expeditiousness; and Public Trust and Stakeholders Engagement. Under the second pillar, the JoT expresses its commitment to increase access to justice for vulnerable and disadvantaged groups, women and children in particular. Judicial training, aimed at enhancing the capacity of judicial officers in administering justice, is seen as an important tool for attainment of the goals of the Strategic Plan and improving the JoT's transparency and credibility among citizens.

This study assesses gender training in the JoT. The key question for investigation is whether judicial training in Tanzania includes gender awareness programs and if so, to what extent. Before embarking on this question, the chapter discusses, albeit briefly, the conceptual and normative framework underlining gender training, and the state of affairs and justification for gender training in Tanzania. The chapter will analyze the training programs conducted by the Institute of Judicial Administration (IJA), Lushoto, Tanzania and the Tanzania Women Judges Association (TAWJA). The focus of this analysis is to examine what the training programs cover, who participates in such trainings, and the effectiveness of these training programs in addressing gender inequality and enhancing access to justice for all. The last part identifies the gaps and provides recommendations.

Conceptual and normative framework on gender and judicial training

The unique role of courts in advancing equality between men and women has been highly acknowledged in the gender justice discourse. Underlying this discourse

DOI: 10.4324/9780429327865-16

is the proposition that the law adjudicated in these courts is not necessarily a neutral arbiter of disputes or a positive instrument of social change, as it has been deemed to be. Rather, it has historically been a powerful conduit for transmission and reproduction of the dominant ideology, male power structures, and gender inequality (Thornton, 1986). The feminist theorists have maintained that the justice systems all around the world reflect the power imbalances inherent in their society and in so doing, underpin male dominance over women (Banakar & Travers, 2002). Unequal distribution of power and resources between women and men and the public–private divide that is prevalent in almost all jurisdictions exacerbate gender inequality in courts. Because of the public–private divide, injustices against women, such as domestic violence, rarely attract attention, as they happen in the private sphere and are deemed acceptable norms of respective communities. Culture is often given as justification.

In Africa, as in many other parts of the world, the situation of women is dire. Many injustices against women, including sexual assault, often go unnoticed, and the level of impunity is high (Hodgson, 2011) According to the Gender Status Index (GSI), which measures the gender gaps within countries and assesses the extent to which women have the same opportunities as men in education, health, economic empowerment, and access to resources, inequality and women's empowerment still remain among the biggest challenges facing African states (Economic Community for Africa, 2017). In most of the countries, the inequalities manifest themselves in women's limited access to, and control over, productive resources, unequal access to social services and socio-economic opportunities, as well as low representation in politics and decision-making spheres.

The Convention on the Elimination of All Forms of Discrimination against Women (CEDAW) adopted by the United Nations General Assembly in 1979 provides a normative framework to address gender inequality. It defines what constitutes discrimination against women and sets up an agenda for national action to end such discrimination and to achieve substantive equality. The States Parties to the Convention undertake to embody the principle of equality between men and women in their constitutions and to abhor all forms of discrimination against women. One of the notable features of the Convention is its embodiment of the central role of the judiciary in elimination of discrimination and advancement of the quest for equality between men and women.

Article 2(c) of the Convention specifically obliges States Parties to "ensure through *competent national tribunals and other public institutions* the effective protection of women against any act of discrimination." The specific role of national courts, as exemplified under the General Comment No. 28 of the Committee on Elimination of All Forms of Discrimination against Women, is to ensure substantive equality by upholding the principle of equality in their adjudication and highlighting the inconsistencies that exist between national law, including customary and religious law where applicable.

Emulating this spirit, the Protocol to the African Charter on Human and Peoples' Rights on the Rights of Women in Africa, 2003 (Maputo Protocol), apart from providing specific guarantees for formal equality, specifically obliges states to take appropriate measures to ensure effective access by women to judicial and legal services. Article 2 of the Protocol specifically obliges States Parties to (a)embody the principle of equality in their national constitutions and legislation; (b) curb all harmful practices that endanger the health and general well-being of women; (c) integrate a gender perspective in their national policy decisions, legislation, and development plans; (d) take corrective and positive action to eliminate discrimination against women; and (e) support all initiatives directed at eradicating all forms of discrimination against women at the continental, regional, and national level. According to Article 8 and 25 of the Protocol, the States Parties have a responsibility to equip the courts and other law enforcement organs with the ability to effectively interpret and enforce gender equality rights and to protect effective remedy to women whose rights and freedoms are violated.

These two instruments provide a solid normative framework for realization of justice by women. However, the extent to which national courts have lived up to this expectation is debatable. While most States Parties have complied with the obligation to embody the principle of equality in their national constitutions, translation of these embodiments of equality into substantive justice has remained a challenge. In Africa, the situation is dire. It has been reported that there are significant gaps between the provisions of the Protocol, its domestication at the national level, and women's enjoyment of their human rights in practice. Even in countries where the principles enshrined in the Protocol have been domesticated, they are often not enforced, and institutional mechanisms to promote the human rights of women are often underfunded. The main factors for this gap include patriarchal socio-cultural, economic, rigid gender roles justified on the grounds of tradition, customs, and religion; uneven educational attainment for women and girls; poverty; and political unrests and conflicts (African Union and the United Nations Office of the High Commissioner for Human Rights, 2016; Bond, 2010; Ndulo, 2011), Existence of gender-biased laws, limited physical access to justice delivery centers, lack of awareness, and delay in dispensation of justice have been consistently cited as major impediments. Attitudes of judicial officers toward gender issues and lack of knowledge on specific gender dimensions of the law and how it undermines justice are also among the major barriers (Judicial Service of Ghana et al., 2008).

Measures adopted to address these barriers have included programs to enhance judicial responsiveness to gender equality. Responsiveness in this context entails the ability of the judiciary not only to respond to the demands of the dominant sections of society but also the ability to recognize and respond to the needs encountered by marginalized sections of the society, women and girls in particular (UN Women, 2019). Such efforts have encompassed, among others, gender training, increasing the number of female judges and magistrates, creation of special courts to deal with specific gender-based crimes/issues, and compilation and sharing of reference materials in such forms as gender bench books, feminist judgments, and many others. This chapter focuses on gender training.

For the purposes of this chapter, I contextualize judicial training broadly to include continuing judicial education specifically tailored to orient and build the capacity of judges and magistrates by equipping them with skills to identify and address gender issues in their adjudication. The emphasis on judicial training draws on existing research, which has demonstrated that due to the uniqueness of the dynamics of gender, it is crucial for judges to understand and develop skills related to a wide range of legal and social issues. The importance of specialized educational programs for judges is well founded in the literature (Dawuni & Bauer, 2016; Wallacet, 2003; Dawson, 2015; Wallace, 2000; Armytage, 1995; Jaffe & Claire, 2018; Wikler, 1989; Minamino, 2012). Judicial training is deemed an inevitable tool for addressing adjudicators' built-in and often strongly held sets of values, preconceptions, opinions and prejudices, and other inaccurate perceptions that influence judicial reasoning (Cameron, 1990).

The state of affairs in the Judiciary of Tanzania

Tanzania has been an active player in the gender justice discourse. By signing and ratifying the CEDAW and the Maputo Protocol, the country has demonstrated its commitment to the pursuit of gender equality.[2] In line with obligations stemming from these two instruments, Tanzania has embodied the principle of equality between men and women in its constitution. Discrimination on the basis of sex is expressly prohibited under Article 13 (5) of the Constitution of the United Republic of Tanzania, 1977. Enactment of discriminatory laws and laws with discriminatory effect is also explicitly prohibited.[3] In 1998, the parliament enacted the Sexual Offences (Special Provisions) Act, No. 8 of 1998, which introduced several provisions to safeguard the personal integrity, dignity, liberty, and security of women by, among other things, introducing stiff sentences for sexual offenses. The land law reform carried out in the late 1990s, which resulted in the enactment of the Land Act, No. 4 of 1999 and the Village Land Act, No. 5 of 1999, ushered a positive change in land ownership and administration. It affirmed the rights of women to acquire and register land in their own names.[4] It also annulled discriminatory customary rules denying women the ability to own, transfer, and use land and introduced a mandatory requirement for representation of women in land adjudication bodies, the Village Land Council and the Ward Tribunal in particular.[5]

While these measures are laudable, as they signal a strong commitment and political will to combat discrimination, gender inequality has remained obstinately high (UNDP, 2017). There is a predominance of gender inequality, mainly perpetuated through patriarchal systems, customs, and traditions (Nkoma-Wamunza, 1998; TAWLA, 2014; LHRC & ZLSC, 2019). Rape, sexual harassment, domestic violence, child/forced marriage and pregnancies, and denial of property ownership and inheritance are pervasive forms of violence. According to the 2016 Tanzania Health and Demographic Survey (THDS), 40% of women aged 15–49 years have experienced physical violence, and 17% have experienced sexual violence. Half of all ever-married women have experienced spousal violence in the form of physical violence, emotional violence, or both (MoHCDGEC, 2016). In most communities, these incidents are deemed acceptable norms. The THDS report reveals that 58% of women believe that a husband is justified in beating his wife if she burns food, argues with him, goes out without obtaining his permission, neglects the children, or refuses to have sex with him. This is far above the regional sub-Saharan African average of 43.5% (MoHCDGEC, 2016). Consequently, these offenses are rarely reported. Because of cultural influences, limited resources, sheer ignorance of rights, fear, and intimidation, most of the victims prefer amicable settlement at the family level instead of seeking help from law enforcement organs.

Those who defy the cultural barriers and seek redress are not guaranteed a timely and positive outcome due to the structural barriers embedded in the justice system. Customs and practices perpetuating gender inequality form part of the substantive law. Just as is the case in most jurisdictions in Africa, in Tanzania, statutory law, customary law, and Islamic law co-exist. The Judicature and Application of Laws Act [Cap 358 R.E. 2019] (JALA) recognizes and mandates the courts to apply customary laws when resolving disputes between members of the same community or between members of different communities if the rule of customary law of both communities is similar. These rules have been codified under the Local Customary (Declaration) Order of 1963, which serves as a source of customary law applicable in courts. As most of these rules emanate from patrilineal communities, they inherently encompass gender-discriminatory components deeply entrenched in the respective communities. For instance, the customary rules of inheritance applicable in patrilineal societies as codified in schedule 2 to the Local Customary Law (Declaration) (No. 4) Order, 1963 systematically prefer male over female family members on matters of inheritance and administration of estates.[6] Some of these rules entirely deny widows any share of inheritance from their deceased husbands' estates and place them under the care of the children or male relatives of the deceased husbands. Others deny women and daughters the right to inherit clan land.[7]

Adjudication of these rules and other laws with similar effects is a complex process. It involves multifaceted issues with far-reaching consequences, not only for the rights of women and for gender relations between the litigants who come before the court, but also for their respective families and the society at large. Determination of rights of the parties tends to require more than the basic legal analysis skills. Knowledge of the gender dimensions of the law and how it undermines women is fundamental in ensuring that the outcome of litigation does not further the injustices sanctified by these rules. Such a requirement is not always available, because not all the judges and magistrates are sufficiently equipped with gender skills. Professional training for lawyers in Tanzania does not provide a foundation for appreciation of the gender dimensions of the law.

Courses with greater bearing on gender are rarely taught in the Bachelor of Law (LL.B) degree, which is the foundation course for a legal career. The law faculties focus on providing students with broad education in law. As there is no nationwide LL.B curriculum, the law faculties are at liberty in deciding what to teach, provided they include in their respective curricula the traditional legal subjects such as administrative law, civil law, criminal law and procedure, evidence law, and law of contract. These have been designated as compulsory courses by the Council for Legal Education (CLE). With the exception of family law, which has been included in the list of compulsory courses, other courses deemed important for fostering gender equality such as human rights law, probate and succession, law of the child, and gender and law are electives. The teaching of these courses is not guaranteed and tend to be predicated upon factors such as priorities of the respective law faculty or school, availability of lecturers, and the interest which the respective course is capable of generating amongst students. There is currently no accurate empirical data on the extent to which these courses are able to generate interest among students. However, based on the author's experience from the University of Dar es Salaam, which is the oldest and major law faculty in the country, only a few students study these subjects at the LL.B level. Students find these courses less attractive due to their perceived low ability to generate well-paying clients compared with business-oriented courses such as banking law, tax law, insurance law, investment law, and intellectual property law.

At the Law School of Tanzania, which offers a practical Postgraduate Diploma in Law, human rights and probate law are taught as compulsory subjects for all law graduates who join the School. However, this does not offer a comprehensive solution either. Training at this level does not focus on theoretical issues that have long-lasting impacts. It is exclusively centered on procedural aspects of law specifically meant to expose students to certain practical aspects of law in preparation for legal practice. Arguably, very few law graduates in the country can claim to have the required competence in gender, or human rights in general for that matter. Moreover, since specialization in gender is not a prerequisite for recruitment as a judge or a magistrate, it is possible that only a marginal number of LL.B graduates who join the judiciary have had an exposure to the gender aspects of the law.

Dire skills deficiency in the JoT compounds this further (Pedersen & Haule, 2013). The Judicial Training Policy reveals that as of 2018, over 60% of sitting magistrates do not have an LL.B degree, which is the minimum educational standard for a magistrate in the country.[8] Statistics obtained in the course of this research show that as of May 2020, the proportion has dropped to 53.3%.[9] Most of these functionaries of the judiciary have a Certificate or Diploma in Law, mainly acquired from the former Institute of Development and Management Mzumbe (IDM Mzumbe), which used to serve as the training hub for primary court and district court magistrates.[10] Training at this level was confined to introducing students to general principles of law with no exposure to the gender aspects of law. What is alarming is that magistrates in this cohort are mainly based in primary courts, where customary law is applicable in resolving disputes. Disputes such as probate, domestic violence, divorce, and related disputes, which have a great bearing on gender relations, are mostly adjudicated at this level. The majority of women in rural areas are potential users of these courts, because they are geographically closer to them, unlike district courts, which are located in urban areas, mostly at district headquarters. A combination of these factors means that disputes involving gender issues in the country are adjudicated by persons who literally have no exposure to the gender aspects of the law. What is more alarming is the fact that magistrates at this level sit with court assessors who not only advise them on matters of customary law but also participate in decision-making process with voting powers equal to the magistrate (Kyando & Peter, 1994). As magistrates do not have a strong background on gender, ethnic biases and gender stereotypes that the assessors bring along can easily influence the outcome of adjudication processes in general, and this is the case even where the assessors are women (Tenga & Peter, 1996). A convergence of these factors underlines the need for robust gender training programs to build the capacity of judges and magistrates.

Narrowing the gap: JoT and the Institute of Judicial Administration–IJA Lushoto

The JoT attaches importance to training as a tool to address skills deficit and build the capacity of its staff. In-service trainings organized and coordinated by the Department of Administration and Human Resource, which is responsible for staff welfare and development, has been an integral part of JoT activities and programs. However, due to the absence of a well-defined training policy, these programs were haphazardly conducted with little regard to the actual training needs of judges and magistrates. To address this problem, in 1998, the Parliament of Tanzania enacted a law for establishment of the Institute of Judicial Administration (IJA)–Lushoto.[11] Being the national institution for judicial training, IJA was expected to spearhead judicial capacity building and skills gap enhancement within the judiciary. However, for many years after its inception, it focused exclusively on offering certificate and diploma courses in law, meant to prepare court clerks and primary court magistrates. Continuing education for judicial officers, which is pivotal in improving the capacity of judicial officers, remained untraversed.

With this background, repositioning IJA and strengthening its capacity to enable it to assume its central role in enhancing the skills of judicial and non-judicial officers is considered as central in realization of the reform envisaged in the World Bank–supported Citizen-Centric Judicial Modernization and Justice Service Delivery Project and the JoT's Strategic Plan. When the JoT passed its Five-Year Strategic Plan (2015/2016–2019/2020), it specifically identified the need to strengthen IJA's capacity to conduct judicial training as one of the key strategies under pillar one of the three pillars of the Strategic Plan. In 2019, the JoT passed its first ever Training Policy (JoT, 2019c) together with a three-year training program (JoT, 2019d). The policy is very ambitious and holds great potential for refining and restructuring judicial training in the country to respond to societal needs. The policy underlines the importance of induction, orientation, and mentoring programs.

The orientation and induction programs are offered as part of a mandatory program for newly recruited judges and magistrates. Its aims are two-fold, namely, to familiarize and integrate new judges and magistrates into the JoT and to equip them with judicial and managerial principles, procedures, and practice as well as judicial ethics and conduct. The mentorship program is yet to be implemented. It entails placing the newly recruited members under a senior and experienced employee for purposes of practical guidance and imparting knowledge, skills, and experience for ultimate change of attitudes of less experienced employees in order to ensure their growth within the Judiciary Service (JoT, 2019).

On its part, IJA has responded by establishing a directorate responsible for continuing judicial education. Through this directorate, IJA and the JoT have passed a three-year training program. Some of the programs have already been rolled out, the mandatory induction program for judges being among them. Considering the pervasiveness of gender inequality and gender-based violence/violence against women (GBV/VAW) cases, it was envisaged that gender training would be integrated in these trainings. However, the attention to gender in both programs is obscured. The focus has, rather, been on substantive and procedural laws and judicial skills of judging ("judge's craft"). Topics covered include the conduct of criminal and civil trials, judgment writing, procedures guiding the adjudication of labor cases, land matters, commercial disputes, economic and organized crimes, human rights, and constitutional petitions. Also included are emerging legal issues such as the use of information and communication technology (ICT) in the dispensation of justice.

To some extent, gender issues are covered under the topic on matrimonial causes, probate, and inheritance. As the main focus of the induction programs is on procedural aspects, coverage of gender issues tends to be minimal and dependent on the trainer's level of exposure to gender. Trainers who have been well oriented on the gender aspects of judging have a tendency to bring gender perspectives into their respective topics. In contrast, the approach taken by trainers who have little exposure to gender issues and women's rights is mainly gender neutral. Time constraints are also a major barrier for coverage of gender aspects of adjudication in induction programs. Constrained by time, the trainers limit their topics to the general principles of law, procedure, and evidence. Techniques of handling trials with sensitive gender issues such as rape cases and other sexual violence are not covered. The eschewed attention to the techniques of handling such trials is a lost opportunity. The judges assume their adjudicatory roles oblivious of gender inequality issues likely to confront them in the course of adjudication.

Considering that judges come from different backgrounds, and some have had no exposure to gender issues, the omission is fraught with danger for undermining the achievement recorded so far. As alluded to earlier, adjudication in these areas involves multifaceted gender issues that cannot be fairly and equitably adjudicated upon if the adjudicator is not adequately equipped with knowledge on the gender aspect of the law. For instance, a judge or magistrate dealing with a domestic violence case needs to be mindful of the high risk of repeated abuse, retaliation, and threats against the victim due to the fact that the victim not only knows the offender but has had an intimate relationship with him. Limited attention to gender is also apparent in other continuing legal education programs conducted by IJA and JoT. For instance, between 2016 and 2019, the continuing education programs jointly conducted by JoT and IJA focused on conventional areas such as criminal trial and practices, evidence law, and judgment writing. Other areas covered include labor law, practices and procedure, case flow and management, handling of cases involving offenses against wildlife, corruption offenses, and illicit drug trafficking cases (IJA, 2017, 2018, 2019).[12] It is worth noting that the IJA has started to embrace gender in its trainings; for instance, in 2018, when the JoT and the IJA organized a five-day training on constitutional litigation. The training was attended by all judges of the High Court. Constitutional petitions, including those in which the parties litigated over gender-insensitive and discriminatory laws, were discussed in the course of training. From 2018 to 2019, IJA conducted trainings for juvenile justice frontline workers. These trainings were organized under a tripartite collaboration between the JoT, IJA, and the United Nations Children's Fund (UNICEF) and were conducted in all High Court zones with the aim of equipping the participants with knowledge and skills for effective implementation of the Law of the Child Act, 2009.

IJA's support for gender training has gained more momentum following its partnership with the South African–based Centre for Reproductive Rights. Through this partnership, IJA and the Centre for Reproductive Rights will provide training in access to justice, reproductive and health rights in Africa and beyond. Under the auspices of this partnership, in the fiscal year 2019/20, the IJA in collaboration with the Centre for Reproductive Rights (South Africa) organized a regional workshop on gender issues and reproductive health rights. Moreover, in 2020, the IJA in collaboration with the Centre for Reproductive Rights and the UN Human Rights Office of the High Commissioner organized an Africa/Asia Cross Regional Judicial Webinar on Access to Justice and Protecting Reproductive Rights during the COVID 19 Health Crisis. A number of judicial officers from Tanzania were invited and participated. This partnership has great potential for building the capacity of IJA to handle gender-specific trainings.

There are two explanations for the limited focus on gender equality topics. First, with regard to the compulsory induction program, time is the major constraint. The program runs for only three weeks. Experience has shown that the time allocated to the program is not sufficient to cover all the topics. Instructors do not get enough time to cover the topics allocated. As a result, they cannot stretch beyond general principles of their respective topics. The second problem is inadequate funding, which is a persistent problem in JoT and IJA alike.

The Chief Justice of Tanzania and the entire JoT management team have demonstrated high commitment toward the advancement of the agenda for gender equality in the JoT. The Chief Justice, who also serves as patron for TAWJA, has on numerous occasions appealed for gender equality in adjudication as an important goal to be achieved in dispensation of justice. Further commitment is demonstrated through the JoT's outstanding support for TAWJA's work. In spite of its meager resources, the JoT has on numerous occasions supported TAWJA's activities. As will be shown in the next part, in 2004 to 2006, the JoT financed TAWJA's training. Also, in 2018, it sponsored TAWJA to host the Regional Conference on "Gender and the Judiciary in Africa" held in Arusha in 2018. On the IJA's side, the top management has demonstrated strong commitment to gender equality. The Chairman of the Council and the Principal are part of the TAWJA's team of trainers. They all actively participate in TAWJA's trainings and other activities.

Gender training in the JoT: TAWJA winnowing gender into judicial training

TAWJA was formed in 2000 as an umbrella organization for women judges and magistrates in Tanzania. It is also a national chapter for the International Association of Women Judges (IAWJ). TAWJA's key objectives are to advance women's rights by conducting legal research on gender equality and human rights; exchanging information on issues of critical concern to women; and uprooting gender bias from the judicial system and the community (TAWJA, 2000, 2015). In line with these objectives, TAWJA has been a positive force in the advancement of substantive gender equality. It has played a distinctive role in narrowing the gender skills gap in JoT through advocacy for increment of female adjudicators; promoting women's access to the courts; advocating for the increase of the number of women judges at all levels; developing judicial leadership; and capacity building on gender aspects of adjudication.

TAWJA was the first organization to introduce gender training in the JoT in early 2000 and has remained highly committed to the advancement of gender training for judicial officers. Its main focus has been to build the capacity of judges, magistrates, and law enforcement officers by equipping them with the knowledge and skills required in the handling of disputes with gender elements and in particular, sexual offenses, dissolution of marriage, custody of children, maintenance and inheritance rights, and other forms of violence against women. TAWJA's training programs have been helpful in introducing the participants to relevant regional and international norms, most especially the norms contained under the CEDAW and the Maputo Protocol. The participants are also introduced to comparative jurisprudence from other jurisdictions, particularly from within the Commonwealth.

In the first 3 years of its existence, TAWJA trained about 250 judicial officers and officials of the law enforcement organs, on the application of national, regional, and international legal norms in resolving gender-related disputes (TAWJA, 2015). This training was part of the IAWJ's Jurisprudence for Equality Programme (JEP), which highlighted the IAWJ's JEPs implemented in Kenya, Tanzania, and Uganda. The program was funded by UN Women (then UNIFEM). The remarkable success registered in the initial three years (2001–2003) prompted the judiciary to extend the training program for two years from 2004 to 2006. The completion of the two-year extension ushered in a remarkable training program conducted through a two-year project named "Jurisprudence on the Ground (JOG)" (TAWJA, 2015; Yoon, 2016). The project was funded by United Nations Democracy Fund (UNDEF) and was implemented in partnership with the IAWJ and a local non-governmental organization named the Society for Women and AIDS in Africa-Tanzania (SWAA-T) from September, 2008 to August, 2010. Approximately 60 magistrates and judges were trained in human rights law and women's rights (TAWJA, 2015). Between 2010 and 2012, TAWJA, with funding from the royal Danish government, implemented a successful training program through a project named *Sextortion: Naming, Shaming and Stopping Sexual Exploitation by Abuse of Authority* (TAWJA, 2015). The project, which became a flag bearer for TAWJA's training, was extended for three years to 2015 through funding from UN Women, Tanzania. Numerous seminars and workshops covering diverse categories of people including judicial officers, policymakers, officials from law enforcement organs, legislators, community leaders, religious leaders, teachers, doctors, and law students were conducted. A sextortion toolkit prepared in simple language was used in awareness raising. With yet more support from UN Women, TAWJA has implemented a three-year training program under Strengthening the Court System in Management of Cases involving Gender Based Violence and Violence Against Women. A total of 345 justice sector personnel (including 12 judges and 274 magistrates) have been trained. A wide range of topics were covered during this training. They include international and domestic human rights regimes, prevalence of stereotypes and implications for judicial process, community response to sexual and gender based violence (SGBV) cases, sextortion, and the role of courts in crafting effective remedies.

These trainings are conducted by trainers with vast knowledge and skills in adjudication and gender issues. TAWJA's team of trainers comprises female and male Justices of Appeal and Judges of the High Court, who are either in service or in retirement. There are also registrars, deputy registrars, and magistrates. All these are inducted through an intensive training of trainers' program conducted to equip them with knowledge and skills on gender training. A participatory and engaging approach is mostly preferred to stimulate interest and active participation. A combination of training methods, including group activities, case studies, role plays in the form of moot trials, and plenary sessions, is used to enable the participants to relate what they have learned to the realities on the ground.

In addition to judicial training, TAWJA has recorded remarkable success in enhancing understanding of women's rights through outreach programs conducted in schools, villages, and moot courts and printing and dissemination of brochures on law and procedures on gender-based violence and violence against women. Also notable are Radio and TV programs on response to violence against women and gender-based violence. The programs are aired across the country most especially during the 16 days of activism against Gender-Based Violence[13] and during the week preceding the official opening of the new judicial year (Law Week).[14] From January 31 to February 5, 2020, in celebration of Law Week,

TAWJA members across the country conducted outreach programs in primary schools and through TV programs and community radios. These programs have earned TAWJA commendation from within the JoT and beyond. TAWJA also prepared and distributed reference materials in the form of case books and journals for distribution to its members, other adjudicators, and stakeholders.

TAWJA is yet to conduct an evaluation of its training programs. Therefore, at the moment, it is difficult to assess the actual impact of these programs. However, there has been a significant change in the jurisprudence. There is now a positive change in judicial analysis and interpretation of laws that inhibit gender equality and negatively affect the rights of women. As most of these developments have happened after the introduction of gender training programs, which the majority of judges (male and female) have attended, it can be safely argued that there is a correlation between these developments and TAWJA's trainings.

The first area in which significant achievement has been recorded is child marriage. The breakthrough happened in 2016 when the High Court of Tanzania issued a landmark decision in *Rebeca Gyumi Z. Gyumi v. The Attorney General.*[15] In this case, the provisions of Sections 13 and 17 of the Law of Marriage Act, 1971, which sanctioned marriage of girls of 14 and 15 years of age, were declared a nullity for violating the principle of equality embodied under Articles 12 (1) and 13 (1) and (2) of the constitution. In addition to these constitutional provisions, which were used as benchmarks, the court found inspiration from the principle of equality embodied in Article 6 of the Maputo Protocol and the prohibition of child marriage embodied in Article 21 of the African Charter on the Rights and Welfare of the Child, 1990. A similar approach was used on appeal, whereby the Court of Appeal upheld the judgment of the High Court.[16] In its judgment, the Court of Appeal boldly stated that the impugned provisions can no longer be sustained because, apart from being inconsistent with the constitution, they conflict with the principles embodied in international and regional instruments and in particular, the United Nations Convention on the Rights of the Child, 1989, the African Charter on the Rights and the Welfare of the Child, 1990, and the Maputo Protocol, 2003. The decision has been widely celebrated in the country and beyond.[17] It is regarded as an emancipatory tool for girls who would, in the absence of such law, be forced into marriage during their childhood on the pretext that such marriages were legally recognized.

Notable strides have also been made in adjudication of sexual offenses. In this area, progressive jurisprudence is manifested in three areas: determining the probative value of the victim's testimony, proof of penetration in rape cases, and effect of late reporting of rape incidents. With regard to the evidential value of the victim's testimony, the Court of Appeal has now established a principle that recognizes evidence rendered by a victim of rape and sexual offenses as the best evidence.[18] With this liberal jurisprudence, an offender can be convicted based solely on uncorroborated testimony of the victim. In the past, such evidence was held insufficient to secure a conviction if it was not corroborated by other evidence, especially a medical report showing that there was penetration and testimony of a doctor who medically examined the victim. Articulating this principle in *Godi Kisangela v. R.*[19] the Court held that courts should not be bound by the evidence of medical experts, because such witnesses are most often not the actual witnesses to the incident and their evidence mainly constitutes opinions.[20]

In *Abilahi Mshamu Mnali v. R.*,[21] the Court of Appeal dealt extensively with the victim's delay in reporting the incidence. In this case, the appellant, who was then a head teacher of a primary school in Mtwara Region, allegedly raped and impregnated a pupil of his school. The appellant sought to impeach the victim's credibility on account that for over one year she did not disclose the incident to any person. The Court rejected this argument and held that delayed reporting or disclosure does not necessarily cast doubt on the credibility of the prosecutrix. The court reasoned that although timely reporting is desirable, it is not always possible. Victims may be inhibited from reporting by multiple and complex factors such as duress, threat or fear of retaliation, trauma, psychological conditions, and fear of being ostracized. The court cited with approval the decision of the Supreme Court of India in *State of Uttar Pradesh v. Chhoteyeal*,[22] which held that in dealing with rape cases, the court has to be mindful of the fact that the victim loses value as a person. Inspired by this decision, it concluded that

> [t]o achieve justice, *the court must be sensitive and responsive to the plight of victims. The evidence must be scrutinized objectively and free of any myths or preconception.* When the need arises a plausible explanation for the delayed silence in reporting the incident should suffice. [emphasis is mine]

Also, the Court of Appeal has lifted the veil that used to encumber justice for victims of rape and defilement who, due to such factors as cultural background, upbringing, religious beliefs, age, and other social or cultural constraints, failed to lead elaborative testimony in proof of intercourse/penetration. Currently, words such as "sexual intercourse" or "to have sex" are accepted as proof of penetration of the penis into the vagina.[23] In the past, such statements were held as insufficient proof. The principle, as articulated in *Mathayo Ngalya @ Shabani v. R.*,[24] was that for the offense of rape to be deemed to have been proved, the prosecution had to lead evidence of penetration as opposed to a general statement alleging that rape was committed without elaborating what actually took place. Testimony failing this test was rejected outright. The cases of *Hakizimana Syriverster*[25] and *Melkior Peter v. R.*[26] are illustrative. In *Hakizimana*, the victim testified that the assailant dragged her into a house, where he stripped her naked and had carnal knowledge of her. Similarly, in *Melkior Peter*, the testimony of the victim was that her assailant pulled her to a certain house, where he covered her mouth, undressed her, and raped her. In both cases, the testimony was found to be insufficient proof of penetration. Had these two cases been decided after the aftermath of *Hassani Bakari @ Mamajicho v. R.*, they could have yielded different outcomes. Summarizing this development, the Court of Appeal in *Hassan Kamunye v R*[27] made the following remark:

> There is a paradigm shift in the recent jurisprudence of the Court from the orthodox position where in offences of this nature; sexual offences,

> the victims were supposed to be graphic in narrating the ingredients of the offence. Luckily, the Court has had an opportunity to deal with the point in some cases on rape. The current position is that in proving that there was penetration in a rape case, it is not always expected.

This jurisprudence has indeed revolutionized justice for victims of sexual offenses, ensuring that cultural and technical barriers can no longer be relied upon as tools for perpetuating injustice for victims of rape. All these decisions are from the Court of Appeal, which is at the apex of the court hierarchy. Hence, they form part of the law and are binding upon the High Court and all subordinate courts, including the district courts, which exercise original jurisdiction on sexual offenses.

There is also a steady growth of progressive jurisprudence in matrimonial and inheritance matters. Drawing inspiration from the international and regional instruments and jurisprudence covered in TAWJA trainings and building on landmark authorities such as in *Bi Hawa Mohamed v. Ally Seif,*[28] *Ndewawosia d/o Ndeamtzo .v Emmanuel s/o Malasi,*[29] and *Bernado Efraim v. Holaria Pastory and Gervas Kaizilege,*[30] the judges and magistrates have increasingly employed gender analysis in their pronouncements. For instance, in *Laurence Mtefu v. Germana Mtefu,*[31] the court outright rejected the argument that housekeeping is a purely conjugal obligation and does not entitle the wife to any share in the matrimonial assets. It proceeded to state that such an argument is a clear reflection of the violence and discrimination that women have endured over the years. In *Anna Aloyce v. Zacharia Zebedayo Mgeta,*[32] the court held that by ratifying the CEDAW and the Maputo Protocol, Tanzania assumed an obligation to ensure that men and women are entitled to an equitable share of matrimonial assets. In *Naftal Joseph Kalalu v. Angela Mashirima,*[33] the court relied upon the provision of Articles 12 and 13 of the constitution and Article 1 of CEDAW to assert the right of a widow over the deceased husband's estate even though the couple was not formally married.

Challenges and prospects

Further to the challenges discussed in the preceding parts of this chapter, lack of reliable sources of funding threatens the sustainability of TAWJA's judicial training programs. TAWJA does not have a steady flow of funding. It only generates a little income from members' subscription fees, which is incapable of sustaining the training programs and operational costs. TAWJA's training programs are, consequently, heavily reliant upon external funding. This is a serious impediment considering that the interests of the donors are dynamic and their priorities may not necessarily be aligned to TAWJA's mission/priorities. Funding from the judiciary is minimal and not steady either. The immediate effect is a steady reduction of the number of trainings conducted. For example, as of the date of this publication, most of the judges who were appointed in 2019 and 2020 have not attended TAWJA's gender training programs, which implies that for more than a year, they have had no opportunity to be trained on how to handle gender issues in their adjudication. The situation would have been different if the induction program had been inclusive of training on gender-related aspects of judicial decision-making.

Attitudes toward gender inequality are yet another challenge. In some of the cases, the progressive jurisprudence discussed here is either overlooked or applied with hesitation. Matrimonial cases involving the distribution of matrimonial assets are a typical example. Although three decades have passed since the Court of Appeal formally recognized household work rendered by housewives during subsistence of marriage as a valuable contribution for purposes of assessment of the distribution of matrimonial assets following divorce, annulment, and separation, there are still cases where such contribution is overlooked or accorded lesser weight. For instance, in *Mohamed Rashid Mbita v. Salima Ally*,[34] the trial magistrate, having cited the principle in *Bi. Hawa Mohamed v. Ally Sefu*, unexpectedly changed course and held that family chores and farm work performed by the wife were incapable of entitling her to a share in the matrimonial assets.[35] There is also a tendency to award wives a lesser share of matrimonial assets. In most decisions emanating from subordinate courts, women are awarded a maximum of 40% of matrimonial assets, while 60% go to the male spouse.[36] This happens even in cases where the contribution made by the wife in the acquisition of the assets is higher compared with the contribution made by the husband. Although these percentages are often reversed on appeal, the proportion of women likely to be affected by this tendency is higher because the majority do not appeal due to such factors as ignorance of their rights and other social and economic barriers. More training is required to educate judges and magistrates on the need for objectivity in the exercise of discretion in the assessment and distribution of matrimonial assets.

Wrong attitude is also manifested through a lack of attentiveness in handling trials involving sexual offenses. Of serious concern is the laxity in admitting the evidence of a child prosecutrix and especially compliance with the requirement of Section 127 (2) of the Evidence Act, 1967 [Cap 6 R.E 2002]. The law requires that prior to admitting a child below the age of 14 as a witness, the court must require the child to promise that they will tell nothing but the truth. In the past, the law required the court to administer a *voire dire* test to determine whether the child is possessed sufficient intelligence and understands the duty of speaking the truth. Failure to comply with this requirement vitiates the testimony so adduced and renders it equal to unsworn evidence, which is incapable of earning a conviction. Although the law has been amended to simplify the procedure for the *voire dire* test by only requiring that the child be asked to promise to tell the truth, the level of laxity in this area is alarming. A number of trials are conducted in defiance of this rule. Since in most of these cases the testimony of the child prosecutrix tends to be the only tangible evidence linking the offender to the offense, the laxity invariably defeats the ends of justice for the victim by warranting acquittal of offenders.

To address these vices, it is recommended that judicial training programs implemented by the IJA Lushoto should go beyond equipping magistrates and judges with knowledge on substantive and procedural laws. Specific focus should also be directed at equipping judges and magistrates with knowledge and skills to analyze and interpret the law in the context in which justice is administered. To achieve this, it is important that aspects of specific focus on gender be integrated into the judicial training program, which is currently under preparation. Topics such as handling of SGBV cases, matrimonial cases, and probate and inheritance matters should compulsorily be taught in orientation programs for judges and magistrates to equip them with knowledge and skills to prepare them to effectively respond to gender issues in their adjudication. Instruction on topics with gender relevance, such as criminal trial and judgment writing (analysis of evidence), should also include a gender aspect to prepare the judges and magistrates to respond to gender inequality.

Compilation and distribution of reference materials is yet another avenue for improvement of judges' and magistrates' awareness of gender issues. The IJA, JoT, and TAWJA have a shared interest in the compilation and distribution of reference materials for raising awareness. TAWJA publishes a *Case Book* and a *Journal*, both of which are replete with progressive authorities on gender issues. It is also currently working on a gender bench book. The JoT in collaboration with IJA has recently issued two important publications tiled *A Bench Book for Judges Tanzania* (JoT, 2019a) and *A Quick Reference Guide for Magistrates in the District Courts and Courts of Resident Magistrates in Tanzania* (JoT, 2009e). They have also revised the *Handbook for Magistrates in the Primary Court* (JoT, 2019b). These materials are designed to assist users to acquire the necessary skills, knowledge, and proficiency for a better understanding of legal issues and nuanced interpretation of laws. These publications are replete with progressive authorities on gender issues, particularly in areas such as probate and administration of estates, land cases, and matrimonial proceedings. They provide users with guidance on how to deal with notorious issues such as conflict of laws in probate and administration of estates, annulment of marriages, presumption of the marriage, child custody and maintenance, and property rights of spouses in divorce, separation, and annulment of marriage. The authorities include landmark cases such as *Ndewawiosia d/o Ndeamtzo v. Imanuel s/o Malasi*,[37] in which the High Court in 1968 upheld the right of daughters to inherit from the estate of their fathers;[38] and the case of *Bi. Hawa Mohamed v. Ally Sefu* (*supra*) on the division of matrimonial property at dissolution of marriage, which has been exhaustively discussed. These resources should be used as a foundation for the development of joint research projects and publication on gender aspects of adjudication and wider distribution of the materials so published to adjudicators and all justice sector stakeholders. The publications should include, as far as practicable, all the relevant authorities in areas with a notorious record of gender-based injustice. Arrangements for regular updating and revision of the existing literature should also be put in place.

Efforts should also go into forging collaboration with law faculties to create awareness for potential judges and magistrates and generate knowledge through research. The rich research capacity of the law faculties has great potential for generation of knowledge on key gender issues in the society as well as the actual training needs for the JoT. On the other hand, the JoT can use its adjudication experience to impart knowledge to students by serving as moot courts judges and through other programs as guest speakers.

Conclusion

Judicial training on gender is a relatively recent phenomenon in the JoT. Until 2000, it was not part of judicial training and professional training for lawyers. Gender training was introduced in Tanzania by the TAWJA in 2000 (Yoon, 2016). Since then, TAWJA has spearheaded gender training for its members, other judicial officers, as well as prosecutors and other stakeholders on the gender aspects of the law. TAWJA's training programs mainly focus on introducing the participants to international and regional norms on gender equality and comparative jurisprudence from other jurisdictions. The sustainability of these programs is, however, questionable due to dependence on external funding and support. On the other hand, the JoT's training program implemented by IJA is yet to fully embrace gender in its core trainings, such as the mandatory induction program for judges. While some trainers include gender issues in their respective topics, this is not enough. It is recommended that the JoT should institutionalize gender training in the orientation and in-service training program for judges and magistrates. The experience gained through training programs jointly implemented by IJA and the Centre for Reproductive Rights, and informal collaboration and cordial working relationships between IJA, JoT, and TAWJA, should be used as a foundation for institutionalizing gender in JoT's judicial training program.

It is further recommended that concrete measures should be taken to allocate the necessary resources to TAWJA to sustain its training programs and enable it to reach more adjudicators, especially, those in the primary courts. Strengthening collaboration between TAWJA and IJA in training, preparation, and dissemination of reference materials and collaboration with law faculties is also recommended as a tool for enhancing gender awareness in the judiciary.

Notes

1 See Article 107A (1) of the Constitution of the United Republic of Tanzania, 1977.
2 See Article 1 and 2 of the Convention on Elimination of All Forms of Discrimination against Women, 1979. Also see Article 18 of the Protocol to the African Charter on Human and Peoples' Rights on the Rights of Women in Africa, 2003.
3 See Article 13 (2) of the Constitution of the United Republic of Tanzania, 1977.
4 Section 3 (2) of the two Land Acts 1999 provides that the right of every adult woman to acquire, hold, use, deal with, and transmit by or obtain land through the operation of a will shall be to the same extent and subject to the restrictions as the right of any adult man. Section 3 (3) says that for the avoidance of doubt, it is hereby declared to be the law that where during the course of any marriage, either spouse acquires an interest in land in their own name and for their own occupation and use, whether in practice the spouse shares that occupation or use or not and by whatever lawful means that acquisition occurs, that interest in land belong exclusively to the spouse who

acquired it and shall not under any circumstances be regarded as part of the property of the other spouse.

5 Section 60 (2) says where a village council establishes an elders council, that council shall consist of not fewer than five or more than seven persons, of which not fewer than two shall be women

6 By customary inheritance law, as codified in schedule 2 to the Local Customary Law (Declaration) (No. 4) Order, inheritance rules are patrilineal (rule 1). Rule 5, which pertains to the right to administer the deceased's estates, states that "the administrator of the deceased's property is the eldest brother of the deceased, or his father, and if there is no brother or father, it can be any other male relative chosen with the help of the clan council." Only if there are no male relatives can a sister become the administrator. Men are given the right to administer both property and funerals (rule 2). Msuya, N. (2019). Challenges surrounding the adjudication of women's rights in relation to customary law and practices in Tanzania. *Pioneer in peer-reviewed, open access online law publications (PER/PELJ)*, *22*. Retrieved from http://www.scielo.org.za/pdf/pelj/v22n1/14.pdf

7 Rule 27 deals with inheritance of widows. It states that "the widow has no share of the inheritance if the deceased left relatives of his clan; her share is to be cared for by her children, just as she cared for them." Furthermore, according to rule 51, the deceased's heir is to have the responsibility of taking care of the widow. Under rule 20, women are allowed to inherit, except clan land. They can use clan land without selling it during their lifetime. If there are no men in that clan, a woman can inherit the land completely. Under rule 31, female children may not inherit clan land

8 The breakthrough came from the bold decision by the JoT to assign law graduates to primary courts, which was a "taboo" before, because practising advocates were not allowed to appear in primary courts. This led to a considerable number of law graduates moving to primary courts. In a way, though advocates are still not allowed to appear in primary courts, the presence of graduates in these courts has to some extent improved the quality of the legal discourse in these courts.

9 Information obtained from JoT Department of Administration and Human Resources on May 23·2020.

10 Mzumbe was used as an in-house training for the judiciary, which produced primary court magistrates, court clerks, and other cadres in the lower judiciary and also provided opportunity for up-grading for those who were diligent and hard-working. Therefore, one could move from being a court clerk to primary court magistrate and later, district magistrate. From there, one now required a Bachelor of Laws to become a resident magistrate.

11 Institute of Judicial Administration Act [Cap 405. R.E. 2002].

12 For details, see report on continuing legal education activities by IJA as reported in *Institute for Judicial Administration Lushoto, Annual Activity Report 2016/2017*, p.22; *Institute for Judicial Administration Lushoto, Annual Activity Report 2017/2018*, pp.22–33; and *Institute for Judicial Administration Lushoto, Annual Activity Report 2018/2019*, pp. 1–29.

13 This is an annual international campaign against gender-based violence, starting on the International Day for the Elimination of Violence against Women on November 25 and running until December 10, which is Human Rights Day.

14 The event takes place in early February following the completion of the long judicial vacation.

15 *Rebeca Z. Gyumi v. The Attorney General*, High Court of Tanzania at Dar es Salaam, Miscellaneous Civil Case No. 5 of 2016 (Unreported).

16 *The Attorney General v. Rebeca Z. Gyumi*, Civil Appeal No. 204 of 2017, Court of Appeal of Tanzania at Dar es Salaam (Unreported).

17 In fact, following her success in this case, Rebeca Gyumi was recognized as one of the "100 most influential Africans" in 2019. See Rebeca Gyumi: Winning the battle against child marriages, *New African (London)*, 599, December, 2019/January, 2020, 32.

18 See the following authorities: *Selemani Makumba v. Republic* [2006] TLR 379; *Godi Kasenegala v. Republic*, Court of Appeal of Tanzania, Criminal Appeal No. 10 of 2008 (Unreported); *Alfeo Valentino v. Republic*, Court of Appeal of Tanzania, Criminal Appeal No. 494 of 2002; *Mohamed Haji Alli v. DPP*, Court of Appeal of Tanzania, Criminal Appeal No. 225 of 2018 (Unreported); *Juma Mohamed v. Republic*, Court of Appeal of Tanzania at Tanga, Criminal Appeal No. 4 of 2011 (Unreported); *Ramadhani Samo v Republic*, Court of Appeal of Tanzania, Criminal Appeal No. 17 of 2008 (Unreported).

19 *Godi Kisangela v R*, Court of Appeal of Tanzania, Criminal Appeal No. 10 of 2008 (Unreported).

20 *Ramadhani Samo v. Republic*, Court of Appeal of Tanzania, Criminal Appeal No. 17 of 2008 (Unreported).

21 *Abilahi Mshamu Mnali v. R*, Court of Appeal of Tanzania at Mtwara, Criminal Appeal No. 98 of 2010 (Unreported).

22 *Uttah Pradesh v. Chhoteyeal* (2011) I.S.C.R. 406 at 429.

23 *Hassan Bakari @ Mamajicho v. Republic* Criminal Appeal No. 103 of 2012, *Minani Evarist v. Republic* Criminal Appeal No. 124 of 2007, *Ndikumana Philipo v. Republic* Criminal Appeal No. 276 of 2009, *Minani Selestin v. Republic* Criminal Appeal No. 66 of 2013, *Matendele Nchanga @ Awilo v. Republic* Criminal Appeal No. 108 of 2010, *John Martin @ Marwa v.* Republic Criminal Appeal No. 22 of 2008, *Joseph Leko v. Republic* Criminal appeal No. 124 of 2013, *Jumanne Shaban Mrondo v. Republic* Criminal Appeal No. 282 of 2010, *Baha Oagari v. Republic* Criminal Appeal No. 39 of 2014, *Nkanga Daudi Nkanga v. Republic* Criminal Appeal NO.316 of 2013, *Athuman Hassan v. Republic* Criminal Appeal No. 84 of 2013 and *Simon Erro v. Republic Criminal* Appeal no. 85 of 2012 (all unreported).

24 *Mathayo Ngalya @ Shabani v. R.*, Criminal Appeal No. 170 of 2006, Court of Appeal of Tanzania.

25 *Hakizimana Syriverster v. R.*, Criminal Appeal No. 41 of 2004, Court of Appeal of Tanzania at Mwanza.

26 *Melkior Peter v. R.*, Criminal Appeal No. 9 of 2010, Court of Appeal of Tanzania at Arusha.

27 *Hassan Kamunyu v Republic*, Criminal Appeal No. 277 of 2016.

28 *Hawa Mohamed v. Ally Seif* [1983] TLR 32 (TZCA).

29 *Ndewawosia d/o Ndeamtzo v. Emmanuel s/o Malasi* (1968) HCD 127.

30 *Bernado Efraim v. Holaria Pastory and Gervas Kaizilege* (PC) Civil Appeal No. 70 of 1989, High Court of Tanzania.

31 *Laurence Mtefu v. Germana Mtefu* Civil Appeal number 214 of 2000 High Court of Tanzania, at Dar es Salaam (unreported).

32 *Anna Aloyce v. Zacharia Zebedayo Mgeta* PC. Matrimonial Appeal No. 1 of 2020, [2020] TZHC 851; (30th April, 2020).

33 *Naftal Joseph Kalalu v. Angela Mashirima* High Court of Tanzania at Dar es Salaam Civil Appeal number 145/2001 (Unreported).

34 *Mohamed Rashid Mbita v. Salima Ally*, Kilombero District Court in Civil Appeal No. 42 of 2018, original Matrimonial Cause No. 22 of 2016 Ifakara Primary Court.

35 This decision underlines our argument on the need for proper legal training for judicial officers. Departing from the path set by the Court of Appeal is an indication of lack of understanding of the principle of *stare decisis*.

36 This notwithstanding the decision of the Court of Appeal of Tanzania in *Richard William Sawe v. Woitara Richard Sawe*, Court of Appeal of Tanzania at Dar es Salaam, Civil Appeal No. 38 of 1992 (Unreported), which placed division of matrimonial property at dissolution of marriage at 50%–50%.

37 *Ndewawiosia d/o Ndeamtzo v. Imanuel s/o Malasi* (1967–1968) HCD No. 127.

38 Saidi, J. (as he then was) made the powerful statement that "It is quite clear that this traditional custom has outlived its usefulness. The age of discrimination based on sex

is long gone and the world is now in the stage of full equality of all human beings irrespective of their sex. Creed, race or colour. On grounds of natural justice daughters like sons in every part of Tanzania should be allowed to inherit the property of their deceased fathers whatever its kind or origin, on the basis of equality."

References

Armitage, l. (1995). Judicial Education on Equality. *The Modem Law Review Limited* 58(2), 160–186.

Banakar, R., & Travers, M. (Eds.) (2002). *An Introduction to Law and Social Theory*. Oxford: Oxford, Hart.

Bauer, G., & Dawun, J. (2016). *Gender and the Judiciary in Africa: From Obscuity to Parity?* New York: Routledge.

Bond, J. (2010). Gender, Discourse, and Customary Law in Africa. *Southern California Law Review*, *83*(3), 425–489.

Cameron, E. (1990). Judicial Accountability in South Africa. *South African Journal on Human Rights*, 6(2), 25.

Dawson, T.B. (2015). Judicial Education: Pedagogy for a Change. *Journal of Dispute Resolution*, *2015*(1), 175–190 Available at: https://scholarship.law.missouri.edu/jdr/vol2015/iss1/11 (accessed on July 7, 2020).

Hodgson, D.L. (2011). *Gender and Culture at the Limit of Rights*. Pennsylvania, PA: University of Pennsylvania Press.

IJA. (2017). *Annual Activity Report 2016/2017*. Tanga- Lushoto: IJA.

IJA. (2018). *Annual Activity Report 2017/2018*. Tanga- Lushoto: IJA.

IJA. (2019). *Annual Activity Report 2018/2019*. Tanga- Lushoto: IJA.

Jaffe, P.G., & Claire, V.C. (2018). Enhancing Judicial Skills in Domestic Violence Cases: The Development, Implementation, and Preliminary Evaluation of a Model US Programme. *Journal of Social Welfare and Family Law*, *40*(4), 496–514.

JoT. (2019a). *A Bench Book for Judges Tanzania*. Dar es Salaam: Judiciary of Tanzania.

JoT. (2019b). *A Handbook for Magistrates in the Primary Court: Revised and Updated Version*. Dar es Salaam: Judiciary of Tanzania.

JoT. (2019c). A *Quick Reference Guide for Magistrates in the District Courts and Courts of Resident Magistrates in Tanzania*. Dar es Salaam: JoT.

JoT. (2019d). *Training Policy, 2019*. Dar es Salaam: JoT.

JoT. (2019e). *Training Programme for 2018/2019 2020/2021*. Dar es Salaam: JoT.

Judicial Service of Ghana et al. (2008). *Report of the Partners for Gender Justice Conference: The Role of the Judiciary in Promoting Gender Justice in Africa*. Accra: Judicial Service of Ghana.

Kyando, L.A.A., & Peter, C.M. (1994). The People's Representation in the Courts of Law in Tanzania: The Need to Retain the Assessors. *Commonwealth Law Bulletin*, *20*(1), 317.

Legal and Human Rights Centre (LHRC) & Zanzibar Legal Services Centre (ZLSC). (2019). *Tanzania Human Rights Report 2018*. Dar es Salaam, Tanzania: LHRC & ZLSC.

Minamino, K. (2012). Gender Fairness and Continuing Legal Education. In K Minamino (Ed.) *Comparative Research on Continuing Legal Education*. Tokyo, Japan: Nihon Kajo Shuppan.

Ministry of Health, Community Development, Gender, Elderly and Children (MoHCDGEC) et al Tanzania Mainland, National Strategy for Gender Development,

[Tanzania Mainland], et al. (2016). Tanzania Demographic and Health Survey and Malaria Indicator Survey 2015-2016. Dar es Salaam, Tanzania: MoHCDGEC.

Ndulo, M. (2011). African Customary Law, Customs, and Women's Rights. Cornell Law Faculty Publications Paper 187. http://scholarship.law.cornell.edu/facpub/187

Nkoma-Wamunza, A. et al. (1998). *The Rights of Women and Girls in Tanzania. A Study of Knowledge, Attitudes and Practices with a Gender Perspective in Twelve Selected Districts*. Dar es Salaam: Dar es Salaam University Press (DUP).

Pedersen, R. H., & Haule, S. (2013). *Women, Donors and Land Administration: The Tanzania Case* (DIIS Working Paper No. 19). Copenhagen: Danish Institute for International Studies, DIIS.

Tanzania Women Judges Association (TAWJA) (2000). Dar es Salaam. TAWJA.

Tanzania Women Judges Association (TAWJA). (2015) *Journal of The Tanzania Women Judges Association (TAWJA)*. Dar es Salaam: TAWJA.

Tanzania Women Lawyers Association (TAWLA). (2014). *Review of Laws and Policies Related to Gender-Based Violence*. Dar es Salaam: TAWLA.

Tenga, N., & Peter, C.M. (1996). The Right to Organize as Mother of All Rights: The Experience of Women Organization in Tanzania. *Journal of Modern African Studies 34*(1), 143–163.

Thornton, M. (1986). Feminist Jurisprudence: Illusion or Reality? *Australian Journal of Law and Society 3*, 24.

UN Women (2019). *Justice and Gender in Gender and Security Toolkit*. Geneva: DCAF, OSCE/ODIHR, UN Women.

UNDP (2017). *Human Development Report 2016: Human Development for Everyone*. New York: UNDP.

United Nations Economic Commission for Africa (UNECA). (2017). *African Gender and Development Index Regional Synthesis Report: Measuring Gender Equality and Women's Empowerment in Africa*. Addis Ababa: UNECA.

Wallace, J.C. (2000). Judicial Education and Training in Asia and the Pacific. *Michigan Journal of International Law 21*(4/2), 849–874. Available at: https://repository.law.umich.edu/mjil/vol21/iss4/2

Wallacet, C. (2003). Globalization of Judicial Education. *The Yale Journal of International Law 28*, 355–364.

Wikler, N. (1989). Water on Stone: A Perspective on the Movement to Eliminate Gender Bias in the Courts. *Court Review, 13*(3), 9–26.

Yoon, Y.M. (2016). Tanzania: Women Judges as Agents of Judicial Education. In: G Gretvhen Bauer & Dawuni, J (Eds). *Gender and the Judiciary n Africa: From Obscurity to Parity*. New York: Routledge, 2016 at 99–107.

13 Gender awareness training in Judicial Training Institutes in Kenya and Uganda

Nightingale Rukuba-Ngaiza, PhD

Introduction

The assumption that judges know the law and do not need to be trained has hampered judicial training efforts for a long time (Schultz & Shaw, 2013). Even today, training is limited primarily to magistrates, because higher-ranking judicial officers claim to be adequately prepared for their positions. In common law countries, the assumption is that the judges' law school training, coupled with the practice of law for several years, is adequate, unlike in civil code countries, where an informal internal apprenticeship is offered to aspiring judges as semi-professional staff (Hammergren, 1998, p.6). However, changing recruitment patterns, including recruitment of academics and non-practicing lawyers, increasing workloads, and more complex laws and legal issues have questioned traditional assumptions about the best way to deliver qualified lawyers who are ready to assume responsibilities in the judiciaries (Hammergren, 1998, p.6).

The overarching rationale for investment in education for judicial officers (including magistrates and judges at all levels) at the beginning of their careers and on an ongoing basis is based on the need to have a cadre of competent, independent, ethical, and professional judicial officers. Judicial officers are expected to keep abreast of new developments in law, appreciate the social context of their decisions, and deliver reliable, predictable, and quality justice for all while improving the courts' performance. In some countries, judicial education has been shown to help "eliminate hidden bias from the judicial mind in fact-finding, particularly in relation to gender and ethnic issues" (World Bank, 2003, p.28). For instance, some judicial officers in India participated in a gender and judicial education project for a period of up to six years to improve their gender awareness in judicial decision-making. The results of the project showed that some judicial officers demonstrated sensitivity toward women while working on high-profile cases, and all the judicial officers expressed that they were more ready to proactively pursue their judicial responsibilities and deliver unpopular judgments (Schultz & Shaw, 2013, p.538).[1]

The limitations in some judicial officers' competence in Uganda and Kenya are often due to gaps in their undergraduate law school education (Kameri-Mbote et al., 2019, pp.475–77) and postgraduate legal practice training, both of which

DOI: 10.4324/9780429327865-17

are prerequisites for admission to the judiciary (Owor & Musoke, 2012, p.3).[2] While practical training in law firms is a requirement of the postgraduate diploma program, judicial clerkships are not prioritized in the training of postgraduate students. The limited exposure to gender training in the early parts of judicial officers' careers, coupled with their social and cultural biases, has at times limited their ability to deliver justice that is sensitive to gender issues (Aura, 2017, p.20; Owor & Musoke, 2012, p.3).

This chapter focuses on the judicial training institutes (JTIs) in the two East African countries of Kenya and Uganda. Both JTIs were established around the same time, and both countries were British colonies that gained independence around the same time (Maxon, 2009). The countries have common law systems, law schools with similar curricula, and initially shared one law school, the University of Dar es Salaam, in Tanzania (Tanganyika at the time). In addition, Kenyans and Ugandans have similar cultural beliefs and biases with regard to gender, which are rooted in tradition. Even today, some women and girls are disinherited, are victims of violence and sexual harassment, or are forced to enter into involuntary marriages (UN Women, 2020). To address these challenges, both countries have incorporated gender rights in their constitutions and integrated them into their national development programs. In this context, an analysis of the JTIs can provide insight into the progress the courts in these countries are making in terms of increasing gender awareness in the judicial system, including how JTIs address gender in their training and how the training contributes to the judicial officers' decisions in cases involving gender issues.

Gender as a social construct is entrenched in society, and feminist studies in the region have exposed the ways in which women and men have different lived realities in Kenya and Uganda (Kameri-Mbote, 2013, pp.18, 28). Gender-aware judging entails an understanding of what constitutes gender, gender biases, and stereotypes and the influence they may have on judicial decision-making. Judicial education offers a platform for reflection and education of judicial officers on different issues, including gender bias. The ultimate goal of gender-sensitive judicial education is for judicial officers to identify the inequalities between men and women in their society and use existing legal tools to address them.

The main objective of this chapter is to analyze the role of the Kenya Judicial Training Institute (KJTI) and the Uganda Judicial Training Institute (UJTI) in carrying out gender training in the past ten years. It assesses the potential impact of the training on judgments delivered by judicial officers who have been trained in gender matters, and it highlights constraints to the efficacy of training programs.

This chapter uses three different methods to analyze the potential impact of the JTIs' gender awareness training on judicial officers' decision-making. First, it examines the relevant literature and JTI papers, including training materials and cases. Second, it surveys JTI trainees using questionnaires. Finally, it conducts interviews with key stakeholders, including directors of the JTIs, judges, and trainers.

The survey asked nine questions that required short responses. The questions inquired whether judicial officers had received any training, the number of gender trainings they had received in the last ten years, and whether the training focused specifically on gender or if gender awareness was only one part of the course. The questionnaire also inquired whether the training had influenced the judicial officer's judgments on gender issues, and it requested the judicial officers to share those judgments, if any.

One hundred questionnaires were sent to all judicial officers (magistrates and judges) trained by the UJTI in the last 10 years, of which 48 were completed and returned. Out of these responses, 64.5% were from magistrates, who received most of the training, and 35.5% were from judges. The response rate was higher among female judicial officers (69%) than their male counterparts (31%).

Fifty questionnaires were sent out to judicial officers trained by the Kenya Women Judges Association (on behalf of the KJTI), judicial officers recommended by the chief registrar, and judicial officers recommended during the interview process (as having received training) by judges involved in providing or receiving gender training.[3] Twenty-five questionnaires were completed and returned by judges and magistrates. The response rate was higher among magistrates (76%) than judges (34%). The response rate for the female judicial officers was 52%, higher than 48% for the male judicial officers. The tenure of the respondents in both countries ranged from 5 to 27 years, with one judge in Kenya having served 37 years in the judiciary. The overall low response rate at the JTIs has been attributed to the current environment affected by the COVID-19 pandemic, in which judicial officers are juggling multiple responsibilities during an unprecedented time. In addition, both JTIs raised concerns about their weak record-keeping systems and limited access to the trainees' records.

Interviews were used as a third and final method to measure the impact of the JTIs. Among those interviewed were the directors of the JTIs, judges from the High Court and Court of Appeal, one Supreme Court judge from Uganda and one Supreme Court judge from Kenya, and officials who had trained judicial officers, including at the JTIs. Interviewees were chosen based on their response to the questionnaire or on the recommendation of the directors of the JTIs or the chief registrar. Interviews were conducted via the video conferencing platform Zoom and lasted between 30 and 45 minutes. Some questions posed during the interviews inquired about the interviewees' views on gender training at the JTIs; whether the training provided by the JTIs, or in collaboration with the JTIs, was adequate; the judgments they attribute to the gender training; and what recommendations they have for improving gender training programs. While the interviews were conducted using a set of questions, they also allowed for unstructured conversation.

There are limits in establishing a direct correlation between gender awareness training and judicial officers' decision-making process or gender-aware judging. The author acknowledges that the gender training offered by the JTIs may not be the only factor that influenced gender-aware judgments. Judicial officers who attributed such judgments to the benefits of the training and who shared judgments influenced by such training were the exception rather than the rule. However, the value of gender awareness training in countries like Kenya and Uganda, where negative gender cultural norms are still prevalent, is significant.

This chapter is divided into four parts. The first part provides a historical background on gender inequality in a number of customs and traditions in Uganda and Kenya, the history of legal training, and the evolution of the laws and cases related to gender in both countries. It also describes the motivation for integrating gender awareness into judicial training. The second part outlines the establishment and institutionalization of the JTIs, while the third part reviews the literature on gender training, examines the gender-related courses offered by the JTIs, and presents the results of interviews with trainers, trainees, administrators, and key informants, highlighting the opportunities and challenges of gender awareness training. Finally, the fourth part summarizes the overall findings of the study and concludes with some recommendations.

Historical background and gender inequality

Uganda and Kenya are former British colonies that gained independence in 1962 and 1963, respectively, and they both apply English common law as the foundation of their domestic laws (Maxon, 2009). Both countries still have some discriminatory laws, customs, and traditions related to marriage, succession, and other family matters. Some of these discriminatory customs and traditions are rooted in colonial laws, such as the 1882 Married Women's Property Act of England, which embraced the doctrine of coverture (Mutiso, 2019, p.124). The English common law doctrine of coverture is traceable to the Victorian era in England and provided that a wife had no legal standing or legal claim during the marriage. Her personhood and being were subsumed or incorporated within that of her husband, "under whose wing, protection, and cover, she performs everything" (Zaher, 2002, p.460).[4] Therefore, she could not own assets in her own right or seek legal recourse without her husband's authorization.

Some discriminatory traditions were upheld in early court decisions in both Kenya and Uganda. For instance, *R. v. Amkeyo* (1917) originated in Uganda and was appealed to the colonial East African Court of Appeal (which had binding authority on the judiciaries of Kenya, Uganda, and Tanzania). Justice Hamilton held that women married under customary law were not proper wives under the law; payment of bride price meant that they were themselves property and, therefore, incapable of owning property, as was the case in England (Ombura, 2017). His decision was based on misconceptions and misinterpretation of the payment of dowry as a contract for sale or "wife purchase" (Ombura, 2017).

Case law indicates that most judges in the colonial and immediate postcolonial period in Uganda and Kenya were white men who were ignorant of and averse to customary law. Under the Judicature Acts in both countries, African customary law could only be applied if it was not "repugnant to justice and morality" (Kenya Judicature Act 1967, Section 3 (2); Uganda Judicature Act 1967, Section 15) as defined by colonialists. The history of legal education in Kenya and Uganda indicates that the process of women joining the legal profession, and in particular the judicial service, has been incremental. As a result, even after the appointment of African judges, who might have interpreted the law to ensure gender justice, the discriminatory tradition did not change, because most of the judges were men trained in the patriarchal English tradition.

Judges in both countries have been tasked with implementing laws that are either gender blind, gender neutral, or gender discriminatory in areas such as marriage and inheritance (Kabeberi-Macharia, 1995). In practice, "African women's legal status, social standing, political participation, and national membership were [and still are] largely appended to that of their male relatives" (Tamale, 2004, pp.53–55), prohibiting them from full participation in society.

Legal education and gender

While legal education is supposed to prepare a cadre of lawyers who appreciate human rights, the British colonialists were reluctant to provide legal education to Africans during the colonial period, concerned that they would turn into political troublemakers like Gandhi and Nehru (Ghai, 1981, pp.173–74). Tanzanian President Nyerere's commitment to having trained African lawyers led to the rapid implementation of the recommendations of the *Report on legal education for students from Africa* (hereinafter the "Denning Report") (1961). The Denning Report sought to establish legal training in East Africa for the first time through an inter-territorial college based in Tanzania (Tanganyika at the time). This report recommended that the three East African governments of Kenya, Uganda, and Tanzania contribute to the recurring costs of the college. The University College in Dar es Salaam was established in 1961 as the first law school in East Africa, and its curriculum was adopted from the University of London due to the haste with which the law program was initiated (Fimbo, 2011; Mabirizi, 1986, p.67). This is where the foundational training for African judicial officers for Kenya and Uganda began, and at this early stage, gender was not yet part of the curriculum.

Uganda later established its own Department of Law at Makerere University in 1968, and Kenya established the University of Nairobi Law School in 1970 (Mabirizi, 1986, pp.68–69). The courses offered at both law schools had minimal gender content until the 1990s, when courses on gender and law were introduced (Kameri-Mbote et al., 2019, p.479). However, gender courses were and still are an elective offered in the final year of law school,[5] which means that not all prospective judicial officers take them. The diploma in legal practice that lawyers pursue after law school prepares them for the courtroom and incorporates some practical training, most of which is offered at law firms. However, judicial clerkships are rare in the postgraduate training of lawyers, which means that many judicial officers hired by the judiciary lack practical experience and have few or inadequate judicial skills.

Despite the level of training, judicial officers face the challenge of applying discriminatory laws. The recent study *Women, business and the law 2020*, conducted by the World Bank, analyzes the laws and regulations that affect women's economic opportunities in 190 countries[6] (including Uganda and Kenya) and scores the countries' performance based on selected indicators (World Bank, 2020, p.2). The study assesses formal laws against eight indicators: mobility, workplace, pay, marriage, parenthood, entrepreneurship, assets, and pension (World Bank, 2020, p. 2). The study allocates a positive score for progressive laws and a negative score for discriminatory laws or the lack of progressive laws. The study finds that the results are uneven, with high-income countries having the best scores and developing countries the lowest scores (World Bank, 2020, p.ii). This discrimination leaves "women in many countries with only a fraction of the rights of men" (World Bank, 2020, p.ii). According to the study, Kenya and Uganda score 80.6% and 73.1%, respectively (World Bank, 2020, p.7). Both countries score below North America and Europe and Central Asia, which have come close to providing equal rights to women and men, with overall scores of 96% and 90%, respectively, in 2019.

A review of the World Bank study indicates that the grounds for divorce for men and women are the same in Kenya. However, in Uganda, under Section 4 of the Uganda Divorce Act (1904), a husband can divorce his wife based on her adultery, but a wife can only divorce her husband based on his adultery coupled with either cruelty or desertion without reasonable excuse for two years or longer. For the distribution of marital property, the law in Kenya provides for the valuation of non-monetary contributions such as childcare and other home-making activities, while the law in Uganda does not.[7] Discriminatory laws do not only exist in the area of marriage but also extend to inheritance and choice of domicile. With regard to inheritance in Kenya, sons and daughters have equal rights to inherit assets from their parents (Kenya Law of Succession Act, 2010, Art. 35 (5)), while in Uganda, different standards apply based on the gender of the child (Uganda Succession Act, 1906, Section 2, 26 (1) and Section 38 (2)). In terms of the domicile or choice of where to live, the study found that men and women in Kenya have equal rights and can choose where to live. In Uganda, according to sections 14 and 15 of the Succession Act (Chap. 162), when a woman marries, she acquires the domicile of her husband. This can be disadvantageous to the woman, as a person's domicile determines a host of rights and obligations, such as tax determinations. Although Kenya scores higher than Uganda on progressive legislation related to women's rights, it does fall short in terms of laws regarding a married woman's registration of a business. Article 6 (1)(h) of the Kenya Business Names Act (1990) requires a married woman to include the name of her husband when registering a business.

In cases involving discriminatory laws, progressive judicial officers in both Kenya and Uganda can be constrained in delivering judgments that are gender neutral. While the JTIs were established to provide judicial officers with the relevant skills, including training on gender-aware judging, officers are still obligated to follow the law, including discriminatory laws, although laws can be challenged as unconstitutional.

Establishment and management of Judicial Training Institutes

KJTI

The KJTI in Kenya was established in 2008 through an administrative order (Kenya Judiciary, n.d.) issued by Chief Justice Evans Gicheru. The objective of the KJTI is to institutionalize continuous development training for judges and magistrates and prioritize research, learning, and innovation in the judiciary (Kenya National Assembly, 2019, Ch. 2.6). The Chief Justice also sought to ensure that the training of judicial officers occurred within the judiciary to maintain the courts' autonomy and independence (Kenya Judicial Education Workshop, 2008).

The KJTI was established and operates in an enabling legal environment for gender equality in Kenya. For example, the Sexual Offenses Act was enacted in 2006 and was later augmented by the 2010 Constitution of Kenya, which unequivocally called for gender equality. The 2010 Constitution also created the Kenya National Human Rights Commission (KNHRC) with the mandate to promote gender equality and facilitate gender mainstreaming in national development (Art. 59).

Under the 2010 Constitution of Kenya, the Judicial Service Commission (JSC) is mandated to prepare and implement continuing education and training programs for judges and other judicial officers (Art. 172.1(d)). While the Judicial Service Act of 2011 provides details on the internal workings of the JSC, it does not, however, provide details on the administration of judicial education or the share of the JSC's budget that should be allocated to the KJTI (Part III). In the past, the KJTI's budget was reflected in the judiciary's budget; it was not until 2014 that it was separated. Data on budget allocation to the KJTI from 2014 to date indicates that its budget has been consistently decreasing, with the exception of the last two years.[8] However, despite the slight budgetary increase in the past two years, the KJTI has indicated that its budget allocation is insufficient for it to effectively carry out its responsibilities. In addition, given the JSC's heavy workload, interviews indicate that the JSC has not been effective in implementing its mandate on judicial education or overseeing the performance of the KJTI.[9]

The KJTI's leadership structure includes an executive director, who is appointed by the Chief Justice and supported by three directors in charge of judicial education and curriculum development; research and policy; and finance, planning, and administration. However, the position of director of finance, planning, and administration was moved from the KJTI and placed under the JSC in 2019. The Board of the KJTI consists of the Chief Justice as chair, the executive director, and seven other members drawn mainly from the courts. The Board is the governing council, and its responsibilities include providing management with strategic policy direction, while the executive director is responsible for the day-to-day operations of the KJTI.[10]

For its training programs, the director and deputy director of judicial education and curriculum development of the KJTI shared in an interview that the KJTI relies on sitting judges and magistrates for peer training as well as experts in various fields, including academics, lawyers, international experts, and judges from other jurisdictions. The KJTI maintains a database with all the experts' biographies and calls on them to provide training on topics related to their field or expertise. These experts are compensated for the training they deliver. The KJTI also collaborates with other non-governmental organizations (NGOs) and international agencies, such as UN Women and the Kenya Women Judges Association, a local chapter of the International Women Judges Association, to provide specialized training as needed.[11]

The KJTI uses consolidated data from the evaluation of all training courses offered in the preceding financial year to determine training priorities and identify emerging priority areas. A draft training calendar is then prepared and presented to the presiding judges and registrars of all courts for input before it is discussed with potential donors. The final version of the training calendar is prepared based on available funding and input from internal stakeholders. It is then presented to the JSC for approval. There are, however, no consultations conducted with the public or Court Users Committees (CUCs) on perceived weaknesses in the judiciary that may need to be addressed. The CUCs are tasked with overseeing judicial service delivery (from the high courts to the lower courts), including identifying and addressing factors that impede the effective administration of justice (National Council, 2019, p.3). They are also tasked with improving "access to justice and service delivery by all actors in the justice system and in particular children, women, and persons with disabilities" (National Council, 2019, p.3). Their input would greatly enrich the training program.

UJTI

In Uganda, the UJTI, originally known as the Judicial Studies Institute, was initially established through administrative direction by Chief Justice Ben Odoki in 2004 (Uganda Judiciary Office Instruction, 2004; Kakuru, 2018). It was created to be semi-autonomous and was renamed the Judicial Training Institute in 2017 (Uganda Judiciary Office Instruction, No. 2 of 2017). The UJTI was recently re-established with the mandate to provide specialized and continuous education to the judiciary service (Administration of the Judiciary Act 2020, Section 19).

Like the KJTI, the UJTI was established and operates in an enabling legal environment that was created by the 1995 Constitution of the Republic of Uganda. The country's constitution provides for equality and freedom from discrimination, including gender-based discrimination (Art. 33), and the Gender Mainstreaming Policy 2018 requires public institutions to integrate gender equality into their programs. Uganda's laws and policies provide the UJTI with the mandate and necessary legal provisions to provide training on gender equality.

The UJTI consists of several bodies. The governing council comprises a chairperson, deputy chairperson, executive director, a judge of the High Court, and other government officials and legal professionals. It is responsible for approving the training curriculum and core faculty, approving policies and plans for the UJTI, and appointing committees and sub-committees. The executive director is appointed by the Chief Justice and oversees the implementation of the UJTI's plans, including assessing training needs and monitoring and evaluating programs (Kakuru, 2018, pp.1–2). Finally, the registry is headed by a registrar responsible for conducting training needs assessments, proposing training curricula, and coordinating and managing training programs.

The UJTI, like the KJTI, relies on sitting judges, academics, and experts from NGOs who provide training and receive remuneration for their services. It prepares a list of trainers and in some cases, seeks trainers with specialized expertise. Prior to the establishment of the UJTI, training was offered by various institutions in partnership with the judiciary.

Gender training: Opportunities and challenges

KJTI

The KJTI offers between 40 and 50 training courses each year, of which 1 or 2 may focus on gender. Gender awareness training is delivered as part of other priority areas like land law, access to justice, family law, or domestic violence, leaving little room for a comprehensive treatment of the subject. The majority of the trainees indicate that the training on gender offered by the KJTI is insufficient. The Kenya Judiciary Gender Audit of 2019 (hereinafter "Gender Audit") was carried out to analyze the judiciary's sensitivity and responsiveness to gender in its internal operations. The Gender Audit found that the KJTI provides neither training on gender equality nor training on applying equality standards in judicial services or the workplace. The Gender Audit further indicated that the lack of gender awareness training has led to gender-insensitive language being sometimes used in courts and even in decisions on constitutional principles of equality (National Gender and Equality Commission, 2019, p.2–5).

Interviews with judges confirmed the findings of the Gender Audit. For example, an Appellate Court judge agreed with the Gender Audit's findings and further cautioned that Kenya's judiciary is "conservative, patriarchal, and still has very deep-seated views about gender."[12] She stated that in her 18 years as a judge, she had learned that gender was a fundamental issue, with important implications for the realization of human rights. In her opinion, gender has not been prioritized by the judiciary, and all judges and magistrates should be trained on gender bias.

Interviews with other judges confirmed that there is minimal training at the KJTI[13] on gender justice and how to incorporate gender into judicial decision-making. They attributed their training on gender to the training offered by NGOs such as the Kenya Women Judges Association and the International Association of Women Judges (IAWJ) in their jointly implemented Justice for Equality Project, which linked gender-related aspects of judicial training to human rights. An Appellate Court judge and a judicial officer at the KJTI opined that gender issues in Kenya have been trivialized as "women's issues"[14] instead of "human rights issues."[15] To address deep-rooted gender biases in the judiciary, they argued that stand-alone gender awareness training is just as important as, if not more important than, gender training embedded in other training programs (e.g., programs focusing on land or succession). However, there has been no assessment of the training offered by the KJTI or other NGOs to judicial officers.

The most pressing challenge identified by the interviewees in terms of the training offered by the KJTI is that the quality of the training is dependent on the professional experience (including adult training) and time commitment of the program director. Many interviewees noted that judicial officers with experience in providing legal training perform better in running the KJTI. Since the director is required to perform court work, KJTI programs compete with the often lengthy case list demanding the director's attention. Other challenges include inadequate funding; hosting KJTI training in rented facilities for over eight years; and the lack of adequate and permanent staff.

Interviewees also pointed out that the KJTI's location in Nairobi also makes it inaccessible to judicial officers in other parts of the country who cannot travel on account of their workload. To address this challenge, they recommended investing in information and communication technologies to provide virtual training to judges and other judicial officers outside Nairobi. Interviewees pointed out that during the ongoing global pandemic, virtual courts in Kenya had been effective in taking testimony from witnesses and delivering judgments on time.[16]

UJTI

The UJTI offers several gender awareness training courses on its own or in collaboration with partners. Responses to questionnaires distributed to judicial officers[17] indicate that, on average, the UJTI offers between 10 and 20 courses each year, only 1 of which may focus on gender.[18] According to the respondents, each judicial officer took one to three courses, on average, only one of which may have addressed the issue of gender in judicial decision-making. There was no recent review of the training at the UJTI. The curriculum posted on the UJTI website indicates two key sources of gender training. One source is the *Gender bench book: Women's access to justice in Uganda, 2016*, which was prepared with financing from UN Women. The lead consultant for the preparation of the book was a High Court judge who collaborated with other judges, women's rights activists, lawyers, and academics (Addou, 2018; Uganda Judiciary, 2016, p.iv). The other source of gender training at the UJTI is *Gender, the law and practice in Uganda* (Gender Module). The purpose of the Gender Module is to train judicial officers to promote gender equality by learning about the discrimination and injustice caused by the application of gender-biased laws, gender-blind laws, and practices veiled as gender neutral (Batema et al., n.d., p.44).

The Gender Module, which contains substantive and procedural issues and judicial practices related to gender and judging, is delivered over three days (Batema et al., n.d., p.44). It highlights gender stereotypes and analyzes cases that have had an adverse impact on gender relations. The Gender Module also highlights national and regional legal instruments relevant to Uganda as well as progressive judicial decisions in the region that can be used to guide impartial decisions that promote gender equality (Batema et al., n.d., p.48). Although impressive on paper, discussions with judicial officers involved in the Gender Module[19] revealed that it was last delivered in 2013, and the *Gender bench book* has only been used for training during the last two years. This limited use does not provide adequate time to conduct a comprehensive assessment of their utility, given the time needed to conclude cases.

As confirmed by interviews, the UJTI prepares the curriculum and training priorities based only on discussions with judicial officers. Unlike the KJTI, the UJTI owns its training facilities and, therefore, does not pay exorbitant rental costs. However, the UJTI often rents conference rooms at hotels, given its own facilities' limited capacity and lack of proximity to courthouses, and judicial officers are sometimes deterred from traveling to training sessions due to heavy traffic. Like the KJTI, the UJTI has limited budgetary resources for training. It receives funding from the government of Uganda through the judiciary and the Justice Law and Order Sector Secretariat, which is an umbrella body for all justice-related institutions.[20] Although the share of the judiciary budget 2010/11 appears to have fallen from 0.8% (63.49 billion Uganda Shillings for the judiciary and 7,547.46 billion Uganda Shillings for the national budget) to 0.5% in 2019/20 (129,931 billion Uganda Shillings for the judiciary and 34,304.70 billion Uganda Shillings for the national budget), the national budget more than doubled in the same period, which means that the larger judiciary budget has not translated into additional training resources for the UJTI (Ministry of Finance and Economic Planning, 2010/11 and FY 2019/20 pages XXX11 and 126).

The JTIs in both Kenya and Uganda have relied on other organizations to supplement their limited budgetary resources to provide gender training. These organizations include international organizations, such as UN Women and the International Development Law Organization, and NGOs, such as the IAWJ, the International Federation of Women Lawyers, Equality Now, Women in Law and Development Africa, and the East Africa Judicial Education Committee. Since neither JTI has dedicated training staff or budgets for research and innovation related to training, the support they have received from these organizations has been vital, as it has enabled the JTIs to develop training material and provide training. With dwindling donor resources for judicial reforms and training, and limited budgets for judiciaries, the JTIs need to explore options for self-financing. Interviews with judicial officers at the UJTI[21] confirmed the need for web-based learning that can be anchored in the experiences of the virtual court sessions in Uganda during the COVID-19 pandemic.[22]

Impact of training and gender-aware jurisprudence

Although both JTIs offer gender awareness training, neither has evaluated the effects of the training. Gender-aware judging considers how gender biases and stereotypes can affect the decisions judges make. Without some way of evaluating the training itself or the impact of the training on judicial officers' judgments, it is difficult to determine whether the training has led to more gender-aware judging. Each JTI distributes a questionnaire that assesses the trainers and the quality of the specific training at the end of each training course. However, neither JTI conducts follow-up impact assessments of the training programs. Periodic evaluations of training programs are key to determining their utility and assessing whether additional investments are justified. The KJTI indicated that it is planning to link the evaluation of its performance to the overall monitoring and evaluation of Kenya's judiciary. The 2007 UJTI Judiciary Training Policy, which is still operational,[23] indicates that training programs should be assessed on their ability to affect learning outcomes as well as on their costs and financial benefits.

To assess the impact of the JTIs' gender awareness training, the author reviewed the questionnaires that were distributed to trained judicial officers and followed up with select officers who had shared judgments they attributed to the training, as well as trainers who had received training on gender and judging. Interviews were also conducted with key informants, including directors of the JTIs and several judicial officers who had received and provided training at both JTIs.

Despite the lack of a systematic assessment or evaluation of the training offered by the JTIs, the study finds that gender training influenced some of the judicial officers to render progressive decisions on gender-related cases. In some cases, the training nudged some judges to pursue further gender training, including at the postgraduate level abroad.[24] The research also reveals that some judicial officers interviewed in the study had received training from both the JTIs and international or local NGOs working in the justice sector. Some of the judicial officers who occasionally trained at the UJTI had taken comprehensive postgraduate studies[25] focusing on gender justice, and they had been instrumental in issuing favorable gender-aware decisions and providing gender training at the UJTI.

KJTI

In Kenya, the gender awareness training delivered by the KJTI and other organizations has influenced some judicial officers' decision-making. A Court of Appeal judge[26] discussed her decision while at the High Court and the impact gender awareness training had on her judgments. In *Rono v. Rono & Another* (2008), she made a discriminatory decision against a women's inheritance claim based on her cultural upbringing. She indicated in her judgment that the possibility of girls getting married and inheriting more property from their new families would give them an unfair advantage over their male family members. This discriminatory judgment was rendered before the KJTI was established and exhibits the dangers of a lack of gender awareness. In an interview with this judge, she deeply regretted the decision and emphasized that since that case, she had been trained on gender discrimination and had herself delivered training to new judicial officers to sensitize them on gender justice.

Paradoxically, the Court of Appeal bench, which overturned the High Court decision in *Rono v. Rono* and ruled in favor of the woman, consisted of only men. The lead judge had received gender awareness training under the IAWJ's Jurisprudence for Equality Project. The Court of Appeal ruled that there was no basis in law for discriminating against the children of a deceased person based on their sex or marital status. The judges relied on the materials highlighted in the gender awareness training they had received, such as articles from the Convention on the Elimination of All Forms of Discrimination Against Women (CEDAW), to assert the gender equality and non-discrimination principle. This case is particularly notable because a female judge at the High Court made a discriminatory decision against women's rights that was later overturned by male judges at the Court of Appeal, highlighting the potential deep impact of gender awareness training on judicial decisions.

Another case shared by this same female judge is *Re Estate of Ngetich* (2003), which involved inheritance claims in a marriage of two women under the Kalenjin tribe's customary law. Under this law, a childless woman who is advanced in age can "marry" a younger woman to have children to propagate her lineage. The relationship between the two women is not sexual. Depending on the situation, either woman may choose the father of the children. However, the children born during the relationship are the older woman's children, and she provides for them and their mother. The younger woman looks after the older woman in return. In this case, when the older woman died, the family tried to disinherit the younger woman or "wife." The judge ruled in favor of protecting the "wife" based on customary law, and she attributed this judgment to the gender awareness training she had received.

Another judge who was interviewed[27] attributed a decision he had made at the High Court on the legal recognition and protection of intersex children to the training he had received on gender equality and human rights. In the case of *Baby A (suing through her mother) v. Attorney General & Others* (2013), the judge ordered the government of Kenya to file a report in court within 90 days based on a statute regulating intersex persons as a sexual category with guidelines and regulations for corrective surgery for intersex persons. A task force was then formed, and intersex people were subsequently recognized as a category in Kenya's census in 2019 (Kenya Law Reform Commission, 2018; Yusuf, 2019). The judge explained that following that decision, he had also issued a public apology to an intersex person who had been involved in a criminal trial before him and whom he had ordered to be detained in a men's jail. This judge emphasized that the value of gender awareness training for judicial officers cannot be overemphasized, whether as a separate module or as part of broader human rights training sessions.

Throughout the interviews and questionnaires, judicial officers explained that regardless of the number or duration of gender-aware training courses, they have been critical to their judicial analysis and have influenced how they approached or would approach gender issues in their judgments. In some cases, judicial officers[28] explained that after the training, they began analyzing family and succession-related agreements entered into by women through a gender lens, cognizant of the economic and social limitations that can have an impact on women's bargaining position.[29] One judge[30] indicated that the training enabled him to approach the entire judicial process through a gender lens. For example, he accords priority to hearing to lactating mothers and applies different procedural strategies in cases involving gender-based violence, including protecting the identity of witnesses by hearing cases in camera or in the privacy of the judge's chambers without spectators and jurors.[31] One of the judicial officers shared that the sexual and gender-based violence training offered outside the KJTI had not only improved the quality of her judicial decisions but also prompted her to write a civic education book titled *The predators*, warning communities of gender-based sexual violence.[32]

Despite the positive impact of the few gender awareness training programs, there are judicial officers[33] who have been in the court system for over 20 years and have had no gender awareness training,[34] or they have only received 12 training sessions, of which only 1 focused on gender issues. These officers, who in some instances have handled gender-related cases, could not point to decisions they had rendered that had been influenced by gender awareness training.[35] Invariably, all those who had been trained but had not handled gender-related cases indicated that if an opportunity arose, they would apply the lessons learned from the training, including any other training that provided them with information on relevant local and international law (including international human rights law), to promote gender equality.[36] The progressive and robust provisions on gender equality in the constitutions of both Uganda and Kenya have not led to the elimination of gender biases in judicial decision-making (Constitution of Uganda, 1995, Art. 33; Constitution of Kenya, 2010, Art. 27). Some judicial officers in Uganda (Owor & Musoke, 2012) and Kenya (National Gender and Equality Commission, 2019) are still rendering biased judicial decisions due to their cultural and social background and limited gender awareness training.[37]

UJTI

The effects of the gender awareness training provided by the UJTI and other organizations in Uganda can be evaluated by analyzing the answers provided by judges and magistrates (the latter of which were the majority of the respondents/interviewees) in interviews and questionnaires. For example, in a 1994 sexual assault case, a respondent judge[38] who had not received gender awareness training acquitted the accused on the grounds that the victim could not clearly explain or verbalize the sexual act the accused had committed against her in public due to cultural sensitivities. After receiving training on gender justice and appreciating the cultural sensitivities and the applicable international conventions to which Uganda was a signatory, the same judge was later more sensitive to a girl's testimony on sexual assault. In his ruling in favor of the victim, the judge challenged some of the discriminatory rules that the court was following, such as the requirement that the court be cautious of acting on uncorroborated evidence of victims based on other precedents. He argued that the rule perpetuated the discriminatory view that women are liars, especially in matters involving sexual allegations. He ultimately decided that the rule discriminates against women, who are statistically the most frequent victims of sexual offenses, and is, therefore, inconsistent with Uganda's constitution and international obligations under various conventions.

Another judge attributed her gender-aware judging to her initial training at the UJTI and further postgraduate studies on gender. She shared some of her innovative judgments, including the High Court case of *Ebiju Justine Wilson & Angwedo Mary v. Echodu Surubaberi* (2015), in which she ruled in favor of a widow who had sold land left to her by her husband to their daughter. The land was under the control of the clan and subject to customary law. The clan challenged the sale on the grounds that the widow had no proprietary interest in the suit. The judge ruled that customs that bar widows who have inherited customary land from having proprietary rights are a violation of the constitutional provisions on equality and discrimination based on sex. She also cited CEDAW to affirm these same principles.

Some judges have received postgraduate specialized gender-based training outside the UJTI. One of these judges,[39] who is a trainer at the UJTI, laments the limitations of his undergraduate legal training and the negative impact that his inadequate training had on the judgments he wrote as a chief magistrate. He attributes his progressive judgments on gender, the training he offers at the UJTI, and his role in the preparation of the *Gender bench book* to his postgraduate gender awareness training at a college in South Africa. One of his progressive decisions is *Uganda v. Lomoe Nokopuet* (2016). The case centered on a rape cloaked under the Karamajong cultural practice, where a father, along with his sons, dragged his daughter to a man who had paid them dowry, and they held her to the floor while the man raped her. The judge convicted the accused of rape and sentenced him to 15 years' imprisonment. The judge vehemently condemned the harmful practices of Karamajong's "culture of forcefully chasing, abducting, and raping girls and women to make them wives [as] … a brutal and backward culture promoting violence against women" (*Uganda v. Lomoe Nokopuet*, 2016, p.4). He further stated: "Nobody and no one's daughter, sister[,] or mother deserves being raped in the name of marriage. This vice of cultural rape is a resilient, pervasive, and persistent culture promoting gender stereotypes" (*Uganda v. Lomoe Nokopuet*, 2016, p.4).

Drawing from his training, the judge highlighted that Article 5(a) of CEDAW, to which Uganda is a party, requires governments to modify customs and eliminate stereotypes that promote discrimination against women (*Uganda v. Lomoe Nokopuet*, 2016, pp.4–5). Article 5 also calls on courts of law to fight cultural rape, as it is rooted in harmful, discriminatory views of women (p.5). He also called attention to the fact that under Article 6 of the Maputo Protocol on the Rights of Women in Africa and Article 16 of CEDAW, women and men enjoy equal rights as equal partners in marriage, and women have the same right to freely choose a spouse and enter into marriage with their free and full consent (p.6).

The judge also brought attention to the domestic legal framework that protects the rights of women. He called attention to Article 32 (2) of the constitution, which expressly prohibits laws, cultures, and traditions that are against the dignity, welfare, or interest of women or which undermine their status. He highlighted that cultural rape was a form of torture, cruelty, and inhuman and degrading treatment, as outlawed by the Republic of Uganda's constitution. He even went so far as to call for judicial activism in terms of Article 274 of the constitution to fight backward customs and traditions found in existing customary law (*Uganda v. Lomoe Nokopuet*, 2016, p.5).

Another respondent, a Supreme Court judge,[40] expert on gender awareness training, and occasional trainer at the UJTI, attributes her progressive judicial decisions on gender-related cases to her postgraduate studies outside Uganda and her work with female prisoners in jail for homicides linked to domestic and sexual violence they had experienced. After her training and experience working with women in the criminal justice system, the judge made several progressive rulings, including *Ntambala Fred v. Uganda* (2015). Like the previous judges, she also questioned the legal validity of an old standing rule that requires courts to be cautious of acting on the uncorroborated evidence of a sexual assault victim, and she noted that victims of sexual assault are mainly women (*Ntambala Fred v. Uganda*, 2015, p.2). In her ruling, she explained that the rule violated Uganda's constitutional clause on equality before the law and that the evidence of a victim in a sexual offense must be treated and evaluated in the same manner as the evidence of a victim of any other offense (p.4).

A number of magistrates[41] who benefited from gender awareness training at the UJTI also explained how the training influenced their decisions, and some shared their non-binding judgments. These judgments demonstrated their sensitivity to gender issues in the criminal justice system, such as granting bail to an accused who was heavily pregnant and another who had her four young children with her in court. Neither woman had sureties, but they were released on the court's cognizance of their unique conditions as women and mothers.[42] In another case, the magistrate stated: "Where a widow was chased from her matrimonial home on the grounds that women do not own property, I ordered the return of her cows, goats, and gardens. I also issued orders for compensation for the destroyed crops and issued a permanent injunction."[43] Moreover, another magistrate explained that her sentencing criterion was influenced by the gender training she had received, which resulted in reduced sentencing and the application of international instruments to make up for gaps in national law. In other cases, magistrates[44] were sensitive to the way they interrogated victims of gender-based violence. Magistrates are closer to the people they serve than judges because they hear their cases first, unlike judges, who may review the appeal based only on the record. Magistrates handle many cases in the communities they work in and administer justice on matters such as customary divorce and land under customary tenure, especially during divorce. The value of gender awareness training to this cadre of judicial officers cannot be overemphasized.

Several of these case studies show that gender awareness training offered by either the UJTI or other organizations and postgraduate programs influenced the judges' and magistrates' decision-making process. The effects of the training appear clearest with magistrates, who work closely with plaintiffs and victims.

Overall findings and recommendations

The study found that the UJTI has invested more time than the KJTI in creating pedagogical material on gender-aware judging. In addition, more judicial officers trained in Uganda than in Kenya provided examples of judgments rendered as a result of gender awareness training. The KJTI's interim use of the Women Judges Association to conduct gender training has been useful, but the KJTI has long-term plans to recruit a gender expert and embed gender awareness training in its programs, and it is in the process of developing gender-related training material.

Despite the various challenges facing the KJTI and UJTI, judicial officers in each country appreciated the training offered by the JTIs. The key recommendations made by judicial officers in both JTIs are: (a) make gender training compulsory and offer it at the induction phase and throughout the judicial officers' careers; (b) provide sabbatical or time off to enable judicial officers to obtain training without it competing with their regular workload; (c) select directors for the JTIs who have prior experience in training and adult learning and reduce their judicial duties if they are sitting judges to enable them to focus on the JTIs; (d) provide adequate financial resources and dedicated pedagogical experts; (e) invest in information and communication technologies and virtual training to reach judges outside the capital cities through online courses; (f) link the evaluation of the performance of the JTIs and the training to the overall monitoring and evaluation strategy of the judiciaries; (g) link continuous training to the performance of the judicial officers; (h) attain accreditation for the JTIs so that certificates attained from the JTIs can be linked to promotions; and (i) establish oversight mechanisms for the JTI training programs.

Finally, all the respondents agreed that each judiciary should have a JTI led by a judge, as opposed to substituting the JTIs with a single regional training institute, training institutes run by NGOs, or institutes that have a public–private partnership arrangement. To develop a robust gender training program, the respondents recommended that a number of stakeholders should be consulted, including the judiciary, the bar, court users, the business sector, and the wider public, to ensure that judicial education programs are effective and responsive to community perceptions of judicial weaknesses.

Conclusion

This chapter highlighted the importance of judicial training in orienting newly appointed judges, facilitating their transition to the bench, and informing them of emerging legal issues. More fundamentally, it has underscored the importance of continuous judicial education in building the capacity and professional competence of judges to deal with gender issues and expand opportunities for women's access to justice. The chapter finds that both the Kenyan and Ugandan JTIs have carried out minimal training on gender despite the requirement for gender equality in the countries' constitutions and international obligations. While the overall training offered by the JTIs (including that which addresses gender bias) has not been fully evaluated to determine its impact, this chapter analyzed the available resources and evidence, which linked progressive decisions on gender-related legal issues to the training offered both within and outside the JTIs. It demonstrated that gender awareness training, whether as postgraduate training or continuous judicial training, can play an important role in changing cultural and social biases that judicial officers may have about gender. Some of the cases and approaches cited in this chapter from both countries have challenged dominant discriminatory views about gender and made justice more accessible to women.

Notes

1 The judicial training program included intense gender-based training that required attitudinal and behavioral change, which enabled participants to sustain their involvement for four to six years, and involved international collaboration (Schultz & Shaw, 2013, p.538). This level of involvement may be limited in regular gender-based training proposed at the JTIs, and trainers will have to seek avenues to ensure that short-term targeted gender training attains the same results in the long run.

2 The authors in this case were looking at the postgraduate legal training in Uganda; however, the same conclusions apply to the Kenya School of Law, which offers a postgraduate legal training program. The course content on its website (https://www.ksl.ac.ke/advocates-training-program/) indicates that the program mainly focuses on litigation and legal practice in preparation for a law firm experience.

3 The KJTI recommended approaching the KWJA, which conducted most of the gender training, and key judicial officers who were interviewed recommended judicial officers who had been either trainees or trainers on gender rights.

4 According to the Seneca Declarations, a married woman was considered "civilly dead" under the legal doctrine of coverture (Hoff, 1994; Zaher, 2002).

5 In interviews with Prof. Patricia Mbote, in connection with the Kenya law schools, and Dr. Sylvia Tamale, in connection with Makerere University Law School Uganda.

6 The data in the study are current as of September 1, 2019 (World Bank, 2020, p.15).

7 The study found that no applicable provisions could be located in the laws; however, the courts in Uganda have been progressive and issued decisions that consider a spouse's non-monetary contributions.

8 The KJTI budget in Kenya Shillings was as follows: 234,253,463 Kenya Shillings (KSh) in FY2013/14; KSh 193,407,234 in FY2014/15; KSh 214,431,079 in FY2015/16; KSh 203,551,999 in FY2016/17; KSh 157,941,765 in FY2018/19; KSh 159,678,488 in FY2019/2020; and KSh 172,799,993 in FY2020/21. With the exception of budgetary allocations for 2018/19 and 2019/2020, the budgetary allocations fell in the previous years.

9 Interview with respondents KJTI Nos 2, 8, and 9 (transcript on file with the author). Other functions of the JSC include recommending individuals to the President for appointment as judges; reviewing and recommending the conditions of service of judges and judicial officers (other than their remuneration) as well as the staff of the judiciary; appointing, receiving complaints against, investigating, and removing from office or otherwise disciplining registrars, magistrates, other judicial officers, and other staff of the judiciary; and advising the national government on improving the efficiency of the administration of justice.

10 In an interview with the director of the KJTI.
11 In an interview with the director and deputy director of judicial education and curriculum development at the KJTI.
12 Respondent KJTI No. 6 (transcript on file with the author).
13 Respondent KJTI Nos 1, 2, 5, and 6 (transcripts on file with the author). This is also consistent with the Gender Audit (2019), which confirmed that there was hardly any training on gender at the KJTI.
14 Respondents KJTI No. 1 and 13 (transcripts on file with the author).
15 Respondents KJTI No. 1 and 3 (transcripts on file with the author).
16 Respondents KJTI Nos. 4 and 5 and interviews with Chief Registrar Anne Amadi and Professor Mbote.
17 Respondents UJTI Nos. 1 and 2 (transcripts on file with the author).
18 Courses include mediation, judgment writing, small claims, gender, induction, jurisprudence of equality, plea bargaining, sentence guidelines, recent reforms and practice directions, judicial enforcement of reproductive rights, and training of trainers on the management of gender-based violence.
19 Respondents UJTI 1 and 2 (transcripts on file with the author).
20 The justice law and order sector is a justice sector–wide approach adopted by the government of Uganda, comprising 18 justice-sector institutions, with the objective of promoting access to and administration of justice through a sector-wide approach to planning, budgeting, program implementation, monitoring, and evaluation (Justice Law & Order Sector, n.d.).
21 Respondents Nos. UJTI 1 and 2 (transcripts on file with the author).
22 Respondents UJTI Director (transcript on file with the author).
23 Uganda Judiciary Training Policy, 2007, para. 28.
24 Respondent UJTIs Nos. 47 and 48 both judicial officers (transcripts on file with the author).
25 Respondents UJTIs Nos. 46, 47 and 48 Uganda (transcripts on file with the author).
26 Respondent KJTI No. 5 interviewed as a trainer and trainee and also a key informant (transcript on file with the author).
27 Respondent KJTI No. 2 (transcript on file with the author).
28 Respondents UJTI Nos. 7, 8, and 9 (transcripts on file with the author).
29 Respondents UJTI Nos. 1, 2, 3, 4, 20, 21, and 46. See also KJTI Respondents Nos. 6 and 7 (transcripts on file with the author).
30 Respondent UJTI No. 6 (transcript on file with the author).
31 Respondent UJTI No. 7 (transcript on file with the author).
32 Respondent KJTI No. 12 (questionnaire on file with the author).
33 Respondents UJTI Nos 10, 11, 12, and 13 (transcripts on file with the author).
34 . In the Kenya judiciary, some of the proposed respondents indicated that despite being in the judiciary for over ten years, they had not received any gender training and were removed from the list of interviewees.
35 Respondent UJTI Nos. 5 and 6. See also Respondents Nos. KJTI 6, 7, 8, 9, and 10 (transcripts on file with the author).
36 Respondent UJTI No. 11 (details on file with author).
37 The Kenya judiciary Gender Audit 2019 was commissioned by the National Gender and Equality Commission in collaboration with the International Association of Women Judges–Kenya Chapter with support from the International Development Law Organization (National Gender and Equality Commission, 2019, p.2). As indicated in its executive summary, it sought to analyze the gender sensitivity and responsiveness of the judiciary as a whole in its internal operations and delivery on its external mandate and included a review of how the judiciary manages its workforce and how it delivers to its constituents (National Gender and Equality Commission, 2019, p.5).

38 Account of retired judge's experience and his sharing of these facts with other judicial officers provided by Respondent UJTI No. 47 and corroborated by Respondent UJTI No. 48 (transcript on file with the author).
39 Respondent UJTI No. 48 (transcript on file with the author).
40 Respondent UJTI No. 47 (transcript on file with the author).
41 Respondent UJTI No. 34 (transcripts on file with the author).
42 Respondent UJTI No. 36 (transcript on file with the author).
43 Respondent UJTI No. 18 (transcript on file with the author).
44 Respondents UJTI Nos. 23 and 27 (transcripts on file with the author).

Constitutions, legislation and administrative instruction

Constitution of Kenya. (2010).
Kenya Judicature Act. (1967), Chapter 8.
Kenya Judicial Service Act. (2011). No. 1.
Kenya Law of Succession Act. (2010). Ch. 160.
Kenya Registration of Business Names Act. (1990). Ch. 499.
Uganda Constitution. (1995).
Uganda Divorce Act (1904)
Uganda Judiciary Chief Justice Office Instructions No. 2 of 2017

Case law

Baby A (suing through the mother EA & another) v. Attorney General & 6 Others, Petition No. 206 (2013) and (2014) eKLR
Ebiju Justine Wilson & Angwedo Mary v. Echodu Surubaberi, Civil Appeal No. 43 [2015] UGSC 12
Ntambala Fred v. Uganda, (Criminal Appeal-2015); (2018) UGCA 83
Re Estate of Ngetich (2003 KLR 84)
Rono v. Rono & Another, (Civil Appeal 66 of 2002) (2008) KLR
R. v. Amkeyo (1917), 7 EALR 14 [11]
Uganda v. Lomoe Nokopuet (Criminal Case-2016/109); UGHCCRD 14 (25 January 2019)

References

Addou, H. (2018). International Organizations and Gender-Responsive Legal and Judicial Reforms. In: Conference on Gender and the Judiciary in Sub-Saharan Africa, June 11–13 [panelist], Arusha, Tanzania.

Aura, R. (2017). Situational Analysis and the Legal Framework on Sexual and Gender-Based Violence in Kenya: Challenges and Opportunities. *Kenya Law*, 1–33. http://kenyalaw.org/kl/index.php?id=4512

Batema, N.D.A., Onyango, J.O., Wangutusi, D., & Mulyagonja, I. (n.d.). Gender, the Law and Practice in Uganda.

Fimbo, G.M. (2011). *Fifty Years of Legal Education in Tanzania: Development of the LL.B. Curriculum*. Martisayi Investments Company Limited.

Ghai, Y. (1981). Law and Lawyers in Kenya and Tanzania: Some Political Economy Considerations. In: C.J. Dias, R. Luckham, & D.O. Lynch, & Paul, J.C.N. (eEds.),

Lawyers in the Third World: Comparative and Developmental Perspectives (pp. 144–176). Scandinavian Institute of African Studies.

Hammergren, L. (1998, August). *Judicial Training and Justice Reform*. United States Agency for International Development. https://biblioteca.cejamericas.org/bitstream/handle/2015/5203/hammergren-jud-training.pdf?sequence=1&isAllowed=y

Hoff, J. (1994). *Law, Gender, and Injustice: A Legal History of U.S. Women*. New York University Press.

Justice Law & Order Sector (n.d.). *Our History*. https://www.jlos.go.ug/index.php/about-jlos/our-history

Kabeberi-Macharia, J.W. (1995). *Women, Laws, Customs, and Practices in East Africa: Laying the Foundation*. Women & Law in East Africa.

Kakuru (2018). Kenneth Justice: The Role of the Judicial Training Institute in Contributing to Better Performance of the Judiciary. In: Paper presented at the 20th Annual Judges Conference, 24th January 2018.

Kameri-Mbote, P. (2013). *Fallacies of Equality and Inequality: Multiple Exclusions in Law and Legal Discourses*. Inaugural Lecture, University of Nairobi.

Kameri-Mbote, P., Hellum, A., Stewart, J., Kanyongolo, N., & Munalula, M. (2019). Engendering and Decolonising Legal Education: South–South and South–North Co-Operation. In: T. Halvorsen, K. Skare Orgere, & R. Krøvel (Eds.), *Sharing Knowledge, Transforming Societies the Norhed Programme 2013–2020* (pp. 474–499). African Minds.

Kenya Judicial Education Workshop (2008). July 16–20, Mombasa Serena Hotel, Nairobi, Kenya.

Kenya Judiciary (n.d.). *About Us*. https://www.judiciary.go.ke/about-us/our-history

Kenya Law Reform Commission (2018, April 18). Taskforce on Policy, Legal, Institutional and Administrative Reforms Regarding Intersex Persons in Kenya. https://www.klrc.go.ke/index.php/klrc-blog/613-taskforce-on-policy-legal-institutional-and-administrative-reforms-regarding-intersex-persons-in-kenya-blog

Kenya National Assembly (2019, May). Twelfth Parliament, Third Session. *Report on the Consideration of the 2017/2018 Report of the State of the Judiciary and the Administration of Justice*.

Mabirizi, D. (1986). Some Aspects of Makerere's Legal Education in Development. *Third World Legal Studies*, 5, 63–78.

Maxon, R. (2009). *East Africa: An Introductory History*. 3rd ed. West Virginia University Press.

Ministry of Finance and Economic Development. (FY 2010/11). Approved Estimates of Revenue and Expenditure, National Budget Framework Papers FY 2010/11 and National Budget Framework Paper FY 2019/20/.

Mutiso, B. (2019). Getting to Equal: Resolving the Judicial Impasse on the Weight of Non-Monetary Contribution in Kenya's Marital Asset Division. *Michigan Journal of Gender & Law*, 26(1), 121–173. doi:10.36641/mjgl.26.1.getting

National Council on the Administration of Justice (2019). *Court Users' Committee Guidelines*. https://www.unodc.org/documents/easternafrica//Criminal%20Justice/CUC_GUIDLINES_2019_final.pdf

National Gender and Equality Commission. Kenya Judiciary, & International Development Law Organization (2019, December 21). *The Judiciary Gender Audit Dec 21 2019*. https://www.judiciary.go.ke/download/judiciary-gender-audit-dec-21-2019/

Ombura, f. (2017). Registration of Customary Marriages: 100 Years after R vs Amkeyo. *The Deuteronomy, East Africa Weekly Law Newsletter*, 6(4). https://thedeuteronomy.bi

talaadvocates.com/2017/06/23/registration-customary-marriages-100-years-r-vs-amkeyo/

Owuor, M., & Musoke, D.H. (2012, June 12). The Neglect of Gender Questions in Judicial Education in Uganda. Paper presented at 2012 Law and Society International Conference, Honolulu, Hawaii.

Schultz, U., & Shaw, G. (2013). *Gender and Judging*. Oxford, Portland, and Oregon: Hart Publishing.

UN Women (2020, November). *Facts and Figures: Ending Violence against Women*. https://www.unwomen.org/en/what-we-do/ending-violence-against-women/facts-and-figures

World Bank (2003, January). *Legal and Judicial Reforms: Strategic Directions*. http://documents1.worldbank.org/curated/en/218071468779992785/pdf/269160Legal0101e0also0250780SCODE09.pdf

World Bank (2020). *Women. Business and the Law 2020*. https://openknowledge.worldbank.org/bitstream/handle/10986/32639/9781464815324.pdf?sequence=10&isAllowed=y

Yusuf, M. (2019, August 27). Intersex People Recognized in Kenya Census. *VOA*. https://www.voanews.com/episode/intersex-people-recognized-kenya-census-4006646#:~:text=Kenya%20has%20become%20the%20first,and%20female%20on%20census%20forms

Zaher, C. (2002). When a Woman's Marital Status Determined Her Legal Status: A Research Guide on the Common Law Doctrine of Coverture. *Northern Kentucky University Law Library Journal*, 94(3), 459–486.

Part V

COVID-19 pandemic and gender-related judicial issues

14 The COVID-19 pandemic, courts, and the justice system

Muna Ndulo, DPhil

Introduction

The COVID-19 pandemic has had a deep impact on communities across the world. The virus has now spread to over 177 countries, and it has affected all aspects of daily life, including the economy, education, healthcare, food security, gender inequality, and the administration of justice. The justice system, which is the focus of this chapter, has faced tremendous challenges. The pandemic has forced courts to limit or end jury trials; restrict access to courtrooms; suspend in-person proceedings; grant extensions for court deadlines (including deadlines to pay fees and fines); and encourage or require audio and video conferences in lieu of in-person hearings. It has also resulted in an increased number of persons held in pre-trial detention all over the world. These challenges raise several questions. First, what are the main challenges to accessing the justice system—especially among women and other vulnerable groups? Second, what measures are courts taking to deal with the current challenges, and what is the potential impact of these measures on the delivery of justice and the protection of human rights? Policymakers need to find meaningful answers to these questions to ensure that policy interventions can guarantee the rule of law and access to justice.

Respect for the rule of law and the protection of individual rights are necessary conditions for sustainable economic and social development. Since an effective and efficient justice system is critical to the promotion of rule of law and good governance, the maintenance of such a system is central to inclusive economic growth.[1] This is especially important for developing economies that have limited capacity to absorb systemic shocks. The adoption and strengthening of human rights, the deepening of democracy, and the increased public participation in governance all require an effective judicial system. Indeed, the courts play an important role in strengthening democratic institutions responsible for adopting justice-related policies and adequately protecting and promoting human rights. An effective judicial system has been described as "one that is predictable, resolves cases in a reasonable time frame, and is accessible to the public" (Dakolias, 1999, p.87).

Justice systems worldwide provide essential constitutionally mandated services to the public.[2] They provide countries with mechanisms for people and

DOI: 10.4324/9780429327865-19

corporations to settle both criminal and civil disputes. They also serve as an instrument for the protection of vulnerable groups in society (Banda, 2019, p.4). An effective, efficient, and well-resourced system of justice should guarantee a fair hearing and manifest equality before the courts. While courts should be impartial and treat everyone equally when settling disputes, there are sometimes vast differences in the experience of members of the public when they engage with the courts. For example, racial and socio-economic inequalities in many parts of the world are abetted and sometimes exacerbated by the inability of the justice system to adequately respond to the needs of minorities and economically disadvantaged groups. Overly difficult procedures can sometimes make judicial institutions inefficient and limit access to judicial services. Even in ordinary times, judicial systems are not perfect. For example, many courts face delays in the resolution of disputes, and some courts struggle with large caseloads as well as inadequate courtrooms and personnel. Delays in criminal trials leave many people in jail awaiting trial for long periods of time, which often leads to overcrowded jails.

The pandemic has exacerbated these challenges as courts prioritize the safety of judges, lawyers, parties, court staff, and members of the public. Court officials are faced with the challenge of balancing the need to minimize health risks with the need to keep the judicial system operational. To prevent and control the potential spread of COVID-19 via the courts, countries have instituted several measures. While the adoption of strict measures is important to curb the spread of the disease, it can also negatively affect the delivery of vital public services. As Texas Chief Justice Nathan Hecht observed with respect to the United States, "Since the onset of the pandemic, courts throughout the country have determined to stay open to deliver justice without faltering, no matter the adjustments and sacrifices demanded, but also to protect staff … and the public from the risks of disease. We are learning new technology and practices together" (NCSC, n.d.).[3] At the beginning of the pandemic, courts in most jurisdictions suspended their operations, as many officials thought that the pandemic would be controlled in a few months. Court proceedings were restricted to only urgent cases. For example, many criminal courts only heard pleas for serious cases and bail applications. Even then, they had to comply with state policies on public health. Courts also restricted entry to court buildings to litigants and witnesses only. As time passed and uncertainty around the duration of the pandemic grew, courts began to rearrange the physical layout of their courtrooms to adhere to social distancing and other health measures. Additionally, many resorted to holding proceedings online, which necessitated not only the restructuring of the courts' physical infrastructure but also the upgrading of their information and communication technologies (ICT) infrastructure. As a result of the pandemic, video conferencing and electronic filing have become the default means of conducting court proceedings worldwide. However, this has also lifted the veil on existing problems created by the digital divide and the limited skills and broadband infrastructure in many courts in developing countries. This is exacerbated by the fact that courts in many countries were behind the curve in technology adoption even before the COVID-19 pandemic. Dame Hazel Genn, Professor at University College London, observes with respect to the United Kingdom:

> The COVID-19 pandemic has necessitated a significant increase in the role of technology in the justice system in England and Wales. The ongoing reform program "Transforming our Justice System," which began in 2016, aimed to radically enhance the role of technology. However, when COVID-19 pandemic struck in 2020 the court system was still, in terms of the use of technology, virtually below the sea level.
>
> (Justice Committee, 2020)

One of the most unfortunate results of the COVID-19 pandemic is that it has increased longstanding structural inequalities in society. It is also undermining the progress that has been made in reducing both economic and gender inequality. Moreover, the crisis has made it more difficult for countries to work toward the attainment of the Sustainable Development Goals, as countries have been forced to shift budgetary resources from development priorities to pandemic-related measures. As a result of historical and structural conditions, women have been disproportionately impacted by the pandemic within the household, in the public sphere, and in the courts and the rest of the justice system. The impact of the pandemic on access to judicial services for women and other vulnerable groups is exacerbated by deeply entrenched gender norms and structures. Understanding this structural context is important to determine both the impact of the crisis and the efficacy of policy interventions on women and other vulnerable groups.

This chapter examines the challenges that judicial systems, especially the courts, are facing because of the COVID-19 pandemic. It focuses on the impact of the current crisis on women, mainly in terms of their ability to access courts and the overall justice system, and it evaluates measures taken to ensure that courts are safe and continue to dispense justice and offer effective protection to women and other vulnerable groups. In its concluding section, the chapter looks at whether the crisis brought about by the pandemic provides an opportunity for courts to increase their use of technology to improve their operations. Specifically, the chapter explores the opportunity to improve justice systems by integrating technologies into court proceedings and other judicial services, especially in developing countries. Finally, the chapter considers what post-pandemic courts will look like and what it will take, in terms of resources and infrastructure, to ensure that people, particularly women and other vulnerable groups, have access to fair and efficient judicial services, which will almost certainly require improved capacity for technology.

The challenges posed by the pandemic to the justice system: An overview

The courts, access to justice, and the COVID-19 pandemic

The courts, like many other institutions, have been affected by the COVID-19 pandemic. Judges, court officials, and lawyers are all among those who have been infected by the virus. Courts exist to ensure that all people have access to judicial services and are protected by a country's laws and regulations. However, the court system is unable to function if there is no access to the courts or other justice forums. The COVID-19 pandemic has forced many countries to introduce sweeping measures to control the spread of the virus, including lockdowns, travel restrictions, the prohibition of public gatherings, and the closure of public institutions. These measures have had a huge impact on the delivery of judicial services and the justice system as a whole, as access to courts and prisons has been severely restricted. Access to justice is not just a fundamental right in itself; it is also an essential prerequisite for the protection and promotion of all other rights, including civil, political, cultural, economic, and social rights. Access to courts can be considered the inexorable pathway to justice. Anything that hinders the free movement of citizens in and out of the justice system has implications for the delivery of legal services, socio-economic development, inclusive prosperity, economic growth, and the welfare of a country's citizens. Access to courts promotes stability and political and economic liberalization by guaranteeing the opportunity for all people to seek protection and redress under the law. This is especially important for vulnerable groups, who often only have the justice system to rely on to protect and enforce their rights. The resilience of these communities is, therefore, dependent on the resilience of the overall justice system. Even in ordinary times, judicial systems, especially in developing countries, suffer from inefficiencies and inordinate delays in the processing and hearing of cases. Congestion and unreasonable delays in the court system are unfortunate realities of the judicial process in many parts of the world.

The COVID-19 crisis has resulted in increased delays and the lengthy adjournment of trials. Shelter-in-place orders have led to the shutting down of courts, postponement of trials, and delays of other judicial proceedings. Additionally, prison visits and the ability of police and judicial officers to inspect properties and crime scenes have also been negatively impacted by the pandemic. The need to prioritize safety has meant that courtrooms must observe social distancing measures, which has led to a shortage of available courtrooms, as some courtrooms are too small to enforce social distancing. Trials must be conducted in a manner that is not only safe but also observes constitutional safeguards. Some pandemic-related measures have caused specific problems with criminal trials, including victims dropping out of sensitive sexual and domestic abuse cases, resulting in further persecution at the hands of the offenders. Many detention centers also suffer from overcrowding and uninhabitable conditions. This is especially the case for persons awaiting trial. One of the concerns when cases are delayed is the possibility of the misuse of the practice of plea bargaining. There is an increased tendency for people awaiting trial to plead guilty to escape the rigors of trial and long pre-trial detention periods, which have become more prevalent during the current crisis. There is a danger that prosecutors will take advantage of people's situations and force them to agree to guilty pleas in exchange for freedom, which could result in innocent people pleading guilty to avoid trial. It has been observed that some litigants in family matters have taken advantage of the pandemic to secure emergency court orders for temporary sole custody, citing safety concerns of the child. Some courts have also refused the filing of non-essential and non-emergency cases. When deciding whether to pivot to remote proceedings, officials need to consider all intended and unintended consequences and their likely impact on the rights of defendants. Of particular importance is the likelihood that the defendants' pre-trial detention period will be protracted. Other considerations include the actual length of any delays; the nature of the hearing, including the complexity of the case and the matter being dealt with; the need to call witnesses; the likely impact of the hearing on individual rights and deprivation of liberty; and the existence of impairments or other factors that could negatively affect the defendant's ability to participate effectively in court proceedings.

Distancing and space

As courts reopen, they are faced with logistical challenges in terms of complying with government health directives. Courts must adapt their physical spaces as well as entry protocols to adhere to safety guidelines, including installing acrylic barriers; providing staff with safety kits; offering masks to visitors; improving ventilation systems; taking temperature at courthouse doors; and adopting procedures to protect jurors (e.g., pre-screening them through questionnaires before bringing them into the courthouse). However, there is limited space in the courts, which means that adhering to social distancing (e.g., maintaining two meters of distance) is extremely difficult, considering the number of litigants, lawyers, court staff, and legal staff involved in the justice system. Moreover, some court infrastructure is old and cannot be adjusted or modernized with the technology necessary to meet the new standards. There is also the need for numerous other measures to enable courts to function in a safe environment, such as improved cleaning procedures and education of staff about how the virus spreads.

Courts have taken a number of measures designed to protect staff. These include advisory notifications on the restriction of trials, the implementation of telework arrangements, and the restriction of entry to courthouses or their closure altogether. The effects of the pandemic extend beyond the courtroom to a noticeable shift in some of the usual litigation trends, including (a) the promotion of alternative dispute resolution mechanisms, such as arbitration and mediation; and (b) a fall in the number of new claims, which could be due to the de-prioritization of less important cases or because people are waiting for the end of the pandemic to file cases.

Specific problems with criminal trials

For countries that have jury systems, there are concerns about exposure and operational issues involved in maintaining two meters of distance among jurors. These issues can also lead to distracted jurors, which could result in unsound judgments if jurors are more concerned about their health and safety than the case before them. However, the current circumstances could also incentivize prosecutors to drop minor charges, although this is quite difficult to evaluate, since many justice departments may not have proper records of cases they decided not to pursue. Human rights that guarantee a speedy trial, liberty, an impartial jury, and right to counsel are at stake in many countries because of the pandemic. People's rights may be compromised due to inadequate technology, limited access to jurors, lack of digital skills, low levels of literacy, and lack of access to digital services, especially among women and vulnerable groups. For example, the use of technology in courts may not always be tailored to the needs of the most vulnerable users of the justice system, such as people with learning disabilities. Emergency orders may also delay speedy trials, leading to more time in prison and delays in bail hearings. The unemployment crunch, resulting in a lack of bond money, further contributes to prison overcrowding.

The impact of COVID-19 on women and girls and their access to the justice system

Women, girls, and COVID-19

While the COVID-19 pandemic has had a devastating impact on all people around the world, it has especially affected the lives of women and girls. Crises, conflict, disasters, and unrest are always linked to an increased incidence of violence against women and girls, including intimate partner violence. The United Nations (UN) has observed that policies such as lockdowns, quarantines, stay-at-home orders, and travel restrictions adopted by countries in response to the pandemic increase the risks of gender-based violence (GBV) (Vaeza, 2020). The United Nations Population Fund (UNFPA) projects that millions of new cases of GBV will occur globally for every year that lockdown measures continue (UNFP, 2020). The drivers of violence include increased levels of economic insecurity and lengthy periods of quarantine. Data from multiple countries already show an alarming increase in demand for helplines, protection orders, and emergency shelters.

A UNFPA report further observed that COVID-19 disruptions would delay the implementation of programs meant to prevent other forms of GVD, including child marriages in countries where they are prevalent. Poverty is a known driver of child marriages, so pandemic-related economic stress may increase the risk of families marrying off their daughters to alleviate the perceived burden of caring for them. The increase in GBV is likely to push back fragile progress made on gender equality, strain already overburdened justice systems, and exacerbate the economic impact of COVID-19. Access to judicial services requires financial resources to pay for lawyers and court fees, which disproportionally affects the poor and vulnerable groups, including women, children, juveniles, and persons living with disabilities. Reports indicate that the pandemic has made it harder for especially women to access judicial services,[4] and it has resulted in rising GBV and discriminatory laws that have affected the lives of women and other vulnerable groups, including lesbian, gay, bisexual, transgender, queer, and intersex (LGBTQI) individuals.

Due to lockdown and unemployment, domestic violence has increased significantly around the world. Unemployment increases tensions in the household and relationships, which can lead to violence. A lack of privacy in shared accommodation can also lead to an increase in the reporting of violent incidents. An increase in caregiving responsibilities, such as during the current crisis, without a corresponding increase in protection for caregivers exacerbates the situation. In its special submission to the UN Special Rapporteur, Human Rights Watch identifies the following categories of vulnerable women: domestic workers, older women, women working from home, women without technology, women facing housing issues, and women facing overlapping discrimination or inequalities.

Shelter-in-place orders and escaping violence

Shelter-in-place orders have in some cases undermined women's ability to respond to domestic violence by confining them to their homes. The threat has been acknowledged by the UN Secretary-General António Guterres, who stated that while "we know lockdowns and quarantines are essential to suppressing COVID-19 … they can trap women with abusive partners" (Guterres, 2020a, para. 8). In another presentation, the Secretary General stated that court closures have made it more difficult for women to obtain protection orders against their abusers, and that "gender equality and women's rights are essential to getting through this pandemic together, to recovering faster, and to building a better future for everyone" (Guterres, 2020b, para. 19). The COVID-19 pandemic has created a toxic brew of circumstances that have directly and indirectly affected almost every group in the world. Moreover, violence against women increases during emergencies, and the current pandemic is no exception (UN Women, 2020). Gendered disadvantages have increased at an alarming rate during the crisis, and these disadvantages have been acknowledged as a "shadow pandemic" (Mlambo-Ngcuka, 2020, para. 1) by the executive director of UN Women, Phumzile Mlambo-Ngcuka. She observed further: "Confinement is fostering the tension and strain created by security, health, and money worries. And it is increasing isolation for women with violent partners, separating them from the people and resources that can best help them" (para. 3). Additionally, the COVID-19 crisis puts women and children at further risk of violence, as it restricts women's ability to deploy their usual safety strategies, such as staying with relatives or sending children out to play when the level of abuse is escalating.

The COVID-19 pandemic has disrupted or severed many social, legal, and educational support networks. For example, school closures have made young people vulnerable to abuse by family and other household members, and teen pregnancies and early marriages have increased. Communication restrictions by their abusers have meant that many women have been unable to access support systems, and the closure of courthouses and/or delayed court hearings have made it difficult for women to obtain legal redress. It has been widely acknowledged that some measures countries have put into place to mitigate the socio-economic impact of the pandemic, including restrictions on movements and isolation measures, have had an adverse effect on especially women (UN Department of Global Communications, 2020).

Among the measures implemented around the world to mitigate the effects of the pandemic, some have restricted court operations to prevent the spread of the virus, which has had a detrimental impact on those seeking timely justice and resolution. In Uganda, officials suspended all court hearings and appearances for 32 days, effective on March 20, 2020 (Supreme Court of Uganda, 2020). While courts continued to hear urgent cases, judgments and rulings were issued to parties online or through email. Judiciary staff were banned from traveling except under exceptional circumstances (Karugaba, 2020). Moreover, the Chief Justice in South Africa announced through a circular that only urgent matters related to disaster management could be heard during the extended lockdown period. Both criminal and civil trials were postponed, and the circular encouraged parties to try to settle matters out of court. For example, the parties already in agreement may request the Registrar of the High Court to bring their case before a judge to grant a consent order (Mogoeng, 2020, paras. 6–7).[5]

The shutting down of courts has made it more difficult for women to protect themselves from their abusers. Many courts have restricted their functions to urgent matters, limited access to courthouses, and imposed online filing requirements. For example, in the Democratic Republic of the Congo, courts provided only minimal services, with no public hearings and no witnesses for cases that needed a hearing.

Groups dealing with domestic violence have had to file protection orders for domestic abuse victims remotely and use innovative ways to contact victims in cases when the primary means of communication are controlled by the abuser. In normal circumstances, victims can seek help at shelters and through colleagues, families, and other support systems. Such support is often no longer available, and many domestic violence groups have had to find innovative solutions to file cases and contact victims, such as working with local courts to set up e-filing for protection orders, relying on neighbors and delivery persons to contact victims, and setting up support hotlines through text-messaging.

Domestic workers around the world, most of whom tend to be women, have also been negatively impacted by COVID-19. The U.S. National Domestic Workers Alliance survey of late March found that almost three-quarters of domestic workers in the United States have lost their jobs because of the pandemic (Schwabish & Anderson, 2020). Globally, with schools closed, many have taken on added household work and childcare duties. They have also been subjected to increased abuse and face economic insecurity because of delayed wages and the possibility of deportation. Lebanon and Jordan are hosts to some of the largest populations of migrant domestic workers in the world. In Lebanon, hospitals have refused to test undocumented workers for COVID-19 without their employers' consent. Although documented, some live-in migrant domestic workers in Lebanon have had their identification documents seized by abusive employers. A 2016 International Labour Organization (ILO) study found that out of 1,200 employers surveyed in Lebanon, more than 94% withheld their workers' passports

(ILO, 2016). The ILO reports that the COVID-19 crisis has increased the price of food and basic hygiene products, making it difficult for migrant workers to access a balanced and healthy diet. The ILO has also found that the pandemic has increased xenophobia across the country (Stoevska, 2020).

The COVID-19 pandemic has led to an environment in which human trafficking thrives. According to the National Center for Missing and Exploited Children in the United States, there was a 90% increase in "online enticements" between January and June 2020 (O'Donnell, 2020). School closures, unemployment, food insecurity, homelessness, and travel restrictions all tend to be perfect catalysts for enticing and exploiting victims. The vacuum left by school closures is filled by predators who offer food, security, and money in exchange for abuse and exploitation. Human trafficking has also been impacted by court closures. Limited legal services result in delayed or abandoned evidence collection and limited translating and interpreting services. Efforts aimed at combating human trafficking have also been negatively impacted by the pandemic. Traffickers benefit from border closures because of delayed, reduced, or lack of communication between neighboring countries. A report by the Organization for Security and Cooperation in Europe's Office for Democratic Institutions and Human Rights (OSCE ODIHR) reports that 102 countries are struggling to provide trafficking survivors with basic services and support during the pandemic (OSCE ODIHR & UN Women, 2020).

The COVID-19 pandemic has had an especially negative effect on the reproductive, emotional, and mental health of women (Mittal & Sigh, 2020). Women have missed regular health visits because of the crisis, including breast cancer screenings and reproductive health treatments. The pandemic has also caused delays in the contraceptive supply chain, affecting access to birth control pills, condoms, and other reproductive medication. For example, lockdowns in Nepal and India have forced clinics operated by Marie Stopes International—the largest provider of family planning services in India outside the public sector—to close. A new study conducted by investigators from CARE, a non-profit international aid organization, has found that while almost nobody is spared from the anxiety, worry, and overall emotional fatigue of the pandemic, women are almost three times as likely as men to report suffering from significant mental health issues that are attributable to the current crisis (Kluger, 2020). A recent Kaiser poll shows that 53% of women who responded report a significant negative impact on their mental health, compared with only 37% of men (Panchal et al., 2020).

Approaches to deal with challenges facing women

A number of approaches are being taken to mitigate the impact of the pandemic on women around the world. These include (i) increasing the use of hotlines for reporting incidents related to GBV; (ii) enabling chat-based reporting tools to make it easier for victims who lack privacy to seek help; (iii) training personnel to deal with cases involving GBV; (iv) providing alternative options for shelters; (v) leveraging ICT to allow victims and judges to communicate directly with each other and enable special protection units to carry out interviews and psychological evaluations remotely; (vi) using social media platforms to share information on legal support available in cases of domestic violence and to refer victims to emergency hotlines; and (vii) creating remote applications for issuing protection orders and filing complaints through hotlines. In Australia, policymakers have enacted changes to the criminal code that made it possible to submit restraining orders online, and they increased the penalty and extended the limitation period for prosecuting breaches of restraining orders.

Pandemic-related measures taken in the justice sector and their impact on human rights: An evaluation

While measures are needed to protect litigants, court personnel, and the public from exposure to COVID-19, some measures taken by countries have posed serious human rights concerns. This section examines some of these concerns. In response to the COVID-19 pandemic, prisons and detention centers across the world have been limiting or banning visits. These measures are no doubt understandable given the need to protect detainees, prison staff, and court personnel from the virus, but they have also interfered with the right of detainees to access essential services, including legal assistance. Restrictions and bans on in-person visits make defendants increasingly reliant on telephones and other forms of remote communication to maintain contact with their lawyers and families. In many countries, telephone services in prisons are not free, and the telephone infrastructure in many developing countries is not well developed, making it difficult for defendants to access their legal support. In most cases, this will mean that defendants are disincentivized, if not outright prevented, from communicating with their lawyers and families. There is also a risk that a reliance on remote communication will undermine the quality of legal assistance. Restrictions on the frequency and length of telephone calls, for example, could affect the ability to provide and obtain legal advice, and the lack of in-person meetings may make it harder for lawyers to establish a good rapport and working relationship with their clients. Moreover, video-link hearings can make it harder for lawyers and clients to communicate discreetly during hearings, and there are concerns about the confidentiality of video-based consultations between defendants and their lawyers before and during hearings. A fear that someone may be listening in during consultations impedes honest communication between lawyers and their clients.

Digital communication means that the parties are not going to be in the courtroom in person. The physical absence of defendants from the courtroom is likely to have an impact on their ability to participate effectively in their own criminal proceedings. This is a particularly serious challenge in cases where the defendant is unrepresented by a lawyer. Without legal assistance, defendants are likely to find remote hearing isolating, stressful, and disorienting. The poor quality of video conferencing infrastructure in many countries, especially developing countries, will also mean that litigants could find it difficult to follow and understand the proceedings, and they could even be prevented from observing the courtroom in its entirety. This deprives parties, lawyers, judges, and juries of the opportunity to read non-verbal clues from others in the courtroom, which is often important for lawyers to mount an effective defense.

Technology and its implications for privacy

With video conferencing, privacy is always an issue. The possibility that outsiders may find a way to listen in on hearings poses important privacy and security concerns, and improper access to digital court records and the interruption of internet services could stall or derail court processes. In addition, judges and staff may lack the necessary training to fully take advantage of new technologies, and lack of access to or inappropriate use of technology could hamper efforts to speed up trial proceedings. Even scheduling a date to enter a plea by video from prison can take three or four weeks, as the entire prison system may have a limited number of video links. Also, there may not be enough staff available to accompany prisoners to and from communication facilities.

There are also concerns about how to adequately protect witnesses testifying over video and how to ensure they are not coached, intimidated, or otherwise compromised. Limiting the number of people who can come to the courtroom may have the adverse effect of creating significant barriers for people seeking to use courts to protect or defend themselves and their rights. Not everyone involved in the justice system has access to or the ability to use the technology required to communicate electronically with the courts. This is especially true in domestic violence cases, where the accused could still be present in the same household as the victim.

Another challenge with remote hearings is how to ensure equal access to information for all parties. It can be particularly challenging for defendants to access information when files can only be accessed at a specific location (e.g., the courthouse or police station) or need to be brought to detention centers. Travel restrictions and the closure of certain facilities (e.g., the courthouse) could have a significant impact on the right of access to information, particularly for defendants in detention. Remote procedures have implications for the rights of all defendants, especially vulnerable defendants and those who need access to special services such as interpretation and translation. Defendants with mental impairment, in particular, face serious barriers to effective participation in most normal court settings. Depending on the defendant and the type of impairment, remote justice procedures could severely worsen these challenges, making it even more difficult for them to understand and follow court proceedings. There are similar challenges for defendants with other language-assistance needs, who face additional barriers to communication.

Human rights implications of remote hearings in criminal trials

Most countries' constitutions or laws guarantee the right to a public trial and the right to confront witnesses during trial. These are central provisions in all human rights conventions, including the International Covenant on Civil and Political Rights and the Universal Declaration of Human Rights. These rights are designed to ensure the rigorous testing of evidence presented in court against a defendant. Efforts to introduce digitization in the judicial process, especially for key parts of a trial such as criminal adjudication, could jeopardize the rights of defendants and victims alike.

On the other hand, technological innovations can greatly improve court procedures. In courtrooms worldwide, video conferencing is being implemented as a way to speed up proceedings. The use of video conferencing allows numerous users to express their thoughts in a more naturally occurring atmosphere (e.g., their homes), and it can improve the protection of witnesses. If a prisoner is known to be violent, it could be safer to hold trials and hearings remotely, with the prisoner attending proceedings in jail through a video link. Moreover, digital communication can improve the speed and efficiency of court proceedings and help relieve the pressure of a large backlog in cases. Using video conferencing tools could offer a better solution than waiting for a specific date or period when police officers are available to bring suspects or parties to the courtroom. The challenge is to find the right balance between the advantages and disadvantages posed by technology.

Delays and prison overcrowding

In its report on preparedness, prevention, and control of COVID-19 in prisons and other places of detention, published on March 15, 2020, the WHO identifies people deprived of liberty, such as people in prisons, to be especially vulnerable to COVID-19. The report recommends that

> [e]nhanced consideration should be given to resorting to non-custodial measures at all stages of the administration of criminal justice, including at the pre-trial, trial, and sentencing as well as post-sentencing stages. Priority should be given to non-custodial measures for alleged offenders and prisoners with low-risk profiles and caring responsibilities, with preference given to pregnant women and women with dependent children.
>
> (WHO, 2020, p.4)

The Council of Europe anti-torture Committee's statement of principles relating to the treatment of persons deprived of their liberty in the context of the COVID-19 pandemic also reiterates that

> [a]s close personal contact encourages the spread of the virus, concerted efforts should be made by all relevant authorities to resort to alternatives to deprivation of liberty. Such an approach is imperative, in particular, in situations of overcrowding. Further, authorities should make greater use of alternatives to pre-trial detention, commutation of sentences, early release, and probation; reassess the need to continue involuntary placement of psychiatric patients;

> discharge or release to community care, wherever appropriate, residents of social care homes; and refrain, to the maximum extent possible, from detaining migrants.
>
> (CE, 2020)

Despite their benefits, governments and the courts will have to consider the impact of virtual hearings on the rule of law and the right to a fair trial. The risk of procedural unfairness during remote hearings in the United Kingdom was noted in the case *Hyde and Murphy v. Nygate and Rayment* (2020). In that case, the judge asserted that the risk affected both sides equally and that the parties were both well resourced and well placed to manage a remote trial. Another case in the United Kingdom, *SC v. University Hospitals Southampton NHS Trust* (2020), further explored the concept of fairness during remote hearings. Justice Johnson concluded that the requirement of fairness was satisfied when a remote hearing can, with careful management, take place in a way that is fair to all parties. The judge went on to say that the hearing could be conducted remotely in a way that was fair but stressed that this did not mean that it should be conducted remotely.

The UN Special Rapporteur on the Independence of Judges has suggested seven guidelines to ensure that court staff, prosecutors, and lawyers maintain functioning judicial systems during the current crisis (UN Human Rights, 2020). He recommends an immediate streamlining of justice services to prioritize essential cases and that the prosecution of minor, civil, or economic cases should be postponed. He also argues that the increased risk of COVID-19 infection in crowded prisons could be lowered if pre-trial detentions were minimized and political prisoners, minor offenders, and those who have served most of their terms were considered for early release. Judges, magistrates, public prosecutors, and their staff should be tested for COVID-19 regularly, given that they have to participate in hearings and interact with lawyers and other authorities and groups. Finally, he recognizes that innovation and online procedures are essential in the current environment, but lockdown and social distancing should not prevent the judicial system from guaranteeing due process.

Conclusions and recommendations

The COVID-19 pandemic has disrupted judicial operations worldwide. Courthouses have been closed, cases suspended, and trials postponed. However, courts in many countries were already in crisis before the current pandemic. Many were underfunded, operating with insufficient infrastructure, and generally behind the curve in technology adoption. Similarly, many countries' prison systems were overcrowded and insufficiently resourced. There are several ways the justice system could slow the spread of COVID-19, including by (i) reducing the number of people in prison; (ii) eliminating face-to-face contact (e.g., for attorneys and staff); (iii) making correctional healthcare more accessible; (iv) subsidizing phone calls; and (v) increasing the use of ICT. Nevertheless, the current crisis may present an opportunity for the judiciary to implement technological solutions and streamline processes to ensure that cases are managed properly and in an efficient and timely manner.

Many litigants seem to prefer virtual court hearings because they can attend them without having to take a lot of time off work or find childcare. In some places, the pandemic has even led to bail reforms, easier documentation, and fewer non-appearances in courts. There is a need for the legal profession and the judiciary to look at the current challenges as an opportunity to "reskill and upskill by embracing technology" (Sikri, 2020). The COVID-19 pandemic is only one of many crises the world is likely to face in the coming years. It is, therefore, imperative that governments are prepared and create systems capable of mitigating the effects of future emergencies.

Going forward, policymakers need to focus on not only minimizing delays in the judicial system but also ensuring that courts safeguard the rights of all parties. Long-term planning should be more than about how to reopen courts and must include efforts to make them more efficient, more user-friendly, and better than before. One positive effect of the COVID-19 pandemic has been the courts' increased use of technology and their implementation of e-filing and video conferencing solutions, although human rights and privacy challenges remain. The Chief Justice in the United Kingdom has expressed doubts that the courts will operate in the same way as they did before the pandemic. He argues that many courts have found virtual hearings convenient and overall successful (Holland, 2020).[6] The use of technology may also help alleviate the financial pressures on courts, but the question is, especially for developing countries, whether technology will widen or narrow the gap between the rich and the poor. It is imperative that governments and international development banks prioritize investments in technological infrastructure to ensure that poorer countries and communities also benefit from improved communication.

The authorities should ensure that post-COVID-19 courts are more robust and efficient by reducing paper-based requirements and fully embracing ICT solutions wherever possible. Additionally, increased use of ICT will hopefully reduce the incidence of lost files, destroyed records, etc. The courts in the post-COVID-19 era may be faced with a surge in litigation related to the pandemic. Cases related to failing businesses, divorce, consumer credit, evictions, debt collection, bankruptcy, and domestic disturbances are likely to increase substantially. While few courts will resume in-person-only hearings and proceedings, hearings only via video conferencing are also not a viable solution. Instead, a balanced approach is needed, and the current crisis can be an opportunity for judiciaries to leverage new technologies to streamline processes and reduce delays in the court system.

If courts are to take advantage of technological advances, they will require huge investments in infrastructure, including better bandwidth for e-courts, to be able to hold virtual sessions. Since many rural areas, especially in developing countries, do not have adequate internet connections or facilities, governments need to make internet services more accessible to ensure that everyone can access virtual court sessions (Murungi & Tusiime, 2020). Additionally, people need to be made aware of available internet-based legal services. Access to technologies such as video conferencing and monitoring may not be available to all lawyers and, more importantly, litigants, and many people may lack the necessary skills to use new systems, or they may be uncomfortable using them. In countries with low levels of education, unfamiliarity with technology is likely to be high.

There is a need for increased financial support for services that address violence against women and girls. The experience of the COVID-19 pandemic has demonstrated the importance of digital connectivity and the role of digitally enabled solutions in facilitating access to justice and other healthcare, education, and government services. Limited access to the internet in most developing countries has prevented them from fully leveraging the benefits of improved connectivity. Some governments have taken short-term measures to alleviate connectivity constraints, but medium-term policies are also needed to expand digital infrastructure and adopt digital technologies targeting groups for which provision of services is not commercially viable.

Before the pandemic, the gender gap in internet and mobile phone usage was already significant. In the least developed countries, women are, on average, 30% less likely than men to use the internet. The increased reliance on digital services in almost all aspects of daily life, from healthcare and transportation to the justice system, has disproportionately benefited men. Continued digital exclusion of women will widen the gender gap in access to legal services.

Strategies are also needed for disseminating information about the challenges people face in accessing the justice system and tools available to help them overcome these barriers. Lack of access to information during emergencies such as the current COVID-19 pandemic can significantly hamper recovery efforts. It is, therefore, important that government institutions put measures in place that allow them to quickly and efficiently disseminate accurate information during emergencies. Civil society organizations should be supported because they can play a pivotal role in information dissemination and the provision of training that complement efforts by state institutions. Moreover, governments need to ensure that the most vulnerable people have the necessary legal support and access to judicial institutions by strengthening the provision of basic legal services that target the needs of these groups. Failing to do so risks deepening social and economic inequalities in society. Long-term judicial reforms are likely needed to effectively respond to the threats posed by the current pandemic and its economic fallout.

Worsening financial, family, and health conditions are likely to lead to an upsurge in violence against women and girls, and policymakers need to ensure that courts are able to address the problems confronting women and other disadvantaged groups. The COVID-19-induced recession and unemployment are liable to reduce people's ability to pay alimony and child support, requiring courts to enforce or amend earlier decisions. In addition, women may find it difficult to access social protection payments and other crisis-related benefits if they lack legal forms of identification, are excluded from public information initiatives, or lack the financial resources to seek legal assistance.

Women's financial constraints are likely to worsen, as the pandemic is likely to widen existing economic gender gaps, further limiting women's access to justice. The current crisis presents an opportunity to evaluate different strategies to improve women's access to judicial services. This will, however, require countries to implement monitoring and evaluating mechanisms to measure the impact on women of arrangements adopted to address the effects of the pandemic on judicial systems. Measures that have helped to narrow the gender gap in access to judicial services should be made permanent and scaled up as appropriate rather than being regarded as temporary and reversible. Since the measures outlined in this chapter would require increased funding, countries should be encouraged to include and mainstream expenditures related to domestic violence and the COVID-19 pandemic in national budgets.

Notes

1 Whether it relates to the enforcement of contracts, criminal justice, or the review of allegations of infringement of fundamental rights, courts are the engine of justice and vital for seamless interactions in the society.
2 Since the courts regulate the use of power within a democratic society, judicial powers are often expressed in constitutional provisions, with rigid restrictions on amendments. For example, the Constitution of South Africa from 1996 establishes the powers of the Judicature in Chapter 8, sections 165-180.
3 Texas Chief Justice Nathan Hecht is co-chair of the national Pandemic Rapid Response Team.
4 This is explored in greater depth in the UN Women's press release of May 21, 2020.
5 The directives were issued by the South African Chief Justice Mogoeng Mogoeng in terms of Section 8 (3)(b) of the Superior Courts Act 10 of 2013 for the Management of the Superior Courts During the Extended Lockdown Period, April 9, 2020. See Section D (ii) (11–12) of the Directive.
6 There are, however, also human rights and security challenges associated with remote hearings for judges, lawyers, defendants, and victims.

Case law

Hyde and Murphy v. Nygate and Rayment, EWHC 845 (Ch.) (2020).
SC v. University Hospitals Southampton NHS Trust, EWHC 1445 (2020).

References

Banda, T. (2019). *Access to Justice in Zambia: Court Efficiency In Zambia*. The Cornell Institute for African Development. https://ecommons.cornell.edu/handle/1813/69970

Council of Europe (CE), European Committee for the Prevention of Torture and Inhuman or Degrading Treatment or Punishment (2020, March 20). *Statement of Principles Relating to the Treatment of Persons Deprived of Their Liberty in the Context of the Coronavirus Disease (COVID-19) Pandemic*. https://rm.coe.int/16809cfa4b

Dakolias, M. (1999). Court Performance Around the World: A Comparative Perspective. *Yale Human Rights and Development Journal*, *2*(1), 87, Article 2.

Guterres, A. (2020a). *Make the Prevention and Redress of Violence against Women a Key Part of the National Response Plans for COVID-19*. https://www.un.org/en/un-coronavirus-communications-team/make-prevention-and-redress-violence-against-women-key-part

Guterres, A. (2020b). *Put Women and Girls at the Centre of Efforts to Recover from COVID-19*. United Nations. https://www.un.org/en/un-coronavirus-communications-team/put-women-and-girls-centre-efforts-recover-covid-19

Holland, N. (2020). COVID-19 and the Courts: The Impact of Lockdown on Justice. *McDermott Will & Emery*. https://www.jdsupra.com/legalnews/covid-19-and-the-courts-the-impact-of-22359/

International Labour Organization (ILO) (2016, September 19). *A Study of the Employers of Migrant Domestic Workers in Lebanon: Intertwined*. https://www.ilo.org/wcmsp5/groups/public/---arabstates/---ro-beirut/documents/publication/wcms_524149.pdf

Justice Committee, House of Commons (2020, July 30). *Coronavirus (COVID-19): The Impact on Courts*. https://publications.parliament.uk/pa/cm5801/cmselect/cmjust/519/51903.htm#_idTextAnchor000

Karugaba, P. (2020, March 28). Uganda Legal Implications of COVID-19. *Uganda Legal Information Institute*. https://ulii.org/blogs/phillip-karugaba/28-march-2020/uganda-legal-implications-covid-19

Kluger, J. (2020, September 24). The Coronavirus Pandemic's Outsized Effect on Women's Mental Health Around the World. *TIME*. https://time.com/5892297/women-coronavirus-mental-health/

Mittal, S., & Singh, T. (2020, September 8). Gender-Based Violence During Covid-19 Pandemic: A Mini-Review. *Frontiers in Global Women's Health*. http://www.frontiersin.org/articles/10.3389/fgwh.2020.00004/full

Mlambo-Ngcuka, P. (2020, April 6). Violence against Women and Girls: The Shadow Pandemic. *UN Women*. https://www.unwomen.org/en/news/stories/2020/4/statement-ed-phumzile-violence-against-women-during-pandemic

Mogoeng, M.T.R.M. (2020, April 16). *Directives Issued by Chief Justice Mogoeng Mogoeng in Terms of Section, 8(3)(b) of the Superior Courts Act 10 of, 2013 for the Management of the Superior Courts during the Extended Lockdown Period [2020] ZARC 31*. http://www.saflii.org/za/other/ZARC/2020/31.html

Murungi, E.M., & Tusiime, D.T. (2020, May 4). COVID-19: Law and Technology: Why an Electronic Case Management System Is a Necessity in Uganda. *Bowmans*. https://www.bowmanslaw.com/insights/covid-19-law-and-technology-why-an-electronic-case-management-system-is-a-necessity-in-uganda/

National Center for State Courts (NCSC). (n.d.). *Coronavirus and the Courts*. https://www.ncsc.org/newsroom/public-health-emergency

O'Donnell, B. (2020, July 16). COVID-19 and Missing & Exploited Children. *National Center for Missing & Exploited Children*. https://www.missingkids.org/blog/2020/covid-19-and-missing-and-exploited-children

Organization for Security and Co-operation in Europe (OSCE) Office for Democratic Institutions and Human Rights (ODIHR), & UN Women (2020, July 30). *Addressing Emerging Human Trafficking Trends and Consequences of the Covid-19 Pandemic*. Organization for Security and Co-operation in Europe. https://www.osce.org/files/f/documents/2/a/458434_4.pdf

Panchal, N., Kamal, R., Orgera, K., Cox, C., Garfield, R., Hamel, L., Muñana, C., & Chidambaram, P. (2020, August 21). *The Implications of COVID-19 for Mental Health and Substance Use*. Kaiser Family Foundation. https://www.kff.org/coronavirus-covid-19/issue-brief/the-implications-of-covid-19-for-mental-health-and-substance-use/

Schwabish, J., & Anderson, T. (2020, October). *6 Months in Crisis: The Impact of COVID-19 on Domestic Workers*. National Domestic Workers Alliance. https://domesticworkers.org/sites/default/files/6_Months_Crisis_Impact_COVID_19_Domestic_Workers_NDWA_Labs_1030.pdf

Sikri, A.K. (2020, April 11). Social Distancing Is Leading to Much Needed Judicial Reform. *Sunday Guardian Live*. https://www.sundayguardianlive.com/legally-speaking/social-distancing-leading-much-needed-judicial-reforms

Stoevska, V. (2020, December 9). COVID-19 Is Driving up Food Prices All over the World. *ILOSTAT*. https://ilostat.ilo.org/covid-19-is-driving-up-food-prices-all-over-the-world/

Supreme Court of Uganda, Chambers of the Chief Justice (2020, March 19). *Circular CJ/C.7, Court Proceedings. Guidelines on Conducting Criminal Sessions in Courts of Judicature During the Existence of Covid-19 Pandemic*. https://judiciary.go.ug/files/downloads/CJ%20Guidelines%20on%20Criminal%20Sessions.pdf

UN Women (2020). *COVID-19 and Ending Violence Against Women and Girls*. https://www.unwomen.org/-/media/headquarters/attachments/sections/library/publications/2020/issue-brief-covid-19-and-ending-violence-against-women-and-girls-en.pdf?la=en&vs=5006

United Nations Office of the Commissioner for Human Rights (UN Human Rights) (2020, April 22). *UN Expert Outlines Urgent Steps to Ensure Justice Systems Are Not Paralysed by COVID-19*. https://www.ohchr.org/EN/NewsEvents/Pages/DisplayNews.aspx?NewsID=25816&LangID=E

United Nations Population Fund (UNFPA) (2020, April 28). *New UNFPA Projections Predict Calamitous Impact on Women's Health as COVID-19 Pandemic Continues* [Press release]. https://www.unfpa.org/pcm/node/24174

Vaeza, M.N. (2020, November 27). Addressing the Impact of the Covid-19 Pandemic on Violence Against Women and Girls. *UN Chronicle*. https://www.un.org/en/addressing-impact-covid-19-pandemic-violence-against-women-and-girls

World Health Organization (WHO) (2020, March 15). *Preparedness, Prevention and Control of COVID-19 in Prisons and Other Places of Detention*. World Health Organization Regional Office for Europe. https://apps.who.int/iris/bitstream/handle/10665/336525/WHO-EURO-2020-1405-41155-55954-eng.pdf?sequence=1&isAllowed=y

15 Sexual and gender-based violence in Uganda during the COVID-19 pandemic

New and old lessons for the criminal justice system

Lillian Tibatemwa-Ekirikubinza, PhD

Introduction

In March 2020, the World Health Organization (WHO) declared the COVID-19 outbreak a pandemic of international concern. The Ugandan government responded by adopting a multi-sectoral approach with 34 policy measures, including the closure of educational institutions, restrictions on vehicle movements, a dawn-to-dusk curfew, and a halt to non-essential economic activities. The government's response to the crisis meant that the majority of Ugandans were confined to their homes.

Global research indicates that national emergencies lead to increased levels of sexual and gender-based violence (SGBV) (32nd RCRC Conference, 2015), and there is growing evidence that the COVID-19 pandemic has led to an increase in the incidence of sexual violence around the world (Peterman et al., 2020). The first part of this chapter deals with the impact of pandemic-related restrictions on the incidence of rape and defilement in Uganda.[1] The chapter also evaluates the response of the criminal justice system—the Uganda Police, the Office of Public Prosecution (OPP), and the judiciary—to the current crisis. In Uganda, each police station has a gender desk that receives and manages sexual assault cases. A case file is compiled for each sexual assault reported, which is then investigated and finally forwarded to the prosecutor office for review. The OPP is mandated to institute criminal proceedings against suspected offenders. While this chapter is primarily based on an analysis of records from the Uganda Police, the OPP, and the judiciary, information was also gathered through interviews with officials from these three institutions.

The second part of the chapter places sexual violence against women within the socio-cultural context of Ugandan society. This is important, because emergencies may escalate women's vulnerability to sexual abuse, but they are often not the cause of the abuse. Like any other social phenomenon, rape can only be fully understood by considering the broad social context within which it occurs. To understand sexual encounters between men and women in Uganda, the discussion must be placed within the discourse of gender in a patriarchal society. While the

DOI: 10.4324/9780429327865-20

country's judiciary is being called upon to play a central role in protecting women's right to protection against sexual violence during the current crisis, violence is not rooted in the pandemic. This chapter interrogates the theory that a judge's decision is grounded in the society in which it takes place, and that gender stereotypes and myths are embedded in judicial processes. To demonstrate a correlation between gender notions and the outcome of a rape trial, the results of a study I conducted on community perceptions of rape are juxtaposed with an analysis of judicial processes applied in rape trials. It is assumed that a judge's preconceived notions on gender, sex, and sexuality in a patriarchal society may affect the outcome of a trial and hamper women's access to justice. Any recommendation for improving women's access to justice during emergencies must, therefore, unearth the failures of the justice system to protect the rights of victims of sexual abuse in non-emergency situations.

Pandemic-related restrictions and sexual violence against women

A survey by the Uganda Association of Women Lawyers reveals that the pandemic led to a spike in cases of domestic and sexual violence during the lockdown (Musiime, 2020). For example, teenage pregnancies are reported to have increased during the school closures. The closure of schools can result in girls spending more time with the opposite sex, increasing the likelihood that they will engage in risky sexual behavior and be exposed to sexual violence and exploitation (World Vision, 2020). School closures also heighten the vulnerability of children to sexual abuse by people living in close proximity to their homes. According to the United Nations Population Fund (UNFPA), teenage pregnancies in Uganda increased by an estimated 1.62% in 2020 compared with the last three years (UNFPA, 2020).

Despite the increase in domestic and sexual violence, the incidence of rape and defilement reported to the police in Uganda fell in the first half of 2020. A report by Uganda's Criminal Investigation Directorate shows that reported cases of defilement fell by 5.2% between January and June 2020. In this period, a total of 6,838 cases of defilement were reported to the police, lower than 7,216 cases reported between January and June 2019 (Figure 15.1). The records also show that 749 rape cases were reported to the police in the first half of 2020, lower than 770 cases reported in the same period in 2019, representing a decrease of 2.7%. It is, therefore, clear that the escalation of sexual assault reported at the community level during the pandemic has not been fully reflected in the number of cases reported to the police. The decrease in the level of reporting was likely due to victims being unable to access the police and other services as a result of restrictions on movement, as the number of cases increased sharply once the restrictions were eased.

Police trends: Kabalagala and Katwe police stations

Data collected in collaboration with the Criminal Investigation Department reveal that Katwe and Kabalagala police stations[2] recorded a drop in reported

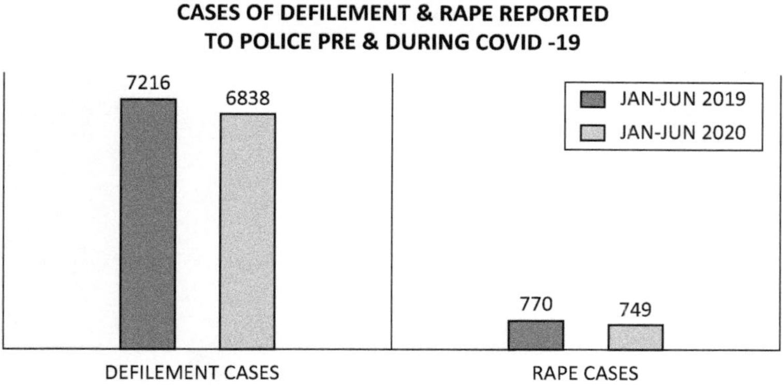

Figure 15.1 Incidence of rape and defilement reported to the police *Source: Uganda Criminal Investigation Directorate, September, 2020.*

rape and defilement cases, although they did show a possible link between stay-at-home orders and the sexual offenses committed. A review of 50 case files (33 related to defilement, 19 to aggravated defilement, and 17 to rape) at both police stations shows that most incidents of rape and defilement during the lockdown were committed by people who knew or resided or worked close to the victim, such as family members, friends of the family, neighbors, or service providers (e.g., barbers, *boda* riders,[3] food vendors, etc.) (Figure 15.2).[4] The abuse frequently took place at private residences, although pathways, football pitches, and plantations were also recorded as crime sites. Most of the incidents occurred during the daytime, and children were often defiled in either their parents' or neighbors' homes. Assaults committed by people close to the victim, coupled with the continued proximity of the perpetrator to the victim, may have made it difficult for some victims to report the assault to the police.

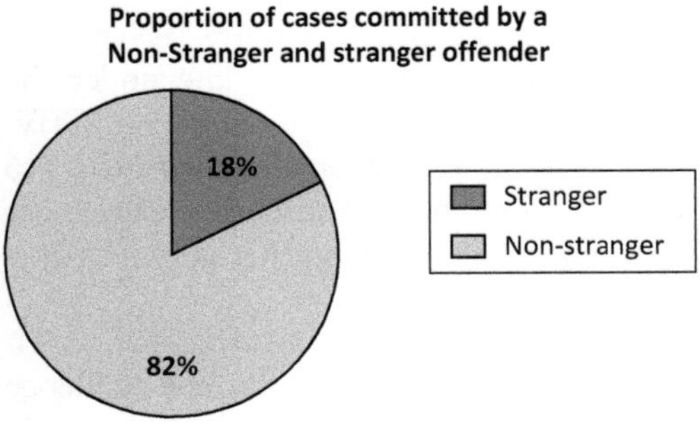

Figure 15.2 Proportion of cases committed by a non-stranger or stranger *Source: Kabalagala and Katwe police records, accessed September, 2020.*

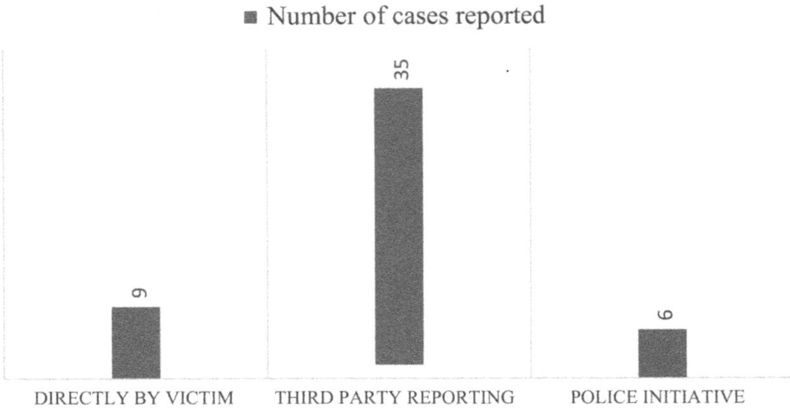

Figure 15.3 Cases of rape and defilement by source of reporting *Source*: Kabalagala and Katwe police records, accessed September, 2020.

Data also show that restrictions on economic activities, which led to the need for alternative sources of income, increased women's vulnerability to sexual abuse. For example, some women were assaulted by men who had promised to help them acquire employment in essential sectors. Furthermore, confinement at home led to an increase in the use of the internet and social media such as WhatsApp and Facebook. With this came an increase in the sharing of nude images, which was interpreted by some perpetrators as implied consent to sex.

Most rape and defilement cases processed at the Katwe and Kabalagala police stations were reported by third parties. Out of the 50 cases reviewed, 9 were reported by the victims, 35 were reported by third parties, and 6 were the result of community policing (Figure 15.3). This may be an indication that the police need better tools and training to identify signs of abuse as they engage with members of the community.

Use and limitations of technology

The police in Uganda have set up a 24/7 toll-free support line under the Department of Child and Family Protection Unit to receive reports of SGBV. It has been popularized on various social media platforms, along with the 116 Sati toll-free support line established in 2014 by the Ministry of Gender, Labor and Social Development (MGLSD) to encourage the reporting of child rights violations.

In September, 2020, the MGLSD scaled up the digital platform SafePal, which was created in 2015 with support from the UNFPA, to respond to the challenge of low levels of reporting of sexual violence (Songa, 2020). SafePal enables survivors to report cases confidentially and access information on psychosocial, legal, and medical services. Participating organizations include ActionAid, Naguru

Teenage Center and Center for Domestic Violence Prevention, and the Uganda Police Child and Family Protection Unit. When a case is submitted, SafePal instantly notifies the relevant service provider so that they reach out to the victim. Incident reports submitted are usually attended to within 72 hours. The identity of the person who reported the incident is recorded with a unique code for use when there is a need to contact them to gather evidence.

While the use of technology can make it easier and more efficient to report and manage sexual abuse cases, innovative applications must be grounded in the lived realities of the targeted group. For example, many solutions that utilize information and communication technologies (ICT) assume that victims have access to phones. However, *Groupe Speciale Mobile Association* reports that women have a harder time accessing digital technologies and the internet than men because of high financial costs and high levels of technology illiteracy. A 2015 Uganda Communications Commission survey on access and use of ICT revealed that 44% of women owned and could use a phone, much lower than 62% of men (Women of Uganda Network, 2020). The survey also showed that only 15% of women interviewed had used a computer or the internet in the last three months preceding the survey, lower than 21% of men. Therefore, the digitalization of judicial practices can especially limit women's access to justice.

The use of phone services to report instances of abuse also has logistical and privacy challenges. The chief executive officer of the Uganda Association of Women Lawyers, Ms. Lilliane Adriko, has observed that it may be difficult for officers to follow up with victims who have reported their abuse by using a phone from a third party. For example, there could be a breach of privacy if the owner of the phone wants to know why the victim or the police need the phone. In addition, toll-free support lines are unevenly distributed across the country, and counseling services are harder to provide to victims over the phone. Finally, there may be inadequate capital and human resources to meet the demand created by digital platforms. For example, a survivor who calls a service center may expect to be physically rescued, but the police may not have the resources to transport and support the victim. Nevertheless, mobile applications to report sexual abuse have been increasingly used during the lockdown, especially by urban youth, university students, and women in the corporate sector. The perception that these applications can protect the identity of users has made them popular throughout the country (Songa, 2020).

Community policing

As a member of the National Joint Security Task Force and charged with enforcing COVID-19 prevention measures, the police have unrestricted access to communities. Using this privilege, the Department of Sexual and Child Offences has scaled up community policing and prioritized the reporting of sexual abuse. However, the success of the department's interventions has been limited by challenges such as a shortage of fuel to facilitate the continuous and timely response of the police. The unfavorable public opinion of the police has also made it more complicated for community liaison officers to investigate reports of sexual abuse (Kamya, 2020).

Social media as a source of information

During the lockdown, the police in Uganda have followed leads on social media and investigated cases that trended online, with some cases forwarded to the OPP. These efforts were, however, hampered by the limited ability of the police to collect and verify information from social media platforms. Furthermore, the training offered to the Uganda Police Force on identifying sexual assault on the internet has been very limited.

Media campaigns

In August and September 2020, the MGLSD spearheaded media campaigns to raise awareness and respond to the increase in SGBV during the COVID-19 pandemic. The campaign adopted a multi-sectoral approach, and experts from the different government agencies, including the police, shared data on reporting and information on adopted strategies.

Office of Public Prosecution

There was an increase in the number of cases of SGBV that were sanctioned by the OPP for the prosecution during the COVID-19 lockdown (Figure 15.4).[5]

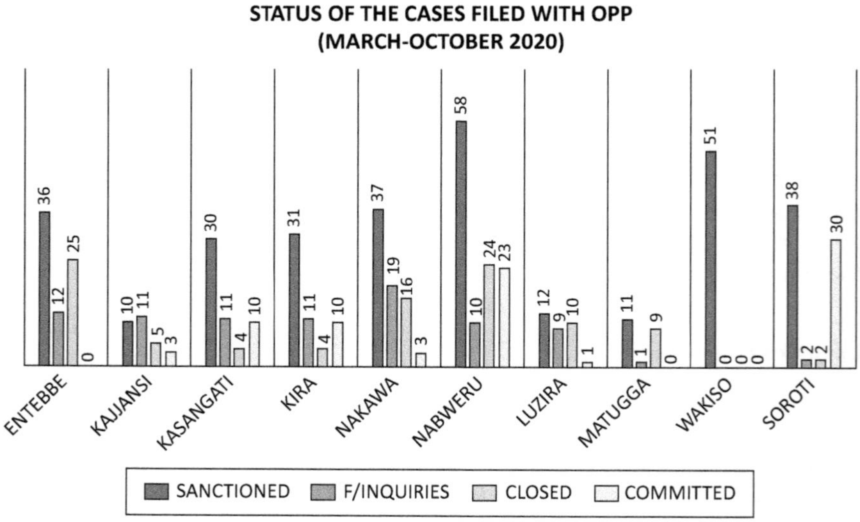

Figure 15.4 Cases filed with the OPP between March and October, 2020 by status *Source: OPP, November, 2020.*

Data from ten police stations across Uganda, which show that more women than men were sexually assaulted, also point to a correlation between the number of SGBV cases sanctioned and urbanization. The OPP sanctioned more cases in large cities such as Entebbe, Nakawa, and Nabweru than in smaller cities such as Kajjansi, Luzira, and Matugga. This is expected, since judicial systems are more concentrated in urban areas, and residents of major metropolitan areas tend to be more knowledgeable about the justice system than people living in small towns or rural areas. Urban residents are also less likely than their rural counterparts to subscribe to a culture of silence when dealing with sexual assault.

During the lockdown, there were 314 cases sanctioned by the OPP in 10 jurisdictions, of which 118 cases (37.5%) were withdrawn. This means that for every three cases sanctioned by the OPP, one case was closed. The unwillingness of the witness to testify was the main reason for the withdrawal of sexual assault cases.

Pandemic-related measures and restrictions on the prosecution

The OPP is not recognized as an essential service in the country's COVID-19 National Response Plan. According to Ms. Wakooli, head of the Sexual Offences Department, this compromised not only the work of prosecutors but also that of the criminal justice system as a whole. She stated: "It is important to note that the prosecutors 'own' criminal cases, a case cannot be tried in court unless it has been filed by the OPP." Restrictions on movement made it difficult for prosecutors to access their chambers and the courts and interview witnesses. As a result, even cases that made it to court suffered significant delays.

To cope with the challenges imposed by pandemic-related restrictions, the OPP increased its use of technology to facilitate a safe work environment. Some prosecutions were conducted online using digital tools such as Zoom, although these efforts had a minimal impact on proceedings outside of Kampala due to limited training of prosecutors in the use of technology. The government should consider prosecutors essential workers during emergencies, and they must be properly trained in the use of digital tools (e.g., a training module on virtual prosecution could be developed). The OPP should also procure relevant ICT equipment to ensure that its offices around the country can utilize remote technologies.

The courts

The Chief Justice issued guidelines for courts during the lockdown to prevent the spread of COVID-19. For criminal cases, all in-person court appearances were suspended; proceedings were to be conducted using video conferencing whenever possible, and courts were instructed to continue to handle certificates of urgency and taking pleas for serious cases and bail applications, although only the parties and their lawyers could be present in court.

Although in-person court appearances were suspended, the police continued to arrest criminal suspects. This meant that courts had to use audio and video conferencing to take the pleas of those arrested. The Judicature Audio-Visual

Rules No. 26 of 2016 enumerate the circumstances under which witnesses can give evidence through electronic means. These include proceedings relating to sexual offenses. An audio-visual link facility was established at the Buganda Road Chief Magistrate's Court. While launching the facility in 2016, the Chief Justice emphasized its value in promoting the rights of child witnesses who are victims of sexual violence. At the launch, a 16-year-old victim of defilement became the first person in Uganda to give evidence in court through an audio-video link.

However, following the issuance of the COVID-19 guidelines, not a single case of sexual assault has been handled using the audio-video link facility at the Buganda Chief Magistrate's Court. While the facility has been used by all the courts in Kampala and its surrounding areas, the heavy traffic has made it near impossible to conduct full trials. Instead, the facility has been used for plea taking, hearings for bail applications and plea bargains, and the delivery of judgments. As is the norm in criminal justice, the judicial system has focused on the rights of accused persons and failed to acknowledge the need to expedite the adjudication of sexual assault cases.

Magistrate Courts in Nabweru and Makindye

Between March 21 and June 2020, over 200 criminal cases were registered in the Chief Magistrate Court in Nabweru, of which only 33 cases involved sexual assault (Table 15.1). In 32 of the sexual assault cases, the victim and the perpetrator knew each other, and 32 offenses occurred at the perpetrator's residence. In 28 of these cases, the victims were school-going adolescents. These findings validate the argument that school closures increase the vulnerability of school-going children to sexual abuse by people living in close proximity to them. Sixteen of the victims were reportedly pregnant as a result of the defilement, which is supported by UNFPA data that project an increase in teenage pregnancies in Uganda in 2020. Also, a 2020 study by World Vision International shows that school closures during crises can result in girls spending more time with the opposite sex, increasing the likelihood of engaging in risky sexual behavior and raising the risk of sexual violence and exploitation (World Vision, 2020).

Table 15.1 Nabweru Chief Magistrate's Court

Offense	*Number of cases*
Aggravated defilement	2
Simple defilement	27
Attempted defilement	2
Rape	0
Attempted rape	2
Child-to-child sex	0

Source: Nabweru Chief Magistrate Court records, accessed September 2020.

Table 15.2 Makindye Chief Magistrate Court

Category of offense	*Number of cases*	%	*Total cases*	%
Aggravated defilement	15	33.3	**39**	**87**
Defilement	24	53.3		
Rape	4	9	**6**	**13**
Attempted rape	2	4.4		
Grand Total	**45**	**100**	**45**	**100**

Source: Makindye Chief Magistrate Court records, accessed September, 2020.

During the lockdown, 45 sexual offenses were reported to the Chief Magistrate Court in Makindye, 39 of which (87%) involved defilement and 6 (13%) involved rape (Table 15.2). The majority of the accused (64.4%) were subjected to pre-trial detention, compared with more than one-third (35.6%) who were granted bail pending trial. Under normal circumstances, it is rare in Uganda to grant bail to people accused of serious offenses before they have spent 180 days in pre-trial detention. According to interviews with the magistrates in Nabweru and Makindye, the trend of judicial officers being more willing to grant bail was the result of efforts to curtail the spread of COVID-19 by reducing the prison population. This trend is similar to that reported by Save the Children International in the northern district of Adjumani—the police released men suspected of defilement back into the community after 48 hours because the OPP was closed due to the pandemic (Save the Children, 2020).

Both magistrates reported an increase in bail jumping during the lockdown, and there were more instances of witnesses not showing up to court when suspects did turn up. The economic hardship caused by the pandemic has made it harder for victims to afford transportation to court. This has been exacerbated by the rising cost of public transportation linked to the adoption of social distancing measures, which has resulted in vehicles carrying fewer passengers on each route. The OPP needs to ensure that victims and witnesses have the means necessary to be in court when they are needed. One case that clearly shows the negative impact of COVID-19 restrictions on the administration of justice in Makindye was the release of a 48-year-old man who defiled a 14-year-old girl. The court was informed by the prosecution that there was no available transport to the prison for the accused, which meant that prosecutors could not object to the bail application.

Aside from efforts to reduce the prison population, there are also other factors that have led officials to be more willing to grant bail, accept plea bargains, and make use of non-custodial sentences. For example, in some defilement cases involving girls aged between 16 and 18 and men in their early twenties, there was evidence that the sexual act was consensual, even though a technical offense had been committed. However, no person accused of rape was granted bail pending trial during the lockdown period. Efforts to reduce the prison population have also resulted in an increase in the use of plea bargaining, which has led to shorter prison sentences (e.g., the average sentence of sexual assault offenders at both courts is six months) and more frequent use of non-custodial sentences such as cautions and community service orders.

Delay in adjudication is one potential reason for the high attrition rate in sexual assault cases in Uganda. Policymakers need to study best practices from other countries that have implemented effective strategies to enable women to access judicial services during the current crisis. For example, Ethiopia has continued to hear domestic violence cases with minimal interruption (Huaxia, 2020). Other countries are using virtual means to enable domestic violence survivors to utilize teleconferencing during court proceedings. A report by the United Nations High Commissioner for Refugees (UNHCR) points out that Burundi and Ethiopia have recognized SGBV services as essential in their COVID-19 national response plans. Both countries have facilitated access to judicial services and personal protective equipment and lifted movement restrictions for SGBV case workers (UNHCR, 2020).

Sexual violence, the socio-cultural context, and the judicial system

The police and the OPP have discretion in determining which cases are worth pursuing. When determining which cases to pursue, officers are aware of the principles that guide the courts in their decision to acquit or convict an accused. Officers file cases in court where, in their view, there is a reasonable chance of conviction. Therefore, any attempts to improve the quality of justice for victims of sexual abuse must include an evaluation of the workings of the judicial system. Moreover, judges are influenced by social norms, and their preconceived notions on gender, sex, and sexuality in a patriarchal society may negate women's access to justice in a rape trial.

To show the correlation between gender notions and the outcome of a rape trial, the results of a rape study that I conducted, which included interviews with 120 Ugandans on community perceptions of rape, were juxtaposed with the results of an analysis of judicial processes applied in rape trials. The interviews focused on the respondents' understanding of consent in sexual encounters, and the analysis of judicial processes focused on the Zuma rape trial (*The State v. Jacob Gedleyihlekisa Zuma*) because of the global interest it elicited. Mr. Jacob Zuma, the former President of South Africa, was charged in the High Court on December 6, 2005. He was accused of raping a 31-year-old woman. He admitted to having had sexual intercourse with the complainant but stated that it was consensual. While the trial was in South Africa, the effect of patriarchy on notions of sexuality in South Africa is assumed to be similar to that in Uganda.

Gender, patriarchy, and gender justice

The rape study adopted a generally accepted definition of gender as the socially constructed roles, behaviors, and attributes that a given society typically associates with and considers appropriate for males and females, respectively. Ugandan society has cultural norms that determine gender expression and roles. Gender is hierarchical and produces inequalities that intersect with other social and economic inequalities. A patriarchal society is defined as that which consists of a male-dominated power structure throughout organized society and in individual relationships. Under patriarchy, men have power over women simply because they are male. Ugandan society is defined as patriarchal, and its structure is based on a hierarchical system of oppression, where men as a class have power over women. To mitigate the effects of patriarchal society, Uganda's constitution enshrines the equal rights of women and men and prohibits laws and cultural, customary, and traditional practices that undermine the status of women (Constitution of Uganda, 1995).

Socially constructed roles shape women's access to justice. An understanding of gender and patriarchy by actors in the justice system is critical to any discussion of gender justice. Also, to understand sexual encounters between men and women, it is crucial that the discussion is placed within the discourse of gender in a patriarchal society. In its narrowest sense, access to justice refers to the formal ability to appear in a court of law. More broadly, however, access to justice interrogates the wider social context of a legal system. It probes the systemic barriers faced by different groups in the community in their attempt to use the services made available by the established institutions. Access to justice looks beyond equality of opportunity and aims to achieve equality of outcomes by addressing the barriers faced by those trying to access the judicial system (McHale, 2016). True access to justice must be considered in light of social variables that have historically had a negative impact on the ability of certain groups to access justice. It follows that gender justice involves efforts to end the inequalities between women and men that are produced and reproduced in the family, the community, and state institutions such as courts. In the context of a rape trial, it is important to evaluate the experiences of female victims as their complaints are processed through the justice system.

Statutory law on rape

Uganda's Penal Code Act (1950) defines rape as having sexual intercourse with a woman without her consent (Section 123). Prosecutors must prove that as a matter of fact there was no consent. They must also deal with the state of mind of the accused and prove that he knew that the woman was not consenting or was reckless as to whether or not she was consenting. If the accused establishes that he held an honest belief that the complainant was consenting, even if that belief was not reasonable, he would be free of criminality (*DPP v. Morgan*, 1976). The position of the law, as stated by the House of Lords in the United Kingdom, has been adopted by Ugandan and South African courts as well as many other commonwealth jurisdictions.

Myths, beliefs, and stereotypes on sex and sexuality

A man may wrongly believe a woman is consenting to sexual relations because of stereotypical beliefs and rape myths held in society. Lonsway and Fitzgerald

(1994) define rape myths as "attitudes and beliefs that are generally false but are widely and persistently held, and that serve to deny and justify male sexual aggression against women" (p.134). The rape study that I conducted, which consisted of interviews with 120 men and women in Uganda, reveals that a slight majority (52%) agree that a man is entitled to sex with a woman on whom he has spent money. With 55% of men and 48% of women agreeing with the statement, the difference between men and women is insignificant. The majority (60%) of respondents under the age of 35 did not agree with the statement, while more than two-thirds (70%) of respondents over the age of 35 agreed.

In terms of perceptions, one male respondent asked, "Why would a man who is neither your father nor brother give you money?" Other respondents said that men feel used by women who repeatedly accept financial favors and then refuse to have sex with them. Many women also held the view that to accept numerous favors from a man and then deny him sex was dishonest: "if you have no intentions of sleeping with him, reject his favors." It is clear that many in Uganda perceive financial favors as an investment and that the woman's consent is thereafter assumed. Because Uganda is a patriarchal society, men have greater access to the country's socio-economic resources. Within the context of rape, men's economic privilege is often translated into entitlement to women's bodies. It is, therefore, no surprise that a man who promised to help an unemployed woman access work during the pandemic would expect sex in return.

To the question of whether a man has the right to insist on sex after he and a woman have returned to his apartment after a date, the majority (53%) of the respondents answered yes, with 63% of men and 42% of women saying yes—a significant difference between men and women. Fewer younger people answered in the affirmative, as only 30% and 40% of young women and men, respectively, said yes.

Date rape is closely linked with the issue of men raping women on whom they have spent or "invested" money. In Uganda, it is generally expected that the man pays for dinner or other activities when the parties have an intimate relationship or where there are indications of a romantic relationship. Also, the man is usually the person who will suggest that the two go out. Therefore, some of the observations made regarding the economic context of rape are also relevant in the context of date rape.

The majority of respondents also interpreted a woman's voluntary presence at a man's home as "asking" for it, meaning that the woman had agreed to sex by visiting the man's home. According to many of the interviewees, "A mature woman knows that if butter is placed near fire, it melts—if you go to a man's house but resist his sexual advances and he forces you into sex, you cannot blame him." One female respondent said that "she would have taken herself to the man's house and by so doing she stimulated him to have sex with her." Others asked, "How can you give a dog meat and then instruct it not to eat it?" Ironically, this opinion is in stark contrast to a picture of a disciplined dog next to a bucket of meat, which appeared in a local daily newspaper in 2015 (Figure 15.5).

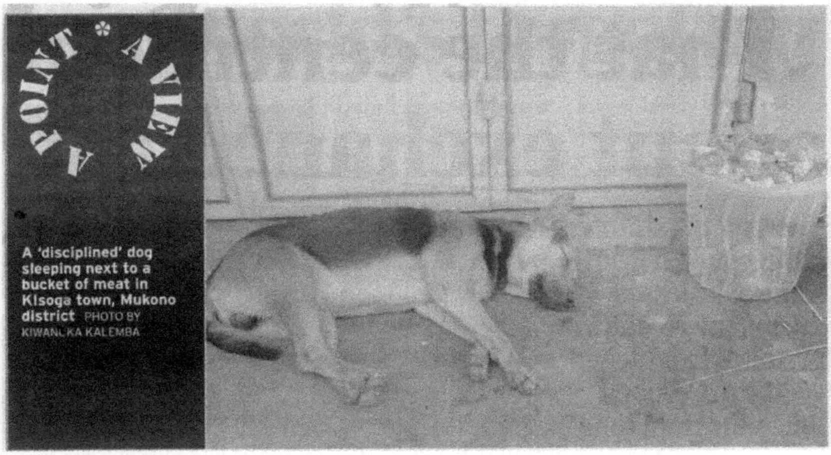

Figure 15.5 Picture of a disciplined dog *Source*: Kalemba, K. (2015, December 19). A "disciplined" dog sleeping next to a bucket of meat in Kisoga town, Mukno district. *Saturday Vision*.

The prevailing argument expressed by many of the respondents is that a woman should not go to a man's home after a date if she does not want to have sex with him, and a woman should know that sex is expected if she goes to a man's house. This perception was crudely supported by one male respondent, who stated that a woman cannot undress in the presence of a man and then claim she is scared of an erect penis. In the eyes of the majority, a woman's voluntary presence in a man's private space and/or relationship to the man in question can function as a stand-in for consent, or it renders her consent unnecessary. Others saw the woman's presence in the man's home as implied consent and stated, "Women will not verbally communicate consent to sex and if you make sexual advances and she rejects you, consider it feigned resistance; women say no when they mean yes; if in such circumstances you do not 'force' her into action, she would believe that you are impotent." The results of this study are in line with observations made by Moore et al. (2007) in a study of sexual relationships in sub-Saharan Africa. She found that the relationship between individuals and the circumstances under which sexual intercourse occurs influence an individual's perception of what constitutes sexual coercion. Similarly, Giarruso et al. (1979) report that some Americans do not regard non-consensual sex within a dating relationship as rape, even if a man coerces the woman. Moreover, a study carried out by Stets and Pirog-Good (1989) in the United States shows that some Americans believe it is justified for a man to have sex with a woman against her will if the woman allows the man to pay for all expenses during a date.

In response to the question of whether kissing and fondling in a secluded place indicate that a woman is willing to have sexual intercourse, 85% of the respondents said yes, and a majority did not consider it rape if under these circumstances the man uses force to have sex with the woman. Interestingly, more women (97%) than men (73%) answered yes, with one female respondent stating, "Girls are very cautious; if she is not ready for sex, she cannot engage in such deep intimacy and in a secluded place." While a slim majority (53%) of respondents younger than 35 years old answered no, all the young women perceived kissing and fondling in a secluded place as an indicator that the girl was ready for sex, and an overwhelming majority (87%) of respondents aged 36 and older answered yes.

In Ugandan culture, kissing is an activity thought to be done exclusively in private, which means that it is perceived differently than in most Western societies. Many Ugandans perceive penetrative sex as the next step after kissing, and many believe that a man cannot control his sexual urges once they have reached a certain point, which is used to excuse men's aggressive sexual actions. This myth about men not being able to control their sexual urges also affects perceptions of the severity of rape and may result in the refusal to label an act as rape.

Societal expectations of masculinity and femininity influence the conduct of men and women in sexual encounters. In a discussion on gender, the terms masculinity and femininity are used to identify a set of characteristics that are associated with men and women. In patriarchal societies, to be masculine is to possess qualities and traits associated with men, such as strength, dominance, aggression, control, courage, and being active and assertive, while femininity is associated with being submissive, passive, emotional, etc. The pressure to conform to these stereotypes can have negative consequences for both women (e.g., sexual assault) and men (e.g., jail time).

In a community where men are valued within the context of sexual virility, it may not be surprising that a man would be aggressive in his demand for sex. In a society that praises men for their sexual prowess, any possibility that a man's conduct may be interpreted as evidence of sexual "weakness" may cloud a man's interpretation of a woman's conduct. In such a context, a man is likely to opt for behavior that re-affirms his masculinity. Indeed, as argued by Ilkkaracan and Jolly (2007):

> The societies we live in construct the right and wrong way to behave as men and women and these are mapped onto "right" and "wrong" sexual practices, beliefs and behaviors. Ideas that men should be macho can mean that sexual violence is expected rather than condemned. (p.3)

The 120 respondents were asked if women say no to sex when they mean yes, and 80% of them said yes, with 75% of men and a staggering 85% of women agreeing with the statement. A slighter larger share of people aged 35 and younger (83%) agreed that a woman's no may be an agreement to sex. The perception that a woman's "no" to sex means "yes" could be rooted in the fact that women and men are socialized into believing that a virtuous woman is uninterested in sex or at the very least does not express her sexual desires. This is exacerbated by the stereotype of women as submissive and passive. In Uganda, a woman is not expected to make decisions, which means that her decision not to have sex can be safely ignored. These findings are in line with the observations of Ashlyn Olson (2009), who states:

> Men are under the social impression that women mean yes when they say no. This is related to women's learned role of being passive and shy. It is related to the notion that a virtuous woman does not show interest in sex – feigns disinterest. (p.1)

Varga (2003) observes that cultural gender norms in many sub-Saharan African countries make girls feel that they cannot be in charge of their own sexuality or assertively communicate their sexual interests. These cultural norms promote an environment where a girl's "no" is reinterpreted as a "yes," which, combined with the perception that men cannot control their sexual urges, results in an environment supportive of "soft rape," or situations where a girl can be thought of as having sexually "teased" a boy into coercive sex (Balmer et al., 1997).

A study in South Africa found that one in four adults agree that rape usually happens because of something the woman has done or said (Kalichman et al., 2005). Similar to this finding, one of the young women I interviewed in the rape study stated: "We ladies often confuse men. Men never know what we want because we think it is a shame to say, 'I want.'" She supported the sentiment that it is not rape if a man forces a woman to have sex with him if she is in his house. Many of the respondents said that it is in the "nature" of women to feign lack of interest in sex. In their view, even when a woman consents to sex, she will first have to show resistance. Another female respondent said, "The girl was not forced to go to the man's house. Why did she go there? She brought the rape upon herself." Another woman said, "When a man is not related to a girl, it is not easy for her to go to his house, she must have intended to have sex with him. The man's act is not rape because she took herself for the man." Finally, one young male respondent compared a sexual encounter between a man and a woman to what cocks and hens do. He said, "A rooster will dance, the hen will at first run around and around and the rooster will give chase. But eventually the hen will sit down and allow the cock to get on top." He interpreted the hen running around as the female searching for assurance that the rooster was serious in its pursuit.

These opinions are also in line with the observations made by Olson (2009), who stated:

> Men think women play games to get them aroused and this leads to a whole jumble of confusion for both parties. There is a cultural view that women are timid but seductive which can lead men to believe a woman wants to be sexual when she does not. (p.1)

The views of the respondents also echoed what Mungwini and Matereke (2010) observe about the Shona of Zimbabwe:

> Among the Shona, there are cultural expectations that girls and women will resist any sexual advances from their male counterparts in order to prove that they are not sexually weak and promiscuous. It is for this reason that when a boy makes sexual advances to his girlfriend, he does not take seriously her attempts to say "no" because he anticipates them anyway, and this adds to his aggression. Commenting on these expectations in Zimbabwe, Musarurwa wrote that a woman has to struggle as a matter of duty and honor to defend her chastity. There is also the feeling that if she quickly and cheaply gives in her man will think she is a cheap woman who will sleep with anybody on request. Men are always faced with the problem to determine the amount of force they have to use. If it is too much it becomes rape. If it is too little it achieves nothing. They are in a dilemma. The mid-point is very elusive (Mungwiri and Matereke, 2020). Mungwiri and Matereke's (2020) opinion is that there are challenges in drawing boundaries between reasonable/acceptable force and the kind of force which constitutes rape. (pp.1–19)

The majority of the participants in the rape study opined that a woman would likely lose a court case if she testified that the purported rape occurred in the man's house. The message from society is that men cannot be expected to control their sexual desires. In a patriarchal society, men learn to be aggressive in their sexual pursuits because they have been socialized to believe the myth that they cannot control their sexual urges. The findings in the rape study about the Ugandan society mirror what Mann (1994) said of American society, namely that extremely early in life, boys learn that they cannot control their hormones and are rarely expected to do so. And according to Olson (2009), there is an argument that hormone levels are to blame for sexual aggression that leads to rape. Many of the respondents in my rape study opined that if the man was not aggressive in terms of sex, that would be evidence of him not being a "real" man—he would be a "cock which does not crow." As a result, the man cannot be blamed for forcing a girl to have sex with him if she has led him on (e.g., kissing and/or going to the man's house), as he would (i) not be in position to control himself; and (ii) "naturally" interpret the woman's resistance as mere pretense, since a woman never says yes even when she wants sex. He would be entitled to interpret the romance and the location as consent and presume that the woman is pretending not to want to have sex. Surprisingly, a 70-year-old man was firm in his belief that as long as a woman makes it clear that she does not want to have sex, even if she expressed interest and led him on, using force would be considered rape.

Among the relatively few respondents who did not think that a man should force a woman into sex under the described circumstances, a staggering 97% of women and 62% of men said that the matter should not be handled in court, with 88% of respondents aged 35 years and older and 70% of respondents younger than 35 years old agreeing that the courts should not be involved. Some of the reasons given for not involving the courts include: (i) it was the woman's fault since she "led" the man on; and (ii) the two were lovers, which makes it a private matter.

Prevailing social views of right and wrong ways to behave as a man or a woman influence sexual behavior. As revealed in the rape study, the idea that men should act "macho" often leads to tolerance rather than condemnation of male sexual violence against women. Like many other societies, Ugandan society has constructed an entire mythology that blames women for acts of sexual violence by men. One such myth is that in sexual matters, once a man starts, he cannot stop, since he has an uncontrollable sex drive. A woman should, therefore, make sure a man's sexual urge is not ignited. This means that a woman who exchanges nude pictures with a man and then visits his home must be blamed if the man forces her into sexual activity. Whatever the interpretation of non-consensual sex, these types of justificatory narratives are rooted in patriarchal practices that legitimize violence by men (i.e., the dominant group) against women (i.e., the disempowered group). The non-consensual sex act can, therefore, be viewed as an expression of power disparities between different groups based on social status, age, gender, etc.

Judicial construction of gender and sexuality

Community perceptions can affect judicial interpretations of a sexual encounter between a man and a woman. Judges must ensure that the defendant's right to a robust defense does not eclipse the victim's rights to be treated with dignity and respect. Unfortunately, several myths and stereotypic beliefs have found their way into the judicial construction of sexual encounters between men and women, which Barn and Kumari (2015) refer to as the infusion of rape mythology into the court process. An overwhelming majority of the 120 respondents believed that women often give mixed signals and that the circumstances in which a sexual encounter takes place can be the basis of inferred consent. For example, in the view of many of the respondents, the voluntary presence of a woman in a man's private space such as his home, the continuous acceptance of money and other favors from a man, and a woman's voluntary engagement in intimacy in a secluded place all justify a man's belief that the woman has provided her consent (albeit implied) to penetrative sex. These views implicitly support the legal notion from *DPP v. Morgan* (*supra*) that a man should not be convicted of rape if he believed that the woman was consenting to sex. The implicit message is that it is the responsibility of women to refrain from doing anything that may be interpreted as readiness to engage in penetrative sex.

In the Zuma rape trial, the accused stated, "The complainant visited my home … and stayed over for the night. This was of her own volition. At no stage did I believe that the sexual intercourse was against the will of the complainant" (*The State v. Jacob Gedleyihlekisa Zuma*, 2006). The complainant stated that the accused had invited her to his house, and she testified that it was the accused who suggested that she stay over for the night. More importantly, the complainant testified that the accused had not asked for her consent before he had intercourse with her. She answered "no" to the question: "Did you give him your consent or was there anything in your conduct which could have led the accused to believe that you gave him consent to have intercourse with you?"

In the rape trial, one of the factual issues that seemed important in determining the guilt of the accused was whether the woman's presence in the accused's home was initiated by the complainant. After analyzing the evidence of the accused and the complainant, the judge stated:

> It is in dispute as to whether the accused invited (the complainant) to go his home or whether she invited herself. It is common cause that the complainant stayed for the night. It is in dispute whether the accused invited her to stay over or whether the complainant indicated that she would be staying over. The testimony of the accused's daughter supports the accused's evidence that it was the complainant who decided to stay the night.

The results of the rape study show that many Ugandans believe a woman's consent to sex is implied rather than explicitly given. In the Zuma rape trial, the judge emphasized:

> Prior to the rape and in the preceding two months, the complainant had sent 54 sms messages to the accused. It appears that a change in the tone of the sms messages had also taken place in that they ended off with "love, hugs and kisses." It appears as if the complainant was seeking to make regular contact with the accused. In the accused's house the complainant walked around in a kanga with no underwear which prompted Duduzile Zuma (the accused's daughter) to say that she was inappropriately dressed.

One can infer that in the opinion of the judge, the complainant's conduct prior to the sexual encounter was evidence that she was interested in sex with the accused.

The ruling in the *DPP v. Morgan* case was restated in the Zuma trial: "Rape … means … intentional sexual intercourse had to take place with the accused knowing that there was no consent by the complainant." This is in line with the inherent message from many of the participants in the rape study that a woman should not lead a man on if she is not willing to have sex.

In summarizing the evidence of the complainant, the judge in the Zuma rape trial noted:

> She also stated that the accused did not ask her for her consent before he had intercourse with her. The leading question was then put "Did you give him your consent or was there anything in your conduct which could have led the accused to believe that you gave him consent to have intercourse with you?" The answer was "No I did nothing to make him believe that, no."

The specific question put to the complainant is especially revealing. Mr. Zuma said that the sex act occurred in his bedroom and that the woman had entered the room on her own accord. He also testified that she had signaled her interest in sex earlier in the evening by wearing a skirt and sitting with her legs uncrossed as she faced him. Furthermore, the judge noted that the complainant confirmed that she only had on a kanga[6] without any underwear when she went to the accused before the sexual encounter. The message of the judge to the complainant (albeit implicit) was that it was her fault and that her conduct led the man into believing she consented to sex.

The societal perception that sex is expected in exchange for financial favors, which means that the woman's consent to sex is assumed, may also have played a part in what took place in the Zuma–Kwezi sexual encounter. The complainant had requested financial assistance from the accused to attend university, and Mr. Zuma had agreed to fund her. It was also reported that the accused at one time paid the airfare for the complainant to travel and see her mother. The monetization of women's bodies is also clearly exhibited during events that happened after the alleged rape. For example, the complainant's mother and the accused had discussed compensation for the alleged rape. The accused testified that during the meeting with the complainant's mother, he said he was prepared to assist the complainant to go to London for further studies. He had also said to the mother that he was willing to assist with a fence at the complainant's parental home in KwaZulu Natal.

Another finding from the rape study is that many respondents believed that women sometimes show a fake lack of interest in sex. This can be interpreted to mean that women tell lies about sexual encounters. It is a trite principle of the law of evidence that a conviction can be based on the testimony of a single witness. To prove any fact, what matters is the quality and not the quantity of evidence. And yet historically, courts have as a matter of practice warned themselves of "the danger" of acting on the uncorroborated evidence of a complainant in a sexual assault case, which has been the cautionary rule in cases involving sexual offenses.[7]

Reasons given for the need of evidence that is independent of the victim's story in sexual assault cases have their origin in the opinion of the Chief Justice of England, Sir Mathew Hale, who said that rape must be examined with greater caution than any other crime, as it is easy to charge and difficult to defend (Tibatemwa-Ekirikubinza, 2015, p.38). A similar opinion was expressed by Lord Justice Salmon: "In cases of alleged sexual offences human experience has shown that in these cases girls and women do sometimes tell an entirely false story which is very easy to fabricate but extremely difficult to refute" (R v Henry and Manning, 1969, p.153). The belief that women lie about sexual encounters has dire consequences for victims of rape, because most acquittals depend on the credibility of the complainant as a witness.

Next steps

The United Nations Convention on the Elimination of All Forms of Discrimination's (CEDAW) General Recommendation No. 33 on women's access to justice urges countries to modify or transform harmful gender stereotypes and eliminate wrongful gender stereotyping (CEDAW, 2015). Gender stereotyping is harmful when it results in violations of human rights. An example is the failure of the justice system to hold perpetrators of sexual violence accountable because of stereotypes of women's appropriate (sexual) behavior. Courts in the common law legal system operate on the basis of the doctrine of *stare decisis*,[8] which obligates courts to be guided by precedents when determining cases. Inherent in this principle is the expectation that courts will decide cases according to consistent principled rules, so that similar facts will yield similar and predictable outcomes. One of the negative consequences of this doctrine is that it can result in the judicial perpetuation of harmful stereotypes.

Judges, just like all people, hold preconceived and often strongly held values and beliefs. Judicial authorities must take steps to ensure that prejudices and harmful gender stereotypes do not undermine the credibility of victims of SGBV. Judges must address biases that lead to victim-blaming or mistrust in the victim's story and ultimately, putting the victim on trial. This, however, presupposes that judicial officers are aware of the unintended consequences of *stare decisis*. They need to be willing to interrogate previous court decisions from a human rights perspective and, where appropriate, rule that previous decisions are unconstitutional.

Efforts to improve women's access to justice often call for judicial activism—the process by which new juristic principles evolve and are used to amend existing laws to bring them in conformity with current expectations of society (Ukey, 2015). For example, the historical rule on corroboration in sexual assault cases was nullified through judicial activism in the case of *Uganda v. Peter Matovu*. In this case, Judge Lugayizi declined to apply the rule on corroboration because of its discriminatory effect on women, which was considered a violation of both the country's constitution and Uganda's obligations under CEDAW. The judge recognized the inherent stereotyping of women and stated that the

> Court had not come across any empirical data or basis for the belief that women are greater liars than men or, for that matter, that they are much more likely to lie than to say the truth in matters concerning sexual allegations. For that reason, it seems that both the belief and the resultant rule have no logical basis.
>
> (*Uganda v. Peter Matovu*, 2001)

Moreover, in the case of *Ntambala v. Uganda* (2015), the Supreme Court stated that the court needed to depart from its previous decision, which held that the cautionary rule was a requirement in sexual assault prosecutions because the rule violated Uganda's constitutional provisions of equality before the law and equal protection under the law. It is clear that in both *Uganda v. Peter Matovu* and *Ntambala v. Uganda*, there was a deliberate decision by the courts not to follow precedent.

An effective judicial response to sexual assault calls for efforts to ensure that judges have the required expertise to understand SGBV. For judges to be able to challenge judicial precedents from a gender perspective, they need the skills and tools necessary to recognize gender bias in judicial practice and apply human rights and gender mainstreaming to improve women's access to justice.

Conclusion

A positive effect of the pandemic is that it has re-energized efforts to evaluate the systemic barriers faced by women in their attempt to access justice. For example, the Medical-Legal Committee on Gender Based Violence was established in August 2020 under the MGLSD to coordinate efforts of various partner institutions[9] related to SGBV, especially during the pandemic. The committee shares information on victims of SGBV who are in need of medical and legal assistance; advocates for gender-based budgeting; and performs field assessments on the prevention of and response to SGBV. Committee members have visited various districts to ensure that medical and legal services are available to survivors of SGBV, identify key challenges, and suggest policy recommendations. However, the barriers to women's access to justice in Uganda were not created by the current emergency but are rooted in women's subordination in a patriarchal society. To ensure that women are treated fairly in the justice system, all judicial authorities need to adopt a gender perspective in their work and assess the implications for both women and men of any planned policy action, including legislation, administrative process, policy program, or emergency measure to mitigate the impact of the COVID-19 pandemic.

Notes

1 Defilement refers to sexual activity with a person under the age of 18, while rape refers to having sexual intercourse with a woman without her consent.
2 The Katwe and Kabalagala police stations were selected because the heads of the two stations responded promptly to the request for information and were willing to allow their officers at the gender desk to be interviewed. To process data from 50 case files covering the period of March to October, 2020, a data collection tool was developed that included information on (i) date of occurrence; (ii) nature of the offense; (iii) relationship between the perpetrator and victim; (iv) age of the perpetrator and victim; (v) place of occurrence; and (vi) a brief narrative on how the offense was committed.
3 *Boda bodas* are bicycle and motorcycle taxis commonly found in East Africa.
4 With movement restrictions and the lockdown of small businesses, service providers such as hair salons and restaurants started offering their services in people's homes.
5 Based on an interview with the Assistant Director of Public Prosecution/Head of Gender, Children and Sexual Offences at National Level, Ms. Samali Wakooli, and data collected from ten police stations: Entebbe, Kajjansi, Kasangati, Kira, Nakawa, Nabweru, Luzira, Matugga, Wakiso, and Soroti.
6 The kanga is a colorful fabric worn by women and occasionally by men throughout the African Great Lakes region. *Source*: https://en.wikipedia.org/wiki/Kanga_(garment). In East Africa, it is also referred to as Leso or lesu.
7 In East Africa, the leading authority on this rule has been the decision of the East African Court of Appeal in Chila and *Another v. R.*[49]
8 *Stare decisis* means let the decision stand.
9 The Ministry of Health, the Office of Public Prosecutions, the Ministry of Gender, and the Uganda Police.

Constitutions and legislation

Constitution of the Republic of Uganda. (1995).
Penal Code Act. (1950). Uganda Legal Information Institute.

Case law

DPP v. Morgan, AC. No. 182, (House of Lords, 1976).
Ntambala v. Uganda, Cr. App. No. 34 of 2015. [2018] UGSC 1 (UGSC, Jan. 18, 2018).
R v. Henry and Manning, 53 Cr. App. R. 150 (1969).
Uganda v. Peter Matovu, Criminal Case No. 146, (High Court, 2001).
The State v. Jacob Gedleyihlekisa Zuma, (High Court of South Africa, Witwatersrand Local Division, May 8, 2006). (Unreported)

References

Abrams, D., Viki, G.T., Masser, B., & Bohner, G. (2003, January). Perceptions of stranger and acquaintance rape: The role of benevolent and hostile sexism in victim blame and rape proclivity. *Journal of Personality and Social Psychology*, *84*(1), 111–125. https://pubmed.ncbi.nlm.nih.gov/12518974/

Balmer, D.H., Gikundi, E., Billingsley, M.C., Kihuho, F.G., Kimani, M., Wang'ondu, J., & Njoroge, H. (1997). Adolescent knowledge, values, and coping strategies: Implications for health in Sub-Saharan Africa. *Journal of Adolescent Health*, *21*(1), 33–38. https://pubmed.ncbi.nlm.nih.gov/9215508/

Barn, R., & Kumari, V. (2015). Understanding complainant credibility in rape appeals: A case study of high court judgments and judges' perspectives in india. *The British Journal of Criminology*, 55(3), 435–453.

Constitution of Uganda (1995). https://statehouse.go.ug

Convention on the Elimination of All Forms of Discrimination against Women (CEDAW) (n.d.). *General Recommendation No. 33 on Women's Access to Justice*, 23 July 2015. *CEDAW/C/GC/33*, https://tbinternet.ohchr.org/Treaties/CEDAW/Shared%20Documents/1_Global/CEDAW_C_GC_33_7767_E.pdf

Giarruso, R., Johnson, P., Goodchilds, J., & Zellman, G. (1979). Adolescents' cues and signals: Sex and assault. presented at Western Psychological Association Meeting Symposium. Acquaintance Rape and Adolescent Sexuality, San Diego, CA, April 1979.

Huaxia (2020, March 18). Ethiopia closes federal courts for 15 days in latest anti-COVID-19 measures. *Xinhua.Net*. http://www.xinhuanet.com/english/2020-03/18/c_138892587.htm

Iikkaracan, P., & Jolly, S. (2007, January). *Gender and Sexuality*. Bridge. https://www.bridge.ids.ac.uk/reports/CEP-Sexuality-OR.pdf

International Conference of the Red Cross and Red Crescent (32nd RCRC Conference) (2015, December 8–10). 32IC/15/R3. Resolution 3: Sexual and gender-based violence: Joint action on prevention and response. http://rcrcconference.org/app//uploads/2015/04/32IC-AR-on-Sexual-and-gender-based-violence_EN.pdf

Kalemba, K. (2015, December 19). *A 'Disciplined' Dog Sleeping next to a Bucket of Meat in Kisoga Town, Mukno District*. Saturday Vision.

Kalichman, S.C., Simbayi, L.C., Kaufman, M., Cain, D., Cherry, C., Jooste, S., & Mathiti, V. (2005). Gender attitudes, sexual violence, and HIV/AIDS risks among men and women in Cape Town, South Africa. *Journal of Sex Research*, *42*(4), 299–305. https://doi.org/10.1080/00224490509552285

Kamya, J.R.Y. (2020). *SGBV During the COVID-19 Pandemic in Uganda* [Unpublished report]. ICGLR-RTF.

Lonsway, K.A., & Fitzgerald, L.F. (1994). Rape myths: In review. *Psychology of Women Quarterly*, *18*(2), 133–164. https://doi.org/10.1111/j.1471-6402.1994.tb00448.x

Mann, J. (1994). *The Difference: Growing up Female in America*. Warner Books.

McHale, M.J. (2016, February 2). What does access to justice mean? *UVicACE*. http://www.uvicace.com/blog/2016/2/2/what-does-access-to-justice-mean

Moore, A.M., Biddlecom, A.E., & Zulu, E.M. (2007). Prevalence and meanings of exchange of money or gifts for sex in unmarried adolescent sexual relationships in Sub-Saharan Africa. *African Journal of Reproductive Health*, *11*(3), 44–61.

Mungwini, P., & Matereke, K. (2010, August). Rape, sexual politics and the construction of manhood among the Shona of Zimbabwe: Some philosophical reflections. *African Journals Online*, *2*(1). https://www.ajol.info//index.php/tp/article/view/57662

Mungwiri, P., & Matereke, K. (June 2020). *Thought and Practice : A Journal of the Philosophical Asssociation of Kenya (PAK) New Series*, *2*(1), 1–19. http://ajol.info/index.php.tp/index

Musiime, E. (2020). The disruption of women's rights in the face of the COVID-19 pandemic in Uganda. *Institute for African Women in Law*. https://www.africanwomeninlaw.com/amp/the-disruption-of-women-s-rights-in-the-face-of-the-covid-19-pandemic-in-uganda?__twitter_impression=true

Olson, A. (2009). Gender socialization and rape. *Wolf's Sociology*. *204*. http://www.srwolf.com/wolfsoc/soc204/204archives/2009/03/19/gender_socialization_and_rape.php

Peterman, A., Potts, A., O'Donnell, M., Thompson, K., Shah, N., Oertelt-Prigione, S., & Gelder, N. van (2020, April 1). *Pandemics and Violence Against Women and Children*. (Working paper 528). Center for Global Development. https://www.cgdev.org/sites/default/files/pandemics-and-vawg-april2.pdf

Save the Children (2020, May). *Keeping Children Safe in Uganda's Covid-19 Response*. Save the Children Resource Center. https://resourcecentre.savethechildren.net/node/17615/pdf/Joining%20Forces%20-%20Protecting%20children%20during%20Covid-19%20in%20Uganda.pdf

Songa, M. (2020, September 28). *Ministry of Gender Launches Mobile App to Strengthen Reporting of Sexual Violence and Dissemination of Reproductive Health Information*. United Nations Population Fund. https://uganda.unfpa.org/en/news/ministry-gender-launches-mobile-app-strengthen-reporting-sexual-violence-and-dissemination

Stets, J.E., & Pirog-Good, M.A. (1989). Patterns of physical and sexual abuse for men and women in dating relationships: A descriptive analysis. *Journal of Family Violence*, 4(1), 63–76. https://doi.org/10.1007/BF00985657

Tibatemwa-Ekirikubinza, L. (2015). *Criminal Law in Uganda: Sexual Assaults and Offences Against Morality*. Fountain Publishers.

Ukey, K.L. (2015). Judicial activism: Principles and practice: A Bird's Eye view of theory, practice and current trends in global/Indian scenario. *Online International Interdisciplinary Research Journal*, ISSN 2249-9598. http://www.oiirj.org/oiirj/july-aug2015/19.pdf

United Nations High Commissioner for Refugees (UNHCR) (2020, August 11). *East and Horn Of Africa, and the Great Lakes Region SGBV: Regional Overview, March-July 2020*. Reliefweb. https://reliefweb.int/report/burundi/east-and-horn-africa-and-great-lakes-region-sgbv-regional-overview-march-july-2020

Varga, C.A. (2003). How gender roles influence sexual and reproductive health among South African adolescents. *Studies in Family Planning*, *34*(3), 160–172. https://pubmed.ncbi.nlm.nih.gov/14558319/

Women of Uganda Network (2020, February). *Bridging the Digital Gender Gap in Uganda: An Assessment of Women's Rights Online Based on the Principles of the African Declaration of Internet Rights and Freedoms*. https://africaninternetrights.org/sites/default/files/Bridging-the-Digital-Gender-Gap-in-Uganda-WOUGNET.pdf

World Vision (2020, August 21). *COVID-19 Aftershocks: Access Denied Teenage Pregnancy Threatens to Block a Million Girls Across Sub-Saharan Africa from Returning to School*. Reliefweb. https://reliefweb.int/report/world/covid-19-aftershocks-access-denied-teenage-pregnancy-threatens-block-million-girls

Index

Abebreseh v. Kaah 42–43
Abilahi Mshamu Mnali v. R 245
Abuja Declaration 108, 117–118n6
access to justice: COVID-19 pandemic and 281–283, 317; gender and 307
Achiampong v. Achiampong 42–43
activism 5, 13, 89, 95, 168, 171–173, 219; human rights defenders (HRDs) 174–175; judicial 133, 316; *see also* social media
Addadzi-Koom, M. E. 7, 10
Adom v Kwarley 42
affirmative action 6; two-thirds rule 6
Africa 8
African Charter on Human and People's Rights *see* Banjul Charter
African Charter on Human People's Rights on the Rights of Women in Africa *see* Maputo Protocol
African Charter on the Rights and Welfare of the Child (ACERWC) 150
African Commission on Human and Peoples' Rights (ACHPR) 8, 69, 144, 152, 161, 162, 176; human rights defenders (HRDs) 174–175; maternal and infant health 104–105; representation of women in 162–165, 168–170; special mechanisms 171; Special Rapporteur on Human Rights Defenders in Africa 173–175; Special Rapporteur on Rights of Women in Africa 170–173; women's participation and representation in 166–168; *see also* Banjul Charter
African Committee of Experts on the Rights and Welfare of the Child 175
African Court 69, 142, 144, 172–173, 175; *APDF and IHRDA v Mali* 151–153
African Union 166, 167, 169, 172; gender equity mechanisms 176–177
Alapini-Gansou, R. 8, 174
Albertyn, C. 29
Algeria 14
Aminata Diantou Diane (represented by APDF & IHRDA) v Mali 150–151
Andrews, P. 14, 15
Anna Aloyce v. Zacharia Zebedayo Mgeta 246
anti-essentialism 99–102, 116
Anto Furundzija 101
apartheid 6, 180, 191, 193, 195, 196, 198
appointment of female judges 212–213, 216–217; skepticism about 217–218
appointments 5
Argentina 9
Arthur case 46, 48, 53
Article 19 v. Eritrea 69
Asuagbor, L. 164, 172, 174
Ayer v. Kumordzie 42, 43

Banaszczyk, S. 81
Bangalore Principles on Judicial Conduct 211
Banjul Charter 69, 150–152, 161; Article 2 162; Article 42 165; Article 45 161–162; claw-back clause 69
Baraza, N. 10, 26, 28–29
Barn, R. 313
Bauer, G., *Gender and the Judiciary in Africa: From Obscurity to Parity* 5
Beckley v Beckley 43
Beijing Conference 57, 163, 171
Benin 9
Boafo v Boafo 47–48
Bonsu, O. 123–124
Botswana 9, 62, 68
Brock, A. 83, 84
Bulley-Neequaye v. Acolatse 44
Byamugisha, C. 115

cases 4, 10; *see also* African Court of Human Rights; Community Court of Justice (CCJ)
cautionary rule 101
CEHURD v. The Executive Director, Mulago National Referral Hospital 112–113
Centre for Health Human Rights and Development (CEHURD) v. Attorney General 106, 109–111, 114, 115
Centre for Reproductive Rights 241
Cheborion, B. 115
Chibesakunda, L. 220–222
child marriage 244
Chile 9
Chiluba, F. 221
civil law, revenge porn and 131
civil society organizations (CSOs) 162, 164
C.K. (A Child) Through Ripples International as Her Guardian and Next Friend) & 11 Others v. Commissioner of Police/Inspector General of The Equality jurisprudence by Kenyan courts 35 National Police Service & 3 Others 34–35
claw-back clause 69
Clerk v. Clerk 42–43
colonialism 27, 32, 191
Committee on Economic, Social and Cultural Rights 103
Committee on Elimination of All Forms of Discrimination against Women 234
Community Court of Justice (CCJ) 142–144; *Aminata Diantou Diane (represented by APDF & IHRDA) v Mali* 142, 150–151; *Dorothy Njemanze & 3 Ors. v. Nigeria* 142, 144–146, 153, 154; *Hadijatou Mani v Niger* 142, 146–148, 153; *Mary Sunday v Nigeria* 142, 148–150, 154
community policing, COVID-19 pandemic and 301–302
consent 309, 310, 314; revenge porn and 125, 135, 136, 137–138n6
Constitutional Court of South Africa 15, 189, 193–194, 203; jurisprudence on discrimination against women 200–202; jurisprudence on equality 197–202
constitutionalism 2, 10, 195, 197–198; "transformative" 29–30
constitutional law, revenge porn and 129
Constitutional Rights Project v. Nigeria 69
constitutional transformation projects 1–2; customary laws and 9–10; gender and 2–3; "transformation" and 29–30
Constitution of Ghana 40; Article 17(2) 6–7; Article 18 53; Article 18(2) 129; Article 22 41, 44–45, 47, 48, 50–51; Article 27(3) 7; Article 33 133; Article 33(5) 129; Article 35(6)(b) 6–7; Directive Principles of the State 7
Constitution of Kenya 10, 25, 260; Article 2(5) and (6) 28; Article 10 27; Article 21(3) 34; Article 27 27, 33, 35; Article 27(4) 27; Article 27(6) 6, 27; Article 27(8) 6, 27; Article 29(c) 34, 92; Article 82 27; Article 259 26, 28; gender equality principles 27–28; judicial interpretation 28
Constitution of South Africa 6, 10, 67, 193, 195, 197–198; Bill of Rights 6
Constitution of the Federal Republic of Nigeria 67; s. 37 67; s. 39 68; s. 45(1) 68
Constitution of the United Republic of Tanzania, Article 13(5) 236
Constitution of Uganda 107–108, 261; Article 32(2) 268–269; Article 33(3) 109
constitutions 5, 6; and gender equality 7; gender-specific provisions 8–9; judicial interpretation and 7
constructive interpretation 30
Convention on the Elimination of All Forms of Discrimination against Women (CEDAW) 28, 93, 150, 153, 166–167, 171, 242, 266, 268, 315–316; Article 1 246; Article 2(c) 234; maternal and infant health 103–104
Convention on the Rights of the Child 104, 167
Cook, B. B. 212
Coontz, P. 190
copyright law, revenge porn and 132
"corrective rape" 61
Counting Dead Women Kenya 79
coverture 257
COVID-19 pandemic 5, 8, 271, 297; access to courts and 281–283, 317; community policing and 301–302; criminal trials and 283–284; domestic workers and 286–287; human trafficking and 287; impact on courts in Uganda 303–304; impact on human rights 288–289; impact on the judicial system 280–281; and incidence of rape and

defilement cases 298–300; mitigating the impact on women 287–288; prison overcrowding and 290–291; recommendations and technological solutions 291–294; remote hearings and 289, 291, 292; reproductive health rights and 287; and restrictions on prosecutions in Uganda 303; sexual and gender-based violence (SGBV) and 304–306; shelter-in-place orders 285–287, 298; social distancing and 283; structural inequality and 281; United Nations Population Fund (UNFPA) report 284; women and 284–285
criminal law, revenge porn and 129–131
criminal trials, COVID-19 pandemic and 283–284
critical technocultural discourse analysis (CTDA) 83–84
cultural norms, gender and 311
cultural rape 268–269
customary laws 1, 40, 198, 236, 257; Akan 42; constitutional transformation projects and 9–10; discrimination against women and 30; distribution of marital property and 41–42; judging and 93; Kenya and 30; marriage and 32; in Tanzania 237
cyber-harassment: revenge porn 124–126; *see also* revenge porn

Daniels, E.W.C. 44
Dawuni 202–203; *Gender and the Judiciary in Africa: From Obscurity to Parity* 5
Deborah Takyiwa v. Kweku Adu 44
decisions 15; patriarchy and 30; property rights of Ghanian wives and 45–47
Declaration on the Elimination of Violence Against Women (DEVAW) 93
democratization 1–2; fourth wave of 1; third wave of 5–6
Denning Report 258
difference 4, 203–204n1
differential theory 100–101, 115
digital intimacy 123
discrimination against women 6, 27, 67, 142, 167, 169, 170, 179, 198–202, 234, 236, 267–268; customary laws and 30; education and 177–178; female judges and 191–192; HIV status and 65; in Kenya 25–26; lesbians 60–62, 64–65, 70–71; prostitution and 200–201; slavery 146–148; unconscious gender bias 13; in the workplace 61; *see also* employment discrimination; racial discrimination
distribution of marital property: and Article 18 of the Constitution of Ghana 52; and Article 22 of the Constitution of Ghana 50–51; customary law and 41–42; equity and 44; inheritance and 33; in Kenya 31–32, 35–36; property rights of Ghanian wives after 1992 44–49; property rights of Ghanian wives before 1992 41–44; revenge porn and 126; rhetoric and 47–49; self-acquired property 40; statute law and 43–44; substantial contribution doctrine 42–43, 48–49
diversity 5, 210; gender 5, 14–15; judicial 194–196, 211
doctrine of trust 31
domestic violence 7, 148–150; COVID-19 pandemic and 285, 286; pandemic-related restrictions and 298; shelter-in-place orders and 285–287
domestic workers, COVID-19 pandemic and 286–287
Domfe v. Adu 44
Dorothy Njemanze & 3 Ors. v. Nigeria 144–146, 153
DPP v. Morgan 313, 314
Duarte, V. 163, 164, 168
Dworkin, R. 30

Eagly, A. H. 222
Ebiju Justine Wilson & Angwedo Mary v. Echodu Surubaberi 268
Echaria v Echaria 31
Economic Community of West African States (ECOWAS) 13, 15, 106, 142; Supplementary Protocol 143; *see also* Community Court of Justice (CCJ)
education: discriminatory practices against women 177–178; *see also* judicial training
Egypt 14
el Cheikh, A. 163
Electroland v Adomako 48, 49, 53
employment discrimination 11
England, Married Women Property Act (MWPA) 31, 257
equality 2, 4, 6–7, 27, 193, 200, 233–234; in the Constitution of Kenya 27; gender and 5; judicial training and 10–13;

jurisprudence of the Constitutional Court of South Africa 197–202; in marriage 35–36; threats to the judiciary's efforts to uphold 36–37
equity 6; distribution of marital property and 41, 44; judicial training and 10–13
Eric Gitari v. NGO Board & 4 others 68
essentialism 192
ethics of care 4, 190
Eunita Geko & Another v Philip Orinda Petition No. 237 of 2014 35–36
Evans, A. 210, 214
evidence, social media as 93–95
exclusion 2

Facebook 81, 95; *see also* social media
family law: perceptions of illegitimacy 223; revenge porn and 132–133
female judges 4, 189, 212; appointment of 217–218; discrimination and 191–192; establishing validity of the skepticism regarding 218–220; exclusion of in South Africa 191–192; jurisprudence on equality 197–202; perception of 90–95; perceptions of illegitimacy 209–210, 213–214, 221–225; perspectives 202; political networks 219; prejudice toward 222–223; as role models 202–203; in South Africa 194–197; in Zambia 209; *see also* appointment of female judges
femicide 79, 80, 91, 95, 96n1; hashtags and 81–82, 84–90; *Open Africa* report on 85
feminism/feminist scholarship 95, 115–116, 190, 204–205n12, 234; approaches to judicial interpretations 28–29; critical technocultural discourse analysis (CTDA) 84; situating social media in 81–83
Fiske, J. 80–81
Fitzgerald, L. F. 307
Ford Foundation 11
fourth wave of democratization 1
Fynn 53

gender 1, 2, 15, 255, 306; and access to justice 307; anti-essentialism and 99–100; conceptual and normative framework on judicial training and 233–236; cultural norms 311; difference and 4; diversity and 5, 14–15; employment discrimination 11; equality and 5; essentialism 192; intersex 266; judging and 3, 4, 99–102, 114–116; judicial construction of 313–315; judicial diversity and 3–4; judicial training and 12–13; and law 3; legal education and 258–259; sensitization training 12; sex and 2; stereotyping 315–316
Gender and Development (GAD) 12
gender-based violence (GBV) 35, 83–84, 95, 177; domestic violence 148–150; hashtags and 81–82, 84–90; in Kenya 33–34, 79–81; revenge porn 124–128; *see also* revenge porn
Gender Status Index (GSI) 234
Genn, H. 281
Germany 11
Ghana 5, 7, 10, 124; Criminal Offences Act (1960) 129–130; customary laws 40; Domestic Violence Act (2007) 7, 132–133, 135; Electronic Transactions Act (2008) 130; gender equality in 6–7; gender sensitization training 12; Intestate Succession Act (1985) 43; Marriages Act 43; Matrimonial Causes Act (1971) 43; property rights of wives after 1992 44–49; property rights of wives before 1992 41–44; revenge porn 127–137
Giarruso, R. 309
Gicheru, E. 260
Gilligan, C. 4, 100; *In a different voice: Psychological theory and women's development* 99
Gisege Angoi v Macella Nyomenda 35–36
Global Judicial Integrity Network (GJIN) 11
Godi Kisangela v. R 245
Godsil, R. D. 224
Gor-Digen 59
Gusse, J. 81
Guterres, A. 285

Hadijatou Mani v Niger 146–148, 153
Hague, The 11
Hakainde Hichilema & Others v Edgar Lungu & Others 218
Happee v Happee 43
hashtags 95; #ArrestNzomo 94; #CampusMeToo campaign 79; #CountingDeadWomenKenya 80; judging and 85–90; #TotalShutdownKE 91–92
Hassan Kamunye v R 245–246
Hecht, N. 280
HIV/AIDS 60, 65, 198
Hon. Bernard Mulengani v. Attorney General and 2 others 112

human rights 1, 2, 142, 161, 169, 176, 279; claw-back clause 69; COVID-19 pandemic and 288–291; justiciability 105–107; maternal and infant health 102–107; progressive realization 103–105; promotion of 105; protection of 104–105; remote hearings and 289–290; *see also* African Commission on Human and Peoples' Rights (ACHPR); Banjul Charter
human rights defenders (HRDs) 174–175, 178, 179
human trafficking, COVID-19 pandemic and 287
Hyde and Murphy v. Nygate and Rayment 291

Ibrahim, M. 26
Iddrisu, H. 124
Ifeanyi Orazulike v. Inspector General of Police & Abuja Environmental Protection Board 64–65
inclusivity 2, 15; in the constitution-making process 8
India 62
infant mortality 10
inheritance 31, 33, 151–153, 250n6, 250n7
In Re George Ntim 46
Institute of Judicial Administration (IJA) 233, 239, 249; continuing judicial education 240, 241; gender issue training 241; partnership with the Centre for Reproductive Rights 241
International Association of Women Judges (IAWJ) 262; Jurisprudence Equality Programme (JEP) 242–243
International Commission of Jurists 167–168, 181n26
International Covenant on Economic, Social and Cultural Rights (ICESCR) 103
intersectionality theory 59–60

Jacinta Wanjiku Kamau v Isaac Kamau Mungai 31
Jackson, S. 81
Johm, J. 174
Jonas v. Ofori 42
Jonathan, G. 64
Joshua Cheruiyot v Rachel Korir 33
Joyce Nakacwa v. Attorney-General & Others 109
judging: anti-essentialism and 99–102; Bangalore Principles on Judicial Conduct 211; cautionary rule 101; criteria for 216–217; customary laws and 93; differential theory and 100–101; gender and 3, 4, 15, 99–102, 115–116; gender-aware 255, 264–265; judicial training and 265–270; perception of women judges 90–95; relationship between gender and maternal infant health jurisprudence 114–116; revenge porn and 133–137; social media and 85–90; *sub judice* rule 94; *see also* female judges
judicial activism 133, 316
judicial construction of gender 313–315
judicial diversity, gender and 3–4
Judicial Institutes for Africa (JIFA) 11
judicial interpretation 5, 7, 15; constructive 30; feminist approaches 28–29; in Kenya 26, 28; positivist approach 30; as a process for gender equity 9; transformative 30
judicial training 5, 7, 233, 235, 236, 249, 256; advocates 194; challenges and prospects 246–249; conceptual and normative framework on gender and 233–236; Denning Report 258; gender and 12–13, 233–236; gender training 242–246, 254, 255; Global Judicial Integrity Network (GJIN) 11; for magistrates 269; on-the-bench 11; orientation programs 248; as prospect for gender equity 10–13; recommendations 270; reference materials 248; *see also* Judiciary of Tanzania (JoT); Kenya Judicial Training Institute (KJTI); Uganda Judicial Training Institute (UJTI)
Judicial Training Institutes (JTIs) 11–13, 255, 271; evaluation of training programs 265; gender training 256–257; recommendations 270
judiciaries 1, 8; COVID-19 impact on 281–283, 286; female representation in 14, 15, 210–211; role of in contemporary times 210–212; services provided by 279–280; South African 192–194, 196–197
Judiciary of Tanzania (JoT) 236, 237, 249; continuing judicial education 241; gender equality topics 241–242; gender training 240–246; Judicial Training Policy 238, 239; mentorship program 240; orientation and induction programs 240; reference materials 248; Strategic Plan 233

justice 5–7, 89, 134, 235; lesbians' access to in Nigeria 64–67
justiciability 105–107

Kabiito, B. 112, 115
Kameri-Mbote, P. 27, 31
Kamore v Kamore 31
Kang, A. 9
Kanyamugule and Another v. Attorney-General and 3 Others 111–112
Karau, S. J. 222
Kasonde, L. 215
Katanekwa, T. 220
Katey 46
Kayitesi, S. 164
Kenney, S. J. 3
Kenya 5, 9, 10, 12, 37; Business Names Act (1990) 259; customary laws 257–258; customary laws and 30; customary marriages 32; discriminatory traditions 25–26, 257, 259; distribution of marital property 31–32, 35–36; division of matrimonial property in 35; English law and 35; equality in marriage 35–36; Evidence Act 94; femicide in 79; gender-based violence (GBV) in 33–35, 79–81; gender inequality in 257–258; inheritance 33; judging and social media in 85–90; Judicare Act 36; Judicial Services Act (2011) 260; Judicial Training Institutes (JTIs) 255; Law of Succession Act 36; Matrimonial Property Act (2013) 35; perception of women judges in 90–95; Protection from Domestic Violence Act (2015) 34, 35; Sexual Offences Act (2006) 35, 79, 80, 260; social media 81, 84–85; *sub judice* rule 94; threats to the judiciary's efforts to uphold gender equality 36–37; transformative constitutionalism 29–30; two-thirds rule for gender equality 6; woman-to-woman marriage 32; women's right to land and property ownership 25–26; *see also* Judicial Training Institutes (JTIs)
Kenya Judicial Training Institute (KJTI) 255; curriculum development 260–261; establishment and management of 260–261; gender-awareness training 262–263; impact on judging 265–267; leadership structure 260; recommendations 270
Kenya National Human Rights Commission (KNHRC) 260
Khalfallah, M. 174
Kimani v Kimani 31–32
King, J. 164
Kisaakye, E. 115
Kivuitu v Kivuitu 31
Klare, K. 197–198
Kumari, R. 313
Kyobiika, W. N. 10

Langa, P. 29
Laurence Mtefu v. Germana Mtefu 246
law 6; gender and 3; *see also* legislative acts
lawmaking 15
leadership, women and 214–216
legal education 254–255; gender and 258–259; Law School of Tanzania 238; *see also* judicial training
legal instruments 5, 8
legislative acts 6, 7
legitimacy 213–214; judicial governance and 223–225
lesbians 57–58; access to justice in Nigerian courts 64–67; constitutional rights protection and 67–69; criminalization of 62; discrimination and 60–62, 64–65, 70–71; experiences of discrimination 60–62; intersectionality theory and 59–60; same-sex marriage and 63–64; workplace discrimination 61–62, 64
Letsweletse Motshidiemang v Attorney Genera 68
LGBTQ: constitutional rights protection and 67–69; discrimination against lesbians 60–62; intersectionality theory 59–60; in Nigeria 57–58
locus standi 66; *see also* justiciability
Lonsway, K. A. 307
Lorde, A. 13
Lumbu, R. 174
Lungu, E. 215

Magaji v. The Nigerian Army 62–63
magistrates 269
male judges 4
Mali 150–151; Family Code (2011) 151–153
Malleson, K. 212
Mambilima, I. 215
Mandela, N. 199
Manu v. Kuma 42
Manuela, M. 164
Maputo Protocol 8, 10, 93, 104, 146, 150–152, 166–168, 171, 181n25, 234, 242; Article 2 235; Article 8 235

Margaret Mumbi Kagiri v Kagiri Wamairwe & 3 othe 31
Maria Angoi v Macella Nyomenda 32
marriage 40, 200, 247; child 244; coverture 257; division of matrimonial property 31, 35; divorce and 259; equality in 35–36; equal rights and 151–153; same-sex 63–64; violence and 80; woman-to-woman 32; *see also* distribution of marital property; gender-based violence (GBV)
Mary Rono v Jane Rono & another 30–31
Mary Sunday v Nigeria 148–150, 154
Masabo, J. 12
Masengu, T. 14, 15
Matereke, K. 311
maternal and infant health 10, 100, 117; African Commission of Human and Peoples' Rights 104–105; Convention on the Elimination of All Forms of Discrimination against Women (CEDAW) 103–104; human rights and 102–107; jurisprudence 114–116; justiciability and 105–107; Maputo Protocol 104; in Uganda 108–113
Mathayo Ngalya @ Shabani v. R. 245
Mcloughlin, K. 212–213
media 13
Melkior Peter v. R 245
Melo, A. 164
Mensa-Bonsu, H. 10
Mensah 46, 47, 53
Millennium Development Goals (MDGs) 102–103
Minamino, K. 11
Miwa, A. 11
Mlambo-Ngcuka, P. 285
Mohamed Rashid Mbita v. Salima Ally 247
Mohammed, W. F. 84–85
Moore, A. M. 309
"morph porn" 125
Mtikila v The United Republic of Tanzania 69
Mugambe, L. 100, 115, 116
Muigai, G. 28
Mumba, F. 213
Mungwini, P. 311
Muriungi, M. 27, 31
Mutanga, W. 26
Mutuna & Others v. Attorney General 220–221

Naftal Joseph Kalalu v. Angela Mashirima 246
Namibia 14, 15
Nanor v. Nanor 49
National Coalition for Gay and Lesbian Equality v. Minister of Justice 67–69
Ndewawiosia d/o Ndeamtzo v. Imanuel s/o Malasi 248
Ndiaye, Y. 163
Ndulo, M. 8, 212, 221
Ndungu, N. 26
Nguema, I. 163
Ngulube, M. 217, 221
Nigeria 10, 69, 145–146, 148–150; Armed Forces Act (1993) 62; #CampusMeToo 79; constitutional rights protection 67–69; Criminal Code Act (1916) 57, 62; erasure of women in 62–64; Fundamental Rights (Enforcement Procedure) Rules (2009) 66; HIV/AIDS (Anti-Discrimination) Act (2014) 65; lesbians' access to justice in the courts 64–67, 70–71; LGBTQ movement 57–58, 60; Same Sex Marriage (Prohibition) Act (2013) 62, 63, 65, 67, 71; Same Sex Marriage Prohibition Act (2014) 7–8; same-sex marriage in 63–64, 66–69; Shari'a law 62; under-representation of lesbians in 57–58; Violence against Persons (Prohibition) Act (2015) 65; *Yan Daudu* 59
NML v Peter Petrausch 34
non-consensual pornography *see* revenge porn
non-governmental organizations (NGOs) 68, 144, 148, 151–154, 162, 164, 261
Ntambala Fred v. Uganda 269
Ntambala v. Uganda 316
Nyabola, N., *Digital Democracy, Analogue Politics: How the Internet Era Is Transforming Kenya* 95
Nzomo, M. 25

Obani, P. 7–8, 10
O'Connell, C. 146
Ojigho, O. 8, 13
Ojwang, J. 26
Olson, A. 311, 312
on-the-bench training 11
Onziel-Gnelenga, J. 163–164, 171–172
Open Africa report on femicide 85
Owusu v. Nyarko 44

Pacey, A. 84
Pamela Adie v. Corporate Affairs Commission 58, 66
"parasite porn" 125

patriarchy 25, 193, 306–308, 313; judicial decisions and 30; in Nigeria 60
Patriotic Front (PF) 214–215
perceptions of illegitimacy, female judges and 209–210, 213–214, 221–225
Peter Keingati & 4 Others Vs Ann Nguthi & 3 Others 33
Peter Mburu Echaria vs. Priscilla Echaria 35
Philippines 11
Pillay, N. 84, 101
Pirog-Good, M. A. 309
political networks 219
positivist judicial interpretation 30
power 224, 234; female leadership and 214–216; legitimacy and 213–214, 223–225
prejudice toward female judges 222–223
prison overcrowding, COVID-19 and 290–291
privacy: Ghanaian constitutional law and 129; revenge porn and 124, 136–137; video conferencing and 289
progressive realization 103–105
property rights 150–151, 250n6; customary law and 41–42; division of matrimonial property 31–32; divorce and 31–32; equity and 41; in Ghana 41–49; inheritance 31, 33, 250n7; judicial rhetoric and 41; Married Women Property Act (MWPA) and 31; patriarchy and 30; universal partnerships and 190
proportionality principle 68–69
Prosecutor v. Akayesu 101
prostitution 145–146, 200–201
Purohit and Moore v. The Gambia 104, 105

Quaico v. Fosu 42
Quartey v. Martey 41–42, 44–47, 49
Quartson 46, 47, 50–51

R v Amkeyo 32, 257
racial discrimination 14
racism 2, 14
Rackley, E. 213
rape 244–246, 297, 298, 305, 307; consent and 314; "corrective" 61; COVID-19 lockdowns and 298–300; cultural 268, 269; date 308; myths 308, 311–314; socio-cultural context 306–307; "soft" 311; Zuma trial 313–315
Rebeca Gyumi Z. Gyumi v. The Attorney General 244
re Estate of Francis Mbaria 33
Re Estate of Ngetich 266
Reindorf alias Sacker v. Reindorf 44
remote hearings 291, 292, 303–304; COVID-19 and 289; human rights implications 289–290; procedural unfairness and 291
reproductive health rights 177, 241; COVID-19 and 287
Republic v Johana Mweni 35
revenge porn 10, 123, 124; aggravation and 135–136; application of Ghanaian laws on 128–133; child pornography and 130; civil action against 135; consent and 125, 135, 136, 137–138n6; consequences of 127–128; copyright law and 132; definition of 124–125; extortion and 130; family law and 132–133; in a gendered context 125–126; in Ghana 127–137; Ghanaian civil law and 131; Ghanaian constitutional law and 129; Ghanaian criminal law and 129–131; multi-jurisdictional approach to 135; obscenity laws and 129–130; role of the court in addressing 133–137; tort law and 131–132
rhetoric: outcomes for women and 49; spousal rights and 41–43, 47–49
role congruity theory 222
role models, female judges as 202–203
Rono v. Rono & Another 265–266
Rukuba-Ngaiza, N. 12
Rwanda 9

Sadaka 148
SafePal 300–301
Sahli-Fadel, M. 164
same-sex marriage, in Nigeria 63–64
Sangwa, J. 218–219
Sata, M. 215, 220
SC v. University Hospitals Southampton NHS Trust 291
Schultz, U. 11
self-acquired property, distribution of marital property and 40
Senegal, *Gor-Digen* 59
SERAP v. Nigeria 106
"sexting" 123, 137n1
sextortion 243
sexual and gender-based violence (SGBV) 8, 316; consent and 309, 310; COVID-19 pandemic and 297–300, 304–306, 317; media campaigns 302; myths and

309–313; pandemic-related restrictions and 298; reporting 300–301; SafePal 300–301; school closures and 304, 305; socio-cultural context 306–307; *see also* violence against women
sexual harassment 79; *see also* discrimination against women
slavery 146–148
social distancing, COVID-19 pandemic and 283
social media 80, 81, 96n2, 300; #CampusMeToo campaign 79; #CountingDeadWomenKenya 80; critical technocultural discourse analysis (CTDA) 83–85; feminist scholarship and 81–83; hashtags 81–82, 84; judging and 85–90, 93–95; perception of women judges and 90–95; for police casework 302; "sexting" 123, 137n1; technoculture 89; *see also* hashtags
South Africa 2, 6, 9, 14, 189; advocates 194; appointment of female judges 196–197, 203; exclusion of female judges in 191–192; judicial diversity in 194–196; Judicial Service Commission (JSC) 6, 196, 197; Legal Practice Act (2018) 194; transformation of the legal and judicial system 192–194; *see also* Constitution of South Africa
Southern African Chief Justices Forum (SACJF) 211
Southern African Development Cooperation (SADC) Protocol on Gender and Development 211
spousal rights 41; *see also* distribution of marital property; marriage
Srinivasan 84
stare decisis 316
State of Uttar Pradesh v. Chhoteyeal 245
statute law: distribution of marital property and 43–44; erasure of women in 62–64
stereotypes 298, 307–308; gender and 315–316; women and 214–215
Stets 309
structural inequality, COVID-19 pandemic and 282
sub judice rule 94
substantial contribution doctrine 42–43, 48–50
Sudan 14
Sunkutu, E. 220
Supreme Court of Kenya 26
Supreme Court of Zambia, Justice Lombe Chibesakunda's tenure as Acting Chief Justice 220–222
Sustainable Development Goals (SDGs) 102–103, 281; no. 5 211

Tabury 46
Tanzania 12, 13, 233, 236; child marriage 244; Council for Legal Education (CLE) 238; customary laws 237; gender inequality in 236–237; Institute of Judicial Administration (IJA) 239; Land Act (1999) 236; Law of Marriage Act (1971) 244; Local Customary Order of 1963 237; magistrates 239; Sexual Offences Act (1998) 236; violence against women in 236–237; *see also* Institute of Judicial Administration (IJA); Judiciary of Tanzania (JoT)
Tanzania Women Judges Association (TAWJA). 12, 233, 241, 246, 249; funding 246–247; judicial training 242; outreach programs 243–244; reference materials 248; *Sextortion: Naming, Shaming and Stopping Sexual Exploitation by Abuse of Authority* 243; training program assessment 244–245; *see also* Judiciary of Tanzania (JoT)
technoculture 89
technology: critical technocultural discourse analysis (CTDA) and 84; remote hearings 289, 290, 292, 304; SafePal 300–301
Teriah Joseph Ebah v Federal Government of Nigeria (FGN) 66
third wave of democratization 5–6
Tibatemwa-Ekirikubinza, L. 8, 101, 113
tort law, revenge porn and 131–132
transformation 29–30; *see also* constitutional transformation projects
treaties 6, 8, 28
Tunoi, P. 26
Twitter 79, 93–94; #BlackLivesMatter 81; *Counting Dead Women Kenya* 79; hashtags 81–82, 84; *see also* social media

Uganda 5, 8–10, 99, 100, 297, 298; community policing 301–302; COVID-19 pandemic and 303–304; customary laws 257–258; discriminatory traditions 257, 259; Divorce Act (1904) 259; funding 264; gender inequality in 257–258; gender justice in 306–307;

guidelines for courts during lockdown 303–304; Judicial Training Institutes (JTIs) 255; maternal and infant health data 108; maternal and infant health jurisprudence 114–116; Office of Public Prosecution (OPP) 302, 303; pandemic-related measures and restrictions on prosecution 303; rape and defilement cases in 298–300; rights-based legal framework 107–108; right to maternal and infant health jurisprudence 109–113; SafePal 300–301; sexual and gender-based violence (SGBV) in 304–306; social media campaigns 302; statutory law on rape 307; stereotypical beliefs on sex and sexuality in 307–313; Zuma rape trial 313–315; *see also* Judicial Training Institutes (JTIs)
Uganda v. Lomoe Nokopuet 268
Uganda Judicial Training Institute (UJTI) 255, 256, 261; curriculum development 264; establishment and management of 261–262; gender-awareness training 263–264; governing bodies 261–262; impact on judging 267–270; recommendations 270; reference materials 263–264
unconscious gender bias 13
United Nations Declaration on Human Rights Defenders (UNDHRD) 173
United Nations Office on Drugs and Crime (UNODC) 11
United Nations Security Council, Resolution on Women, Peace and Security (2000) 8
United Nations Women Global Gender Equality Constitution Database 7
Universal Declaration of Human Rights (UDHR) 34, 101, 103
universal partnerships 189–191
Uzebu-Imarhiagbe, E. 14

Varga, C. A. 311
Vial, A. C. 214
video conferencing, privacy and 289
violence against women 63, 65, 70, 150–151, 178–179, 193–194, 267–268; "corrective rape" 61; COVID-19 and 284–285; COVID-19 pandemic and 297; cultural rape 268–269; domestic violence 148–150; hashtags and 81–82, 85–90; marriage and 80; revenge porn 125–126; slavery and 146–148; in Tanzania 236–237; *see also* gender-based violence (GBV); revenge porn; sexual and gender-based violence (SGBV)
voire dire test 247

Wahiya 148
Wanjala, S. 26
Watsemwa and anor v. Attorney General 111
Williams, R. 83
Wing, S. 9
women 1, 4, 5; in the African Commission on Human and Peoples' Rights 163–170; COVID-19 pandemic and 284–285, 287–288; in positions of leadership 214–216; "rights" 2; symbolic representation of 4; violence against 126; *see also* discrimination against women; gender-based violence (GBV)
Women and Development (WAD) 12
women's rights 15
workplace discrimination 61; against lesbians 64
World Bank 11, 36, 149–150, 259; Gender and Poverty Assessment (2016) 25; Women in Law and Business project 15
World Health Organization (WHO) 102, 297

Yan Daudu 59
Yaotey v. Quaye 42
Yeboah v. Yeboah 42–43

Zambia 210; appointment of judges in 216–217; criteria for judges 217; female judges in 209, 212; gender equity in the Superior Courts 212; Judicial Service Commission (JSC) 216–217, 220, 224, 225; Justice Lombe Chibesakunda's tenure as Acting Chief Justice 220–222; Patriotic Front (PF) 214–215; perception of female judges in 223–225; prejudice toward female judges in 222–223; women in positions of power in 214–216
Zimbabwe, Shona 311–312
Zuma, J. 196
Zuma rape trial 313–315
ZWN v PNN 35

For Product Safety Concerns and Information please contact our EU representative GPSR@taylorandfrancis.com
Taylor & Francis Verlag GmbH, Kaufingerstraße 24, 80331 München, Germany

www.ingramcontent.com/pod-product-compliance
Ingram Content Group UK Ltd.
Pitfield, Milton Keynes, MK11 3LW, UK
UKHW020154200926
475702UK00016B/2702
* 9 7 8 1 0 3 2 1 2 9 5 2 5 *